Ius Gentium: Comparative Perspectives on Law and Justice

Volume 79

More information about this series at http://www.springer.com/series/7888

Lei Chen · André Janssen
Editors

Dispute Resolution in China, Europe and World

Springer

Editors
Lei Chen
City University of Hong Kong
Hong Kong, China

André Janssen
Faculty of Law
Radboud University Nijmegen
Nijmegen, The Netherlands

ISSN 1534-6781 ISSN 2214-9902 (electronic)
Ius Gentium: Comparative Perspectives on Law and Justice
ISBN 978-3-030-42973-7 ISBN 978-3-030-42974-4 (eBook)
https://doi.org/10.1007/978-3-030-42974-4

This Springer imprint is published by the registered company Springer Nature Switzerland AG
The registered company address is: Gewerbestrasse 11, 6330 Cham, Switzerland

Contents

Recent Developments in the International Commercial Courts

Commercial Courts in Germany 3
Gerhard Wagner and Arvid Arntz

Recognition and Enforcement of International Commercial Court Judgments 31
Anselmo Reyes and Kevin Tan

The New Chinese International Commercial Court and the Future of Dispute Resolution in the Belt and Road Initiative 51
David Holloway

The Netherlands Commercial Court (NCC): Its Challenges and Perspectives 81
Jeroen A. van der Weide

Further Developments in International Commercial Arbitration

The Efficient Conduct of the Arbitration Proceedings and the 'New' Role of Arbitrators: A Challenging Journey Through Promises and Expectations 111
Paolo Marzolini

Reflections on the Key Ingredients for Successful Reform of International Commercial Arbitration in the Asia Pacific 131
Weixia Gu

Interim Remedies in the People's Republic of China 153
Fang Zhao and Han Ma

Anti-suit Injunctions in Support of Arbitration and EU Law 171
Pietro Ortolani

Overseas Recognition and Enforcement of China's Arbitral Awards—From the Perspective of the Enforcement of SCIA Arbitral Awards in Hong Kong 191
Xiaochun Liu and Xiongfeng Li

Navigating Conflict of Laws in International Commercial Arbitration in China 209
Patrick Zheng, Charles Qin, and Han Li

Developments in International Investment Arbitration

Investor-State Arbitration in China: A Comparative Perspective 231
Leon E. Trakman, Qiao Liu, and Lei Chen

For Whom the Bell Tolls: Any Hope Left for Investment Arbitration After *Achmea*? 263
André Janssen and Christian Johannes Wahnschaffe

Editors and Contributors

About the Editors

Lei Chen is Associate Professor at School of Law, City University of Hong Kong until June, 2020. He becomes Chair of Chinese Law and co-Director of Centre for Chinese Law and Policy, Durham University, UK since July, 2020. He is also Eastern Scholar Professor of Law at East China University of Political Science and Law. He is on the Law Panel of Hong Kong Research Assessment Exercise 2020. His research areas are Chinese and comparative private laws and dispute resolution. He is a seasoned arbitrator at a number of arbitration institutions in Asia and Europe.

André Janssen is Chair Professor at the Radboud University Nijmegen, the Netherlands. He has previously held positions at the Universities of Bayreuth, Göttingen, Münster, and at the City University of Hong Kong. Furthermore, he was a visiting scholar at the Universities of Nijmegen, Oxford and Turin and Member of several international research networks. He taught and presented at international conferences on four continents and published more than 100 books and articles. He is Co-chief-editor of the *European Review of Private Law* (ERPL), Member of the editorial board of the *International Arbitration Law Review* (IALR) and Head of the German Redaction Committee of the Italian Law Journal *Contratto e impresa/Europa*.

Contributors

Arvid Arntz Faculty of Law, Humboldt-Universität zu Berlin, Berlin, Germany

Lei Chen School of Law, Hong Kong Special Administrative Region, City University of Hong Kong, Kowloon Tong, People's Republic of China

Weixia Gu Faculty of Law, The University of Hong Kong, Hong Kong, People's Republic of China

David Holloway Birmingham Law School, University of Birmingham, Birmingham, UK

André Janssen Faculty of Law, Radboud University Nijmegen, Nijmegen, The Netherlands

Han Li Llinks Law Offices, Beijing, People's Republic of China

Xiongfeng Li Shenzhen Court of International Arbitration, Shenzhen, People's Republic of China

Qiao Liu School of Law, City University of Hong Kong, Kowloon Tong, People's Republic of China

Xiaochun Liu Shenzhen Court of International Arbitration, Shenzhen, People's Republic of China

Han Ma Hui Zhong Law Firm, Shanghai, People's Republic of China

Paolo Marzolini Patocchi & Marzolini, Geneva, Switzerland

Pietro Ortolani Radboud University, Nijmegen, The Netherlands

Charles Qin Llinks Law Offices, Shanghai, People's Republic of China

Anselmo Reyes Singapore International Commercial Court, Singapore, Singapore

Kevin Tan Rajah & Tann Singapore LLP, Singapore, Singapore

Leon E. Trakman University of New South Wales, UNSW Law, Sydney, Australia

Jeroen A. van der Weide Leiden Law School, Leiden University, Leiden, The Netherlands

Gerhard Wagner Faculty of Law, Humboldt-Universität zu Berlin, Berlin, Germany

Christian Johannes Wahnschaffe Faculty of Law, University of Münster, Münster, Germany

Fang Zhao Hui Zhong Law Firm, Shanghai, People's Republic of China

Patrick Zheng Llinks Law Offices, Beijing, People's Republic of China

Recent Developments in the International Commercial Courts

Commercial Courts in Germany

Gerhard Wagner and Arvid Arntz

Abstract This chapter contains a plea for establishing commercial courts in Germany, as a branch of the German judicial system. The existing commercial chambers, which are divisions of the general courts of first instance, are ill-suited to serve the needs of business. Empirical data clearly show that sophisticated parties involved in high-value commercial disputes increasingly flee the German court system. The creation of a German commercial court that employed excellent and experienced judges, offered the speedy and flexible resolution of disputes and possessed state-of-the-art facilities, including IT, holds the promise to stop the decline. This chapter describes the current state of reform in Germany and elsewhere and explores the key features of a commercial court that meets the expectations of potential litigants.

While commercial disputes are becoming more and more international and commercial courts emerging around the world compete for these cases, Germany's more than a century old *Kammern für Handelssachen* are lacking behind. This chapter is organized as follows: After a short glance at the world's most important commercial courts in London and New York (Sect. 1), we will analyze the current state of commercial courts in Germany (Sect. 2) and their decline (Sect. 3). In Sect. 4, we are considering the impact of arbitration on public commercial courts. In Sect. 5, we are recalling the modest reform activities taken in Germany, to conclude with 11 aspects that should be taken into account to establish a real, i.e. competitive, commercial court in Germany (Sect. 6).

G. Wagner · A. Arntz (✉)
Faculty of Law, Humboldt-Universität zu Berlin, Berlin, Germany
e-mail: arvid.arntz@rewi.hu-berlin.de

G. Wagner
e-mail: wagner@rewi.hu-berlin.de

L. Chen and A. Janssen (eds.), *Dispute Resolution in China, Europe and World*,
Ius Gentium: Comparative Perspectives on Law and Justice 79,
https://doi.org/10.1007/978-3-030-42974-4_1

1 The Concept of Commercial Courts

1.1 Definition and Basic Features

Commercial courts are a significant economic factor. They contribute to the infrastructure of a business location, just as traffic conditions, communication networks and taxes do. Unlike a conventional court of general civil jurisdiction, the jurisdiction of commercial courts is specialized, and obviously in commercial litigation. Thanks to their specialization, the judges sitting on commercial courts are particularly knowledgeable in commercial law. Judges in these courts are either professional judges that have gained special expertise in commercial matters throughout their career; or they are merchants or other business persons that join the courts as lay judges and contribute their practical experience gathered while going after their business affairs. There can also be a mix of professional judges and lay judges on the bench. The procedural framework within which commercial courts operate is often wider when compared to the rules of procedure for the courts of general civil jurisdiction. This is meant to better serve the needs of business. The primary goals are to speed up the procedure and make it more flexible. Last but not least, commercial courts often have their own buildings and are, depending on their appreciation by the other branches of government, well equipped with staff and office facilities. Especially a state-of-the-art information technology (IT) system is a staple feature of modern commercial courts, or at least it ought to be so. For these reasons, commercial courts usually enjoy a somewhat special position vis-à-vis the courts of general jurisdiction. Nonetheless, they remain embedded in the public court system.

The most famous and renowned commercial courts of present times are the English Commercial Court in London and the Commercial Division of the Supreme Court in New York State. They shall serve as reference points for an analysis of commercial courts. Besides the firmly established courts in London and New York, there has been a world-wide trend in setting up commercial courts within national judicial systems. In the past decade, the Dubai International Financial Centre Courts, the Qatar International Court, the Abu Dhabi Global Market Courts and the Singapore International Commercial Court opened their doors to the world's companies that find themselves involved in a commercial dispute. Within Europe, the Netherlands are about to create a commercial court in Amsterdam.[1] Likewise, Belgium is in the midst of the political process of building the Brussels International Business Court which is planned to take off by 1 January 2020.[2] In France the *Chambre Internationale de la Cour d'Appel* Paris was established on 1 March 2018. This drive towards commercial courts in Europe was further boosted by the upcoming departure of the United Kingdom (UK) from the European Union (Brexit) which could substantially

[1] See https://netherlands-commercial-court.com.

[2] See http://arbitrationblog.kluwerarbitration.com/2018/06/25/the-belgian-government-unveils-its-plan-for-the-brussels-international-business-court-bibc.

weaken London's predominant position in the market of judicial dispute resolution. The waning attraction of the English Commercial Court has spurned efforts in Continental-European jurisdictions, including Germany, to reform the existing institutions for the judicial settlement of commercial disputes.[3]

1.2 The English Commercial Court as a Prototype

Notwithstanding current Brexit turmoil, the prototype of a commercial court offering high-quality judicial service remains the English Commercial Court in London. The Commercial Court was established as early as in 1895. Its establishment was meant to respond to the urge of the business community that, in the late 19th century, pressed for a court and a procedure better tailored to its needs. The practice of the then-existing courts of general jurisdiction was characterized by expensive and time-consuming court proceedings guided by judges unfamiliar with business practice and had led to growing frustration.

In terms of institutional set-up, the Commercial Court is a subdivision of the High Court, which again is one branch of the Royal Courts of Justice. Its jurisdiction extends to 'commercial claims', as defined in Rule 58.1 of the Civil Procedure Rules. These include claims arising out of or relating to business contracts and documents, export or import of goods, purchase and sale of commodities, carriage of goods, exploitation of natural resources, insurance and re-insurance, banking and financial services, operation of markets and exchanges, construction of ships, business agency and arbitration. The commercial judges are recruited from amongst the members of the Bar, with a view on those practitioners who are most experienced in commercial matters. In this way, the Commercial Court managed to attract and develop a judiciary of particularly high caliber. The human capital vested in its judges—in addition to its long tradition—is considered to be its strongest advantage in international judicial competition. The mechanisms and procedures that are exclusive to the Commercial Court have been compiled in the 'Commercial Court Guide'.[4] It vests broad discretionary powers in the individual judge handling a particular case. One of the hallmarks of Commercial Court practice is the case management conference which, pursuant to Rule D3.1 of the Commercial Court Guide, shall be scheduled six weeks after the last defendant has filed his or her defence.[5]

Since 2011, the seat of the Court is the Rolls Building in the City of London. It shares the building with other subdivisions of the High Court serving its commercial and property business. The facilities include three 'super-court' rooms to handle

[3]Cf. Podszun and Rohner (2018, p. 450).

[4]The Commercial Court Guide (10th edn., 2017), https://assets.publishing.service.gov.uk/government/uploads/system/uploads/attachment_data/file/672422/The_Commercial_Court_Guide_new_10th_Edition_07.09.17.pdf (hereafter 'The Commercial Court Guide').

[5]The Commercial Court Guide (2017, p. 26).

international and domestic cases which are characterized by highest complexity and exorbitant stakes.[6]

London's Commercial Court has seen a remarkable success. It has become one of the most important courts of the world in complex and large-scale commercial disputes. A glance at the number of international cases at the Commercial Court and, more significantly, the amounts of money involved, reinforces this assessment. While, in 2005, there were 981 new cases, numbers peaked in 2009 with 1256 new cases. As of late, this number decreased to 719 new cases in 2017.[7] Although the caseload has fluctuated over the years, a general downward trend cannot be identified. The ups and downs seem to correlate with the general business cycle, or rather, the cycle of legal disputes. However, even in 2017, no less than 23 of the cases filed in the Commercial Court involved amounts in dispute exceeding GBP 100 million.[8] This is robust evidence of how attractive the English Commercial Court remains to parties disputing over claims of highest values. Notably, in around three quarters of the cases before the Commercial Court one of the parties was domiciled overseas, and half of the cases did not even have any connection whatsoever to the UK.[9]

The UK government is well aware of the attractiveness of the Commercial Court, and of the contribution the Court makes to the domestic economy. As a consequence, it actively takes measures aimed at maintaining and even expanding its excellent position in the global competition for commercial cases. Not surprisingly, therefore, the former Chief Judge of England and Wales, Lord Cwmgiedd, titled his 2017 speech before the Grand Court of the Cayman Islands 'Giving Business What It Wants'.[10] The speaker left no doubt that there is an international competition among commercial courts, and that the English Court can only remain on top of that competition by strictly and constantly adapting to the 'needs of business'.[11] He stressed that close contact and exchange with the users of the court were crucial to understand their constantly changing needs. As far as procedure was concerned, he diagnosed a highly persistent demand for expediency—speed—and efficiency, i.e. limits on costs.[12] Moreover, the court's application and interpretation of the respective law and contractual agreement in question should be compelling enough to earn the respect of the parties. In his view, 'Getting the law right' was just as important a maxim as its procedural counterpart, i.e. 'Getting procedure right'. Lord Cwmgiedd called for judges with a particular understanding for and experience with the needs and interests of companies. He said that, in order to attract such personalities to the Commercial Court, remuneration would have to be adequate, and the facilities would

[6]See https://www.judiciary.uk/you-and-the-judiciary/going-to-court/high-court/the-rolls-building/facilities.

[7]Royal Courts of Justice Annual Tables—2017, https://assets.publishing.service.gov.uk/government/uploads/system/uploads/attachment_data/file/738615/2017_RCJ_tables.xlsx.

[8]Royal Courts of Justice Annual Tables–2017.

[9]Vogenauer (2013, p. 59).

[10]Lord of Cwmgiedd (2017).

[11]Lord of Cwmgiedd (2017).

[12]Lord of Cwmgiedd (2017).

have to be up to date and of excellent quality. This is particularly true with a view to IT and staff. When necessary, judicial clerks or assistants should be assigned to a sitting judge, in order to alleviate his or her workload. Such clerks should help with the management and the organization of the proceedings and prepare analyses of the facts and the applicable law, including precedent, in order to facilitate the ultimate decision of the judge.

1.3 New York's Commercial Division

On the other side of the Atlantic and around a century later than the English High Court, the New York Supreme Court, which is the senior court of first instance of the state of New York, created a Commercial Division of its own. In the 1990s, the local advocacy pressed for this move in order to attract more high-value cases into the New York court system. The idea behind this was to offer top-notch adjudication of high-stakes commercial disputes, which in turn would attract a larger number of complex cases involving large amounts of money, which in turn would add to the attractiveness of the court and thus attract even more of the desired cases. In this way, a virtuous circle would be unleashed. And indeed, the Commercial Division became a success story. Again, the key was close coordination and cooperation between lawyers and potential parties from the business community:

> As the foregoing indicates, the Commercial Division has benefitted from extensive communications with the commercial Bar and Bar associations across the State over the years. [...]. The Office of Court Administration structured the Focus Groups to promote candid dialogue among judges, lawyers and clients to generate new ideas, identify potential areas of improvement and assess application of 'best practices' that have evolved in the Commercial Division to the court system as a whole. Focus Group sessions spanned the State, bringing together lawyers, former and current judges and in-house counsel of major corporations.[13]

In 2014, a commission was constituted to make the Commercial Division 'fit for the future'. This drive for reform was initiated because, in 2010, the Chancery Court of Delaware had established a 'Complex Commercial Litigation Division', thereby entering the competition for complex commercial cases. The ensuing threat to New York's Commercial Division was particularly serious in view of the fact that the Delaware judiciary is dominating the United States (US) market for corporate charters and corporate law disputes. No less than 50% of the large US corporations have their seat in Delaware and are hence subjected to the jurisdiction of the Delaware courts regarding corporate (intra-firm) disputes. Delaware clearly wanted to take on New York in the arena of commercial litigation as well. In reaction to that, New York established a reform commission which arrived at the following recommendations: adding more judges, improving case management, boosting the efficiency of the

[13]See Commercial Division—NY Supreme Court: History, http://nycourts.gov/courts/comdiv/history.shtml (hereafter 'New York Commercial Division History').

discovery process, improving IT, strengthening mediation and imposing a threshold value of at least USD 500,000 for new cases.

The implementation of the reform proposals outlined above seems to have born fruit. Up until today, the New York Commercial Division has managed to maintain its predominant position in the American theatre of the market for the judicial resolution of commercial disputes. Adding pride to success, it promotes itself just as private service providers would be expected to:

> "The Commercial Division serves as a forum for resolution of complicated commercial disputes. Successful resolution of these disputes requires particular expertise across the broad and complex expanse of commercial law. [...] The caseload of the Division is thus very demanding, requiring of the court scholarship in commercial law, experience in the management of complex cases, and a wealth of energy. The Commercial Division has actively sought to employ advanced technology to assist in handling its caseload effectively. [...] The Commercial Division has been a leading force in electronic filing of court documents in New York State. [...] The Commercial Division also utilized an Alternative Dispute Resolution Program ('ADR') first established in New York County in early 1996."[14]

Against this background it is not surprising that New York's local advocacy celebrates the Commercial Division as a full success.[15] This assessment is corroborated by empirical findings. Eisenberg and Miller conducted a study of 2865 high-value contracts of different type with a view to choice of law and forum selection agreements.[16] They found an almost perfect correlation between choice of law and choice of forum.[17] In other words, the parties selected the law and the forum as a package. In substance, the parties to the contracts examined by Eisenberg and Miller favored New York over any other jurisdiction. New York turned out to be the most attractive jurisdiction by far, with 46% of the contracts choosing New York law and 41% choosing New York courts.[18]

2 Commercial Courts in Germany: The Status Quo

The idea of commercial courts has a long tradition in Germany. At the outset of the 19th century, when Napoleon conquered Germany, so called *Kommerztribunale* (Commerce Tribunals) modelled after the French *tribunaux de commerce* were established in Germany, too.[19] The *Reichsjustizgesetze* (Imperial Judiciary Acts) of 1871 overhauled the German court system. After fierce debates in parliament, it was decided to establish the so-called *Kammern für Handelssachen* (Commercial Chambers) at the courts of first instance. The Commercial Chambers were incorporated

[14] New York Commercial Division History.

[15] Bach and Applebaum (2004, p. 158) with reference to Loomis (2002, p. 5).

[16] Eisenberg and Miller (2009, pp. 1487–1489).

[17] Eisenberg and Miller (2009, p. 1503).

[18] Eisenberg and Miller (2009, p. 1504).

[19] Fleischer and Danninger (2017, p. 550).

into the *Landgerichte* (Regional Courts), with their legal basis in Sections 93–114 *Gerichtsverfassungsgesetz* (German Court Act, GVG). The Regional Courts serve as courts of first instance for civil disputes exceeding a threshold amount of modest proportions (currently EUR 5000). Pursuant to Section 109 of the GVG, every registered merchant, or board member or director of a registered company over 30 years of age is eligible to serve as honorary judge at the *Kammer für Handelssachen*. The Commercial Chambers have remained in place until the present day. Ever since their adoption, there have been no major reforms.

The fundamental objective of Germany's Commercial Chambers is to introduce laymen, drawn from the ranks of the business community, into the judiciary. The purpose behind the recruitment of laymen is the provision of more inputs into the decision-making process, namely business expertise and entrepreneurial experience. The legislative materials of the GVG explicitly state:

> "Courts, at which diligent and experienced businessmen take part, will without further ado and certainly be able to reach a reasonable judgment in commercial disputes that duly considers the conditions of commercial trade [...]."[20]

The participation of lay judges in the Commercial Chambers also promised benefits running in the other direction. The framers hoped that the bringing together of professional judges with representatives from the business community would help to improve confidence in the court system. The Commercial Chambers would gain a foothold in the business community and hence contribute to the independence of the court from the other branches of the government.[21]

The jurisdiction of the Commercial Chambers lies in the hands of the parties: According to Section 96 of the GVG, the claimant may request the dispute to be brought before a Commercial Chamber. The defendant has the same right if the claimant has initially brought a commercial dispute before an ordinary court (Section 98, GVG). In both cases, the consent of the other party is unnecessary. The option to resort to the Commercial Chamber is only available where the case actually involves a commercial dispute. Section 95 of the GVG defines commercial disputes by supplying a catalogue. The most prominent category are the so-called two-sided commercial transactions, as defined in Section 95 paragraph 1 No. 1 of the GVG. These are transactions that involve a registered merchant on both sides. In this way, the jurisdiction of the Commercial Chambers relates to the status of the parties as registered merchants.

---

[20] Hahn (1879, p. 111): "Gerichte, bei welchen tüchtige und erfahrene Kaufleute mitwirken, werden ohne Weiteres und mit Sicherheit zu einem sachgemäßen, die Gestaltung des kaufmännischen Verkehrs richtig würdigenden Urtheil gelangen können [...]".

[21] Pernice (2019), before S 93 GVG, para 2.

3 The Decline of Commercial Litigation in Germany

From the outset, the *Kammer für Handelssachen* in Germany served the same purpose as the Anglo-Saxon Commercial Court. The basic rationale of these special units of the civil justice system is to provide the business community with a judiciary that is tailored to its needs and willing and able to decide commercial cases expediently, efficiently and proficiently. This proclaimed goal of the Commercial Chambers remains compelling to the present day. Speed, cost, and accuracy are still the main parameters against which to assess the quality of a court hearing commercial cases. While the overarching goals of the Commercial Chambers continue to be valid, the institutions used for their achievement have become ineffective, insufficient, and outdated.

So far, Germany has not found an answer to the emergence of commercial courts of the Anglo-Saxon type. It seems that Brexit will not help to improve the competitive weakness of the German Commercial Chambers. The reason is that Germany's neighbors, particularly the Netherlands, have already moved to reform their court system with a view to offer an efficient and attractive judicial body to the parties of complex and high-value disputes. The establishment of the Netherlands Commercial Court will put further pressure on the German judicial system.

Corresponding to its function as a quasi-commercial court, the *Kammer für Handelssachen* is expected to decide 'as fast as possible', and 'as accurate as possible' and to 'keep an open mind for the circumstances under which businesses operate'.[22] Yet, the idea that a court automatically proceeds and decides expediently and proficiently, for the simple reason that lay judges are involved, is naïve and unwarranted. Furthermore, the assumption that the resolution of modern commercial disputes requires the participation of lay judges, or at least profits from their involvement, is misguided. The participation of lay judges does not facilitate or improve the resolution of commercial disputes.[23] The commercial parties of today expect a court to professionally manage procedure and to accurately apply the law, rather than dispensing with old mercantile wisdom and experience. Admittedly, there is also a demand for amicable dispute resolution that does not aim for accurate law enforcement but for a commercially reasonable settlement. Yet, the *Kammer für Handelssachen* is not apt to satisfy this demand, and it should not be. Mechanisms of dispute resolution that are focusing on financial or other interests instead of legal positions are widely available in the thriving private market offering ADR-alternatives to litigation. Mediation and conciliation are pertinent examples. In addition, the parties may opt for arbitration which allows them to hand-pick the decision-makers. Parties who are interested in

---

[22]Sommermeyer (1966, p. 75): "Von der Kammer für Handelssachen wird […] erwartet, dass sie möglichst schnell entscheidet. […]. Dass die Kammer trotzdem möglichst gut entscheiden soll, ist eine Selbstverständlichkeit. Dazu gehört wirtschaftliches Verständnis und Einfühlungsvermögen, ein offenes Auge und Ohr für die wirtschaftlichen Gegebenheiten und die sich laufend verändernde Struktur und Lage der Wirtschaft, ein guter Einblick in die Wirtschaftslage und aktuelle Probleme der Wirtschaft und des Marktes […]".

[23]Cf. Hoffmann (2010, p. 99 ff.), Hoffmann (2011, p. 39 ff).

having technical experts or people from the business community with commercial experience to decide their case may opt for expert arbitrators or install a dispute board. Against this background of a broad menu of ADR tools, the proper role of the public courts is not to compete with the providers of informal, business-savvy dispute resolution mechanisms but to excel in the feature that ADR cannot offer, namely a binding decision by a publicly authorized judge or judicial panel that is rendered after a formalized and fair procedure and based on a thorough investigation of the facts and an accurate application of the law. Public courts fail to meet the demand for their specific services if they try to model their procedure and their parameters for decision-making on what is common in ADR. The involvement of lay judges in Germany's *Kammern für Handelssachen* is an element that is more adequately referred and left to the rich world of ADR. Consequently, they fall short of meeting the demand of parties that are actually interested in an authoritative decision of a public court.

The conclusion that the Commercial Chambers fail to live up to the goals they were designed to serve is not merely supported by theory and abstract reasoning. Rather, it is confirmed by empirical data. The number of cases filed with the *Kammern für Handelssachen* has been declining constantly over the course of the years. In the decade from 2007 to 2017 the number of cases resolved by Germany's commercial chambers annually has dropped by 42% or 19,500 cases.[24] This decline cannot be explained by shifts in economic conditions such as the robust performance of the German economy since the financial crisis of 2008/2009.

In addition to the overall decline of the demand for the Commercial Chambers there is other, more specific evidence for the conclusion that the involvement of lay judges has become outdated. Even the most fervent supporters of the Commercial Chambers concede that in 90% of the cases arriving at these courts the parties opt out of the participation of lay judges. If they do so—as they are authorized under the applicable law—the presiding judge decides the dispute all by him- or herself.[25] In the few remaining cases in which the lay judges remain involved, their actual participation and impact is cut to a bare minimum. Usually, the lay judges never even see the court files. Instead, they have to rely on an oral or written report of the case provided by the presiding judge. Moreover, the *Kammern für Handelssachen* hardly ever make use of their authority to decide questions that require business expertise on their own, based on their own knowledgeability.[26] Instead, the Chambers rely on expert witnesses in much the same way that an ordinary panel would. Under these circumstances, the participation of merchants on the court's bench has become a farce.

The fact that the parties shun the participation of lay judges is strong evidence that the Commercial Chambers no longer meet a demand. Since the dispense with lay judges as decision-makers needs the consent of both parties,[27] it is blatantly obvious

[24]Statistisches Bundesamt (2018, p. 42 f).

[25]Cf. S 114, GVG; Lindloh (2011, p. 40).

[26]Lindloh (2011, p. 41 f).

[27]Cf. S 349 para 3, Zivilprozessordnung (Code of Civil Procedure, ZPO).

that these parties do not consider the participation of lay judges as a benefit, but rather as a burden. One reason for the parties' frustration with lay judges might be that it is impossible for them to pick an individual with particular experience and expertise in the field that relates to the dispute in question.[28] In any case, it does not make sense to force a panel of decision-makers upon the parties which they do not want. The empirical evidence just discussed amply proves that parties to proceedings in public courts are seeking a legal decision by professional judges who are experienced in the resolution of commercial disputes.

These bleak conclusions reached for the German Commercial Chambers are well in line with developments elsewhere. France's *Tribunaux de Commerce* (Commercial Courts), that are historically related to the German Commercial Chambers, are experiencing a comparable slump in case numbers. The lack of demand for the *Tribunaux de Commerce* is even more remarkable as the overall number of cases in the French civil courts is not in decline.

The development of the commercial courts of the Anglo-Saxon world proves that the demand of business parties for a special court tailored to their specific needs still exists. It is just the model of the Continental-European commercial chambers and tribunals that has become obsolete. In contrast to the Franco-German model, it is a distinctive feature of the business courts in London and New York that only professional judges are involved. This is all the more noteworthy as the Anglo-Saxon civil procedure is normally quite open to the participation of lay judges. In the US, civil actions at common law are still decided by juries, provided that the parties do not opt out of jury trial. Quite obviously, the framers of the business courts in London and New York worked from the assumption that business parties do not want lay judges to decide their disputes. Instead, business parties prefer professional judges with solid legal training and much expertise and experience in the resolution of complex cases.

The inevitable conclusion to be drawn from the empirical data discussed is that the model of the German *Kammern für Handelssachen* is outdated and no longer competitive. The objective of the framers of the German Commercial Chambers back in the 19th century, i.e. to offer a court sensitive to the needs of the business community, is still valid. It may even be more urgent than before. Yet, the means deployed to reach this end, i.e. the participation of lay judges drawn from the business community, is no longer apt to achieve this goal.

4 The Role of Arbitration

Notably, the decline of cases before the *Kammer für Handelssachen* correlates with a surge in case numbers of arbitral institutions. Cases filed with the German Arbitration Institute (DIS), the most important German arbitration institution, more than doubled

[28] This would be a violation of the German procedural principle of the *gesetzlicher Richter* (lawful judge), which is manifested in Art 101 para 1 sentence 2 of the Grundgesetz (German Basic Law).

between 2005 and 2017.[29] A similar pattern can be observed at the leading arbitration institution for cross-border cases, i.e. the International Chamber of Commerce (ICC). The ICC saw an increase in the number of filings of 57% during this time period.[30] Five per cent of the parties involved in ICC-proceedings are domiciled in Germany. The leading arbitration association for the English market is the London Court of International Arbitration (LCIA). The workload of this organization almost tripled in the time between 2005 and 2017.[31] However, German parties account for only one to two per cents of the total number of parties involved in LCIA arbitrations. Finally, the Swiss Chambers' Arbitration Institution (SCAI) is a relevant player in the market for the arbitral resolution of commercial disputes. The SCAI registered a total number of 937 filings in the years between 2005 and 2015.[32] German companies account for a large share of the parties involved in disputes pending at this arbitration organization. All in all, arbitration has been growing strongly in Europe. This development stands in stark contrast to the decline of case numbers at German public courts, especially at the *Kammer für Handelssachen* (see Sect. 3 above).

These observations, i.e. an increase of filings with arbitral institutions and a decrease of case numbers in the public courts, suggests that disputes have migrated from public commercial courts to private arbitration. Yet, the data clearly refute the conclusion, sometimes voiced by representatives of the judiciary, that the decline of the public courts corresponds with the rise of arbitration. In terms of absolute numbers, the impact of arbitration on the dispute resolution market in total remains marginal. All the cases filed with the DIS, the ICC and the LCIA in the year 2017 added together results in a total of 1255 cases. Even on the assumption that all of these cases would otherwise have ended up in German courts—which is clearly wrong for the large majority of ICC and LCIA cases—they would not have made much of a difference. This is so as the total loss of cases of Germany's Commercial Chambers in the years between 2007 and 2017 is a staggering 19,500.[33] Thus, the total number of cases filed with major arbitration institutions in Europe amounts to no more than five per cent of the decrease in demand for the German Commercial Chambers. In conclusion, the growing demand for private dispute resolution through arbitration cannot be the cause of the decline of the public courts. In other words, the cases lost by the German Commercial Chambers did not migrate to private arbitration.[34]

In light of the above analysis, the idea to restrict or even eliminate arbitration with a view to shift disputes back into the public court system, is misguided. It is certainly true that the arbitration organizations just mentioned do not form an oligopoly and thus do not register every dispute that goes to arbitration. In particular, ad hoc arbitrations that take place without the support of institutions do not enter

---

[29] In 2005: 72 cases; in 2017: 134 cases—DIS (2018, p. 1), http://www.disarb.org/upload/DIS-Verfahrensstatistik%202017.pdf.

[30] In 2005: 521 cases; in 2017: 810 cases—ICC (2018).

[31] LCIA, Director's General Reports 2005–2011; LCIA (2018).

[32] Swiss Chambers' Arbitration Institution (2016).

[33] Statistisches Bundesamt (2018, p. 42 f).

[34] See also, Schubert (2016, p. 30).

the publicly available statistics. The number of ad hoc arbitrations involving parties domiciled in Germany remain outside of the view. Still, it is highly unlikely that the dark field of arbitration cases, i.e. the number of cases that are resolved in arbitration, but are not captured by the statistics, is so high that it could possibly explain the decline of the Commercial Chambers. Surveys among corporate counsels support this view: Corporate counsels reported that they overwhelmingly preferred institutional to ad hoc arbitration. In no less than 86% of the cases going to arbitration, parties chose institutional arbitration and only in the remaining 14% parties opted for an ad hoc procedure.[35]

Finally, the impact of arbitration seems to be strongest in the category of high-profile disputes, involving high stakes. The 160 cases administered by the DIS during the year 2017 represented a total value of more than EUR 1 billion (EUR 1,040,861,397), which translates into an average of EUR 6,505.383 per case.[36] The average value of cases filed with SCAI in 2015 is in the same ballpark, at around CHF 15 million (ca. EUR 14 million).[37] The 810 arbitration cases of 2017 at the ICC represented an average value of USD 137 million.[38] 24% of these cases involved a value of more than USD 5 million, out of which 7.2% had a value of more than USD 100 million and another 1.7% had a value of more than USD 500 million.[39] At the LCIA, 31% of the 2017 claims were for amounts exceeding USD 20 million.[40] Even if the thriving business of arbitration cannot be held accountable for the decline of commercial disputes in the public courts, the figures suggest that arbitration nevertheless attracts the very large cases.

5 Introduction of English as a Court Language

Some of the German *Bundesländer* (states) have understood that the *Kammer für Handelssachen* is in dire need of reform. In 2010, the states of Northrhine-Westphalia, Hesse, Lower Saxony and Hamburg submitted a legislative proposal to create a sister court alongside the *Kammer für Handelssachen*, namely the *Kammern für internationale Handelssachen* (International Commercial Chambers).[41] The key feature of these courts would have been that English was accepted as a court language, provided that the parties settled on this language (cf. Section 184 of the GVG draft).

[35] International Arbitration: Corporate Attitudes and Practices 2008, p. 8. Other research can approve of this ratio: Schmidt-Doemitz (1999, p. 370): 90% of the respondents claimed to have never or rarely opted for an ad hoc arbitration.

[36] DIS (2018).

[37] Swiss Chambers' Arbitration Institution (2016, p. 1).

[38] ICC (2018, p. 61).

[39] ICC (2018, p. 62).

[40] LCIA (2018, p. 1).

[41] Deutscher Bundestag (2010).

The official justification of the bill acknowledges the fierce competition for commercial disputes that takes place between the court system and ADR offerings, but also between the civil justice systems of several jurisdictions:

> Germany as a venue for the settlement of legal disputes will gain in attractivity as a result of introducing English as a court language. International Commercial Chambers will attract major commercial disputes, that hitherto have been referred to arbitration or have been filed with public courts of the English-speaking world. The growing number of cases involving the selection of a German forum will entail the growing choice of German substantive law in international commercial contracts. The choice of a familiar legal system offers German companies the valuable advantage of higher legal certainty in international commercial transactions.[42]

Unfortunately, the proposal became moot when the parliamentary session ended without a vote of approval.

In evaluating the proposal to allow for English as a court language it is important to avoid misunderstandings. It was not the primary goal of the proposal to lure foreign parties into German courts, i.e. parties that are illiterate in German. The objective rather is to make litigation in German courts easier and more efficient for parties based in Germany and for disputes which bear some relation to Germany. This objective must be seen against the background of modern commercial practice. In the business world as well as in legal work related to international business transactions, English has evolved into the *lingua franca*. Thus, even contracts between German nationals, or rather corporations based in Germany, are often written in the English language. In case a dispute arises from such an English-language contract, it is simpler and cheaper to use English also as the language of dispute resolution. It is no longer necessary to engage in the time-consuming and cost-intensive translation of numerous documents, for instance written communications that were exchanged in the course of contract negotiations. But the use of English as the language of the court not only saves costs, it also promises benefits in terms of accuracy, i.e. a more truthful interpretation of the contract and a more precise application of the law. The parties can also use the language of the contract when offering their competing interpretations of its true meaning. It is a welcome side effect of proceedings held in the English language that the process of dispute resolution becomes more transparent and easier to follow for third parties who are unfamiliar with the German language, but have interest in the outcome of the dispute, such as foreign shareholders in a German corporation. In the long run, the decisions of the International Commercial Chambers would convey a proper impression of dispute resolution in Germany to the international business community. Provided that the quality of the courts and their operation is perceived

[42]Deutscher Bundestag (2010): "Der Gerichtsstandort Deutschland wird durch die Einführung von Englisch als Gerichtssprache in hohem Maße an Attraktivität gewinnen. Deutsche Kammern für internationale Handelssachen werden bedeutende wirtschaftsrechtliche Verfahren anziehen, die bisher entweder vor Schiedsgerichten oder im englischsprachigen Ausland verhandelt werden. Die zunehmende Vereinbarung des Gerichtsstandortes Deutschland wird auch die vermehrte Wahl des deutschen Rechts als auf internationale Vertragsverhältnisse anwendbares Recht nach sich ziehen. Das ihnen vertraute Rechtssystem bietet deutschen Unternehmen dabei den wertvollen Vorteil der erhöhten Rechtssicherheit im internationalen Wirtschaftsverkehr".

to be fair and adequate, this may make the German judicial system more attractive as a venue for the resolution of cross-border disputes.

On the other hand, it must be admitted that a model project for International Commercial Chambers at the *Oberlandesgerichte* (Higher Regional Courts) of Cologne and Düsseldorf resulted in disappointment, as these Chambers failed to attract cases. Still, this failure must not be interpreted to imply that the introduction of English as an optional court language for business disputes that are pending in German courts would be useless. The competitive disadvantage of German courts in the area of international commercial disputes cannot be made up or even narrowed overnight. In addition, it takes years for contract practice to pick up new options, as forum selection clauses must be re-drafted and negotiated successfully. It takes even more time for a dispute to grow out of a contract that does include a forum selection clause designating International Commercial Chambers. Finally, the fact that the Dutch established the Netherlands Commercial Court where English also will be the standard court language is evidence of the fact that the demand for dispute resolution procedures in English is recognized elsewhere, too. The same can be said of the newly established chambers in Brussels and Paris as well as for the commercial courts in the Gulf Region.[43]

The modest performance of model International Chambers of Commerce in Cologne and Düsseldorf rather suggests that the introduction of English as an optional court language is not enough to close the competitive gap separating the German courts from their traditional Anglo-Saxon competitors and their newly established Continental-European peers. Allowing for proceedings held in the English language alone will not transform the German Commercial Chambers into commercial courts Anglo-Saxon style. Jurisdictions like England and Wales as well as New York, where English is the everyday language anyway, do acknowledge the need for specialized commercial courts. They also perceive a demand for courts offering a higher degree of proficiency and experience, together with higher-quality facilities than is common among rank-and-file courts. This view is obviously shared by the Dutch lawmakers: The Netherlands Commercial Court stands for the attempt to integrate the major qualities of the English Commercial Court and the New York Business Division into a Continental-European judicial system.

If German courts shall participate successfully in the competition for high-stakes commercial disputes, it takes more than simply introducing English as an optional court language. Establishing a business court in Germany that is truly attractive to the business community and ready to compete with the well-established institutions in England and elsewhere is no mean feat. It would require a number of steps beyond the resolution of the language question. The following section will provide an outline of the basic elements of a successful German commercial court.

---

[43]Brussels International Business Court; *Chambre Internationale de la Cour d'Appel* Paris; Dubai International Financial Centre Courts; Qatar International Court; Abu Dhabi Global Market Courts—See Sect. 1 of this chapter.

6 Reform Proposal: A German Commercial Court

The proposal to create a commercial court in the Anglo-Saxon style in Germany is not new.[44] The following considerations build upon suggestions that were made earlier in order to carry them further. The aim is to provide guide posts for the establishment of a true commercial court in Germany.

6.1 The Interests of the Parties

The starting point for the design of a German commercial court should be the interest of the parties. The prime interest of the parties is not the minimization of the costs of dispute resolution. A business that wants to settle a dispute at the lowest possible cost can choose from a wide range of ADR mechanisms, such as negotiations, mediation, and conciliation. These mechanisms are much cheaper than dispute resolution via arbitral or judicial decision making as they neither require a full investigation of the facts nor a truthful application of the law. Parties who are willing to incur the costs of judicial dispute resolution do so because they value a binding decision by a neutral institution based on a thorough investigation of the facts and a truthful application of the law. It goes without saying that the parties will want to spend more on the resolution of a dispute with a value of EUR 10 million than on one worth EUR 20,000. As always, the parties aim for the optimal balance of costs and benefits.

The officials and executives responsible for successful business courts are well aware of the parties' preferences. In the speech mentioned earlier,[45] Lord Thomas Cwmgiedd's works from the premise that the parties are much interested in curtailing costs, speeding up procedures and reducing procedural complexity, e.g. by avoiding time consuming and expensive satellite litigation about trivial matters. This list of concerns matches with the theoretical considerations on the decision-process of rational process parties.[46] But what do the parties expect to receive in return? Implicit in Lord Cwmgiedd's speech is the assumption that the parties prefer a fair and adequate procedure for the establishment of the true facts of the case—'getting the procedure right'. In addition, the parties expect a 'correct' application of the law to the facts at hand—'getting the law' right. In interpreting the contract made by the parties, and in construing the applicable law, the court must remain faithful not only to the established rules of legal interpretation but also to the needs and the expectations of the particular parties and the business community at large.

Consistently adapting the law to the needs of the business community seems to call for a biased and partial interpretation and application of the law, something that seems to run against the rule of law. However, it must be borne in mind that commercial

---

[44] See especially: Callies and Hoffmann (2009, p. 52), Hoffmann (2009, p. 331); more comprehensive, Hoffmann (2011, p. 175 ff.), Kötz (2010, p. 7).

[45] Lord of Cwmgiedd (2017).

[46] Wagner (2017, p. 46 ff).

courts exercise their jurisdiction in cases which only involve commercial parties. Disputes between businesses and consumers can never make it into a commercial court proper. With a view to legal relations between business parties, a business-oriented interpretation and application of the law is innocent and fully adequate. This is not only true for the default rules of contract law from which the parties may derogate anyway. It also applies to the interpretation and application of mandatory rules as, even here, the parties retain the authority to settle their dispute in any way that they seem fit. Consequently, a court should try, in its decision, to replicate the outcome that rational parties could have agreed in settlement.[47]

6.2 Excellent Judges

Whatever else the parties may expect from a commercial court, they certainly value the court's ability to structure the procedure efficiently and to decide their dispute proficiently. For both aspects, the qualification of the judges is of imminent importance.[48] Consequently, the Netherlands Commercial Court places great emphasis on the training, proficiency, and experience of the judges to be appointed.[49] The aim is to attract personalities who possess not only outstanding legal qualifications, but also extensive practical experience in handling complex procedures. Moreover, they need the ability to conduct the proceedings in the English language and to issue a judgment in this language. The individuals who are in command of such capabilities will automatically be wordly-wise. In fact, the framers of the Netherlands Commercial Court expect the judges serving on that court to possess legal training in comparative law in general, to be familiar with the characteristics of the systems of civil procedure operated in various jurisdictions and to have obtained some experience in communicating with foreign lawyers.[50]

As explained in Sect. 3 above, the German Commercial Chambers fail to live up to the standard just described. The layperson-system of the *Kammern für Handelssachen* offers the opposite of what parties expect from an attractive forum for commercial disputes. By definition, laypersons work full-time in another job and thus have less time and energy to devote to their judicial services. They definitely lack the time and expertise to handle complex large-stakes disputes efficiently and expediently. Moreover, laymen are not remunerated adequately for their services but merely reimbursed for expenses incurred.[51] This may now and then attract individuals that are truly compassionate about making fair and accurate decisions, but surely does not lead to a competition among those individuals who would be most able and qualified to serve as commercial judges. For those who do serve, the lack of

---

[47] Cf. Wagner (1998, p. 106 ff).

[48] Hoffmann (2011, p. 177), Gibbons (1995, p. 45).

[49] Cf. Wagner (2017, p. 198).

[50] Raad voor de Rechtspraak (2015, p. 13).

[51] Commercial lay judges only receive compensation for travel expenses.

an adequate salary weakens their incentives to work hard and diligently. To put the point bluntly: It cannot seriously be expected from an unpaid judge to put in the effort that would be needed to efficiently handle a complex large-stakes dispute to the satisfaction of the parties.

6.3 Workload

At least as important as the selection of the judges is the management of their workload. The current system of workload-management that is operated in the German courts determines the workload of judges by the amount of completed cases. Each judge has to dispose of a certain number of cases annually. Under such a system that largely relies on a quantitative parameter, the proper handling of complex cases is practically impossible.

In Germany, a judge serving at first instance, at a district court, has to process and resolve a dispute of ordinary nature within an average of 569 min or 9.48 h, provided that he or she wants to comply with the scheduled workload. This translates into an annual workload of 180 cases. For certain categories of cases that are more complex than others, such as medical malpractice, construction disputes, company law and competition law cases, the official allocation of time is 1193 min or approximately 20 h. Resolving a dispute from these legal areas should on average not cost more than 20 h. The average number of such cases, involving high complexity, is 86 per annum.[52]

Obviously, it is impossible to adequately handle complex cases with an investment of 20 h of judicial time. A single judge at a Regional Court, who has to deal with 180 cases of ordinary complexity per year, is simply unable to exclusively devote his time and energy to a complex case, not even for a few days, let alone weeks or even months. Even complex cases are supposed to be settled with judicial effort equivalent to 20 h or 2.5 working days! An oral hearing continuing for longer than a few hours would create a serious problem for a judge as he or she would unduly neglect other cases that are also awaiting resolution. It is simply self-defense that the judges burdened with such a workload has no choice but to work towards a settlement. However, pressure to settle is the last thing that parties expect from a high-quality commercial court. Business enterprises are repeat players in the dispute resolution market and thus turn to the court only after chances for an amicable resolution of the dispute have been exhausted. What parties rather expect from a commercial court is high-quality decision-making within a reasonable time and at reasonable cost.

With a view to the existing court system in Germany, the need for reform is patent and urgent. The workload of commercial judges would have to be reduced to a level that enables them to spend the time necessary for a proper management and resolution of complex cases. The requirements of proper dispute handling and resolution must be the benchmark for the assessment of the judges' workload, rather than budgetary

---

[52]Wagner (2017, p. 219).

constraints imposed by the respective Ministry of Finance. Under the current system, a fair performance-based competition between public courts and arbitral tribunals is out of reach. As arbitration is a creature of the parties who have to front the entire costs of arbitral proceedings, tribunals do not labor under a budgetary constraint.

In contrast to arbitral tribunals, public courts are funded by the taxpayer. Any reduction in the judges' workload would therefore increase the number of judgeships and, in the form of wages and other costs, inflate the budget of the judiciary. This raises the question whether the taxpayer should pay for the high-quality management and resolution of complex cases, that are often the ones that also involve high stakes. In Germany, parties to civil disputes bear much of the financial burden of civil litigation anyway, as court fees are comparatively high.[53] Within such a framework, it would be an easy step to burden the parties to high-stakes disputes with the additional cost that a high-quality commercial court would cause for the budget of the judiciary. Thus, the parties to complex disputes should bear the full costs of a commercial court via increased court fees.[54]

6.4 Facilities and Resources

The facilities and technological resources that the German courts have at their disposal vary from state to state, but are often found wanting. The gap between the judicial system and the private sector has been growing in recent years, thanks to budget-tightening policies on the one hand and rapid advances in IT on the other. Large law firms take advantage of these technologies by implementing them quickly. And in arbitration practice, memoranda, other submissions, written witness statements and expert reports, are nowadays submitted in electronic form. A commercial court aspiring to high standards needed IT on par with that of large law firms, and it needed to be accessible via electronic communication. For oral hearings, it must have premises at its disposal which can accommodate multi-member teams of lawyers and representatives of the parties, and for more time than just a few days.

The current state of the German courts in terms of facilities and technology is far from satisfactory. They are lacking modern IT as well as large courtrooms for extensive hearings. At this point, investments in infrastructure are necessary. The Netherlands have also acknowledged the need for such investments in their own court system and committed to a little more than what is absolutely necessary. The Netherlands Commercial Court was designed to shine a little—*en allure uitstralen*. Such an approach would help a German sister court, too.

[53] For a comparative overview cf. Reimann (2012, p. 3).

[54] Cf. Wagner (2017, p. 243).

6.5 Procedure

In principle, the German *Zivilprozessordnung* (Code of Civil Procedure, ZPO) offers an adequate and reliable procedural framework, which allows for a proper and efficient management of complex proceedings. Sections 272 to 276 of the ZPO provide the court with a toolbox for hands-on and tailor-made management of the respective legal dispute.[55] This framework is flexible and adaptable enough to enable the court to adequately manage complex cases. Thus, there is no need to reform the procedural framework for complex cases in a perceived commercial court through legislative measures. The rules and routines that are most adequate for a commercial court should be developed by the judges dealing with complex cases in an iterative case-by-case process of trial and error. With experience, certain guardrails will develop. If necessary, they can be written into law in due time.

However, legislation is necessary to change the routine of court reporting. The common practice in German courts is that the presiding judge summarizes the statements of witnesses and experts in his or her own words. The resulting risk that the statements of witnesses and experts will be distorted somehow by the judicial summary is obvious. In international civil practice, such indirect court-reporting is unacceptable. Here, the verbatim protocol, which documents the testimony word for word, is regarded as indispensable for the purpose of providing a truthful record. In the world of German arbitration, it is already common to hire a court reporter and prepare verbatim record of the evidentiary hearing, or even of any hearing.[56]

The German way of reporting witness' and expert testimony indirectly, through summaries of the presiding judge is not based on better insight, but simply on the ever-present shortage of funds. A verbatim record is much more ambitious and costlier than a protocol dictated by a judge because a highly qualified court reporter has to attend the hearing. With a view to a perceived commercial court, budget constraints should again not stand in the way of reasonable solutions. As with the costs needed for state-of-the-art IT systems, the additional financial burden caused by verbatim protocols should be shifted to the parties in the form of higher court fees. Rational parties will stand ready to bear these costs, as they are outweighed by the additional accuracy of fact-finding that a verbatim record promises. In a multi-million Euro case no rational party would avoid the fees of a court reporter in exchange for the risk of inaccurate fact finding.

6.6 English as the Court Language

Germany's attempts to introduce English as an optional court language were outlined in Sect. 5 above. So far, these attempts have not born fruit. In substance, there is no doubt that such a step is necessary, considering that the Netherlands Commercial

[55] Cf. the legislative materials in Deutscher Bundestag (1974, p. 34).

[56] Wieczoreck and Schütze (2014, S 1047, para 26).

Court will use English as its standard court language, with the possibility for the parties to opt out and to select Dutch as the language of their proceedings.[57]

Nevertheless, the topic of 'English as a court language' has given rise to passionate discussions about the significance of the German language and the self-assertion of German culture in a world dominated by the English language and Anglo-Saxon culture. Skeptics have gone so far as to raise constitutional concerns against the use of a foreign language in domestic courts.[58] They argue that the admission of English as a court language violated the constitutionally guaranteed principle of open access to court proceedings. However, it should be remembered that very few people use their right to eye-witness judicial proceedings. Instead, information about the work of the courts is disseminated by the media that in turn rely on the reports of journalists who are present at court hearings. This kind of indirect information of the public about the courts is unlikely to suffer should English be allowed as an optional language of proceedings.[59] After all, there are certainly enough journalists around who are able to follow a hearing conducted in the English language and to subsequently prepare a report in the German language.[60]

The practical consequences of English being added to German as a court language should not be overestimated. It seems rather unlikely that many parties would opt to substitute English for German as the language of the entire proceedings. In any event, German courts will continue to be selected as a venue of choice in cases only in which German law is the chosen law of the contract. In those cases, i.e. where German law applies, there are good reasons to prepare written statements on German law in the German language. As every lawyer with experience in international legal work knows, the translation of legal terms from one language into another hardly ever works without loss or other distortions. This prediction, that the demand for proceedings that are entirely conducted in English will remain low, is confirmed by the model projects for International Commercial Chambers in Cologne and Düsseldorf where the number of cases brought ranges in the low single-digits.[61] But this does not imply that permission to choose English as the court language would be meaningless. Such permission would at least signal that there is the possibility to submit English-language documents in their original form, without translation, as well as to allow witnesses and experts who do not speak German to testify in the English language without using an interpreter. As one hears from the courts operating International Commercial Chambers, this version of a 'hybrid procedure' is actually well-received by the parties and much in use there. While it is true that the options to submit English-language documents and to interrogate witnesses in English already

[57] See Sect. 5 of this chapter.

[58] Flessner (2011a, p. 3544), Flessner (2011b, p. 1913), Handschell (2010, p. 398), Hirtz (2011, p. 41), presumably also Jacobs (2016), before S 184 GVG, para 4.

[59] Ewer (2010, p. 1324 f.), Armbrüster (2011, p. 103 f.), Hoffmann (2011, p. 183 ff).

[60] Bundesverfassungsgericht (2001, p. 1636), Prütting (2010, p. 114), Armbrüster (2011, p. 104), Mayer (2018, S 169, para 85): 'The media coverage (press, radio, television) is of significant importance to achieve the means, that the principle of public hearing serves' (English translation by the authors).

[61] Hau (2012, p. 59).

exist within the current framework of Section 184 and paragraph 2 of Section 185 of the GVG,[62] it would help to go a step further. It would send a strong signal to the parties that the commercial court is willing and able to accommodate the English language whenever the parties wish for it. Contracts for large-volume transactions are increasingly being negotiated and drafted in English, even where German law is chosen as the substantive law. In these cases, the parties have already done the necessary work of translating German legal terms into English. Thus, the risk that the quality of the judicial process will suffer if the proceedings are entirely conducted in English is only minor. Under these circumstances, the parties should be allowed to proceed in English. The parties should not be deprived of this option without good reason.

6.7 Exclusion of the Public

An essential motivation to choose private arbitration is confidentiality. In particular, hearings before arbitral tribunals are only open to the parties and counsel. They remain closed to the public at large. In contrast, hearings before German courts are open to the public (Section 169, GVG). The public can only be excluded in certain narrowly-defined circumstances. The exclusion of the public is warranted where the court is about to discuss personal or even intimate facts from the life of a party or witness (Section 171b, GVG) or an important business, trade or tax secret (No. 2 of Section 172, GVG). In these cases, the court has discretion to conduct the proceedings in camera. The established categories of confidential court proceedings do not seem to satisfy the parties' interests in confidentiality. Otherwise, it would be difficult to explain why the parties prefer arbitration over litigation even in purely domestic cases, where the neutrality of the forum is not an issue. In fact, Section 171b and No. 2 of Section 172 of the GVG only permit the exclusion of the public from the oral hearings. The judgment of the court must be made public, and it will contain the same facts that were shielded from the public during oral trial, provided that they are relevant for the decision that the court made.

In the literature, it is argued that the principle of publicity of court proceedings, as enshrined in Section 169 of the GVG, may be derogated through party agreement.[63] If the parties were authorized to waive publicity, they could simply agree on in-camera trials, and use this option to protect proceedings in a German commercial court as well. However, to allow such waivers would seriously undermine the principle of publicity of proceedings and is hardly defensible under constitutional law. The German *Bundesverfassungsgericht* (Federal Constitutional Court, BVerfG) vests the principle of publicity of court proceedings not in the rights of the particular parties but in the rights of the general public. The right to publicity of court proceedings is

---

[62] See e.g. Mayer (2018, S 184, para 9).

[63] Ewer (2010, p. 1324).

classified as a 'legal position of the people' and placed within the perimeter of the constitutional principles of democracy and the rule of law.

The perceived commercial courts should turn these constitutional limitations around and sell them as a benefit rather than a burden: The commercial courts would attract high-stakes disputes into the German court system in order to process and decide them under the eyes of the public. This purpose would be missed if public courts would act like an arbitral tribunal, i.e. would work outside of public view. The criticism launched at commercial arbitration, namely that the migration of whole subject-matter areas such as post merger and acquisition disputes into private arbitration, seriously undermines the public interest in the interpretation, application and development of the law,[64] is an advantage for a public court in competing for these same disputes.

6.8 *The Appeals Process*

In every system of civil justice, the question of appeals arises. Should there be levels of appeal against judgments reached further below, and if so, how many? These questions are anything but trivial. On one hand, the appeals process is an advantage of the public judicial system. Allowing for appeals against judgments at first or second instance enables the judicial system to maximize the quality of outcomes under a budget constraint.[65] If all resources would be concentrated at first instance, then cases of little interest and complexity would attract the same degree of attention and effort as more complex and ambiguous ones. A system of staggered appeals allows for deciding a great number of cases with little effort at first instance in order to then put in more effort for those cases where at least one party is dissatisfied with the judgment reached at the lower court. In this way, it is possible to concentrate scarce judicial resources on those cases which actually deserve more attention. The exact limits of this category of case are determined by the lawmakers, who define the prerequisites for launching an appeal, and by the parties for whom launching an appeal is always an option, but no duty.

The obvious disadvantage of the appeals process is a multiplied effort in time and cost for each individual case that goes to appeal. In the situation *ex ante*, before a dispute has arisen, the parties negotiating a dispute settlement clause have the authority to decide for themselves whether the benefit of the chance to correct mistakes on appeal is worth the additional cost. Parties that opt for arbitration apparently do not think that this is the case. This preference does not necessarily apply to dispute resolution by a public commercial court. After all, commercial courts are designed as an alternative to arbitration. As a result, decisions of the English Commercial Court are subject to the same rights of appeal as other judgments of the High Court. The

[64] Duwe and Keller (2005, p. 16).

[65] For a thorough analysis, see Wagner (2009, p. 157 ff).

Netherlands Commercial Court is set up in a similar way, with access to the higher courts of the Netherlands being guaranteed.

Against this background, there are strong reasons to locate the German Commercial Court at the level of the *Oberlandesgerichte*, which are normally acting as an appeals court in the German system of civil justice. Thus, the parties would miss the district courts as first instance and would have only one appeal, directly to the *Bundesgerichtshof* (Federal Supreme Court, BGH). Dispensing with a second appeal seems adequate for complex proceedings. The effort in time and money necessary to accurately determine the facts of the case is usually very high. It should only be incurred once, in this case in first instance proceedings before the Higher Regional Courts. The parties would then have one appeal to the BGH which would be limited to a review of the judgment for legal error. The gathering and evaluation of the evidence would not be repeated on appeal.

Charging the Higher Regional Courts with proceedings at first instance is exceptional, but not impossible. The Higher Regional Courts already operate as courts of first instance in selected areas, such as arbitration and important matters of corporate law.[66] It seems that the lawmakers choose the Higher Regional Courts as courts of first instance with a view to the complexity of the case, the weight of the interests involved, and the interest of the parties in an expedient resolution of their dispute. It would be consistent with these principles to include complex commercial disputes in the list of cases for disposition by the Higher Regional Courts.

6.9 Institutional Anchor

The examples of commercial courts in England, New York and the Netherlands suggest to establish one single German Commercial Court in the Federal Republic of Germany.[67] However, this solution would be in conflict with the German tradition of decentralized judicial administration under the control of the several states. Due to the constitutional principles of separation of powers and of federalism, the federal government lacks the competence to establish a centralized commercial court as a federal forum. This bar could only be lifted through constitutional reform.

Below this high threshold, there is the possibility to empower the states to establish commercial courts. A legislative act authorizing the states to do so would have to make sure that the commercial courts receive a sufficient amount of cases and that they are able to cooperate with a specialized bar. With no cases and the lack of experienced counsel, it is impossible for a specialized forum to thrive. The conditions for the establishment of a successful commercial court can be met in a few places in Germany

[66]Those are: arbitration questions according to S 1062 of the ZPO; corporate approval procedures according to S 246a para 1 sentence 3 and S 319 para 6 sentence 7 of the *Aktiengesetz* (German Corporate Company Act), S 16 para 3 of the *Umwandlungsgesetz* (German Transformation Act).

[67]Belgium also recently established the Brussels International Business Court, see Hoffmann (2018, p. 59).

only. It is neither possible nor desirable to establish a commercial court at each and every Higher Regional Court in the Federal Republic. By definition, the demand for excellent judges with practical experience in handling complex proceedings cannot be satisfied at any town that is home to a Higher Regional Court. The case numbers for any single commercial court would be far too low. Concentration on a few venues is therefore inevitable.

Looking at a map of Germany, it is apparent that none of the 16 German states should be home to more than one commercial court. With a high degree of fragmentation, German commercial courts would certainly loose out in the ensuing competition with sister institutions in neighboring countries. Thus, the federal lawmakers should authorize the states to establish one commercial court in their respective territory. It must be hoped that not every state used this authority and actually established its own commercial court. The competitive opportunities would be greatest if there were as few commercial courts as possible. Potential venues for commercial courts in Germany are Frankfurt, Düsseldorf, and Hamburg, perhaps also Munich and Berlin.

6.10 Competence and Choice of Court Agreements

As described in Sect. 2 above, the competence of the already-existing Commercial Chambers extends to, among other cases, two-sided commercial transactions. For the future, it would be preferable to open up the competence of the commercial court to all disputes between businesses in the sense of Section 14 of the *Bürgerliches Gesetzbuch* (German Civil Code) that require and justify increased judicial effort.

Selecting the cases which fall into the jurisdiction of a commercial court can be done in different ways. One conceivable solution would be that, the commercial court assesses the complexity of the case and, when it denies the required level of complexity, remits it to the ordinary courts. An alternative would be to set value thresholds as, in general, the size and complexity of party submissions grow proportionally with the value of the claim. The higher the stakes, the more the parties invest into the litigation. Finally, one could eschew any objective measure and instead regulate the workload of commercial courts through (higher) court fees. If court fees are set at a level that covers the full cost of the court, there would be no incentive to bring simple cases before these fora. On the contrary, an opulent—and costly—procedure should not be forced upon the parties. A plain offer would be sufficient.

No matter which instrument is chosen to regulate access to the commercial court, the parties have to be able to assess its jurisdiction *ex ante*, at the time of contract formation, with certainty. Only then are the parties in a position to write their contract with a view to the level of accuracy to be expected from the potential decision-maker, in case a dispute arises in the future. A right of the parties to choose the competent court is guaranteed in Section 38 of the ZPO and Article 25 of the Brussels Ia Regulation.

Depending on the institutional anchor of commercial courts within the German justice system, it could be argued that such choice of court agreements would run counter to the principle that the parties lack the authority to choose the judicial panel within the court organization. While this objection is not convincing,[68] a statutory clarification that such contracts are in fact valid and binding would be desirable.

The domicile of the parties should be of no concern to the jurisdiction of commercial courts. It should be no obstacle to its jurisdiction that both parties have their respective seats outside of Germany.

Finally, the jurisdiction of the commercial courts should also extend to disputes associated with arbitral proceedings and awards. These cases are within the jurisdiction of the Higher Regional Courts already pursuant to Section 1062 of the ZPO. It is reasonable and necessary to combine the jurisdiction for complex commercial cases and for disputes evolving out of arbitral proceedings as both cover essentially the same kinds of disputes and require the same expertise and experience on the part of the decision-makers. To combine the two in one hand would enable the judges to gain broader experience which would be welcome considering the low frequency of complex commercial disputes.

6.11 *Financing*

Last but not least, courts have to be funded. The Dutch *Raad voor de Rechtspraak* lays great emphasis on the fact, that the new Commercial Court of the Netherlands will cost the taxpayer not a single penny.[69] The Netherlands Commercial Court charges court fees that are designed to cover its full costs. Germany should follow this model. There is no reason to subsidize the judicial resolution of high-value disputes with taxpayer money. The fees should be sufficient to cover the salaries of the judges and other personnel, and the additional costs of modern IT systems and the like. The parties of large commercial disputes will be willing and able to finance these costs in full, provided that they receive a service in return that is worth its price.

References

Armbrüster C (2011) Englischsprachige Zivilprozesse vor deutschen Gerichten? Zeitschrift für Rechtspolitik (ZRP) 102–104

Bach ML, Applebaum L (2004) A history of the creation and jurisdiction of business courts in the last decade. Bus Lawyer 60:147–275

Bundesverfassungsgericht (2001) Judgement of 24 January 2001, 1 BvR 2623/95. Neue Juristische Wochenschrift (NJW) 54:1633–1639

Callies GP, Hoffmann H (2009) Justizstandort Deutschland im globalen Wettbewerb. Anwaltsblatt 52–53

[68]Wagner (2017, p. 564), Lüke (1990 p. 361) and Hoffmann (2011, p. 193 ff) also argue for the possibility of parties to dispense from the case assignment plan.

[69]Raad voor de Rechtspraak (2015, p. 15 ff).

Deutscher Bundestag (1974) Entwurf eines Gesetzes zur Vereinfachung und Beschleunigung gerichtlicher Verfahren (Vereinfachungsnovelle). Drucksache 7/2729

Deutscher Bundestag (2010) Entwurf eines Gesetzes zur Einführung von Kammern für internationale Handelssachen (KfiHG). Drucksache 17/2163

DIS (Deutsche Institution für Schiedsgerichtsbarkeit) (2018) Statistiken 2017. http://www.disarb.org/upload/DIS-Verfahrensstatistik%202017.pdf

Duwe C, Keller M (2005) Privatisierung der Justiz—bleibt die Rechtsfortbildung auf der Strecke?—Ein Beitrag zur Auflösung des Spannungsverhältnisses von Privatautonomie und Rechtsfortbildung in der Schiedsgerichtsbarkeit. Zeitschrift für Schiedsverfahrensrecht (SchiedsVZ):169–178

Eisenberg T, Miller GP (2009) The Flight to New York: An Empirical Study of Choice of Law and Choice of Forum Clauses in Publicly-Held Companies' Contracts. Cardozo L Rev 30:1475–1512

Ewer W (2010) Das Öffentlichkeitsprinzip—ein Hindernis für die Zulassung von Englisch als konsensual-optionaler Gerichtssprache? Neue Juristische Wochenschrift (NJW) 63:1323–1326

Fleischer H, Danninger N (2017) Handelsgerichte in Frankreich und Deutschland zwischen Tradition und Innovation. Status quo und zukünftige Perspektiven im Rechtsvergleich. Recht der Internationalen Wirtschaft (RIW) 63:549–557

Flessner A (2011a) Deutscher Zivilprozess auf Englisch — Der Gesetzentwurf des Bundesrats im Lichte von Staatsrecht, Grundrechten und Europarecht. Neue Juristische Wochenschrift (NJW) 64:3544–3545

Flessner A (2011b) Deutscher Zivilprozess auf Englisch—Der Gesetzentwurf des Bundesrats im Lichte von Staatsrecht, Grundrechten und Europarecht. Neue Juristische Online Zeitschrift (NJOZ) 1913–1924

Gibbons JJ (1995) The quality of the judges is what counts in the end. Brooklyn L Rev 61:45–51

Hahn C (1879) Die gesammten Materialien zu den Reichsjustizgesetzen, vol 1. Materialien zum Gerichtsverfassungsgesetz. Von Decker, Berlin

Handschell T (2010) Die Vereinbarkeit von Englisch als Gerichtssprache mit dem Grundgesetz und europäischem Recht. Deutsche Richterzeitung (DRiZ) 395–400

Hau W (2012) Fremdsprachengebrauch durch deutsche Zivilgerichte – vom Schutz legitimer Parteiinteressen zum Wettbewerb der Justizstandorte. In: Michaels R, Solomon D (eds) Liber Amicorum Klaus Schurig. De Gruyter, Munich, pp 49–62

Hirtz B (2011) Englisch sollte nicht zu einer deutschen Gerichtssprache werden. Anwaltsblatt 41

Hoffmann H (2009) Rechtsfortbildung im internationalen Wirtschaftsrecht—ein Plädoyer für die Einrichtung von Kammern für internationale Handelssachen. Deutsche Richterzeitung (DRiZ) 329–332

Hoffmann H (2010) Schiedsgerichte als Gewinner der Globalisierung? Eine empirische Analyse zur Bedeutung staatlicher und privater Gerichtsbarkeit für den internationalen Handel. Zeitschrift für Schiedsverfahrensrecht (SchiedsVZ) 96–101

Hoffmann H (2011) Kammern für internationale Handelssachen. Nomos, Baden-Baden

Hoffmann H (2018) Von 'Law—Made in Germany' zu 'Commercial Litigation in Germany'. Zeitschrift für Internationales Wirtschaftsrecht (IWRZ) 58–62

ICC (2018) Dispute resolution statistics 2017. https://cdn.iccwbo.org/content/uploads/sites/3/2018/07/2017-icc-dispute-resolution-statistics.pdf

Jacobs M (2016) In: Bork R, Roth H (eds) Stein/Jonas, Kommentar zur Zivilprozessordnung, vol 6, 22nd edn. Mohr Siebeck, Tübingen

Kötz H (2010) Deutsches Recht und common law. Anwaltsblatt 1–7

Lindloh K (2011) Der Handelsrichter und sein Amt, 6th edn. Vahlen, Munich

LCIA (London Court of International Arbitration) (2018) Casework report 2017

Loomis T (2002) Commercial division: high-profile case casts spotlight on well-regarded court. NY Law J

Lord of Cwmgiedd T (2017) Giving business what it wants—A well run court for commercial and business disputes. https://www.judiciary.uk/wp-content/uploads/2017/03/grand-court-of-the-cayman-islands-guest-lecture-march-2017.pdf

Lüke G (1990) Unorthodoxe Gedanken zur Verkürzung der Prozeßdauer und Entlastung der Zivilgerichte. In: Prütting H (ed) Festschrift für Gottfried Baumgärtel zum 70. Geburtstag. Heymann, Cologne, pp 349–362
Mayer H (2018). In: Kissel R, Mayer H (eds) Kommentar zum Gerichtsverfassungsgesetz, 9th edn. C. H. Beck, Munich
Pernice I (2019) In: Graf JP (ed) Beck'scher online-Kommentar Gerichtsverfassungsgesetz. C. H. Beck, Munich
Podszun R, Rohner T (2018) Nach dem Brexit: Die Stärkung staatlicher Gerichte für wirtschaftsrechtliche Streitigkeiten. Betriebsberater (BB): 450–454. http://www.jura.hhu.de/fileadmin/redaktion/Fakultaeten/Juristische_Fakultaet/Podszun/Podszun_Rohner_Paper_Staatliche_Gerichte_staerken.pdf
Prütting H (2010) Englisch als Gerichtssprache. Anwaltsblatt 113–117
Raad voor de Rechtspraak (2015) Plan tot oprichting van de Netherlands commercial court. https://www.rechtspraak.nl/SiteCollectionDocuments/plan-netherlands-commercial-court.pdf
Reimann MW (2012) Cost and fee allocation in civil procedure: a synthesis. In: Idem (ed) Cost and fee allocation in civil procedure. Springer, Berlin, pp 3–56
Schmidt-Diemitz R (1999) Internationale Schiedsgerichtsbarkeit—eine empirische Untersuchung. Der Betrieb (DB) 52:369–372
Schubert W (2016) Gehen der Justiz in Deutschland die Zivilverfahren aus? Fakten, Überlegungen, Maßnahmen insbesondere mit Bezug zu Sachsen-Anhalt. In: Höland A, Meller-Hannich C (eds) Nichts zu klagen? Nomos, Baden-Baden, pp 21–33
Sommermeyer HC (1966) Die Kammer für Handelssachen. Stoytscheff, Darmstadt
Statistisches Bundesamt (2018) Fachserie 10, Reihe 2.1: Rechtspflege—Zivilgerichte. https://www.destatis.de/DE/Themen/Staat/Justiz-Rechtspflege/Publikationen/Downloads-Gerichte/zivilgerichte-2100210177004.pdf?__blob=publicationFile&v=5,41f
Swiss Chambers' Arbitration Institution (2016) https://www.swissarbitration.org/files/515/Statistics/SCAI%20Statistics%202015%20and%202004_2015_20160731.pdf
Vogenauer S (2013) Regulatory competition through choice of contract law and choice of forum in Europe: theory and evidence. Eur Rev Private Law (ERPL) 21:13–78
Wagner G (1998) Prozessverträge. Mohr Siebeck, Tübingen
Wagner G (2009) Ökonomische Analyse der Rechtsmittel. In: Bork R et al (eds) Ökonomische Analyse des Verfahrensrechts. Mohr Siebeck, Tübingen, pp 157–194
Wagner G (2017) Rechtsstandort Deutschland im Wettbewerb. C.H. Beck, Munich
Wieczoreck B, Schütze RA (2014) Zivilprozessordnung und Nebengesetze, vol 11, 4th edn. De Gruyter, Berlin, Boston

Gerhard Wagner is Professor of Civil Law, Economic Law, and Economics at Humboldt University since 2013, where he is the founder and academic director of the English-language LL.M.-program "International Dispute Resolution". Before joining the Humboldt faculty, Wagner served as executive director of the Institute of Civil Procedure and Dispute Resolution at the University of Bonn. He was Visiting Fellow at University College in London, UK (2003), Visiting Professor of Law at the University of Chicago Law School, Chicago, IL (2010/11), Professor of Fundamentals of Private Law at Erasmus University, Rotterdam, Netherlands (2009/14), Honorary Professor of Law at Renmin University School of Law, Beijing, China (2008/11) and Visiting Scholar at New York University School of Law, NY (2018). Since 2015, he is a Member of the Max Planck Institute for Comparative and International Private Law in Hamburg. Wagner is president of the Private Law Teachers' Association (Zivilrechtslehrervereinigung) and a board member of the German Institution of Arbitration (DIS). For more information: https://plone.rewi.hu-berlin.de/de/lf/ls/wgn/wagner.

Arvid Arntz is a Ph.D. candidate at the faculty of law of the Humboldt University Berlin. He holds a position as a research assistant at the Chair of Civil Law, Economic Law, and Economics (Prof. Gerhard Wagner) of the same university. Before joining Humboldt University, Arntz was a research assistant at the Max Planck Institute for Comparative and International Private Law in Hamburg. He studied law at the University of Freiburg. Currently Arntz researches in private law, economic analysis of law and the digitalization of the economy. His Ph.D. on the regulation of online intermediary platforms is funded by the German National Academic Foundation. For more information: https://www.rewi.hu-berlin.de/de/lf/ls/wgn/ma/arvid-arntz.

Recognition and Enforcement of International Commercial Court Judgments

Anselmo Reyes and Kevin Tan

Abstract International commercial courts have emerged in different parts of the world. Such courts have typically been established to address a 'market failure', viz, by dealing with the peculiarities of international commercial dispute resolution that are not being met by international commercial arbitration. An oft-asked question about such courts is whether their judgments will be recognised and enforced elsewhere. Recent developments suggest that there is much to be optimistic about the recognition and enforcement of their judgments. In the absence of treaties and conventions, the judgments of international commercial courts should still generally be capable of recognition and enforcement under the principles or codes of many common law and civil law jurisdictions. There is more to recognition and enforcement than simply counting the number of Contracting States to treaties or conventions to which a country with an international commercial court is party.

1 Introduction

International commercial courts, which are judicial bodies that resolve transnational commercial disputes having little or no connection with the jurisdiction in question, have emerged in different parts of the world. It has been said that such courts have been established by various countries to address a 'market failure', viz, by dealing with the peculiarities of international commercial litigation.[1]

[1]Ramesh (2018, para 5).

A. Reyes (✉)
Singapore International Commercial Court, Singapore, Singapore
e-mail: reyes.anselmo@gmail.com

K. Tan
Rajah & Tann Singapore LLP, Singapore, Singapore
e-mail: kevin.tan@rajahtann.com

L. Chen and A. Janssen (eds.), *Dispute Resolution in China, Europe and World*,
Ius Gentium: Comparative Perspectives on Law and Justice 79,
https://doi.org/10.1007/978-3-030-42974-4_2

In the past 15 years alone, we have seen the establishment of more than half a dozen international commercial courts. Some examples of international commercial courts include[2]:

(1) The English Commercial Court (ECC) (established in 1895);
(2) The Dubai International Financial Centre Courts (DIFCC) (established in June 2004);
(3) The Singapore International Commercial Court (SICC) (established in January 2015);
(4) The Astana International Financial Centre Court (AIFCC) (established in December 2017);
(5) The International Chambers of the Paris Commercial Court and the Paris Court of Appeal (collectively, the 'Paris ICCs') (established in 2010 and February 2018 respectively);
(6) The China International Centre Court (CICC) (established in June 2018); and
(7) The Netherlands Commercial Court (NCC) (established in January 2019).

International commercial courts are to be welcomed. First, while international commercial arbitration has generally been the go-to mode of resolving transnational commercial disputes, there has been mounting dissatisfaction. For instance, users have highlighted concerns with the high costs, delays, and technicality of arbitration proceedings.[3] Indeed, in view of the wide spectrum of transnational disputes, some cases would invariably be better suited for litigation than arbitration. In addition, the competition from international commercial courts as another alternative dispute resolution mechanism would bring down the cost of arbitration.

Second, international commercial courts generally have features which render them attractive to parties. Such features include: (i) the possibility of making submissions in English, the *lingua franca* of transnational commerce; (ii) the appointment of foreign judges to the bench (thus allowing users of the court to benefit from international judicial diversity and experience); (iii) allowing foreign lawyers to represent parties; (iv) simplified and streamlined rules of procedure in line with the best practices of the common and civil law systems as well as that of international arbitration; (v) pro-active case management which increases efficiency and lowers costs; and (vi) the use of modern technology as part of the adjudication process.[4]

Unsurprisingly, a crucial indicator of the attractiveness of international commercial courts is the enforceability of their judgments: if a successful party is unable to

---

[2]Other international commercial courts include the United States District Court for the Southern District of New York (established in 1789), the Delaware Court of Chancery (established in 1792), the Qatar International Court (established in 2009) and the Abu Dhabi Global Market Courts (established in 2015).

[3]Queen Mary, University of London and White and Case, '2018 International Arbitration Survey: The Evolution of International Arbitration' lists costs as the worst feature of arbitration followed by lack of effective sanctions during the arbitral process, lack of power in relation to Third Parties and 'lack of speed'.

[4]Reyes (2018, pp. 4–5).

readily enforce judgments in jurisdiction(s) where the defendant has assets, the judgment would be of little use to him. In this regard, it cannot be overlooked that international commercial court judgments do not have the same wide-reaching enforceability as arbitral awards, which can be enforced in 159 countries pursuant to the New York Convention 1958 (NYC 1958). Nonetheless, this does not mean that the enforcement of international commercial court judgments is necessarily an uphill task for users of those courts. Indeed, the enforceability of international court judgments should not be viewed as just a numbers game, i.e. by adding up countries to a treaty or convention that provides for their enforcement.

Against this backdrop, this Chapter examines: (i) the general methods for the recognition and enforcement of foreign judgments; (ii) the regimes in the common law and civil law jurisdictions; and (iii) the enforceability of judgments of some key jurisdictions with international commercial courts.

2 General Methods for the Recognition and Enforcement of Foreign Judgments

When considering the general methods for the recognition and enforcement of foreign judgments, it is important to first set out the meaning of the terms 'recognition' and 'enforcement'.

'Recognition' means that the court addressed gives effect to the determination of the legal rights and obligations made by the court of origin. Therefore, parties bound by the judgment of the court of origin are estopped by *res judicata* from contradicting it in subsequent proceedings before the court addressed.[5]

'Enforcement' refers to the application of the legal procedures of the court addressed to execute the judgment given by the court of origin. While not every judgment that is recognised may be enforced,[6] every judgment that is to be enforced must first be recognised.[7]

Foreign judgments can be recognised and enforced pursuant to bilateral agreements, multilateral conventions, or a particular country's domestic law.

2.1 *Bilateral Agreements*

A state may enter into bilateral treaties with other states (especially those whose nationals and corporations the state wishes to attract as investors) for the mutual recognition and enforcement of judgments. This is useful as countries can then tailor

[5]Briggs (2013, p. 140).

[6]For example, the remedy ordered by the rendering court may not be one which can be enforced in the enforcing court.

[7]Briggs (2013, p. 141).

the terms for such mutual recognition and enforcement on a case-by-case basis. For example, China has entered into around 36 treaties providing for the recognition and enforcement of judgments and arbitral awards with countries such as France, Italy, Russia, Mongolia, Kyrgyzstan, Tajikistan and Uzbekistan.[8]

However, the difficulty with the bilateral treaty route is that such treaties are time-consuming to negotiate and must thereafter be signed and ratified by each party. To illustrate, if one considers the number of countries that form part of China's Belt and Road Initiative (BRI)—and if its objective was to create a network of bilateral regimes for the mutual recognition and enforcement of judgments among the BRI countries—that would mean that each country would have to negotiate and enter into more than 60 separate bilateral treaties. This is evidently not an easy task and may not provide any short-term benefits to the BRI.[9]

2.2 *Multilateral Conventions*

A more effective way of recognising and enforcing judgments is for countries to enter into multilateral conventions such as the Hague Choice of Court Agreements Convention (2005) (HCCA 2005). Indeed, the HCCA 2005 has been described as a 'mini version of the [NYC1958] for the enforcement of court judgments',[10] and a 'game-changer in the international enforceability of court judgments'.[11]

The HCCA 2005 came into force on 1 October 2015. There are presently 31 states and one regional organisation (the European Union (EU)) which are parties to the HCCA 2005. Under the HCCA 2005, the judgment of an international commercial court in a Convention State can be recognised and enforced in key cities such as London, Paris and Singapore. The United States (US), Ukraine and China have signed the HCCA 2005 but have not ratified it yet.

There are a number of notable features of the HCCA 2005.

To begin with, the HCCA 2005 applies to cases that are international in nature and relate to civil or commercial matters. It does not apply to, among others, disputes relating to family law, insolvency matters, anti-trust (competition) matters, personal injury claims and the validity of intellectual property rights other than copyright and related rights.[12] The HCCA 2005 also makes clear that it does not apply to interim measures of protection such as injunctions.[13]

It is also important to note that the HCCA 2005 only applies where commercial parties have entered into exclusive choice of court agreements designating the court

[8]Song (2018).
[9]Reyes (2019, pp. 1–16).
[10]Hwang (2015, p. 199).
[11]Menon (2015, para 58(c)(i)).
[12]Articles 1 and 2, HCCA 2005.
[13]Article 7, HCCA 2005.

of a Contracting State as the forum to resolve their disputes.[14] Where parties have designated the court of a Contracting State in an exclusive choice of court agreement, the HCCA 2005 requires the said court to exercise jurisdiction unless the said agreement is null and void under the law of that state.[15] Conversely, Article 6 of the HCCA 2005 provides that a court of a Contracting State other than that of the chosen court shall suspend or dismiss proceedings to which an exclusive choice of court agreement applies unless the exceptions therein apply.[16] In this way, the HCCA 2005 ensures that only the court designated by the parties pursuant to the exclusive choice of court agreement will hear a dispute arising out of their transactions.

The general principle of the HCCA 2005 is that a judgment from the chosen court must be recognised and enforced in other Contracting States unless certain limited and narrow grounds apply. Article 9 provides the grounds for the refusal of recognition and enforcement including the following: (i) the judgment was obtained by fraud in connection with a matter of procedure; (ii) public policy grounds; and (iii) the judgment is inconsistent with an earlier judgment from the requested state or with an earlier judgment given in another state between the same parties on the same cause of action.

The HCCA 2005 should not be confused with the 1971 Hague Convention on the Recognition and Enforcement of Foreign Judgments in Civil and Commercial Matters (HC 1971), which is a multilateral treaty that facilitates the mutual recognition and enforcement of judicial decisions. Unlike the HCCA 2005, the HC 1971 operates without the need for an exclusive choice of court agreement. The difficulty with the HC 1971, however, is that it has not been widely ratified—it only has five parties at present.[17] Further, another drawback is that it requires states to enter into a supplementary agreement with another state to become operative. Similar to the downside of bilateral agreements mentioned above, such a requirement may potentially be time-consuming.

An interesting development that is worth highlighting is the comprehensive Convention of 2 July 2019 on the Recognition and Enforcement of Foreign Judgments in Civil or Commercial Matters (2019 Convention). Like the HCCA 2005, the premise of the 2019 Convention is that judgments of Contracting States shall be recognised and enforced in another Contracting State and may only be refused on specified grounds.[18] The 2019 Convention contains a list of non-applicable matters (which

[14] Article 1, HCCA 2005.

[15] Article 5, HCCA 2005.

[16] These exceptions are: (a) the agreement is null and void under the law of the State of the chosen court; (b) a party lacked the capacity to conclude the agreement under the law of the State of the court seised; (c) giving effect to the agreement would lead to a manifest injustice or would be manifestly contrary to the public policy of the State of the court seised; (d) for exceptional reasons beyond the control of the parties, the agreement cannot reasonably be performed; or (e) the chosen court has decided not to hear the case.

[17] The parties are Albania, Cyprus, Kuwait, Portugal and the Netherlands.

[18] Article 4(1), 2019 Convention.

overlap with the HCCA 2005) such as family law matters, insolvency, anti-trust matters and intellectual property matters.[19] The key difference between the HCCA 2005 and the 2019 Convention is that the latter allows for the recognition and enforcement of foreign judgments relating to civil or commercial matters without the need for an exclusive choice of court agreement.

Article 5(1) of the 2019 Convention also stipulates an exhaustive list of bases for indirect jurisdiction which includes establishing that: (i) the person against whom recognition and enforcement is sought was habitually resident in the State of origin at the time that person became a party to the proceedings in the court of origin, or (ii) the defendant expressly consented to the jurisdiction of the court of origin in the course of the proceedings in which the judgment was given. Commentators have, however, observed that the exhaustive nature of Article 5(1) runs the risk of being overly prescriptive given the dynamism of international trade and rapid change in concepts of legal persons, methods of communication and technical means for the delivery of contents and services. This is compounded by the fact that the text of the 2019 Convention can only be amended by treaty, which is a complex process, especially if there are a large number of Contracting States.[20]

The grounds for refusal of recognition and enforcement under the 2019 Convention are broadly similar to that of the HCCA 2005.[21] These include: (i) the judgment was obtained by fraud; (ii) incompatibility with public policy; (iii) lack of due process (including inadequate notice of the proceedings before the rendering court such that the defendant was not able to present his defence); and (iv) inconsistency with a judgment of the enforcing state or an earlier judgment of another state which would be recognised in the enforcing state.

While the 2019 Convention merits widespread support as it expands the scope of the HCCA 2005, it has been observed that it will probably take some time before a sufficient number of states adopt the convention for it to become truly effective. This is because countries typically adopt a 'wait and see' approach and do not come on board until a number of other states have done so.[22]

In addition to the Hague Conventions, mention should be made of the regimes for the mutual recognition and enforcement of foreign judgments that exist in the EU and the European Free Trade Association (EFTA) namely, Regulation EU 1215/2012 (the Brussels I Recast Regulation) and the Lugano Convention.

The Brussels I Recast Regulation, which came into force on 10 January 2015, is the successor to the Council Regulation (EC) 44/2001. Much of the previous regulation, which governed the recognition and enforcement of judgments in civil and commercial matters within the EU, remains the same. The Brussels I Recast Regulation, however, made a few key changes to the previous regulation, such as streamlining the process for the enforcement of member state judgments in other

[19] Article 2(1), 2019 Convention.

[20] Brand (2019, pp. 19–20).

[21] Article 7, 2019 Convention.

[22] Reyes (2019, pp. 1–16).

member states,[23] and extending the scope of the previous regulation to cover cases where neither party is domiciled in the EU.

The Lugano Convention, which was designed to facilitate cross-border litigation between the EU and the EFTA in 1988 (and updated in 2007), extends the previous regulation (i.e. EC 44/2001) to Iceland, Norway and Switzerland. Notably, the Lugano Convention has not been adapted to reflect the key changes brought about by the Brussels I Recast Regulation.

In the Middle East, two conventions are worth noting in relation to the recognition and enforcement of foreign judgments: (i) the 1983 Riyadh Arab Agreement for Judicial Cooperation[24] (the Riyadh Convention), and (ii) the 1996 GCC Convention for the Execution of Judgments, Delegations and Judicial Notifications (the 1996 GCC Convention).[25] Both conventions allow for the mutual recognition and enforcement of judgments and contain similar grounds for refusing enforcement such as: (i) a violation of Islamic Sharia or public order in the enforcing state; (ii) lack of due process in failure of proper notification of the defendant; and (iii) the existence of a prior/pending conflicting judgment before the enforcing state.[26]

While Asia does not have such multilateral conventions, it is worth noting that there have been official statements by the Association of Southeast Asian Nations (ASEAN) member states to the effect that greater judicial cooperation in the area of recognition and enforcement of foreign judgments will be fostered. At the 2nd China-ASEAN Justice Forum in Nanning in June 2017, the Chief Justices of China and ASEAN member states issued a statement to the effect that subject to domestic laws, the respective Supreme Courts would keep good faith in interpreting domestic laws, avoid unnecessary parallel proceedings and consider facilitating the appropriate mutual recognition and enforcement of civil or commercial judgments among different jurisdictions (the Nanning Statement). This would be effected (among other ways) through an enforcing court presuming the existence of reciprocity where courts of the rendering state have not refused to enforce judgments of the enforcing state.[27]

2.3 *Memoranda of Guidance*

Judiciaries of different countries have entered into Memoranda of Guidance (MOGs) with one another. MOGs are non-legally binding documents that set out the criteria

[23] See Articles 36 and 39 of the Brussels I Recast Regulation, which provide that judgments given in member states shall be recognised and enforceable in other member states without any special procedures or declarations of enforceability respectively.

[24] The signatories include Algeria, Bahrain, Djibouti, Iraq, Jordan, Kuwait, Lebanon, Libya, Mauritania, Morocco, Oman, Palestine, Qatar, Saudi Arabia, Somalia, Sudan, Syria, Tunisia, United Arab Emirates (UAE) and Yemen.

[25] The signatories include Bahrain, Kuwait, Oman, Qatar, Saudi Arabia and UAE.

[26] Article 30, Riyadh Convention; Articles 1 and 2, GCC Convention.

[27] Article VII of the Nanning Statement.

and procedures that a judiciary will apply when considering whether to recognise and enforce a judgment rendered by a foreign judiciary.

As compared to bilateral treaties, MOGs are less time-consuming to negotiate as they can be entered into between the respective judiciaries on an administrative basis without the need for governmental or legislative intervention or approval. While their non-legally binding nature means that there is no guarantee that MOGs will be adhered to by a relevant court, MOGs are still useful evidence of reciprocity as between the states of the relevant judicial parties.[28] This is a significant factor in the recognition and enforcement regimes of civil law jurisdictions which we consider in detail below.

2.4 Domestic Law

Apart from treaties and conventions, the judgments of international commercial courts may also be capable of recognition and enforcement under a country's domestic law. After all, it has been said that judgments are official state documents and not just ordinary documents which commercial parties have agreed to honour as a matter of contract. International comity requires that judgments of a rendering state, upon meeting certain conditions, should be recognised and enforced in another state.[29]

The next section looks at the general approaches of the common law and civil law jurisdictions in recognising and enforcing the judgments of international commercial courts.

3 Common Law Jurisdiction Approach

3.1 Statutory Registration Regime

Most common law jurisdictions have statutory regimes for the registration of foreign judgments. For example, Singapore has the Reciprocal Enforcement of Commonwealth Judgments Act (RECJA),[30] which facilitates the reciprocal enforcement of

---

[28]Reyes (2019, pp. 1–17).

[29]Reyes (2018, p. 3).

[30]The RECJA covers New Zealand, Sri Lanka, Malaysia, Windward Islands, Pakistan, Brunei Darussalam, Papua New Guinea, India (except the states of Jammu and Kashmir), Commonwealth of Australia (High Court of Australia, Federal Court of Australia and Family Court of Australia), New South Wales (Supreme Court of New South Wales), Queensland (Supreme Court of Queensland), South Australia (Supreme Court of South Australia), Tasmania (Supreme Court of Tasmania), Victoria (Supreme Court of Victoria), Western Australia (Family Court of Western Australia and Supreme Court of Western Australia), Australian Capital Territory (Supreme Court of the Australian Capital Territory), Norfolk Island (Supreme Court of Norfolk Island), Northern Territory (Supreme Court of Northern Territory).

judgments and awards in Singapore and other parts of the Commonwealth, and the Reciprocal Enforcement of Foreign Judgments Act (REFJA)[31] which concerns the enforcement of judgments and awards in Singapore rendered by foreign countries that afford reciprocal treatment to judgments given in Singapore. The RECJA provides for the registration and enforcement of judgments obtained from superior courts in the United Kingdom (UK) and other Commonwealth jurisdictions that the Minister has gazetted, after being satisfied that reciprocal provisions have been made in those other jurisdictions. Currently, the RECJA regime applies to jurisdictions including Malaysia, Brunei, India (except the states of Jammu and Kashmir), New Zealand, and the Commonwealth of Australia. The REFJA presently only extends to the Hong Kong Special Administrative Region of the People's Republic of China.

Similarly, in the UK, the Administration of Justice Act 1920 (AJA 1920)[32] allows for the registration of foreign judgments in some Commonwealth territories including Malaysia, Nigeria, New Zealand and Singapore. The Foreign Judgments (Reciprocal Enforcement) Act 1933 (FJA 1933)[33] covers countries such as Australia, Canada, India, and Pakistan.

In Australia, the Foreign Judgments Act 1991 (FJA 1991) applies where there is 'substantial reciprocity' in the enforcement of judgments between Australia and the other country. The regime currently applies to jurisdictions such as the UK, Singapore, France, Germany and Japan.[34]

Foreign judgments which are registered under the statutory schemes can be enforced as if they are judgments of a court in the enforcing country.[35]

3.2 *Common Law Regime*

In the event a foreign judgment falls outside the scope of the statutory schemes, it may still be enforced under the common law. As Professor Adrian Briggs has stressed, for

[31]The REFJA presently only extends to the Hong Kong Special Administrative Region of the People's Republic of China.

[32]The AJA 1920 covers countries including Anguilla, Antigua and Barbuda, Bahamas, Barbados, Bermuda, Botswana, British Virgin Islands, Cayman Islands, Jamaica, Malaysia, New Zealand, Nigeria, Singapore, Sri Lanka, Lesotho, New South Wales and Western Australia.

[33]The FJA also covers judgments from recognised courts in Israel, Guernsey, Jersey, India and the Isle of Man.

[34]The FJA also applies to Alberta (Canada), Bahamas, British Columbia (Canada), British Virgin Islands, Cayman Islands, Dominica, Falkland Islands, Fiji, Gibraltar, Grenada, Hong Kong, Israel, Italy, Malawi, Manitoba (Canada), Montserrat, Papua New Guinea, Poland, South Korea, St Helena, St Kitts and Nevis, St Vincent and the Grenadines, Seychelles, Solomon Islands, Sri Lanka, Switzerland, Taiwan, Tonga, Tuvalu, and Western Samoa.

[35]See for instance Section 9(3) of the AJA and Section 2(2) of the FJA 1933; Section 3(3) of the RECJA and Section 4(4) of the REFJA.

a foreign judgment to be enforced, it must be a judgment of the enforcing jurisdiction (derived by one means or another from the foreign judgment).[36]

The general position under most common law regimes is as follows: the foreign judgment, if it satisfies certain conditions, gives rise to a debt upon which the judgment creditor can sue for the purpose of enforcement. Such judgments can be enforced through a summary judgment procedure (i.e. there is no trial) as there is generally no defence to the judgment debt. The obligation to pay the debt is separate from the underlying cause of action in foreign judgment, but there is no review of the merits of the foreign judgment. Upon the conclusion of the summary process, the foreign judgment is effectively converted into a domestic judgment which can be enforced in the relevant jurisdiction.

In general terms, foreign judgments will be recognised and enforced if: (1) they are judgments for a fixed sum of money[37]; (2) they are final and conclusive; (3) the foreign court had international jurisdiction to hear the matter; and (4) there are no defences that can be raised against the recognition and enforcement of such judgments.

3.3 Final and Conclusive Nature of the Foreign Judgment

A foreign judgment is 'final' in the sense that the decision cannot be reopened in the court that made the ruling, and 'conclusive' in that it represents the court's settled answer on the substance of the point adjudicated.[38] A judgment is typically deemed as final and conclusive even if there is a possibility of appeal. For example, in Singapore, a judgment may be final for the purposes of *res judicata* even though it may be reversed or varied by an appellate court.[39] A default judgment, which is final unless subsequently altered, will also generally satisfy the conditions.[40]

[36]Briggs (2013, p. 139).

[37]In England, only monetary judgments are enforceable under the AJA and FJA: see Section 12(1) of the AJA and Section 1(2)(b) of the FJA. In Singapore, non-monetary relief such as an injunction may be enforced if it falls within the ambit of the Choice of Court Agreements Act (No. 14 of 2016) (CCAA). In Australia, provision is made under Section 5(6) of the FJA 1991 for the enforcement of non-money judgments '*if the Governor-General is satisfied that ... substantial reciprocity of treatment will be assured in relation to the enforcement in that country of all or some non-money judgments given in Australian courts*', and if so the regulations may provide that the FJA applies to such non-money judgments.

[38]Briggs (2013, p. 168).

[39]See for instance, *Manharlal Trikamdas Mody v Sumikin Busan International HK Ltd.* [2014] 3 SLR 1161 at [140], *cf* section 3(2) of the RECJA and section 6(1) of the REFJA, which provide respectively that the foreign judgment will not be registered or that the registration may be set aside if the judgment debtor satisfies the registering court either that an appeal is pending or that he is entitled or intends to appeal the judgment.

[40]*Humpuss Sea Transport Pte Ltd v PT Humpuss Intermoda Transportasi TBK* [2016] 5 SLR 1322 at [77]; Lord Collins of Mapesbury and Harris (eds) (2012, [14-023]).

3.4 The International Jurisdiction of the Foreign Court to Hear the Matter

The common law also generally requires that the foreign court had international jurisdiction to hear the case. In England, a foreign court has jurisdiction over the judgment debtor if the defendant was present within the territorial jurisdiction of the foreign court on the date which proceedings were commenced.[41] It has been suggested that residence (unaccompanied by presence) would suffice under the common law,[42] but commentators have stated that this is undesirable because a test based on residence would make things less certain and predictable.[43] In Singapore, presence suffices for international jurisdiction under the common law.[44]

Alternatively, international jurisdiction may be established if the defendant submits to the jurisdiction either by taking a step in the proceedings or pursuant to an agreement to submit to jurisdiction. For instance, in England, where the judgment debtor appears before the foreign court to: (a) contest the jurisdiction of the court; (b) ask the court to dismiss or stay the proceedings on the ground that the dispute in question should be submitted to arbitration or to the determination of the courts of another country; or (c) protect, or obtain the release of, property seized or threatened with seizure in the proceedings, this would not, without more, amount to a submission to the foreign court's jurisdiction.[45]

3.5 Defences to Recognition and Enforcement

The defences to recognition and enforcement of foreign judgments are similar under many statutory regimes and the common law. The common defences are that the foreign judgment: (1) was obtained by fraud[46]; (2) contravenes public policy of the forum[47]; (3) was obtained in breach of natural justice and/or due process (e.g. if the

---

[41] *Adams v Cape Industries plc* [1990] 1 Ch 433 at 518B.

[42] *Joint Stock Company Aeroflot Russian Airlines v Berezovsky and another* [2012] EWHC 3017 at [61].

[43] Briggs (2013, p. 170).

[44] *United Malayan Banking Corp Bhd v Khoo Boo Hor* [1995] 3 SLR(R) 839 at [9]; *cf* RECJA s 3(2)(b) and REFJA s 5(2)(a)(iv) which require residence.

[45] Section 33, Civil Jurisdiction and Judgments Act 1982; see also Section 5(2)(a)(i), REFJA.

[46] For the Singapore position, see Section 3(2)(d) of the RECJA, Section 5(1)(a)(iv) of the REFJA and also under the common law [*Hong Pian Tee v Les Placements Germain Gauthier Inc* [2002] 1 SLR(R) 515 (hereafter '*Hong Pian Tee*')]. See also Section 7(2)(a)(vi) of the FJA 1991 and Section 9(2)(d) of the AJA and Section 4(1)(a)(iv) of the FJA 1933.

[47] In Singapore, this defence is provided for in Section 3(2)(f) of the RECJA and Section 5(1)(a)(v) of the REFJA; in Australia, it is provided for in Section 7(2)(a)(xi) of the FJA 1991; in England, it is provided for in Section 9(2)(f) of the AJA and Section 4(1)(a)(v) of the FJA 1933.

defendant was not notified or did not have sufficient time to defend himself)[48]; and (4) conflicts with an earlier judgment from the forum or an earlier judgment entitled to recognition in its own right.[49]

As regards the defence of fraud, various jurisdictions have taken divergent views. Under English law, where fraud is alleged, the traditional rule is that the court may re-open the merits of the foreign decision.[50] This applies even where the judgment creditor has not produced any newly discovered evidence, and even if the fraud was or might have been alleged in the foreign proceedings. The English Court of Appeal has sought to limit the scope of the traditional rule in the case of *House of Spring Gardens Ltd v Waite*,[51] where it held that a judgment debtor who had commenced a second set of proceedings in the foreign jurisdiction to set aside the original judgment (on the basis of fraud) was estopped from re-litigating the same issue of fraud in the enforcing jurisdiction.[52]

Other jurisdictions have departed from the traditional English common law position.[53] The Singapore Court of Appeal affirmed the traditional rule as regards cases of extrinsic fraud (i.e. fraud external to the merits of the case), but held that the traditional rule does not apply to cases of intrinsic fraud (i.e. fraud that affects the merits of the case).[54] Thus, in Singapore, foreign judgments can only be challenged on the ground of intrinsic fraud if there is fresh evidence not discoverable with reasonable diligence at the time of the trial that was likely to make a difference in the result.[55] On the other hand, the Supreme Court of Canada has suggested abolishing the distinction between intrinsic and extrinsic frauds, in favour of simply stating that fraud going to the jurisdiction of the court can always be raised before a domestic court to challenge the foreign judgment, but the merits of the foreign judgment can be challenged for fraud only where the allegations are new and not the subject of prior adjudication.[56]

---

[48]In Singapore, under Section 3(2)(c) of the RECJA and Section 5(1)(a)(iii) of the REFJA, what is required is that the judgment debtor must have been duly served with process. In Australia, under Section 7(2)(a)(v) of the FJA, the judgment debtor must have received notice of the proceedings in sufficient time for him to defend the proceedings. Similarly, in England, Section 9(2)(c) of the AJA requires the judgment debtor to have been duly served with the process of the original court and Section 4(1)(a)(iii) of the FJA 1933 requires the judgment debtor to have received notice of the proceedings in sufficient time to enable him to defend the proceedings.

[49]See Section 4(1)(b) of the FJA 1933; Section 5(1)(b) of the REFJA; and in Australia, under Section 7(2)(b) of the FJA 1991.

[50]*Abouloff v Oppenheimer* (1882) 10 QBD 295 at 304 and 308.

[51]*House of Spring Gardens Ltd v Waite* [1991] 1 QB 241 (hereafter '*House of Spring Gardens Ltd*').

[52]*House of Spring Gardens Ltd.*, 251.

[53]See *Hong Pian Tee* for the Singapore approach.

[54]*Hong Pian Tee*, [30].

[55]*Hong Pian Tee*, [30].

[56]*Beals v Saldanha* [2003] 3 SCR 416 at [50]–[53].

4 Civil Law Jurisdiction Approach

Certain civil law jurisdictions such as Thailand and Indonesia do not recognise and enforce foreign judgments, and the litigant has to sue afresh on the same cause of action despite a foreign judgment in his favour.

In contrast, many other civil law jurisdictions have allowed foreign judgments to be enforced if certain conditions are satisfied. These include requirements similar to the common law jurisdictions such as international jurisdiction and finality of judgments. An additional requirement unique to civil law jurisdictions is the requirement of reciprocity.

With respect to international jurisdiction, civil law jurisdictions such as Japan and South Korea require the foreign court to have had international jurisdiction in hearing the case. In this regard, an international commercial court's jurisdiction will normally arise due to a choice of court agreement, namely, an agreement between the parties to submit disputes arising out of their transactions to a designated court. Such choice of court agreements usually meet the requirement of international jurisdiction in civil law codes.[57]

Another common requirement in civil codes such as those of Japan, South Korea, and the United Arab Emirates (UAE) is that the foreign judgment must be final and conclusive before they can be enforced.[58]

Some civil codes also require that the foreign judgment had been obtained in accordance with due process rules. The UAE Code requires that '[a]dversaries in the lawsuit on which the foreign judgment was passed were summoned and duly represented'.[59] Similarly, the German Code of Civil Procedure provides that a foreign judgment will not be recognised if the defendant, who has not entered an appearance in the proceedings and who takes recourse to this fact, has not duly been served with the document by which the proceedings were initiated, or not in such time as to allow him to defend himself.[60]

In the absence of treaty arrangements for the recognition and enforcement of foreign judgments, certain civil law countries allow for recognition and enforcement by reciprocity. Many civil law states have liberalised the requirement of reciprocity so that this will usually be met if it is shown that the courts of the rendering state are likely to recognise and enforce judgments of the enforcing state.[61] Others have even

---

[57] See for instance Japan, where the treatment of Choice of Court Agreements is dealt with under Article 3–7 of the Code of Civil Procedure.

[58] See Japan: Article 24(3) of the Civil Execution Act which requires proving that the judgment of the foreign court has become 'final and binding' or when the judgment fails to satisfy the requirements listed in Article 118 of the Code of Civil Procedure (Law No. 109 of 26 June 1996 as amended); South Korea: Article 217(1) of the Civil Procedure Act which requires a 'final and conclusive' judgment; UAE: Article 235(2)(d) of the Civil Procedure Code requires that the judgment or order has 'obtained the absolute degree in accordance with law of the issuing court'.

[59] UAE: Article 235(2)(c) of the Civil Procedure Code.

[60] Germany: Section 328(1)(2) of the Code of Civil Procedure.

[61] Elbati (2017, p. 191).

abolished the condition of reciprocity.[62] This has led commentators to argue that reciprocity has become a 'toothless' principle.[63] It has also been said that it is possible to dispense with reciprocity as a requirement altogether and instead abide by the principle of comity.[64] Reciprocity may only be a hurdle in a jurisdiction which adheres to a restrictive recognition and enforcement regime. In China, which has one of the most restrictive reciprocity systems, the courts have regularly denied recognition of foreign judgments (including those from Japan and South Korea) on the basis of reciprocity.[65] However, the situation is expected to change in the light of recent developments: in December 2016, a Chinese Court decided that a Singapore Court judgment could be enforced in China based on the principle of reciprocity because the Singapore Court had previously recognised a Chinese judgment.[66] Shortly after, in 2017, China also recognised a US judgment on the basis of reciprocity.[67] These recent decisions suggest that China is now taking a broader and more flexible approach to establishing reciprocity. Further, the Nanning Statement should also help to enhance the mutual recognition and enforcement of foreign judgments in China (and ASEAN).

Many civil codes also require that the foreign judgment does not violate the public policy of the enforcing state. For example, the UAE Code provides that the judgment must not 'include any violation of moral code or public order'.[68] In China, the foreign judgment cannot contradict basic principles of the law of the People's Republic of China or violate State sovereignty, security or the public interest.[69] The issue of public policy is unlikely to prove a hurdle where international commercial court judgments, which deal with commercial matters, are concerned.

5 Features of Jurisdictions with International Commercial Courts

This section outlines some features relating to the recognition and enforceability of judgments in jurisdictions with international commercial courts.

[62] These include jurisdictions such as Venezuela, Lithuania, Bulgaria and Poland. For more information, see Elbati (2017, pp. 187–188).

[63] Elbati (2017, p. 185).

[64] In Reyes (2019, pp. 1–28), where the author explains that comity means that the requirements of a sovereign state should be accorded due respect and that subject to certain conditions, foreign judgments should be recognised and enforced as a matter of course.

[65] For more information, see Elbati (2017, pp. 201–205).

[66] *Kolmar Group AG and Jiangsu Textile Industry (Group) Import & Export Co., Ltd.* (2016 Su 01 Xie Wai Ren No. 3); see also *Giant Light Metal Technology (Kunshan) Co Ltd v Aksa Far East Pte Ltd.* [2014] 2 SLR 545 which concerned the recognition and enforcement of a Chinese judgment in Singapore.

[67] *Liu Li v Tao Li & Tong Wu,* Intermediate People's Court of Wuhan, Hubei Province, China, 30 June 2017.

[68] Section 235(2)(e) of the UAE Civil Procedure Code.

[69] Article 282 of Chinese Civil Procedure law.

5.1 London

The UK currently can take advantage of the abovementioned EU Regimes (i.e. the Brussels Recast Regulation and the Lugano Conventions), the statutory regimes under the AJA 1920 and FJA 1933, as well as the English common law regime. In addition, in 2013, the ECC entered into a MOG with respect to the enforcement of money judgments with the DIFCC.

However, the enforceability of ECC judgments in the post-Brexit era is uncertain. Upon its departure from the EU, the UK would no longer be able to take advantage of the current EU regimes.[70] The UK government has stated that in the event of a 'no-deal' Brexit, the UK would 'revert' to the existing 'common law and statutory rules'.[71] The government has also acceded to the HCCA 2005 with effect from 1 November 2019.[72] In addition, the UK has stated that it will seek to participate in the Lugano Convention after it leaves the EU but as some of its provisions have been overtaken and it is limited in scope, the UK is keen to explore a new bilateral agreement with the EU, and build on the principles established in the Lugano Convention and subsequent developments at the EU level.[73]

The uncertainty surrounding the enforceability of post-Brexit ECC judgments could potentially cause the ECC to be a less attractive choice for international dispute resolution, at least in the short term.

5.2 Paris

Apart from the multilateral conventions such as the EU regimes, France has entered into various bilateral treaties on the recognition and enforcement of judgments with countries such as China, the UAE, Vietnam, Algeria, Egypt, Brazil and Uruguay. Apart from treaties, foreign judgments can also be enforced under French domestic law.[74]

5.3 Netherlands

The Netherlands, which similarly benefits from the EU regimes and the HCCA 2005, also has entered into bilateral treaties with other countries, including the UK and

---

[70] See the Civil Jurisdiction and Judgments (Amendment) (EU Exit) Regulations 2019 (SI 2019/479).

[71] 'Guidance—Handling civil legal cases that involve EU countries if there's no Brexit deal' (13 September 2018).

[72] See the UK's Declaration dated 12 April 2019 in relation to the HCCA 2005: www.hcch.net/en/instruments/conventions/status-table/notifications/?csid=1318&disp=resdn.

[73] HM Government (2018, paras 147 and 148).

[74] See Article 509 of the French Code of Civil Procedure.

Surinam. If no treaty applies, one must then initiate proceedings in the Netherlands to recognise and enforce the foreign judgment. In the *Gazprombank* case, the Supreme Court of the Netherlands laid down four distinct requirements for the Dutch courts to recognise and enforce foreign judgments pursuant to fresh proceedings: (1) the foreign court's jurisdiction is based on internationally accepted grounds; (2) the foreign judgment is the result of a proper judicial procedure (i.e. fair trial); (3) the foreign judgment does not violate Dutch public policy; and (4) the foreign judgment is final and not inconsistent with any other judgment that is capable of recognition in the Netherlands.[75]

5.4 *DIFC*

Judgments of the DIFCC must be enforced through the Dubai Courts in accordance with DIFC Law (e.g. they must be translated into Arabic).[76] DIFCC judgments benefit from the bilateral and multilateral treaties signed by the UAE such as the 1983 Riyadh Arab Agreement for Judicial Cooperation and the 1996 GCC Convention. The DIFCC has also signed MOGs with other courts such as the ECC, the Singapore Supreme Court, and the US District Court for the Southern District of New York.

Mention should be made of the DIFCC's innovative process of converting court money judgments into arbitral awards.[77] This was described by former DIFC Chief Justice Michael Hwang as 'an experiment without parallel in arbitration history'.[78] Under this process, parties who have elected to submit to the DIFCC's jurisdiction can refer any dispute relating to the enforcement of a DIFCC decision to the DIFC-LCIA Arbitration Centre, which will render an award that in turn is enforceable under the NYC 1958.

In 2016, a Joint Judicial Committee of the Dubai Courts and the DIFCC was established for the purpose of determining conflicts between judgments of the Dubai Courts and the DIFCC in relation to the same parties and subject matter, proposing rules to avoid conflicting jurisdictions between the two sets of courts, and giving opinions in matters relating to cooperation and coordination between the two courts. The establishment of the said committee has led to uncertainty as to what will happen when there is an overlap between the jurisdiction of the DIFCC and the Dubai Courts, especially as regards the enforcement of judgments and arbitral awards.

---

[75] Dutch Supreme Court, 26 September 2014, ECLI:NL:HR:2014:2838.

[76] Article 7, Dubai Law No. 12 of 2004.

[77] See Amended DIFC Practice Direction (2 of 2015)—Referral of judgment payment disputes to Arbitration, which allows parties to refer a 'Judgment Payment Dispute' (defined as any dispute, difference, controversy or claim between a judgment creditor and judgment debtor with respect to any money (including interest and costs) due under an unsatisfied judgment) to arbitration under the DIFC-LCIA Rules.

[78] Hwang (2015, p. 203).

5.5 AIFC

As for the AIFCC, its decisions are to be enforced in the Republic of Kazakhstan in the same way and on the same terms as decisions of the courts of the Republic of Kazakhstan save that a translation of the decision into the Kazakh or Russian language is required.[79] This potentially allows AIFCC judgments to be enforced in jurisdictions which have bilateral or multilateral treaties with Kazakhstan.[80]

5.6 Singapore

The SICC holds a strategically advantageous position in Asia where the enforcement of judgments is concerned. As the SICC is part of the Supreme Court of Singapore, SICC judgments can be enforced in the same manner as other judgments issued by the Singapore High Court. Unlike the DIFCC and AIFCC, no translation of its decisions is required.

SICC judgments can be enforced in most major commercial jurisdictions. Singapore is a Contracting State to the HCCA 2005 which, as mentioned above, has a subscription of 31 states and a regional organisation (the EU). The Choice of Courts Agreements Act (CCAA) enacts the HCCA 2005 into Singapore law. The CCAA distinguishes between mandatory and discretionary grounds for refusing the recognition and enforcement of foreign judgments.[81] Mandatory grounds include where the judgment was obtained by fraud or recognition—which would be manifestly incompatible with Singapore's public policy. Discretionary grounds include situations where a party lacked capacity to enter into the choice of court agreement or the foreign judgment is inconsistent with a Singapore court judgment in a dispute between the same parties.

In addition, SICC judgments can be enforced by registration in courts of the countries under the RECJA (for some commonwealth jurisdictions) and the REFJA (for Hong Kong) and also under the common law or civil law regime. Singapore has also entered into various MOGs with different courts to facilitate the enforcement of money judgments, including the Supreme Court of Bermuda, the Supreme People's Court, the Qatar International Court and Dispute Resolution Centre, Abu Dhabi Global Market Courts and the DIFC.

---

[79] Article 13(8) of the Constitutional Statute of the Republic of Kazakhstan.

[80] For example, Kazakhstan has entered into the Kiev Agreement between the CIS Countries on the Procedure for Settlement of Disputes Associated with Commercial Activities (20 March 1992), which is force between Armenia, Azerbaijan, Belarus, Kazakhstan, Kyrgyzstan, Russian Federation, Turkmenistan, Tajikistan, Ukraine, Uzbekistan and the Minsk Convention on Legal Assistance and Legal Relations in Civil, Family and Criminal Matters. See also the agreement entered into between the Republic of Kazakhstan and the UAE on Judicial Assistance in Civil and Commercial Matters.

[81] See Sections 14 and 15, CCAA.

5.7 China

CICC judgments have the same status as a judgment from the Supreme People's Court of the People's Republic of China. As mentioned above, China has entered into around 36 treaties providing for the recognition and enforcement of judgments and arbitral awards with countries including France, Italy, Russia, Mongolia, Kyrgyzstan, Tajikistan and Uzbekistan. Further, while China has signed the HCCA 2005, it has yet to ratify it.

Without a treaty or convention facilitating the mutual enforcement of judgments, parties may also seek enforcement of a CICC judgment in a foreign jurisdiction on the basis of reciprocity. In this regard, it is worth noting, as mentioned above, that China has adopted a restrictive policy on reciprocity which may in turn affect the enforceability of its judgments in countries which require reciprocity before enforcing judgments. However, China has recently taken a broader and more flexible approach to establishing reciprocity. China has also entered into a MOG with the Singapore Supreme Court to facilitate the mutual recognition and enforcement of money judgments in commercial cases in 2018. These recent developments, which may enhance the enforceability of CICC judgments, are to be welcomed.

6 Conclusion

In the final analysis, recent developments show that there is much to be optimistic about the recognition and enforcement of international commercial court judgments.

The HCCA 2005 is a commendable first step in the recognition and enforcement of international commercial court judgments. The new Hague Convention (if widely adopted) would, in conjunction, with the HCCA 2005, allow money judgments in commercial matters to be widely recognised and enforced. This would enable the Hague Conventions to rival the NYC 1958 in relation to the extent of application.

In the absence of treaties and conventions, judgments of international commercial courts should still generally be capable of recognition and enforcement under the principles or codes of the common law and civil law jurisdictions respectively. As demonstrated above, most common law jurisdictions allow foreign judgments to be enforced in a summary judgment manner (i.e. without trial). Many civil law jurisdictions, on the other hand, allow the enforcement of foreign judgments if certain conditions such as indirect jurisdiction, reciprocity and the said judgment does not violate public policy, are met. The establishment of MOGs between various courts is also a step in the correct direction facilitating the mutual enforcement of judgments from the relevant jurisdictions.

For the reasons stated, it is submitted that when one considers the enforcement of international commercial court judgments, there is more than simply totalling up the number of Contracting States to treaties or conventions. While there are some states that refuse to recognise foreign judgments as a matter of principle, this will likely be the exception rather than the norm. We can therefore be more optimistic about the recognition and enforceability of judgments of international commercial courts in the near future. This will undoubtedly enhance the attractiveness of international commercial courts, which has been in recent years a growing trend that is to be welcomed.

References

Brand R (2019) The circulation of judgments under the draft hague convention. University of Pittsburgh Legal Studies Research Paper No. 2019-02. https://papers.ssrn.com/sol3/papers.cfm?abstract_id=3334647

Briggs A (2013) The conflict of laws, 3rd edn. Oxford University Press, Oxford

Elbati B (2017) Reciprocity and the recognition and enforcement of foreign judgments: a lot of bark but not much bite. J Private Int Law 13(1):184–218

HM Government (2018) The future relationship between the United Kingdom and the European Union

Hwang M (2015) Commercial courts and international arbitration—Competitors or partners. Arbitr Int 31(2):193–212

Lord Collins of Mapesbury and Jonathan Harris (eds) (2012) Dicey, morris and collins on the conflict of laws, vol 1, 15th edn. Sweet & Maxwell, London

Menon S (2015) International commercial courts: towards a transnational system of dispute resolution (opening lecture for the DIFC courts lecture series 2015). https://www.supremecourt.gov.sg/Data/Editor/Documents/opening-lecture—difc-lecture-series-2015.pdf

Ramesh K (2018) International commercial courts: unicorns on a journey of thousand miles. In: Conference on the rise of international commercial courts, 13 May 2018. https://www.sicc.gov.sg/docs/default-source/modules-document/news-and-article/international-commercial-courts-unicorns_23108490-e290-422f-9da8-1e0d1e59ace5.pdf

Reyes A (2018) International commercial courts and the belt and road initiative. In: Speech delivered in Xian on 8 September 2018 at a conference on the China international commercial court and belt and road initiative

Reyes A (2019) Introduction: towards a system for the recognition and enforcement of judgments. In: Reyes A (ed) Recognition and enforcement of judgments in civil and commercial matters. Hart Publishing

Song J (2018) Recognition and enforcement of foreign judgments in China: challenges and developments. http://cicc.court.gov.cn/html/1/219/199/203/1048.html

Anselmo Reyes practises as an arbitrator. He was Professor of Legal Practice at Hong Kong University from October 2012 to September 2018. Before that, he was a judge of the Hong Kong High Court from 2003 to 12, when he was in charge of the Construction and Arbitration List (2004–8) and the Commercial and Admiralty Lists (2008–12). He was Representative of the Hague Conference on Private International Law's Regional Office Asia Pacific from April 2013 to July 2017. He became an International Judge of the Singapore International Commercial Court in January 2015.

Kevin Tan is a partner in Rajah & Tann Singapore LLP. He has acted in wide range of disputes in the Supreme Court of Singapore (including the Singapore International Commercial Court) and in international arbitrations. Prior to entering private practice, he served as a Justice's Law Clerk to the Chief Justice, Judges of Appeal and Judges of the Supreme Court of Singapore, an Assistant Registrar of the Supreme Court and a Deputy Public Prosecutor in the Attorney General's Chambers.

The New Chinese International Commercial Court and the Future of Dispute Resolution in the Belt and Road Initiative

David Holloway

Abstract The Chinese Government established the new Chinese International Commercial Court (CICC) in July 2018 as an integral part of the Belt and Road Initiative (BRI). This Chapter seeks to analyse the key features of the CICC in the context of the BRI and the modern trend of establishing new 'International' Commercial Courts. The Chapter will also examine how the unique approach of the CICC has potential to act as a catalyst for law reform in China.

1 Introduction

The Chinese Government established the new Chinese International Commercial Court (CICC) in July 2018. The launch of the new court represents a confluence of two separate historical trends. Most significantly, the establishment of the Court is a key milestone in the advancement of the Belt and Road Initiative (BRI); the key policy guiding China's approach to international trade and wider foreign policy since 2013. Secondly, it can be seen as a major addition to the family of recently established 'international' commercial courts, following those launched in Dubai (Dubai International

[1] https://www.difc.ae/.

[2] https://www.sicc.gov.sg/.

[3] https://aifc.kz/.

[4] https://netherlands-commercial-court.com/.

[5] Ordentliche Gerichtsbarkeit Hessen (2017); Deutscher AnwaltSpiegel (2018). See also, the official website of the Frankfurt district court about the Chamber for International Commercial Disputes: https://ordentliche-gerichtsbarkeit.hessen.de/ordentliche-gerichte/lg-bezirk-frankfurt-m/lg-frankfurt-m/chamber-international-commercial-disputes.

That chapter was previously published in the Vindobona Journal of International Commercial Law and Arbitration, Volume 22 Issue 2 (2018).

D. Holloway (✉)
Birmingham Law School, University of Birmingham, Birmingham, UK
e-mail: dholloway@36stone.co.uk

L. Chen and A. Janssen (eds.), *Dispute Resolution in China, Europe and World*,
Ius Gentium: Comparative Perspectives on Law and Justice 79,
https://doi.org/10.1007/978-3-030-42974-4_3

Financial Centre (DIFC) in 2014),[1] Singapore (Singapore International Commercial Court (SICC) in 2015),[2] Kazakhstan (Astana International Financial Centre (AIFC) in 2018),[3] the Netherlands (Netherlands Commercial Court (NCC) in 2018),[4] Germany (Chamber for International Commercial Disputes at the Landgericht Frankfurt am Main in 2018),[5] Belgium (Brussels International Business Court (BIBC) expected to be launched in 2020).[6] This Chapter seeks to analyse the key features of the CICC in the context of those trends, to examine how the unique approach adopted has potential to act as a catalyst for law reform in China. The Chapter will also look at the consequences for the practice of dispute resolution in the context of the BRI and internationally.

2 The BRI—Background and Structure

The BRI was announced by China's President Xi Jinping in Kazakhstan in 2013. The Initiative aims at boosting trade and economic growth by reviving the old Silk Trading Routes and connecting Asia, Europe and Africa through a new infrastructure and trade network. The initiative is designed to enhance economic cooperation and to facilitate long-term trade and investment relationships.[7] The Chinese Government has repeatedly stressed that the BRI is open to any country or international organization.[8] There are currently 84 countries who are officially listed as part of the BRI.[9]

2.1 The Land Based Silk Road Economic Belt

This consists of three different routes: The first route connects China and Europe through Central Asia and Russia, the second route connects China and the Middle East through Central Asia and the third route connects China, South East Asia and the Indian Ocean.

[6]http://arbitrationblog.kluwerarbitration.com/2018/06/25/the-belgian-government-unveils-its-plan-for-the-brussels-international-business-court-bibc/.

[7]National Development and Reform Commission et al. (2015); https://eng.yidaiyilu.gov.cn/qwyw/qwfb/1084.htm.

[8]Office of the Leading Group for the Belt and Road Initiative (2017).

[9]List and Country profiles available at the official Belt and Road Portal of the Chinese government, https://eng.yidaiyilu.gov.cn/info/iList.jsp?cat_id=10076&cur_page=1.

2.2 The 21st Century Maritime Silk Road

This consists of two routes, one of them connecting China and Europe through the South China Sea and the Indian Ocean and the other one linking China and the South Pacific Ocean through the South China Sea.[10]

Six 'economic corridors' have been established within the aforementioned routes (Fig. 1).

The New Eurasian Land Bridge Economic Corridor: This Economic Corridor connects China with Europe via an international railway line running through Kazakhstan, Russia, Belarus and Poland, before it reaches a number of European destinations including ports. Several freight rail routes now link China to Germany, Poland and Czech Republic allowing rail-to-rail transport and facilitated declaration, inspection and release of cargo.[11]

China-Mongolia- Russia Economic Corridor: The three countries decided in 2014 to deepen the already existing trade and cross-border cooperation by entering into bilateral agreements and committing to jointly contribute to the BRI, Russia's Eurasia Land Bridge and Mongolia's Steppe Road.[12]

China-Central Asia-West Asia Economic Corridor: Passing through Kazakhstan, Kyrgyzstan, Tajikistan, Uzbekistan, Iran and Turkey, this Economic Corridor links

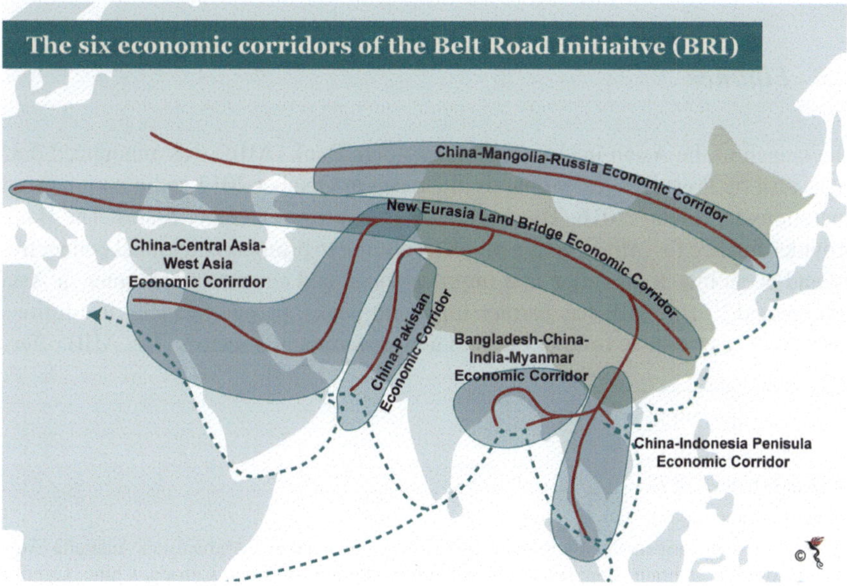

Fig. 1 Map of Six Economic Corridors of the BRI (Gnanasagaran 2017)

[10]National Development and Reform Commission et al. (2015).

[11]Gnanasagaran (2017).

[12]Gnanasagaran (2017).

China and the Arabian Peninsula by using the Central Asian and West Asian railway networks. In 2015, China and the Central and Western Asian Countries along this Corridor agreed on building the BRI and national development strategies in the respective countries, which are all closely connected with the land based Silk Road.[13]

China-Indochina Peninsula Economic Corridor: Linking China with Myanmar, Laos, Vietnam, Thailand, Malaysia and Singapore, this Economic Corridor aims at strengthening the cooperation and boost trade with the ASEAN countries by constructing nine highways across the countries situated at the Mekong Delta in addition to new air and rail routes.[14]

China-Pakistan Economic Corridor: The Chinese government announced the idea of the China-Pakistan Economic Corridor (CPEC) in 2013. The original plan of connecting Kashgar, a city situated in the northwest of China and Gwadar Port in Pakistan has been extended ever since to be the largest economic corridor of the BRI. The two countries have agreed on building rail- and highways, gas and oil pipelines and optic fibre networks and other projects such as an international airport, the Haier-Ruba Economic Zone and an expressway close to Gwadar Port.[15]

Bangladesh-China-India-Myanmar Economic Corridor: This Corridor links China and India, two of the biggest markets in the world, facilitating trade and access to natural resources and paving the way for large infrastructure and sustainability projects.[16]

2.3 Finance

The launch of the Asian International Investment Bank (AIIB) was announced during a visit by President Xi Jinping to Indonesia in October 2013 and it commenced operations in January 2016. There are now 86 approved member States. The Bank provides finance for infrastructure projects, aiming to promoting regional connectivity and economic cooperation and improve social and economic outcomes in Asia and beyond.[17] The AIIB has partnerships with banks, private financial institutions and other organisations from public and non-governmental sectors. The AIIB offers

[13]Gnanasagaran (2017).

[14]Gnanasagaran (2017).

[15]Gnanasagaran (2017).

[16]Gnanasagaran (2017).

[17]https://www.aiib.org/en/about-aiib/index.html. The 67 members are: Afghanistan, Australia, Austria, Azerbaijan, Bahrain, Bangladesh, Brunei Darussalam, Cambodia, Canada, China, Cyprus, Denmark, Egypt, Ethiopia, Fiji, Finland, France, Germany, Georgia, Hong Kong (China), Hungary, Iceland, India, Indonesia, Iran, Ireland, Israel, Italy, Jordan, Kazakhstan, Korea, Kyrgyz Republic, Lao PDR, Luxembourg, Madagascar, Malaysia, Maldives, Malta, Mongolia, Myanmar, Nepal, Netherlands, New Zealand, Norway, Oman, Pakistan, Philippines, Poland, Portugal, Qatar, Russia, Samoa, Saudi Arabia, Singapore, Spain, Sri Lanka, Sweden, Switzerland, Tajikistan, Thailand, Timor-Leste, Turkey, UAE, United Kingdom, Uzbekistan, Vanuatu and Vietnam. The 20 prospective members are Armenia, Argentina, Belarus, Belgium, Chile, Bolivia, Brazil, Cook Islands, Ecuador,

financing (sovereign and non-sovereign) for projects such as rural infrastructure, transportation and telecommunication, sustainable energy and power projects, environmental protection, water supply and sanitation and urban development and logistics.[18] Currently the AIIB has provided funding for 26 approved projects in a total amount of approximately USD 4.59 billion.[19]

A USD 40 billion fund ('The Silk Road Fund') was established by the Chinese Government on 29 December 2014 to finance and invest in the trade and economic cooperation under the BRI. Its founding shareholders are China's State Administration of Foreign Exchange, the China Investment Corp., the Export-Import Bank of China and the China Development Bank. It invests in infrastructure, resources and industrial and financial cooperation together with domestic and international financial institutions and enterprises to enhance trade and investment development in all countries involved in the BRI. The Silk and Road Fund aims at medium to long-term funding through various investment and financing mechanisms such as equity investment, debt investment, investment in funds and others. The total capital of the fund amounts to USD 40 billion and RMB 100 billion (contributed by China). Currently 70 per cent of the committed capital has been invested in infrastructure projects.[20] It is estimated that total net investment in BRI related projects stands in the region of around USD one trillion.[21]

Examples of the infrastructure projects conducted under the auspices of the BRI include:

> *Gwadar Port*: The key point of the Chinese-Pakistan Economic Corridor is Gwadar Port in Pakistan, which will provide an alternative trading route to the Malacca Strait (where tensions exist between China and the United States of America).[22] Gwadar Port is an important link between land-based and maritime parts of BRI. The CPEC stretches from Xinjiang in China to Gwadar Port in Pakistan and an estimated USD 54 billion worth of infrastructure projects planned for this route. The construction of the 3200 km long road between Xinjiang and Gwadar Port has lasted for decades and is now finally partly operational. It passes through regions marked by conflict and with elevations of 5000 m above sea level and is one of the highest roads in the world. Multiple projects planned alongside the road contain the building of gas pipelines, power plants, highways and optic fibre cables. Significant further investments have been made in other ports including Piraeus (Greece),[23] Kumport (Turkey).[24]

Greece, Kenya, Kuwait, Lebanon, Papua New Guinea, Peru, Romania, South Africa, Sudan, Tonga and Venezuela. https://www.aiib.org/en/about-aiib/governance/members-of-bank/index.html.

[18] https://www.aiib.org/en/about-aiib/who-we-are/our-work/index.html.

[19] https://www.aiib.org/en/index.html. For an overview of the AIIB's structure, success and future, see Lichtenstein (2018).

[20] Jin (2018).

[21] Kelly and Puchua (2018).

[22] Kumar and Barry (2017), Chan (2015).

[23] Hosken and Kasapi (2017), Georgiopoulos (2016).

[24] China COSCO Holdings Company Limited (2015).

Khorgos Gateway: The Khorgos Gateway on the border between China and Kazakhstan is an important intersectional transshipment point between the rail networks in China and Kazakhstan (Kazakhstan as a former country of the Soviet Union uses the same railway gauges as Russia, which are wider than those used in Western and China). The gateway is accordingly the biggest dry port in the world. The expected freight volume to be handled at the border of Kazakhstan and China is 15 million tons per annum and might increase up to 30 million tons a year when a second European-China railway link will be opened.[25]

Rail Links to London-Europe-Tehran-Laos: The first trains completed their 18-day-7400 mile journey from Yiwu in China to London in the United Kingdom (UK) via Russia, Kazakhstan, Belarus, Poland, Germany, Belgium and France in 2017. London is the 15th European city being directly connected with China by rail and it is said to be an important economic link between the UK and China, especially in the upcoming post-Brexit phase.[26]

Similarly a 10,400 km long railway network from China to Iran through Kazakhstan, Uzbekistan and Turkmenistan has been completed. The trains leave for their 14-day journey from Western China, pass through the Khorgos dry port and the Kazakh city of Almaty before reaching Tode Bi in Kazakhstan, where one railway branches off to Iran and the other one towards London.[27]

The Laos-China Railway is estimated to be 414 km long. It will connect Boten, the northern Lao town bordering southwest China's Yunnan Province, with Vientiane, capital of Laos.[28] The China-Laos railway will be extended in the south to link Bangkok, capital of Thailand and will connect to Chinese railway network.[29] It is estimated to be operational by the end of December 2021.[30] The total investment of the project is approximately RMB 40 billion (USD 5.8 billion[31]), of which 70 per cent come from Chinese investment.[32]

Bangladesh Bridge Projects: The Padma Bridge is a multipurpose road-rail bridge across the Padma River under construction in Bangladesh. It not only connects the 21 districts of southern Bangladesh with the capital Dhaka, but also ends the history of ferrying between these areas and Dhaka. It plays an import role in deepening cooperation between China and South Asia and neighboring countries.[33] On 9 August 2016, China Railway Group Limited (which is a State-Owned Enterprise (SOE))

[25] Cohen (2018), South China Morning Post (2018).

[26] South China Morning Post (2018), Belt and Road Portal (2018a).

[27] Belt and Road Portal (2018a).

[28] People's Daily Online (2017).

[29] People's Daily Online (2017).

[30] People's Daily Online (2017).

[31] Some articles cite USD 7 billion: Yun (2017).

[32] Xinhuanet (2018).

[33] Belt and Road Portal (2018b).

published an 'Announcement of China Railway Group Limited on Winning of Bid for a Material Overseas Project' on the Shanghai Stock Exchange website.[34]

The Bangladesh-China Friendship Bridge is a long-term infrastructure project between China and Bangladesh, which aims at assisting Bangladesh in achieving its economic development goals and should express the friendship between Chinese and Bangladeshi people. Starting in 1986, China has already helped build seven such Friendship Bridges. The 8th Friendship Bridge is under construction and the funding of the 9th was recently confirmed.[35]

The 'Power-of-Siberia'-Pipeline: The 'Power-of-Siberia'-Pipeline is a natural gas pipeline which is designed to transport gas from Eastern Siberia to the far east of Russia and China. The China National Petroleum Corporation (CNPC) and Gazprom signed a 30-year Sales and Purchase Agreement in 2014 which supplies China with Russian Gas through the more than 3000 km long pipeline, starting in 2019.[36] The estimated total costs of the pipeline amount to USD 55 billion and the project is said to be the largest energy project of our time.[37] Because of China's continuously growing demand for gas, the China-Russia Pipeline will significantly help to ease China's shortage of own natural gas.[38]

The Kyaukpyu Pipeline: The Kyaukpyu Pipeline supplies China with oil from the Middle East and Africa and is one of the strategic energy projects of high importance because it provides an alternative supply route to the Malacca Strait for China's crude oil imports. Its construction began in 2010 and the pipeline officially started operating in 2017 after several years of delay due to opposition in both countries.[39] Starting in Kyaukpyu in West Myanmar, the 771 km long USD 1.5 billion pipeline runs across four states before reaching the Yunnan Province and is expected to carry 22 million tons of oil per year. Parallel to the oil pipeline a twin gas pipeline was built, which began operating in 2015.[40]

2.4 The BRI—Aims

The stated aims of the BRI comprise a long shopping list of largely laudable objectives relating to Chinese and international economic development, regional integration and

---

[34]China Railway Group Limited (2016).

[35]Xinhuanet (2017), Xinhuanet (2016).

[36]http://www.gazprom.com/about/production/projects/pipelines/built/ykv/, Zheng (2017).

[37]Foy (2018).

[38]Zheng (2017).

[39]Hornby (2017).

[40]Zhang (2017), Mangi (2018).

more general international goals such as sustainable development and 'world peace'. Specifically these include developing or promoting[41]:

- economic prosperity in the countries of the BRI;
- exchanges and mutual learning between different civilizations;
- world peace-mutual understanding and friendship among countries;
- cultural exchanges-mutual learning from different civilizations;
- deeper political trust;
- cultural diversity- a multipolar world;
- development-diversified, independent, balanced and sustainable development in the region;
- economic globalization, global free trade, an open world economy;
- a network of free trade areas that meet high standards;
- closer economic ties;
- deep integration of markets;
- economic policy coordination;
- in-depth regional cooperation;
- the connectivity of Asian, European and African continents and their adjacent seas;
- partnerships among the countries along the Belt and Road;
- multi-tiered and composite connectivity networks;
- more profound opening up of China;
- common security;
- improved infrastructure in the region;
- a secure and efficient network of land, sea and air passages.

The Chinese policy statements also contain five cooperation priorities: cultural exchange, financial integration, trade and investment, facilities connectivity and policy coordination.[42] BRI countries are encouraged to promote people-to-people bonds and the spirit of peaceful cooperation through academic, cultural and personnel exchanges, media, science and information cooperation, mutual technical and health support as well as political, social and ecological interaction.[43]

One specific priority is energy cooperation. The BRI aims to improve regional energy safety and to optimize the distribution of energy resources. It will seek to integrate regional energy markets and promote green and low-carbon development

---

[41] National Development and Reform Commission et al. (2015), Belt and Road Portal (2017). See also, Guiding Principles on Financing the Development of the Belt and Road (Issued by Ministry of Finance, May 2017), https://eng.yidaiyilu.gov.cn/zchj/qwfb/13757.htm.

[42] A detailed description of the 5 key areas and their intended impact on the BRI can be found at: http://china-trade-research.hktdc.com/business-news/article/The-Belt-and-Road-Initiative/The-Belt-and-Road-Initiative/obor/en/1/1X3CGF6L/1X0A36B7.htm and in National Development and Reform Commission et al. (2015). News relating to the cooperation priorities can be found on the official BRI homepage of the People's Republic of China: https://eng.yidaiyilu.gov.cn/index.htm.

[43] http://china-trade-research.hktdc.com/business-news/article/The-Belt-and-Road-Initiative/The-Belt-and-Road-Initiative/obor/en/1/1X3CGF6L/1X0A36B7.htm; https://eng.yidaiyilu.gov.cn/index.htm.

of energy. By doing so, the BRI will seek to meet increasing demand for energy and advanced economic development in countries involved in the Initiative.[44] More recent statements have placed increasing emphasis on ecological and sustainable development as goals of the BRI.[45] The Chinese government has sought to stress the compatibility of the BRI with the Sustainable Development Goals of the United Nations (UN).[46] The UN has responded positively, seeking to promote the 17 goals as guiding principles for the future development of the BRI.[47]

Since the launch of the BRI there had been speculation as to whether such a vast initiative could or should be developed on an ad hoc basis, or whether an accompanying legal infrastructure, such as an overarching treaty or political or legal institutions would be necessary or desirable. Looking at the general aims of the BRI as stated above, an emphasis on policy coordination, increased economic connectivity and removing barriers to trade might argue in favour of the establishment of common legal institutions. On the other hand, an emphasis on a 'multipolar' world and cultural diversity would tend to argue against the need for new overarching institutions such as a court or even founding treaty. The divergence could be illustrated by those who envisaged the BRI as the first steps to establishing an international organization or community such as the European Union (EU) and those imagining it as a purely economic or cultural phenomenon, analogous to the Marshall or Colombo plans for economic development in the aftermath of World War II.[48]

During 2016/2017 it became apparent that some legal infrastructure in the form of a Court would be established to sit alongside the vast pieces of physical infrastructure accompanying the BRI projects (roads bridges, pipelines, etc.) but outside observers remained curious as to the form such an institution would take. Would it be a traditional 'Court' hosting judges and litigation or a 'Tribunal' hosting ad hoc arbitration? Would it be a Chinese institution or an 'international' one? The thinking of the Chinese government has only been recently revealed.

3 The Establishment of the CICC

At the end of June 2018, the Chinese authorities published two key documents concerning the legal framework for dispute resolution in the BRI. These were:

---

[44] National Development and Reform Commission and the National Energy Administration of China (2017).

[45] Ministry of Environmental Protection of China (2017).

[46] Ministry of Foreign Affairs of the People's Republic of China (2017).

[47] United Nations (2017).

[48] On the role played by the Court of Justice of the European Union/European Court of Justice in the development of the EU, see Tamm (2013).

(1) *Opinion Concerning the Establishment of the Belt and Road International Commercial Dispute Resolution Mechanism and Institutions (The Opinion).*[49] This was issued by the Communist Party Central Committee and the General Office of the State Council of the People's Republic of China on 27 June 2018. Following extensive discussion and consultation the Opinion was adopted by the Leading Group for Deepening Overall Reform of the 19th Chinese Communist Party Central Committee, chaired by President Xi Jinping. The opinion thus represents the current Chinese thinking on implementation of the BRI and the role of dispute resolution. The Opinion takes the form of an instruction for relevant government departments to follow in the course of their work generally.
(2) *Provisions of the Supreme People's Court on Several Issues Regarding the Establishment of the International Commercial Court (The Provisions).*[50] These were issued on 28 June 2018 in the form of a judicial interpretation and give more concrete guidance on dispute resolution in the context of the BRI.

The key announcement in both instruments is the establishment of the new International Commercial Court of the People's Republic of China as part of wider dispute resolution mechanism for the BRI. New Courts have now in fact been established and inaugurated in both Shenzhen and Xi'an. The choice of these cities as locations appears to be both practical and symbolic. Shenzhen has played a key part in Chinese trade policy since the opening up period in the 1980s and occupies a strategic position in the development of the Maritime Silk Road and China's Greater Bay Area.[51] Xi'an has significant connections with the historic Silk Routes and occupies a strategic position in China's internal development and as a logistic and economic hub for Chinese trade with Central Asia and Europe.

Several general principles and ambitions for BRI dispute resolution are referenced in the Opinion, which are then expanded on in a more concrete manner in the Provisions (the latter can be viewed as a blueprint for a procedural code for the new dispute resolution mechanism).These range from very broad reiteration of some of the aims of the BRI itself (see above) and plans for BRI dispute resolution in general to more to more specific aims of the newly established CICC. The general principles gleaned from the Opinion and Provisions can be summarized roughly as follows:

- promoting the implementation of the BRI;

[49] Opinion Concerning the Establishment of the Belt and Road International Commercial Dispute Resolution Mechanism and Institutions (27 June 2018), http://cicc.court.gov.cn/html/1/219/208/210/819.html.

[50] Judicial Interpretation of the Supreme People's Court of the People's Republic of China—Fa Shi [2018] 11 (Provisions of the Supreme People's Court on Several Issues Regarding the Establishment of the International Commercial Court), http://cicc.court.gov.cn/html/1/219/199/201/817.html.

[51] The Chinese policy of coordinated development in the Southern Guangdong area including Hong Kong, Macau, Guangzhou and Shenzhen. See, Framework Agreement on Deepening Guangdong-Hong Kong-Macao Cooperation in the Development of the Bay Area, signed by the National Development and Reform Commission of the People's Republic of China, the Hong Kong SAR Government, the People's Government of Guangdong Province and the Macau SAR Government on July 1 2017.

- upholding the principles of openness and inclusiveness—promoting the development of an open global economy;
- following a spirit of cooperation ‘the principle of planning together, building together and benefiting together’;
- creating a stable, fair, transparent, and predictable business environment under the rule of law;
- protecting the legal rights and interests of Chinese and foreign parties equally;
- establishing a widely accepted mechanism and institutions for international commercial dispute resolution, suitable for the unique characteristics of Belt and Road participating countries;
- upholding the principle of justice, efficiency, and convenience—resolving cross-border commercial disputes arising in the course of the BRI with fairness and efficiency;
- upholding the principle of party autonomy—respecting the rights of the parties from Belt and Road participating countries in respect of adopting different ways of dispute resolution and choosing domestic or foreign laws familiar to them;
- upholding the principle of diversified dispute resolution—recognizing the diversity of parties in the BRI, the complexity of the types of disputes, and the differences in countries’ legislations, judiciaries, and legal culture and developing diversified dispute resolution mechanisms, which integrate litigation, mediation and arbitration, create a convenient, expeditious and low-cost ‘one stop’ center for dispute resolution;
- learning from existing international dispute resolution mechanisms;
- supporting active participation by experts specializing in international law as well as domestic laws of their respective jurisdictions from the BRI participating countries;
- applying international treaties and customs to protect legitimate rights and interests of all parties;
- promoting of mediation—encouraging law firms with appropriate expertise to take part in the Belt and Road international commercial mediations;
- attracting more outstanding arbitrators, in China and overseas, to provide high-quality arbitration legal services for parties from the Belt and Road countries;
- strengthening the management of information and data analysis over cases in relation to the BRI—providing intelligent service to judges to ensure correct and consistent judgments;
- cultivating a talent pool of legal experts, who are specialized in international law and international trade rules with English-speaking ability—encouraging legal experts to participate in dispute resolutions;
- exploring areas of law reform (e.g. of the Civil Procedure Law, Arbitration Law, and other areas to support the BRI international commercial dispute resolution mechanism and institutions).

The Provisions give a certain amount of detail in some areas as to how these goals are to be realized, but considerable uncertainties remain to be answered by the practice of the Court. Further law reform will also be required to achieve these historic ambitions as will be discussed more fully below.

3.1 Status and Jurisdiction

The CICC is a permanent adjudicative body and part of the Supreme People's Court. (Art. 1, The Provisions).[52] It will have jurisdiction in cases which are 'international' and 'commercial' (Arts. 2 and 3, The Provisions).

The 'international' element for the jurisdiction of CICC is defined in Article 3 of the Provisions as follows:

(a) one or both parties are foreigners, stateless persons, foreign enterprises or other organizations;
(b) one or both parties have their habitual residence outside the territory of the People's Republic of China;
(c) the object in dispute is outside the territory of the People's Republic of China;
(d) legal facts that create, change, or terminate the commercial relationship have taken place outside the territory of the People's Republic of China.

A similar approach to international cases has been adopted to that of the SICC.[53] The definition also corresponds closely to the Chinese jurisprudential concept of disputes involving 'foreign elements' (a concept permitting a choice of foreign law or arbitration).[54] The result appears to be an attempt to encourage parties who would have the right under Chinese law to choose foreign Courts or arbitration, to choose instead the CICC.

---

[52] Like the recent additions in Singapore, Netherlands and Germany, the CICC is in fact a division of the national court system. In this respect, these courts have something in common with the Commercial Court in London, which was established in the 19th Century and which handles large volumes of litigation of an international character.

[53] Order 110, r. 1, Rules of Court (Cap. 322, R 5). It is important to bear in mind that the term 'international' here refers to the business done by the court, rather than the nature of the court itself which remains part of the domestic court structure. This distinction has sometimes caused confusion, see *Amin Rasheed Shipping Corporation v Kuwait Insurance Company* [1983] 3 WLR 241 at p. 250 and Mann (1984, p. 195).

[54] The position appears to be that disputes involving 'foreign elements' may be referred to courts and Tribunals outside the People's Republic of China, but those not involving 'foreign elements' may not be so referred. Article 128 of the Contract Law of the People's Republic of China. Article 271 of the Civil Procedure Law of the People's Republic of China. Supreme People's Court Reply to the Beijing High Court [2013] Min Si Ta Zi No. 64.

The 'commercial' element is largely undefined, in contrast to more detailed provisions used by the English Commercial Court.[55] It has been confirmed by Governmental statements that investment disputes (both State/State and Investor/State) are intended to be excluded from the ambit of the CICC, which is designed to resolve disputes between 'equal commercial parties'.[56] This would correspond with the China's adoption of the New York Convention under the 'commercial reservation' and its stated position that arbitration awards in investor-state disputes are not 'commercial' awards.[57]

According to Article 2 of the Provisions, the jurisdiction of the CICC in international commercial cases will also only apply:

- Where the parties have chosen the CICC *AND* the value in dispute is at least RMB 300,000,000;
- Where the case is of national significance;
- Where the case is referred by a Higher People's Court, which would otherwise have jurisdiction;
- Where the Supreme People's Court considers the case appropriate to be tried by the CICC.

The jurisdiction is clearly reserved only for significant international commercial cases. The financial threshold for party choice of the CICC is a high one (there is no such general threshold for example in the English Commercial Court[58]).

The Provisions also establish jurisdiction of the CICC in certain arbitration related claims (such as applications for the preservation of assets and proceedings for enforcement or setting aside of international commercial arbitration awards). This will be discussed separately and in more detail below.

---

[55]The English Civil Procedure Rules commercial court guide Part 58.1 provides 'commercial claim' means any claim arising out of the transaction of trade and commerce and includes any claim relating to—(a) a business document or contract; (b) the export or import of goods; (c) the carriage of goods by land, sea, air or pipeline; (d) the exploitation of oil and gas reserves or other natural resources; (e) insurance and re-insurance; (f) banking and financial services; (g) the operation of markets and exchanges; (h) the purchase and sale of commodities; (i) the construction of ships; (j) business agency; and (k) arbitration.

[56]China International Commercial Court (2018). See also reports of government press conference dated 28 June 2018: http://cicc.court.gov.cn/html/1/219/208/210/769.html and http://cicc.court.gov.cn/html/1/218/149/192/550.html. It is important to note that such disputes have not expressly been ruled out in the text of the Provisions, which may indicate an intention to revisit this question in future. This will be discussed more fully below.

[57]See, Decision of the Standing Committee of the National People's Congress on China Joining the Convention on the Recognition and Enforcement of Foreign Awards, http://www.newyorkconvention.org/implementing+act+-+china.

[58]The English commercial court was established in the late 19th Century and is one of busiest forums in the world for international commercial litigation. Like the recent additions in Singapore, Netherlands and Germany (and like the CICC), it is in fact a division of the national court system, namely an arm of the High Court. Though the English system does provide small claims courts and Mercantile Courts for lower value claims. The Commercial Court's 'Financial List' also has a comparable threshold of GBP 50,000,000 (CPR Part 63A rule 63A.1(2)(a)).

3.2 *Judiciary and Expert Committee*

The CICC will be presided over by senior Chinese judges, sitting in panels of three or more (Art. 5, The Provisions). The criteria for appointment are that the judges are experienced in trial work, have knowledge of international trade law and investment law and proficient in Chinese and English. (Art. 4, The Provisions). Shortly after the inauguration of the CICC in Shenzhen and Xi'an on 29th June 2018, eight Chinese Judges—two women and six men—were appointed as CICC judges in early July 2018.[59]

The establishment of an international commercial expert committee is one of the more innovative features of the CICC (Article 11, The Provisions; see also The Opinion) The Court is in the process of appointing a standing panel of experts to provide assistance with the work of the CICC on matters of international commercial law and foreign law. Experts may also be called upon to preside over mediations. The Committee members to be selected include experts and scholars from China and countries along the route of the 'Belt and Road' and other legal systems. The experts will be recognized experts in international trade law, international investment law and arbitration practice.[60] The first panel of 20 international experts for the CICC was published in August 2018.[61]

These provisions deal with a number of issues which have caused difficulties in other countries where international Courts have been/are being established, in particular the language of the Court and the desirability of an international judiciary.

3.2.1 Language

English is used as the native forum language of the commercial courts in London and Singapore, which is widely perceived as a competitive advantage of those courts due to the widespread use of English as a common second language by parties in international transactions. Other countries setting up international courts have had to wrestle with legal issues associated with departing from the language of the forum and using another (for example the language of the contract).

China, like most countries, requires court proceedings to be conducted in the language of the forum.[62] This naturally poses problems for foreign litigants unfamiliar with the language of the Court. Additionally, in situations where parties have

---

[59] http://cicc.court.gov.cn/html/1/219/208/210/821.html.

[60] China International Commercial Court (2018). See also reports of government press conference dated 28 June 2018: http://cicc.court.gov.cn/html/1/219/208/210/769.html and http://cicc.court.gov.cn/html/1/218/149/192/550.html.

[61] See http://cicc.court.gov.cn/html/1//291/235/237/index.htmlCICCexpert.

[62] See inter alia Article 139 of the Constitution of the People's Republic of China (2018 Amendment) and Article 262 of the Civil Procedure Law of the People's Republic of China. The latter provides: 'When trying foreign-related civil cases, a people's court shall use the spoken and written languages commonly used in the People's Republic of China. Upon request of the parties, interpretation may be provided at the expense of the parties.'.

communicated and contracted in a neutral language (e.g. English), efficiency is compromised when documents and evidence must be translated for the court (or proved using notarization processes). Whilst parties who are subject to the jurisdiction of a State Court must take its language and laws as they find it, in the world of international dispute resolution, commercial parties have considerable autonomy to choose the forum for the resolution of their disputes. Such parties have the luxury of the additional option of international arbitration, where the language of proceedings can largely be determined by party autonomy, or failing agreement by Tribunals who should attempt to find the most efficient solution unshackled by local procedural requirements (such as notarization of translations etc.).[63] Flexibility in relation to the issue above is likely to be proven attractive to commercial parties.

In seeking to attract litigants to their new courts, some countries have dealt with this issue by simply stipulating English as the language of the 'international' Court. The Rules of the DIFC Courts 2014 (RDC 2014) provide that the court proceedings shall be conducted exclusively in the English language.[64] Similarly in the Court at the AIFC which was inaugurated in 2018, the official language of the court is English and court proceedings take place in English.[65] The same will apply in the new BIBC, scheduled to open in 2018[66] and it is anticipated that a similar new Court under discussion in Germany would (at least potentially) operate in English.[67] The new NCC in Amsterdam adopts English as a default language, with the local language (Dutch) available by party agreement.[68]

The CICC's requirement that judges need to be proficient in both English and Chinese goes some way to address the issue of language. It appears, however, from the Opinion and Provisions that the CICC will operate primarily in Chinese, although materials prepared originally in English may be submitted directly to the court without translation where both parties agree (Art. 9, The Provisions). The Provisions also exempt documents originally prepared overseas from the formalities of notarization (but not translations save in the case of English).

---

[63]See e.g., Article 17, London Court of International Arbitration (LCIA) Rules of Arbitration (2014); Article 20, International Chamber of Commerce (ICC) Rules (as amended 2017).

[64]See part 2 of the Rules, https://www.difccourts.ae/part-2-interpretation/.

[65]The AIFC Constitutional Statute No. 438-V ZRK of 7th December 2015 (Articles 15/19), http://aifc-court.kz/legislation.

[66]Croisant (2018).

[67]Official website of the Frankfurt District Court about the chamber for international commercial disputes: https://ordentliche-gerichtsbarkeit.hessen.de/ordentliche-gerichte/lg-bezirk-frankfurt-m/lg-frankfurt-m/chamber-international-commercial-disputes.

[68]The Rules of Procedure for the International Commercial Chambers of the Amsterdam District Court (Netherlands Commercial Court) and the Amsterdam Court of Appeal (Netherlands Commercial Court of Appeal) (Article 2), https://www.rechtspraak.nl/SiteCollectionDocuments/concept-procesreglement-ncc_en.pdf. It has been suggested that cases which go on appeal to the Superior Courts in the Netherlands may nonetheless need to be conducted in Dutch.

3.2.2 Foreign Judges

The Kazakh and DIFC models have sought to create courts operating along the lines of common law courts in jurisdictions which are primarily civil law in nature. It is perhaps inevitable that expertise from foreign common law judges would be required to establish such courts. Such concerns do not apply in relation to the CICC.

The models in the common law jurisdictions of Singapore and Hong Kong are more nuanced. The SICC has panels of both domestic and foreign judges working together.[69] The foreign judges comprise some of the most eminent common law judges with experience of international commercial cases, in addition eminent judges from civil law jurisdictions have been appointed. The purpose is to increase the capacity of judicial expertise in this specialised field.[70] The presence of foreign judges in Hong Kong originated in colonialism and is not without controversy, but serves a similar purpose at the Superior Court level, and is also designed to ensure the consistent development and application of the common law.[71]

Whilst the level of judicial capacity in international commercial law is a pertinent concern to the CICC as it is in Singapore, Hong Kong and elsewhere, this has been addressed by the emphasis on the development of arbitration and mediation and the appointment of the foreign experts committee, rather than the importing of foreign judges. Cases will therefore be decided by Chinese judges, with supplementary expertise on foreign law and international practices being provided by the panel of experts, arbitration and mediation associations, etc. The issue of the consistent development of the common law is of course not a concern in the context of the CICC, however the Opinion does make reference to a desire to ensure 'correct and consistent judgments'. This is to be achieved through technology, namely the use of 'smart courts' and a 'Belt and Road legal database' as well 'centers for foreign law ascertainment'.

The CICC has thus turned away from the idea of 'international judges' as adopted in for example the DIFC, SICC, and AIFC. This can perhaps be explained by the clear definition of the CICC as a branch of the Chinese Supreme People's Court. Article 9 in Chap. 4 (Qualifications for a Judge) of the Judges Law of the People's Republic of China (Amended 2017) states that a judge 'has to be of the nationality of the People's Republic of China'. This rule will not be relaxed for the CICC. This is indeed in line with the position in the NCC and the proposals in Germany.

There will inevitably remain concerns about the Chinese focus of the CICC and the extent to which the announced composition of the court can deliver the stated aims of internationalization, fairness to Chinese and foreign parties, the correct application of foreign law where chosen and the development of the rule of law in the BRI region. The proof of the pudding will be in the numbers of parties choosing to

[69] https://www.sicc.gov.sg/about-the-sicc.

[70] See https://www.sicc.gov.sg/about-the-sicc. See also the precursor report of the SICC: Singapore International Commercial Court Committee (2013).

[71] The foreign judges of the Court of Final Appeal are referred to as 'non permanent' judges, see: https://www.judiciary.hk/en/organization/judges.htm. For recent debates, see: Lum (2018).

litigate in the CICC. This may well prove to be dependent on the way non-Chinese parties perceive the Court in comparison with the alternatives and particularly with international arbitration. The enforceability of the judgments of the Court in the BRI region and internationally will undoubtedly be a key factor in this regard.

3.3 *Enforceability of CICC Judgments*

BRI disputes will often concern non-Chinese parties and relate to investments outside China. A major question is how easy it will be to enforce the judgments of the CICC internationally. Enforceability is determined by a combination of treaties between China and the BRI countries and (in the absence of treaties) by the national law of those countries.

As of August 2018 China has concluded such international Judicial Assistance Treaties and treaties dealing with Enforcement of Foreign Judgments in civil and commercial matters with 26 of the remaining 83 BRI countries.[72]

Outside those treaties the enforceability of CICC judgments will be possible only by permission of national laws, which are incredibly diverse. Whilst common law legal systems mostly contain a general principle of enforceability in relation to foreign judgments, civil law systems vary with many imposing a reciprocity requirement for enforceability (which itself is interpreted differently in different legal systems).[73]

Given that enforcement of foreign judgments is often predicated on respect, ‘international comity’[74] or ‘mutual trust’[75] concerns about the rule of law and general corruption the BRI region cannot be ignored if progress towards more widespread mutual recognition of judgments is to be made. The World Justice Project has listed 50 out of 74 BRI countries (including China) in their Rule of Law Index for 2017–2018. Whilst 16 of these are in the top third in the global ranking, 15 countries can

[72]Kazakhstan, Kyrgyzstan, Uzbekistan, Tajikistan, Belarus, Russia, Ukraine, Lithuania, Mongolia, Laos, Vietnam, Thailand, Singapore, Korea, Turkey, Poland, Romania, Bulgaria, Hungary, Bosnia-Herzegovina, UAE, Egypt, Kuwait, Morocco, Iran, Ethiopia. A list of the judicial assistance treaties signed by the Foreign Ministry of the People’s Republic of China can be found at: http://www.fmprc.gov.cn/web/ziliao_674904/tytj_674911/wgdwdjdsfhzty_674917/t1215630.shtml.

[73]See Lord Collins of Mapesbury and Harris (2017), Chapter 14(2); Barnett (2001), Chapter 1. Schultz and Redi (2018), Briggs (2012, pp. 145–163). The BRI region comprises only 13 common law jurisdictions, the remainder being largely civil law jurisdictions including Islamic law and post-Soviet legal systems. The countries where reciprocity (by treaty or practice) is required include China (excluding Hong Kong), Vietnam, Kazakhstan, Uzbekistan, Egypt, Qatar, Turkey, Iran, UAE (except DIFC), Saudi Arabia, and Russia.

[74]See the United States (US) case of *Hilton v Guyot*, 159 U.S. 113 (1895) and Lord Collins of Mapesbury and Harris (2017), para 1-008.

[75]See the preamble to the various instruments of EU private international law including the Brussels Recast Regulation 1215/2012 and Brussels Regulation 44/2001: http://eur-lex.europa.eu/homepage.html.

be found on positions between 80 and 113 (113 countries were analysed in total).[76] Absence of judicial corruption and civil justice are some of the factors counted into these overall scores for rule of law but looking at the absence of corruption specifically reveals that the BRI countries have both some of the highest but also lowest scores found in the world.[77]

Despite the uncertainties as to the international enforceability of CICC judgments under the varying national laws of the BRI region there is cause for optimism. If reciprocity is the barrier to widespread enforceability there are signs that this concept is being examined in some jurisdictions with the aim of promoting greater enforceability of judgments.[78] There are also moves among international courts to promote the mutual recognition of their judgments.[79]

Finally mention must be made of the Hague Convention on Choice of Court Agreements (Hague Convention), which came into force on 1 October 2015. The parties to this Convention agree to recognize a choice of court agreement between parties relating to civil or commercial matters and enforce judgments of the chosen court subject to certain limited defenses (such as public policy). The Convention aims at ensuring effectiveness of a choice of court between parties to international commercial transactions and thus enhancing judicial cooperation to support international trade and investment. This Convention neatly side-steps issues of mutual trust on the basis that any court good enough to have been chosen by the parties should be deemed good enough to have its judgments enforced.

[76]The World Justice Project (2018). BRI countries not included in this report are: Turkmenistan, Tajikistan, Laos, Brunei, Maldives, Bhutan, Saudi Arabia, Oman, Israel, Iraq Qatar, Kuwait, Bahrain, Yemen, Syria, Slovakia, Latvia, Lithuania, Montenegro, Azerbaijan, Armenia, Timor-Leste, Palestine.

[77]The World Justice Project (2018). Meaning that a system of mutual judgment recognition for the BRI must recognise that we may be dealing with some of the best and some of the worst performing courts in the world.

[78]See e.g. The People's Republic of China case of *Kolmar Group A.G. v Jiangsu Textile Industry (Group) Import & Export Co Ltd* (2016).

[79]See for example 'Memorandum of Guidance—Enforcement between DIFC Courts and the Supreme Court of Singapore' (21 January 2015), https://www.difccourts.ae/2015/01/21/memorandum-guidance-enforcement-difc-courts-supreme-court-singapore/; 'Memorandum of Guidance between DIFC Courts and the High Court of Zambia' (4 October 2017), https://www.difccourts.ae/2017/10/04/15342-2/; and 'Memorandum of Guidance as to Enforcement of Money Judgments between the Supreme Court of the Republic of Singapore and Qatar International Court and Dispute Resolution Centre' (17 October 2017), https://www.sicc.gov.sg/docs/default-source/guide-to-the-sicc/2017_qatar-mog---enforcement-of-judgements-between-the-qatar-international-court-and-dispute-resolution-centre-and-the-supreme-court-of-singapore35b63033f22f6eceb9b0ff0000fcc945.pdf. See also the work of the Standing International Forum of Commercial Courts—a body of around 25 courts from around the world seeking to provide inter alia greater clarity on the rules of enforcing foreign judgments: https://www.supremecourt.gov.sg/docs/default-source/default-document-library/standing-international-forum-of-commercial-courtsae763033f22f6eceb9b0ff0000fcc945.pdf?Status=Temp&sfvrsn=0.8036344335949836.

At present the Hague Convention applies only in the 12 BRI countries which are also EU Member States and thereby party to the Convention.[80] China, Ukraine and Montenegro have signed but not yet ratified the Convention.

When looked at simplistically in terms of international enforceability of judgments, litigation in the CICC must compare unfavorably with arbitration. The New York Convention of 1958 allows widespread enforceability of arbitral awards in 159 countries worldwide. Only six BRI countries are not parties to the New York Convention (Turkmenistan, Maldives, Iraq, Republic of Yemen, Ethiopia and Timor-Leste).[81] Whilst the national laws in many BRI countries may ultimately not preclude enforcement of the judgment of a foreign court chosen by the parties, the variety in national legal systems as well as lack of clarity will simply not inspire confidence from commercial parties.[82]

The further ratification of the Hague Convention by China and other BRI countries would give an undoubted boost to the enforceability of CICC judgments and therefore the attractiveness of the CICC as a forum for international dispute resolution. Further work also needs to be done on an international level to make the process of enforcement of foreign judgments simpler and or more transparent across the BRI region. Commercial parties will inevitably be more easily persuaded to choose the CICC if confident that judgments will be widely enforceable.

3.4 Promotion of Arbitration and Mediation

In the establishment of the CICC, great prominence has been given in the Opinion and Provisions to the development of mediation and arbitration in the BRI. In relation to arbitration there is specific provision for the jurisdiction of the CICC in relation to the enforcement and setting aside of international arbitral awards (Arts. 11 and 14). Given the high financial threshold for claims in the CICC, it is doubtful whether the CICC is intended to be an exclusive venue for enforcement cases arising out of international (BRI) awards. Similarly, in relation to setting aside actions, it is presumed that the CICC would only have jurisdiction in relation to Chinese awards (perhaps of a certain significance or connection with the BRI). Greater clarity is needed as to which international awards may be enforced in the CICC and which may be the subject of set-aside proceedings.

In relation to mediation, the Provisions make specific reference to the promotion of mediation. There is provision for the mediation of disputes by members of the expert committee or appropriate international mediation institution, with party consent (Art.

[80] Bulgaria, Croatia, Cyprus, Czech Republic, Estonia, Greece, Hungary, Latvia, Lithuania, Poland, Slovakia, Slovenia, Singapore, Ukraine, China, Montenegro.

[81] For all contracting states, see: http://www.newyorkconvention.org/countries.

[82] In Thailand for example, the Civil Procedure Court does not specify a rule for the enforcement of foreign judgments. Although there are cases where the Courts have in fact granted enforcement on grounds similar to those found in common law cases, the legal foundation of the cases is unclear.

12) and for the CICC to issue mediation settlement agreements where the parties have settled the case, or judgments in the form of the settlement where requested by the parties (Art. 13).

There is also a clear drive to involve external stakeholders in building the capacity of the CICC in the fields of arbitration and mediation but a certain lack of clarity of exactly who may be involved. The Opinion calls for 'domestic arbitration institutions' and 'domestic mediation institutions' to step forward to conduct arbitrations and mediations under the BRI umbrella. There is a call to attract 'more outstanding arbitrators, in China and overseas' to provide high quality legal services and for 'law firms with satisfactory qualities' to conduct mediations. This is intriguingly linked to the text of Article 11 of the Provisions which provides:

> The Supreme People's Court will set up an International Commercial Expert Committee and select international commercial mediation institutions and international commercial arbitration institutions that meet certain conditions to build up together with the International Commercial Court a dispute resolution platform on which mediation, arbitration, and litigation are efficiently linked, thereby creating a 'one-stop' international commercial dispute resolution mechanism.

Whilst most legal professionals need little invitation to 'step forward' to accept mandates in international cases, what will be of interest here is the role of international commercial arbitration institutions from outside the People's Republic of China (such as the International Chamber of Commerce (ICC), the London Court of International Arbitration, the Hong Kong International Arbitration Centre (HKIAC), etc.). This is because of the traditional position of Chinese law which has not permitted foreign arbitral institutions to administer arbitrations in the People's Republic of China.[83] Article 11 of the Provisions may be a signal that liberalization of this rule may be in prospect in the context of the BRI—perhaps opening up the possibility of foreign arbitration institutions being licensed to operate in conjunction with the CICC.[84] A further clue is given in the Opinion which makes clear that the development of the BRI will include:

> Exploring the possibilities of amending the Civil Procedure Law, Arbitration Law, relevant laws and administrative regulations, judicial interpretations, and other normative documents in order to provide ample legal basis and protections for the establishment of the Belt and Road international commercial dispute resolution mechanism and institutions.

[83] Article 16(3) of the Arbitration Law of the People's Republic of China (Arbitration Law) requires reference to a 'designated arbitration commission'. Article 10 of the Arbitration Law requires the establishment of an arbitration commission to be 'registered with the administrative department of justice of the relevant province, autonomous region or municipality directly under the Central Government'.

[84] Foreign arbitral institutions such as the ICC, HKIAC and Singapore International Arbitration Centre, have established a presence in the People's Republic of China under a more limited mandate, e.g. to promote arbitration, provide training, etc. These institutions were registered with the Department of Commerce of the relevant Municipal Government rather than the Department of Justice, and have not therefore been designated as an 'arbitration commission' in accordance with the legal requirement.

There is little detail as to how exactly the general principles such as that of 'diversified dispute resolution' and 'integration' are to be realized. True the CICC will have the power (by consent) to issue mediation settlement agreements/judgments or refer the parties to mediation; resolve claims involving certain arbitral awards or issue interim measures in certain arbitral proceedings but it is not entirely clear how this will amount to a 'multi-tiered dispute resolution platform' or 'one stop shop' for dispute resolution as envisaged in the Opinion. It does not seem at present that the CICC is offering parties any more in the field of mediation and arbitration than they already have.

3.5 *Investment Disputes*

Investment disputes appear for the present to be excluded from the ambit of the CICC by virtue of the limitation of its ambit to 'commercial' disputes.[85] It is inescapable that many of the BRI projects can equally be classified as investments as commercial ventures, many involving a public dimension as well as a commercial one. Many such projects involve the completion of projects (the construction of bridges, roads, ports, pipelines, etc.) in foreign jurisdictions. These projects often involve the government of the host State and indeed many are conducted by Chinese SOE's. It is inevitable that disputes arising in the BRI context are likely to involve public and investment law elements as well as purely private, commercial elements. Some disputes may well involve both commercial and public aspects. The question for the CICC then is, whether it makes sense to exclude investor-state disputes from its ambit, in light of the stated desire to promote a 'one stop' dispute resolution forum.

The stated reason for the exclusion was:

> One point that we would like to make clear to all the reporters in particular is that, we have excluded two other types of cases: the trade or investment disputes between countries, and investment disputes between the host country and the investor. These two categories are settled in accordance with existing international dispute settlement rules.[86]

Looking at the existing arrangements for the resolution of investment disputes between investors and States in the BRI region, one finds a complex picture. The mechanisms are to be found primarily in bilateral investment treaties concluded by the BRI States and in their respective national investment laws governing foreign investments.

64 of the 84 BRI countries are contracting states to the International Centre for Settlement of Investment Disputes (ICSID) Convention.[87] Four BRI countries are

---

[85] China International Commercial Court (2018). See also reports of government press conference dated 28 June 2018: http://cicc.court.gov.cn/html/1/219/208/210/769.html and http://cicc.court.gov.cn/html/1/218/149/192/550.html.

[86] See Chinese government press conference of 27 June 2018 http://cicc.court.gov.cn/html/1/218/149/192/550.html.

[87] Contracting BRI states: Afghanistan, Albania, Armenia, Austria, Azerbaijan, Bangladesh, Bahrain, Belarus, Bosnia and Herzegovina, Brunei, Bulgaria, Cambodia, China, Croatia, Czech

signatories only and have yet not ratified the Convention and another 16 BRI members are neither contracting states nor have they signed the Convention.[88] Membership of the ICSID Convention provides the possibility for investors and host States to agree to ICSID arbitration. More importantly where Member States have given consent to ICSID arbitration (e.g. by bilateral investment treaty (BIT) or investment law) a resulting award in favor of an investor is automatically enforceable in all ICSID Member States. Where ICSID arbitration is available it therefore provides a dispute resolution mechanism with 'teeth' for an investor in dispute with a host state.

Where a BIT provides for non-ICSID arbitration (whether institutional such as ICC or ad hoc) the awards will be less easily enforceable than those arising from ICSID arbitration. This is because commercial arbitration awards are always subject to some form of judicial review by the enforcing court.[89] Additionally, by virtue of the 'commercial reservation' in Article I(3) of the New York Convention, whereby reserving states 'will apply the Convention only to differences arising out of legal relationships, whether contractual or not, that are considered commercial under the national law'.[90] The reservation allows the countries to apply the New York Convention only to those disputes, which are qualified as commercial under national law. According to the New York Convention Guide, national courts interpret the term 'commercial' rather broadly.[91] However, the Chinese have made it clear that their interpretation of 'commercial' does not include investment disputes.[92]

Almost all BITs between China and the other BRI countries include separate dispute resolution clauses for state-state disputes and investor-state disputes.[93] Regarding investor-state dispute resolution, 12 out of 71 BITs make reference only to ICSID arbitration, 16 BITs refer to ICSID arbitration as one out of several options to resolve

Republic, Egypt, Estonia, Georgia, Guyana, Hungary, Indonesia, Iraq, Israel, Jordan, Kazakhstan, Korea, Kuwait, Latvia, Lebanon, Lithuania, Macedonia, Madagascar, Malaysia, Mongolia, Moldova, Montenegro, Morocco, Nepal, New Zealand, Oman, Pakistan, Panama, Papua New Guinea, Philippines, Qatar, Romania, Saudi Arabia, Senegal, Serbia, Singapore, Slovakia, Slovenia, Sri Lanka, Syria, Timor-Leste, Trinidad and Tobago, Tunisia, Turkey, Turkmenistan, United Arab Emirates, Ukraine, Uruguay, Uzbekistan, Yemen.

[88] Signatories only: Ethiopia, Kyrgyzstan, Russia and Thailand. Neither Signatories nor Contracting: Antigua and Barbuda, Bhutan, Bolivia, Dominica, India, Iran, Laos, Libya, Maldives, Myanmar, Niue, Palestine, Poland, South Africa, Tajikistan and Vietnam.

[89] Although this review is limited by Article V of the New York Convention to issues of procedure, jurisdiction and public policy, there is no permissible court review of ICSID awards.

[90] 24 of the Countries that have ratified the New York Convention subject to the commercial reservation are BRI countries: Afghanistan, Armenia, Bahrain, Bhutan, Bosnia and Herzegovina, China, Croatia, Hungary, India, Indonesia, Iran, Macedonia, Madagascar, Malaysia, Mongolia, Montenegro, Nepal, Philippines, Poland, Korea, Romania, Serbia, Turkey, and Vietnam.

[91] New York Convention Guide (2018), Pryles (2008, pp. 161, 178–179); Born (2014, pp. 296–297); van den Berg (1981, p. 51).

[92] See Decision of the Standing Committee of the National People's Congress on China Joining the Convention on the Recognition and Enforcement of Foreign Awards, http://www.newyorkconvention.org/implementing+act+-+china.

[93] The 12 countries who do not have BITs with China are Afghanistan, Antigua and Barbuda, Bhutan, Iraq, Maldives, Montenegro, Nepal, Palestine, Panama, Senegal, Timor-Leste and Dominica.

disputes and 25 out of 71 BITs refer to the ICSID Convention as fall back regulations for procedural rules and/or for the appointment of arbitrators.[94]

Looking at the BITs in question in relation to investor-state disputes, 13 BITs make references to arbitration only whereas the majority of the BITs, namely 49, provide a choice for the parties to either arbitrate or litigate their dispute (Table 1).[95]

Where a BIT refers to litigation, it generally is a reference to litigation in the Courts of the State hosting the investment. A common example of the patter of the BIT provisions is the China/Serbia BIT (in force 13 September 1996):

> 2. If the dispute cannot be settled through negotiations within six months, either party to the dispute shall be entitled to submit the dispute to the competent court of the Contracting Party accepting the investment.
> 3. If a dispute involving the amount of compensation for expropriation cannot be settled within six months after resort to negotiations as specified in Paragraph 1 of this Article, it may be submitted at the request of either party to the International Centre for Settlement of Investment Disputes (ICSID) or to an ad hoc arbitral tribunal …

Table 1 .

Number of BRI countries *excluding* China:	83	
Number of BRI countries that have BITs with China:	71	
Number of BRI countries that do not have BITs with China:	12	
Number of BITs referring to arbitration only:	State/State 68	Investor/State 12[a]
Number of BITs referring to litigation only:	State/State 0	Investor/State 0
Number of BITs referring to both arbitration and litigation:	State/State 0	Investor/State 54[b]
Number of BITs referring to neither arbitration nor litigation:	State/State 2	Investor/State 3

[a]Direct ICSID: 1, ad hoc: 0, SCC as fallback: 6; ICSID fallback: 4; choice of SCC/ad hoc/United Nations Commission on International Trade Law (UNCITRAL): 1

[b]Direct ICSID: 13, ad hoc: 22, choice of SCC/ad hoc/UNCITRAL: 1; ICSID fallback: 1; choice of ad hoc/ICSID: 12. Sometimes it is difficult to make a clear distinction either because the wording is not clear or because the clauses differential between different types of disputes (disputes related to expropriation, etc.)

---

[94]Optional reference: Uzbekistan, Myanmar, Brunei, India, Saudi Arabia, UAE, Turkey, Jordan, Bahrain, Serbia, Macedonia, Bosnia and Herzegovina, Russia, Ethiopia, Morocco, Korea. Direct reference: Israel, Romania, Czech Republic, Latvia, Lithuania.

Fallback reference: Mongolia, Laos, Vietnam, Cambodia, Malaysia, Singapore, Indonesia, Philippines, Bangladesh, Sri Lanka, Oman, Iran, Egypt, Qatar, Kuwait, Syria, Hungary, Slovenia, Estonia, Croatia, Albania, Georgia, Azerbaijan, New Zealand, South Africa.

[95]China's BITs with Pakistan and Indonesia do not include any reference to either arbitration or litigation regarding state-state disputes. Chinas BITs with Austria, Thailand and Turkmenistan do not include any reference to either arbitration or litigation regarding investor-state disputes.

A similar position is seen when looking at the investment laws of the BRI countries.[96]

Table 2 shows the tendency of national investment laws to refer the disputes almost equally to both arbitration and litigation. Many of the dispute resolution clauses in the national investment laws refer the dispute to the mechanism the parties agreed to in their investment agreement or are provided in international treaties.[97] If no agreements have been made, the parties have the right to choose whether they want their dispute to be resolved in arbitration or litigation.[98]

The Law on Encouragement and Protection of Foreign Investment of Iran (2002) provides at Article 19:

> If disputes between the government and foreign investors over reciprocal obligations within the framework of investments stipulated in this law are not solved through negotiations, they should be referred to domestic courts unless under a contract, the government and the respective government of the foreign investor have already agreed upon another method for settlement of disputes.

The Law on Investments of the Republic Kazakhstan (with amendments and additions as of 7 November 2014) provides at Article 9:

> (1) Investment disputes can be resolved through negotiations, including the involvement of experts, or in accordance with previously agreed by the parties dispute settlement procedures.
>
> (2) If you cannot resolve investment disputes in accordance with the provisions of paragraph 1 of this article, the resolution of disputes shall be in accordance with international treaties and laws of the Republic of Kazakhstan in the courts of the Republic of Kazakhstan, as well as in international arbitrations, the parties specified in the agreement.
>
> (3) Disputes not related to investment, are settled in accordance with the laws of the Republic of Kazakhstan.

A summary conclusion of the dispute resolution provisions in China-BRI BITs and the BRI investment laws might be that the enforceable remedy of ICSID arbitration is available to investors only in the minority of cases. Investors are more commonly

Table 2 .

Number of BRI countries whose investment law has been analysed:	55
National investment laws with reference to litigation:	33
National investment laws with reference to arbitration:	40
National investment laws referring to both arbitration and litigation:	31
National investment laws without reference to arbitration and litigation:	12

[96] Fifty national investment laws have been analysed for this Chapter. National investment laws (including China's national investment law) are available at: http://investmentpolicyhub.unctad.org/InvestmentLaws.

[97] See for example the national investment laws of Kazakhstan, Turkmenistan, Lithuania, Russia, Timor-Leste, and Georgia: http://investmentpolicyhub.unctad.org/InvestmentLaws.

[98] See for example the national investment laws of Syria, Yemen, Ukraine and Cambodia: http://investmentpolicyhub.unctad.org/InvestmentLaws.

required to choose between ad hoc arbitration (which is less widely enforceable due to its public nature) and litigation in the Courts of the host State. The CICC may be seen as an attractive option to a (Chinese) investor in these circumstances and this might be seen as an opportunity for the CICC.

The difficultly for the involvement of the CICC is not so much the provision in BITs and investment laws for the possibility of arbitration, even ICSID arbitration. The Opinions and Provisions make clear that the CICC is expressly aiming to promote and accommodate the use of international arbitration. The problem is rather that where litigation is provided for in the BITs and investment laws with/of BRI countries, it invariably refers to litigation in the Courts of the host state of the investment, rather than the Court of the investor. Given the mechanics of the BRI, this would mean that a significant amount of work on the reform of BITs and investment laws would be required to smooth the way for the CICC to resolve investment disputes. One option might be to develop a bespoke 'CICC investment dispute settlement model' which parties could choose without prejudice to the provisions of the BITs/investment laws cited above. Recent investment treaties between the EU and Canada and Vietnam have found already contain reference to dispute resolution by a standing body (rather than by ad hoc arbitration) and there is advanced discussion in the investment law community of a multilateral version of such a standing body.[99]

4 Conclusions

There is no doubt that the launch of the CICC is a profound development. That a new specialist division of the Supreme People's Court has been dedicated to significant BRI disputes illustrates how important the BRI is towards Chinese policy making. The likely international impact of the CICC is perhaps more difficult to judge and as the article has hopefully addressed there are a number of inevitable uncertainties at this early stage of the life of the court.

The first one relates to the procedure to be adopted by the Court. The early announcements suggest that an element of flexibility has been introduced to issues of language and evidence, but these do not suggest fundamental departures from the norms of Chinese procedural law. Whilst it is not suggested that the imposition of foreign procedural rules (such as is the case in the DIFC or the AIFC) or even international rules (such as has been proposed in the context of the BIBC) would be appropriate in the Chinese context, perhaps greater attention could have been given to the relaxation of formal domestic rules of procedure and evidence in a wider range of circumstances (as has been done in the SICC) to make proceedings more attractive to non-Chinese parties. The area of civil procedure is one which is crying out for further harmonization and there is an opportunity for the CICC to take a lead here in developing procedure which would be appealing to the commercial community perhaps combining attractive elements of the various legal traditions and

[99]Calamita (2017).

from international arbitration.[100] If the procedural rules off the CICC is a work in progress, these are issues that can be incorporated.

The second uncertainty relates to the enforceability of the CICC judgments. As has been shown, this is another area in which there is great international uncertainty. As has been discussed, one key limb of the jurisdiction of the Court is the existence of an agreement of the parties to litigate there. This will go some way to solve the practical difficulties of enforcing the judgments of the Court international. The remaining part of the solution to this problem requires the hard patient work of law reform, particularly in the context of private international law. The widespread adoption of the Hague Convention would undoubtedly provide a boost to the enforceability of CICC judgments, but it is to be remembered that this would not be a one way street but a reciprocal commitment for the enforcement of judgments, requiring China to also recognise and enforce the judgments from the Courts of the other BRI countries, where those Courts have been chosen by the parties. Again, this requires patient work, not just on law reform, but on reform and improvement of Courts.

There is similar uncertainty surrounding the place of investor state disputes in the BRI. Given the large public interests and levels of public investment in BRI projects, it seems odd that these have been excluded from the ambit of an initiative which aims at a 'one stop' shop for BRI dispute resolution. The existing pattern of investment laws and BITs gives a range of options to parties but those options vary from country to country (BIT to BIT). It would perhaps be difficult or impossible to create an arbitration mechanism within the ambit of the CICC which would be compatible with each of the investment laws and BITs applicable in the BRI (or else require significant revision of same). The laws of State immunity would also preclude CICC court litigation type proceedings by investors against BRI States. Remaining options might include the creation of a standing investment claims Tribunal, which would require much thought as to its composition and international consent to ensure success. Again this is an area which requires the patient work of diplomacy and law reform, but perhaps again one in which China could perhaps take a lead in creating an alternative regional alternative to the ICSID model.

Finally, the idea of the CICC as an element in an integrated dispute resolution mechanism for the BRI needs to be elaborated. More detail is needed as to how arbitration and mediation are to be integrated into the work of the CICC. More detail is required as to which awards (for example) the Court will have jurisdiction to review (the required connection with the BRI, financial limits, etc.). The idea that mediation settlement agreements can be declared binding by the Court is welcome and ties in with the recent work of the United Nations Commission on International Trade Law (UNCITRAL) in this area. The involvement of international experts is of course to be welcomed as advisers to the Court, but there remains a question mark over the involvement of foreign lawyers and foreign arbitral institutions. It does not appear at present that foreign lawyers will be able to appear in the Court (unlike for example the SICC and DIFC). It also remains unclear what exactly will be the relationship

[100] Examples might include the flexible availability of remedies such as injunctions, emergency arbitrator procedures, limited disclosure of documents.

between the CICC and the arbitral institutions which are exerted to help build the new system. Will arbitrations be hosted by the CICC? Will the CICC appoint arbitrators in the same way as they may appoint mediators in BRI disputes? Will there be an arbitral branch of the CICC, perhaps a new arbitral institution with its own panel of arbitrators akin to the announced panel of experts?[101] If so, work needs to be done to ensure the independence of this body (and its members) from the CICC and ultimately from the Chinese government, particularly given the politically and nationally sensitive nature of some of the disputes which would be handled by such a body. If the CICC is instead simply to form loose connections with pre-existing arbitral institutions, then what will be the role of the international institutions? Will they be permitted to administer BRI disputes in mainland China? If not, this is perhaps a serious gap, as the benefit of an arbitration administered by a trusted institution (with concomitant scrutiny of awards, etc.) will be something which the parties will be able to avail themselves of outside China, but not within the CICC mechanism. Any new institution (however eminent its panel of arbitrators) is inevitably going to take time to win the trust of the commercial community.

This is of course a fast evolving landscape. It would be pointless and counter-productive to wait until all the legal, political and diplomatic challenges had been solved before launching such a Court. It is also very clear that significant work is ongoing to develop solutions to some of the problems highlighted (on enforcement of judgments, investment law, procedural law, and international arbitration). It is of great significance that with the BRI and the launch of the CICC, China has an historic opportunity to lead in these debates. It is to be hoped that the CICC will provide not just a theatre for the resolution of significant economic and commercial disputes, but a catalyst for international law reform.

Acknowledgements I would like to thank sincerely Professor Wenhua Shan of Xi'an Jiaotong University for inspiring me to think and write on this topic. I would also like to thank Ms Pia Schwanke and Ms Xiaohe Zheng for their excellent research assistance in the preparation of this Chapter. This article was first published in Vol. 22(2) of Vindobona Journal at pp. 96–125.

References

Barnett P (2001) Res judicata, estoppel and foreign judgments. Oxford University Press

Belt and Road Portal (2017) Building the belt and road: concept, practice and China's contribution. yidaiyilu.gov.cn, 11 May 2017. https://eng.yidaiyilu.gov.cn/zchj/qwfb/12731.htm

Belt and Road Portal (2018a) China Railway Express. yidaiyilu.gov.cn, 20 July 2018. https://www.yidaiyilu.gov.cn/zchj/rcjd/60645.htm

Belt and Road Portal (2018b) Padma bridge and river dredging project. yidaiyilu.gov.cn, 11 November 2016. https://www.yidaiyilu.gov.cn/qyfc/xmal/2456.htm

Born GB (2014) International commercial arbitration, 2nd edn. Kluwer Law International

[101] It is to be noted that the first panel of 20 experts announced at the CICC in August 2018 comprised well known international arbitrators, rather than experts on the law of BRI countries specifically.

Briggs A (2012) The principle of comity in private international law. In: Collected courses of the Hague Academy of International Law, vol 354. Brill/Nijhoff, Leiden
Calamita NJ (2017) The challenge of establishing a multilateral investment tribunal at ICSID. ICSID Rev Foreign Investment Law J 32(3):611–624
Chan M (2015) China launches joint naval drills with Malaysia in Strait of Malacca with more than 1,000 PLA troops. South China Morning Post, 18 September 2015. https://www.scmp.com/news/china/diplomacy-defence/article/1859259/china-launches-joint-naval-drills-malaysia-strait
China COSCO Holdings Company Limited (2015) The formation of a joint venture for the acquisition of equity interests in a container terminal in Turkey. en.chinacosco.com, 17 Sept 2015. http://en.chinacosco.com/jcms/jcms_files/jcms1/web5/site/attach/101/1509170653544833484.pdf
China Daily Online (2016) China provides Bangladesh fund for 8th friendship bridge. chinadaily.com.cn, 8 April 2016. http://www.chinadaily.com.cn/world/2016-04/08/content_24362098.htm
China International Commercial Court (2018) About China international commercial court. cicc.court.gov.cn, 28 June 2018. http://cicc.court.gov.cn/html/1/219/193/195/index.html
China Railway Group Limited (2016) Announcements. Crecg.com, 9 August 2016. http://www.crecg.com/english/2699/index.html
Cohen A (2018) Kazakhstan's new capital is growing up quick. forbes.com, 8 June 2018. https://www.forbes.com/sites/arielcohen/2018/06/08/kazakhstans-new-capital-is-growing-up-quick/#59ea79a71c44
Croisant G (2018) The Belgian Government unveils its plan for the Brussels International Business Court (BIBC). http://arbitrationblog.kluwerarbitration.com/2018/06/25/the-belgian-government-unveils-its-plan-for-the-brussels-international-business-court-bibc/
Deutscher AnwaltSpiegel (2018) The beginning of a new chapter: Frankfurt District Court established English speaking chamber for commercial matters in January 2018. https://www.deutscheranwaltspiegel.de/es-koennte-der-beginn-eines-ganz-neuen-kapitels-sein/
Foy H (2018) Russia's $55bn pipeline gamble on China's demand for gas. Financial Times, 3 April 2018. https://ig.ft.com/gazprom-pipeline-power-of-siberia/
Georgiopoulos G (2016) China's Cosco acquires 51 pct stake in Greece's Piraeus Port. Reuters, 10 Aug 2016. https://www.reuters.com/article/greece-privatisation-port/chinas-cosco-acquires-51-pct-stake-in-greeces-piraeus-port-idUSL8N1AR252
Gnanasagaran A (2017) Dealing with the belt road initiative. The ASEAN Post, 27 Nov 2017
Hornby L (2017), China and Myanmar open long-delayed oil pipeline. Financial Times, 11 Apr 2017. https://www.ft.com/content/21d5f650-1e6a-11e7-a454-ab04428977f9
Hosken A, Kasapi A (2017) Why is China investing heavily in south-east Europe? BBC News, 17 Oct 2017. https://www.bbc.co.uk/news/world-europe-41654346
Jin Q (2018) Building a Golden bridge and pursuing mutual benefit. AIIB Company News, 18 April 2018. http://www.silkroadfund.com.cn/enweb/23809/23812/36341/index.html
Kelly J, Puchua M (2018) Investment protection and dispute resolution on the Belt and Road. http://risk.freshfields.com/post/102f1it/investment-protection-and-dispute-resolution-on-the-belt-and-roadv
Kumar H, Barry E (2017) India, U.S and Japan begin War games, and China hears a message. New York Times, 10 July 2017. https://www.nytimes.com/2017/07/10/world/asia/india-us-japan-war-games-china.html
Lichtenstein NG (2018) A comparative guide to the Asian International Investment Bank. Oxford
Lord Collins of Mapesbury, Harris J (eds) (2017) Dicey, Morris and Collins on the conflict of laws, 15th edn. Sweet & Maxwell
Lum A (2018) Foreign judges key to success of Hong Kong's top court, chief justice says. South China Morning Post, 26 June 2018
Mangi F (2018) China's 'belt and road' gains momentum from Kunming to Mombasa. The Economic Times, 12 July 2018. https://economictimes.indiatimes.com/news/defence/chinas-belt-and-road-gains-momentum-from-kunming-to-mombasa/articleshow/63691956.cms
Mann FA (1984) England rejects delocalised contracts and arbitration. Int Comp Law Q 33:193–198

Ministry of Environmental Protection of China (2017) The belt and road ecological and environmental cooperation plan (May 2017). https://www.yidaiyilu.gov.cn/zchj/qwfb/13383.htm

Ministry of Foreign Affairs of the People's Republic of China (2017) Progress report on implementation of the 2030 agenda for sustainable development (August 2017). http://www.fmprc.gov.cn/web/ziliao_674904/zt_674979/dnzt_674981/qtzt/2030kcxfzyc_686343/P020170824650025885740.pdf

National Development and Reform Commission, Ministry of Foreign Affairs and Ministry of Commerce of the People's Republic of China (2015) Vision and actions on jointly building silk road economic belt and 21st-century maritime silk road. http://en.ndrc.gov.cn/newsrelease/201503/t20150330_669367.html

National Development and Reform Commission and the National Energy Administration of China (2017) Vision and actions on energy cooperation in jointly building silk road economic belt and 21st-century maritime silk road (May 2017). https://eng.yidaiyilu.gov.cn/zchj/qwfb/13754.htm

New York Convention Guide (2018) Commentary to Article 1(3) of the New York convention. http://newyorkconvention1958.org/index.php?lvl=cmspage&pageid=10&menu=617&opac_view=-1#627

Office of the Leading Group for the Belt and Road Initiative (2017). Building the belt and road: concept, practice and China's contribution. yidiyilu.gov.cn, May 2017. https://eng.yidaiyilu.gov.cn/zchj/qwfb/12731.htm

Ordentliche Gerichtsbarkeit Hessen (2017) Strengthening Frankfurt as a venue: English speaking chamber for commercial matters to be established in January 2018. https://ordentliche-gerichtsbarkeit.hessen.de/pressemitteilungen/englischsprachige-kammer-für-handelssachen-ab-januar-2018

People's Daily Online (2017) China-Laos railway project set to be complete by late 2012. en.people.cn, 15 Nov 2017. http://en.people.cn/n3/2017/1115/c90000-9293209.html

Pryles M (2008) Reservations available to member states: the reciprocal and commercial reservations. In: Gaillard E, Di Pietro D (eds) Enforcement of arbitration agreements and international arbitration awards: The New York convention in practice. Cameron May Ltd, London, Chapter 6

Schultz T, Redi N (2018) Comity in US Courts. Northeastern University Law J 10(1):280–365

Singapore International Commercial Court Committee (2013) Report of the Singapore International Commercial Court Committee (November 2013). https://www.sicc.gov.sg/docs/default-source/about-sicc/annex-a-sicc-committee-report.pdf

South China Morning Post (2018) Plugging China into Europe—a visual explainer. http://multimedia.scmp.com/news/china/article/One-Belt-One-Road/europe.html

Standing International Forum of Commercial Courts. https://www.supremecourt.gov.sg/docs/default-source/default-document-library/standing-international-forum-of-commercial-courtsae763033f22f6eceb9b0ff0000fcc945.pdf?Status=Temp&sfvrsn=0.8036344335949836

Tamm D (2013) The history of the Court of Justice of the European Union since its origin. In: Court of Justice of the European Union (eds), The Court of Justice and the construction of Europe: analyses and perspectives on sixty years of case-law - La Cour de Justice et la Construction de l'Europe: Analyses et Perspectives de Soixante Ans de Jurisprudence. T.M.C. Asser Press, The Hague, The Netherlands, pp 9–35

The World Justice Project (2018) The world justice project rule of law index 2017–2018. https://worldjusticeproject.org/our-work/wjp-rule-law-index/wjp-rule-law-index-2017–2018

United Nations (2017) At China's belt and road forum, UN chief Guterres stresses shared development goals. un.org, 14 May 2017. https://www.un.org/development/desa/en/news/sustainable/belt-and-road-forum.html

Xinhuanet (2016) China to help Bangladesh build friendship bridge. Xinhuanet.com, 8 Apr 2016. http://www.xinhuanet.com/english/photo/2016-04/08/c_135261652.htm

Xinhuanet (2017) China to fund Bangladesh for 9th friendship bridge, other infrastructure projects. Xinhuanet.com, 11 May 2017. http://www.xinhuanet.com/english/2017-05/11/c_136274644.htm

Xinhuanet (2018) Laotians expect Laos-China railway to bring tangible benefits. Xinhuanet.com, 4 Feb 2018. http://www.xinhuanet.com/english/2018-02/04/c_136948194.htm
Yun S (2017) Winning projects and hearts? Three cases of Chinese mega-infrastructure projects in Southeast Asia. The ASAN Forum, 3 November 2017. http://www.theasanforum.org/winning-projects-and-hearts-three-cases-of-chinese-mega-infrastructure-projects-in-southeast-asia/#13
Zhang L (2017) China-Myanmar oil pipelines: 'Paukphaw' route. Belt and Road Portal (yidaiyilu.gov.cn), 10 May 2017. https://eng.yidaiyilu.gov.cn/qwyw/rdxw/12628.htm
Zheng X (2017) Gas pipeline to be ready in 3 years. China Daily, 14 Dec 2017. http://www.chinadaily.com.cn/a/201712/14/WS5a31bd3aa3108bc8c6732110.html

David Holloway is Senior Lecturer in Law at the University of Birmingham and Director of post-graduate law programmes at the University's Dubai campus. He is also a barrister and arbitrator practising from Outer Temple Chambers, London, dubai and Abu Dhabi. David graduated in law from Cambridge University and holds a Masters degree in Law and Economics from Erasmus University Rotterdam. He has previously held permanent academic appointments at the Universities of Edinburgh and Essex in the UK, at City University of Hong Kong and is a former Professor of Law at Jiaotong University, Xi'an, PR China. He has significant experience of teaching and research in the fields of international trade law and dispute resolution. He has particular experience of the oil and gas industry and has represented oil majors, State Governments and State Owned Enterprises in major litigation and arbitrations. He has appeared in the English Courts at all levels and before numerous international arbitral tribunals (under ICC, LCIA, UNCITRAL and LMAA rules and in ad hoc arbitrations). He has represented clients in significant mediations and ADR procedures. He spent periods of his early career working in the Lloyds reinsurance market in London and with the marine energy and trade department of a leading City of London law practice. I would like to thank sincerely Professor Wenhua Shan of Xi'an Jiaotong University for inspiring me to think and write on this topic. The author would like to thank sincerely Professor Wenhua Shan of Xi'an Jiaotong University for inspiring him to think and write on this topic and also Ms Pia Schwanke and Ms Xiaohe Zheng for their excellent research assistance in the preparation of the text.

The Netherlands Commercial Court (NCC): Its Challenges and Perspectives

Jeroen A. van der Weide

Abstract On 1 January 2019, the Netherlands Commercial Court (NCC) was launched. The NCC is a specialised division of the Amsterdam District Court and the Amsterdam Court of Appeal that offers high-level international dispute settlement by hearing complex cross-border commercial cases. The NCC proceedings are conducted in English and all cases are heard and disposed of by a three-judge panel that is exceptionally knowledgeable in the field of international commercial litigation. Amidst a sea of commercial courts that are rooted in (English) common law, the NCC finds itself amongst the world's first civil-law based, international commercial courts. This Chapter begins by describing the background and central ideas that underlie the creation of the NCC. The Chapter then moves to the key features of the NCC, such as the content of the Rules of Procedure (NCC Rules), the structure and composition of the NCC and its mode of operation. Finally, the Chapter analyses the NCC's challenges and perspectives. What will be the NCC's success rate? Or should the Dutch judiciary temper its ambitions for the NCC? Is the NCC doomed to failure, or will the NCC be a successful and innovative legal concept?

1 Introduction

On 11 December 2018, the Dutch Senate (*Eerste Kamer der Staten-Generaal*) adopted the Act for the establishment of the Netherlands Commercial Court (NCC).[1] On 1 January 2019, the Act came into force, and the NCC was launched.[2] The NCC is a specialised division of the Amsterdam District Court (NCC District Court) and

[1] Wet van 12 December 2018 tot wijziging van het Wetboek van Burgerlijke Rechtsvordering en de Wet griffierechten burgerlijke zaken in verband met het mogelijk maken van Engelstalige rechtspraak bij de internationale handelskamers van de rechtbank Amsterdam en het gerechtshof Amsterdam. Staatsblad 2018, no. 474: https://zoek.officielebekendmakingen.nl/stb-2018-474.html.

[2] Staatsblad 2018, no. 475: https://zoek.officielebekendmakingen.nl/stb-2018-475.html.

J.A. van der Weide (✉)
Leiden Law School, Leiden University, Leiden, The Netherlands
e-mail: j.a.van.der.weide@law.leidenuniv.nl

L. Chen and A. Janssen (eds.), *Dispute Resolution in China, Europe and World*,
Ius Gentium: Comparative Perspectives on Law and Justice 79,
https://doi.org/10.1007/978-3-030-42974-4_4

the Amsterdam Court of Appeal (NCCA)[3] that offers high-level international dispute settlement by hearing complex cross-border commercial cases in English, that being the language of global business. Amidst a sea of commercial courts that are rooted in (English) common law (London, Singapore, Delaware, New York, Dubai), the NCC finds itself amongst the world's first civil-law based, international commercial courts.[4]

While the city of the Hague presents itself as Legal Capital of the World, hosting the world's main legal bodies such as the International Court of Justice, the Permanent Court of Arbitration and the International Criminal Court, the capital city of the Netherlands, Amsterdam, will claim its share and will on its own terms, by means of the NCC and against the background of an upcoming Brexit,[5] contribute to the strengthening of the position of the Netherlands as a key commercial hub in the European Union (EU).

What are the challenges and the perspectives of this newly created Netherlands Commercial Court? In order to answer that question, this Chapter will first focus on the background and central ideas that underlie the creation of the NCC (Sect. 2). We will then move to the key features of the NCC. What is required to initiate an action before the NCC? What is the content of the Rules of Procedure—the so-called 'NCC Rules'—for the NCC District Court, the NCCA, and the Court in Summary Proceedings in the NCC District Court and the NCCA (CSP)?[6] What is the structure and composition of the NCC and its mode of operation (Sect. 3)? Finally, the

[3]The NCC District Court is a court of first instance, while the NCC Court of Appeal (NCCA) hears appeals against a judgment of the NCC District Court and is a court of first instance, if the matter is eligible for appeal and the parties to the proceedings have not designated the NCC District Court, but the NCCA.

[4]Other examples of civil-law based commercial courts are the Chamber for International Commercial Disputes of the Landgericht Frankfurt am Main, and the *Chambres Commerciales Internationales de Paris* (CCIP) or International Commercial Courts of Paris (ICCP). In Belgium, a draft bill was submitted to the Belgian Parliament on 18 May 2018 to set up a specialised English-speaking court with jurisdiction over international commercial disputes, the so-called 'Brussels International Business Court (BIBC)'. See also Sect. 2 of this Chapter.

[5]On 23 June 2016, the EU referendum took place in the United Kingdom (UK). The people of the UK voted to leave the EU by 51.9% to 48.1%. The UK is due to leave the EU on 29 March 2019. However, it is becoming increasingly likely that the UK will request a deadline extension of Article 50 of the Treaty on European Union (TEU).

[6]According to Article 1.3.2 of the NCC Rules, an action may be initiated before the CSP wherein an interim or protective measure is sought (e.g. an application to grant leave for an attachment or to hear an application for a European Account Preservation Order) or another decision for which the Court in Summary Proceedings is designated by law. Cf. Kuijpers (2019, pp. 47–48) on CSP interim relief proceedings. See also Article 30r(3) of the Dutch Code of Civil Procedure. In its unofficial English translation this provision reads as follows:

> In cases to be decided by the court in summary proceedings, if the parties have agreed for proceedings to be in English and before the Amsterdam District Court or the Amsterdam Court of Appeal as referred to in section 1, the Court in Summary Proceedings of the Amsterdam District Court or the Amsterdam Court of Appeal has jurisdiction to hear the case in English.

challenges (Sect. 4) and the perspectives of the NCC (Sect. 5) will be analysed. What will be the NCC's success rate? Or should the Dutch judiciary temper its ambitions for the NCC? Is the NCC doomed to failure, or will it be a successful and innovative legal concept?

2 Background and Central Ideas

The NCC will be established on fertile soil. According to the latest Global Competitiveness Index (GCI) 2018 of the World Economic Forum, the Netherlands is ranked sixth.[7] The GCI Index tracks the performance of nearly 140 countries on 12 factors ('pillars') of competitiveness, such as innovation, macroeconomic environment, education, and market size. In addition, the Netherlands is home to a large number of multinational companies, such as Royal Dutch Shell, Heineken, Philips, Unilever, and ASML. According to the latest report of the Dutch Central Agency for Statistics (*Centraal Bureau voor de Statistiek* (*CBS*)) multinational corporations account for 40 per cent of jobs in the Dutch private sector.[8] Finally, in the Rule of Law Index 2017–2018, the Netherlands is ranked fifth, with an overall score of 0.85.[9] The same is true for the Judicial Independence Ranking of the World Economic Forum (edition 2017–2018), in which the Netherlands is also ranked fifth, with a score of 6.4 on a scale of 7.0, implying near total independence.[10] These data make clear that the Dutch economy flourishes through openness to global trade and investment and is characterised by an honest and independent judicial system that provides strong protection of private property rights while fostering the rule of law.

In its January 2003 published report 'The Netherlands: A Trading Nation. A Transaction Cost Perspective' (*'Nederland handelsland. Het perspectief van de transactiekosten'*), the Netherlands Scientific Council for Government Policy (*Wetenschappelijke Raad voor het Regeringsbeleid*) emphasized the importance of the establishment of commercial courts to handle international commercial disputes in English:

> Viewed from a (national) trade interest, this may include, within the boundaries of the Dutch judicial system, the possibility to draft contracts in the English language (…) and to conduct court proceedings in English as well.[11]

---

[7] See World Economic Forum (2018, p. xi).

[8] See https://www.cbs.nl/en-gb/news/2018/41/multinationals-account-for-30-percent-of-economy.

[9] See World Justice Project (2018, p. 20).

[10] See World Economic Forum (2017–2018).

[11] Wetenschappelijke Raad voor het Regeringsbeleid (2003, pp. 216 and 226). The original Dutch text reads as follows:

> Vanuit het handelsbelang kan concreet worden gedacht aan de mogelijkheid om binnen het Nederlandse rechtsbestel in de Engelse taal te contracteren … en om in deze taal ook bij Nederlandse rechtbanken te procederen.

Since then, a number of factors have sped up the process of turning the idea—the creation of a Netherlands Commercial Court—into reality. Of particular mention is the growing need of internationally operating Dutch companies for a specialised court that can resolve international trade disputes both within a reasonable time and in a cost-effective manner.[12] A second relevant factor is the large number of complex, cross-border civil and commercial disputes that have been brought before Dutch courts. Some believe that this trend is in decline.[13] This, however, contradicts my own professional experience.[14] Over the past few years, we have seen a considerable number of high profile international commercial cases that were dealt with by Dutch courts. I refer to the *KPNQwest* case (accounting fraud and directors' liability),[15] the *Gazprombank/Bensadon* case (recognition of a foreign judgment),[16] the *Tiffany/Swatch* case (confirmation arbitration award),[17] the *Petrobras* case (class action investors' claim due to corruption),[18] and the *Yukos Oil* case (Russian liquidation order contrary to Dutch public policy).[19] These cases require dedicated and specialised court judges.

A third factor appears to be a clear and world-wide trend toward the establishment of international commercial courts.[20] Amongst several other examples, I refer to the long-established London Commercial Court (LCC) (1895),[21] the Singapore International Commercial Court (SICC) (2015),[22] the Dubai International Financial

---

[12] See, e.g. European Parliamentary Research Service (EPRS) (2018), The Boston Consulting Group (2015).

[13] Bauw (2018, p. 11).

[14] Similarly, Tweede Kamer, vergaderjaar 2016–2017, 34761, no. 3, pp. 1–2.

[15] Amsterdam District Court (*Rechtbank Amsterdam*) 25 April 2012, ECLI:NL:RBAMS:2012:BW3790 (*Cargill Financial Markets; Citibank v KPN; Koninklijke KPN; Qwest; Qwest Communications International*), https://uitspraken.rechtspraak.nl/inziendocument?id=ECLI:NL:RBAMS:2012:BW3790&showbutton=true&keyword=kpnqwest.

[16] Dutch Supreme Court (*Hoge Raad der Nederlanden*) 26 September 2014, ECLI:NL:HR:2014:2838 (*Gazprombank v X*), https://uitspraken.rechtspraak.nl/inziendocument?id=ECLI:NL:HR:2014:2838.

[17] Amsterdam Court of Appeal (*Gerechtshof Amsterdam*) 25 April 2017, ECLI:NL:GHAMS:2017:1496 (*The Swatch Group; Look and Feel v Tiffany*), https://uitspraken.rechtspraak.nl/inziendocument?id=ECLI:NL:GHAMS:2017:1496. The judgment has been confirmed by the Dutch Supreme Court in its decision of 23 November 2018, ECLI:NL:HR:2018:2162, https://uitspraken.rechtspraak.nl/inziendocument?id=ECLI:NL:HR:2018:2162.

[18] Rotterdam District Court 19 September 2018, ECLI:NL:RBROT:2018:7852 (*Stichting Petrobras Compensation Foundation v Petrobras*), https://uitspraken.rechtspraak.nl/inziendocument?id=ECLI:NL:RBROT:2018:7852.

[19] Dutch Supreme Court 18 January 2019, ECLI:NL:HR:2019:54 (*OOO Promneftstroy; Yukos Finance v Yukos Finance*), https://uitspraken.rechtspraak.nl/inziendocument?id=ECLI:NL:HR:2019:54. See also Amsterdam Court of Appeal 9 May 2017, ECLI:NL:GHAMS:2017:1695 (*Yukos Finance*), https://uitspraken.rechtspraak.nl/inziendocument?id=ECLI:NL:GHAMS:2017:1695.

[20] Cf. Kuijpers (2019, pp. 63–67), Requejo Isidro (2019).

[21] See https://www.gov.uk/courts-tribunals/commercial-court. Cf. Lord Phillips of Worth Matravers (2016).

[22] See https://www.sicc.gov.sg/about-the-sicc. Cf. Yee Leong (2016), Yip (2016), Report of the Singapore International Commercial Court Committee (2013).

Centre (DIFC) Courts in Dubai, United Arab Emirates (2006),[23] and the Business Courts in Delaware, USA (1792).[24] In February 2018, the international chambers of the Paris Commercial Court and Court of Appeal, the co-called 'International Commercial Courts of Paris (ICCP)' (*Chambres Commerciales Internationales de Paris* (*CCIP*)) were launched. Their aim is to facilitate access to French commercial courts for transnational commercial disputes involving large international groups and to enhance the attractiveness of Paris as the choice of jurisdiction.[25] Two months earlier, on 1 January 2018, the Chamber for International Commercial Disputes of the Regional Court of Frankfurt (*Landgericht Frankfurt am Main*) was established.[26] On 18 April 2018, a (general) proposal was submitted to the German Parliament (*Bundestag*) to provide for the creation of Chambers for International Commercial Disputes within the German Regional Courts.[27] A month later, on 18 May 2018, a draft bill was submitted to the Belgian Parliament to set up a specialised English-speaking court with jurisdiction over international commercial disputes, the so-called 'Brussels International Business Court (BIBC)'. The BIBC should go into effect on 1 January 2020.[28]

Another relevant factor is that the NCC could be an interesting alternative to what are often far too expensive cross-border arbitration proceedings and/or legal actions (litigation) before other national or international (commercial) courts, such as the aforementioned LCC. In this regard, the upcoming Brexit and the departure of the United Kingdom (UK) from the EU could become a factor for litigating parties that seek a settlement of their international commercial disputes. Finally, with the establishment of an international commercial court, the Netherlands could strengthen its position in cross-border litigation.

In November 2015, the Dutch Council for the Judiciary (*Raad voor de rechtspraak*) launched a 'Plan for the establishment of the Netherlands commercial court, including a cost-benefit analysis' (*Plan tot oprichting van de Netherlands commercial court. Inclusief kosten-batenanalyse*).[29] In this Plan, the Dutch Council for the Judiciary unfolded its vision on the establishment of a Netherlands Commercial Court and addressed several relevant issues, such as litigation-related matters, economic impact, organisational aspects (e.g. selection and recruitment of NCC judges, information and communication technology, staff), a cost-benefit analysis, and court

---

[23] See https://www.difccourts.ae/.

[24] See https://courts.delaware.gov/chancery/. Cf. O'Toole and Kelly (2016).

[25] See https://www.cours-appel.justice.fr/paris/presentation-des-chambres-commerciales-internationales-de-paris-ccip. Cf. Jeuland (2016).

[26] See https://ordentliche-gerichtsbarkeit.hessen.de/ordentliche-gerichte/lgb-frankfurt-am-main/lg-frankfurt-am-main/chamber-international; http://conflictoflaws.net/2017/the-justice-initiative-frankfurt-am-main-2017-law-made-in-frankfurt/.

[27] See http://dipbt.bundestag.de/dip21/btd/19/017/1901717.pdf. Cf. Wagner (2017).

[28] See http://www.lachambre.be/FLWB/PDF/54/3072/54K3072001.pdf. See also http://arbitrationblog.kluwerarbitration.com/2018/06/25/the-belgian-government-unveils-its-plan-for-the-brussels-international-business-court-bibc/.

[29] Raad voor de rechtspraak (2015).

fees. In its Plan, the Council pointed out that one of the main reasons for the establishment of a Netherlands Commercial Court was the fact that a considerable number of complex cross-border disputes are settled by foreign courts or through (international) arbitration.[30] According to the Council, this could lead to a lack of knowledge on the settlement of international commercial disputes within the existing Dutch legal framework. Consequently, Dutch multinational companies and Dutch lawyers might prefer foreign courts or arbitrators to resolve their international trade disputes.[31]

On 17 July 2017, the draft legislation on the establishment of an international commercial court was submitted to the Dutch House of Representatives (*Tweede Kamer der Staten-Generaal*).[32] On 8 March 2018, the draft legislation on the NCC was approved and was sent to the Dutch Senate (*Eerste Kamer der Staten-Generaal*). Nine months later, on 11 December 2018, the Dutch Senate adopted the Act for the establishment of the Netherlands Commercial Court.[33] Shortly thereafter, on 1 January 2019, the Netherlands Commercial Court became a reality.[34]

3 Key Features

3.1 Some General Observations

What are the key features of the NCC, its court rules and its legal proceedings?[35] All cases brought before the NCC will be—for the first time in Dutch legal history—heard and disposed of in English[36] by a three-judge panel specialised in cross-border

[30]For some observations on the relation between arbitration and the NCC (state court litigation), see: Kuijpers (2019), paragraph 12.1; Requejo Isidro (2019), paragraph 3.1; Snijders (2018); Tjittes (2018), paragraph 6.3; Dumoulin (2016, p. 329).

[31]Raad voor de rechtspraak (2015, p. 5). The Dutch Council for the Judiciary estimates the NCC to rule in about 125 cases a year. See Raad voor de rechtspraak (2015, p. 16).

[32]See Tweede Kamer, vergaderjaar 2016–2017, 34761, no. 2 (Draft Bill) and no. 3 (Explanatory Memorandum). The Netherlands is a parliamentary democracy. The Dutch Parliament is called 'the States General' (*Staten-Generaal*). It is bicameral, which means it consists of two chambers: the Senate (*Eerste Kamer der Staten-Generaal*) and the House of Representatives (*Tweede Kamer der Staten-Generaal*).

[33]See Staatsblad 2018, no. 474.

[34]On 11 February 2019, only 6 weeks after the NCC was launched, the first case was submitted to the NCC District Court (Court in Summary Proceedings), see: https://www.rechtspraak.nl/English/NCC/news/Pages/NCC-Update-nr-5.aspx; http://conflictoflaws.net/2019/the-netherlands-commercial-court-holds-its-first-hearing/. On 8 March 2019, the NCC (CSP) gave its first judgment, see https://uitspraken.rechtspraak.nl/inziendocument?id=ECLI:NL:RBAMS:2019:1637.

[35]For articles and publications in English on the NCC, see, e.g., Kuijpers (2019), Antonopoulou (2018), Brouwer and Butijn (2018), van Rhee (2016), Oranje (2016), Ernste and Vermeulen (2016).

[36]According to Article 30r(4) of the DCCP, the litigating parties may, however, request that the proceedings be conducted in Dutch.

commercial litigation.[37] The enactment of the Act for the establishment of the NCC will, in any case, lead to an amendment of the Dutch Code of Civil Procedure (DCCP) (*Wetboek van Burgerlijke Rechtsvordering*) and the Dutch Act on Court Fees in Civil Proceedings (*Wet griffierechten burgerlijke zaken*).[38] Article 30r(1) of the DCCP, that came into force on 1 January 2019, reads as follows:

> If the Amsterdam District Court or the Amsterdam Court of Appeal has jurisdiction to hear a dispute that has arisen or will arise as a result of a particular legal relationship which is within the autonomy of parties to agree, there is an international dispute, and it is expressly so agreed, the parties' proceedings may be in English and before the International Commercial Chamber of that district court ('Netherlands Commercial Court') or that appeal court ('Netherlands Commercial Court of Appeal'). This does not apply to cases that are within the jurisdiction of the subdistrict court. An agreement as referred to in the first sentence is evidenced in writing. A written document containing such a clause or referring to general terms and conditions containing such a clause is sufficient for this purpose, provided that the specific clause has been expressly accepted by or on behalf of the counterparty.[39]

As Article 30r(1) of the DCCP indicates, the NCC does not hear cases that are within the jurisdiction of the Subdistrict Court (a Dutch court in the first instance), such as cases where the claim is EUR 25,000 or less or cases related to consumer disputes, rental disputes, hire-purchase, agency issues and labour or employment-related matters (see Article 93, DCCP). Nor does the NCC hear cases that are within the exclusive jurisdiction of a different chamber, such as the Enterprise Division of the Amsterdam Court of Appeal, the Patents Chamber of the District Court of the Hague, and the highly specialised and well-known Maritime Chamber of the Rotterdam District Court.[40]

The requirements for the jurisdiction of the NCC and its mode of procedure will be regulated by Dutch rules of procedural law, in particular the DCCP (specifically Article 30r)[41] and the 'NCC Rules' that contain the Rules of Procedure for the NCC

---

[37] In 2016, the Maritime Chamber of the Rotterdam District Court agreed to a pilot project, allowing for the use of English as its working language. In July 2017, this pilot project was extended.

[38] See Staatsblad 2018, no. 474.

[39] The official and original Dutch text reads as follows:

> Indien de rechtbank Amsterdam of het gerechtshof Amsterdam bevoegd is kennis te nemen van een geschil dat is ontstaan of zal ontstaan naar aanleiding van een bepaalde rechtsbetrekking die ter vrije bepaling van partijen staat en het een internationaal geschil betreft, kunnen partijen die dit uitdrukkelijk zijn overeengekomen bij de internationale handelskamer van die rechtbank ('Netherlands Commercial Court') of dat gerechtshof ('Netherlands Commercial Court of Appeal') procederen in de Engelse taal. Dit geldt niet voor zaken die tot de bevoegdheid van de kantonrechter behoren. Een overeenkomst als bedoeld in de eerste volzin wordt bewezen door een geschrift. Een geschrift dat een dergelijk beding bevat of dat verwijst naar algemene voorwaarden die een dergelijk beding bevatten, is daarvoor voldoende, mits het specifieke beding door of namens de wederpartij uitdrukkelijk is aanvaard. (See: https://wetten.overheid.nl/BWBR0001827/2019-01-01#BoekEerste).

[40] See the Explanatory Notes to Article 1.3.1(a), p. 32.

[41] For an English translation of selected provisions of the DCCP, see Burrough et al. (2018).

District Court, the NCCA and the CSP (Articles 1.1.1, 1.1.2[42] and 1.2, NCC Rules).[43] The NCC Rules that apply to proceedings both initiated by claim (*vorderingsprocedure*) and by application (*verzoekprocedure*)[44] can be downloaded via the NCC's own website.[45] According to Article 30r of the DCCP in conjunction with Article 1.3.1 of the NCC Rules, an action may be initiated in the NCC District Court where:

(a) the action is a civil or commercial matter in connection with a particular legal relationship within the autonomy of the parties and is not subject to the jurisdiction of the Subdistrict Court or the exclusive jurisdiction of any other chamber or court;
(b) the matter concerns an international dispute;
(c) the parties to the proceedings have designated the Amsterdam District Court as the forum to hear their case (choice of forum) or when the Amsterdam District Court has jurisdiction to hear the action on other grounds; and
(d) the parties to the proceedings have expressly agreed in writing for proceedings to be before the NCC District Court in English.[46]

The NCC will have to test on its own initiative (*ex officio*) whether these four conditions have been satisfied (Article 1.3.4, NCC Rules). If not, then the NCC will have no authority to hear and to dispose of the case.

However, there is another—additional and relevant—element that might be overlooked. Since the cases that will be heard by the NCC are characterised by one

---

[42]Article 1.1.2 of the NCC Rules reads as follows:

> These Rules apply to proceedings in first instance in the NCC District Court. These Rules also apply to proceedings in the CSP and NCC Court of Appeal, except where the provision or the CCP or other legislation indicates otherwise, or the provision would not be appropriate in summary or appellate proceedings. Certain provisions, where indicated, apply specifically to proceedings in the CSP or the NCCA.

[43]Rules of Procedure for the International Commercial Chambers of the Amsterdam District Court (NCC District Court) and the Amsterdam Court of Appeal (NCC Court of Appeal), https://www.rechtspraak.nl/SiteCollectionDocuments/ncc-procesreglement-en.pdf. The NCC Rules were adopted both in Dutch and in English. Both versions are authentic (Article 12.3, NCC Rules). The NCC Rules consist of 12 Sections and 4 Annexes that cover: (1) Scope; (2) Language; (3) Mode of procedure and time limits; (4) Initiating an action; (5) Default and defence; (6) Motions and interim measures; (7) Hearing; (8) Evidence; (9) Judgment; (10) Costs; (11) Discontinuance, withdrawal and restart; and (12) Final provisions. The 4 Annexes relate to the following subjects: (I) Explanatory notes to these rules of procedure; (II) NCC clause; (III) Lawyers' fee; and (IV) eNCC Rules.

[44]See Article 1.1.3 of the NCC Rules and the Explanatory Notes to the NCC Rules, p. 33.

[45]See https://www.rechtspraak.nl/English/NCC/Pages/default.aspx. The NCC can be reached at NCC@rechtspraak.nl.

[46]The same jurisdiction rules apply to both the NCCA and the CSP. See Articles 1.3.2–1.3.3 of the NCC Rules.

or more international elements, the NCC is required to determine its own international jurisdiction, according to Dutch rules of international procedural law.[47] These rules may generally be found either in the Brussels I Regulation (recast) that applies from 10 January 2015[48] or the Hague Convention on Choice of Court Agreements (Hague Choice of Court Convention) that entered into force on 1 October 2015.[49] In order to determine the NCC's competence over a case, the Amsterdam District Court needs to be thoroughly competent to hear the case on the basis of the ordinary rules of Dutch international procedural law, such as the domicile of the defendant (Article 4(1), Brussels I Regulation (recast)) or by a choice-of-court agreement (Article 25(1), Brussels I Regulation (recast)/Articles 3 and 5, Hague Choice of Court Convention).[50]

[47] Cf. Tweede Kamer, vergaderjaar 2016–2017, 34761, no. 3, pp. 5–6. See, however, my observations in Sect. 3.2.2 of this Chapter on the qualification of the term 'international dispute' in Article 1.3.1(b) of the NCC Rules, and in particular footnote 54 below.

[48] Regulation (EU) No 1215/2012 of the European Parliament and of the Council of 12 December 2012 on jurisdiction and the recognition and enforcement of judgments in civil and commercial matters (recast), OJ 2012, L 351/1, https://eur-lex.europa.eu/legal-content/EN/TXT/PDF/?uri=CELEX:32012R1215&from=EN. The Brussels I Regulation (recast) is a 'double instrument' which regulates both the jurisdiction of a court in an EU Member State in civil and commercial matters and the automatic recognition and enforcement of judgments in civil and commercial matters rendered by a court in another Member State. The Brussels I Regulation (recast) implies that full faith and credit is to be given to a judgment delivered by a court in another Member State. An EU Regulation is a legal act of general application which is binding in its entirety and directly applicable to all EU countries. For a general commentary on the Brussels I Regulation (recast), *inter alia*, see Magnus and Mankowski (2016), Dickinson and Lein (2015).

[49] Hague Convention of 30 June 2005 on Choice of Court Agreements, https://www.hcch.net/en/instruments/conventions/full-text/?cid=98. The Hague Choice of Court Convention is also a 'double instrument' that contains both rules of jurisdiction and rules of recognition and enforcement. The Hague Choice of Court Convention may serve as the litigation counterpart of the New York Convention on the Recognition and Enforcement of Foreign Arbitral Awards of 10 June 1958. According to Article 26(6) of the Hague Choice of Court Convention, the Brussels I Regulation (recast) will prevail over the Convention: (a) where none of the parties is resident in a Contracting State that is not a Member State of the EU; or (b) as concerns the recognition or enforcement of judgments, such as between EU Member States. The Hague Choice of Court Convention has been ratified by the EU, Singapore, Mexico and Montenegro. The UK is currently a party to the Hague Choice of Court Convention by virtue of its EU membership. As a non-EU Member State, the UK will participate in the Hague Choice of Court Convention as of 1 April 2019. See also: https://publications.parliament.uk/pa/cm201719/cmselect/cmjust/651/65102.htm. For some critical reflections, see van Bochove and Haentjens (2019).

[50] See also Tweede Kamer, vergaderjaar 2016–2017, 34761, no. 3, pp. 5–6 and Article 1.3.1(c) of the NCC Rules. On rare occasions, the NCC may also have international jurisdiction over a case according to Articles 1-14 of the DCCP (Jurisdiction of Dutch Courts).

3.2 Four Conditions

3.2.1 Civil or Commercial Matter (Article 1.3.1(a), NCC Rules)

The four conditions, set by Article 30r(1) of the DCCP in conjunction with Article 1.3.1 of the NCC Rules, that need to be satisfied in order to initiate an action before the NCC District Court raise some questions that need to be answered. First, what is meant by the words ‘civil or commercial matter … within the autonomy of the parties’ (Article 1.3.1(a), NCC Rules)? According to the Explanatory Notes to the NCC Rules, the term ‘civil or commercial matter’ has been derived from Article 1(1) of the Brussels I Regulation (recast).[51] However, the term that is used in Article 1.3.1(a) of the NCC Rules is obviously broader than the scope of the Brussels I Regulation (recast).[52] All matters dealt with by a commercial chamber of a Dutch court are in the scope of Article 1.3.1(a). The provision requires that a dispute relates to civil law in a broad sense, such as contractual disputes, pre-contractual issues, tort claims, personal property disputes and corporate law matters that will not be subject to the exclusive jurisdiction of the Enterprise Division of the Amsterdam Court of Appeal, such as corporate inquiry proceedings. Insurance, finance, intellectual property, public procurement, competition, telecommunications, transportation, and government liability may be within the scope of civil or commercial matters. Insolvency-related matters such as directors’ liability in bankruptcy or a trustee’s annulment of legal acts may also qualify. Also, claims to set aside an arbitral award may be heard by the NCCA, provided that the Amsterdam Court of Appeal is competent, which is the case where Amsterdam has been designated as the place of arbitration (Article 1064a(1), DCCP).

[51] Explanatory Notes to Article 1.3.1(a) of the NCC Rules, p. 31.

[52] Article 1(1) of the Brussels I Regulation (recast) reads as follows:

> This Regulation shall apply in civil and commercial matters whatever the nature of the court or tribunal. It shall not extend, in particular, to revenue, customs or administrative matters or to the liability of the State for acts and omissions in the exercise of State authority (*acta iure imperii*).

The Brussels I Regulation (recast) does not contain a definition of the term ‘civil and commercial matters’. According to the case law of the European Court of Justice (ECJ), the concept of ‘civil and commercial matters’ is autonomous and independent of the corresponding national legal concepts. See, for example, ECJ 14 October 1976, case 29/76, paragraph 3 (*LTU v Eurocontrol*), http://curia.europa.eu/juris/showPdf.jsf?text=&docid=89285&pageIndex=0&doclang=EN&mode=lst&dir=&occ=first&part=1&cid=10392332. Matters that fall outside the scope of the Brussels I Regulation (recast) are determined by the national laws of each Member State, i.e. Articles 1-14 of the DCCP. Article 8(1) of the DCCP contains a specific provision on choice-of-court agreements which is comparable to Article 25 of the Brussels I Regulation (recast).

3.2.2 International Dispute (Article 1.3.1(b), NCC Rules)

According to Article 30r(1) of the DCCP in conjunction with Article 1.3.1(b) of the NCC Rules, the NCC may only hear cases that concern an international dispute. In order to avoid dogmatic discussions at this particular point, the Explanatory Notes to the NCC Rules provide a non-exhaustive list of matters that would typically be considered an international dispute.[53] A dispute may qualify as 'international' if, for instance, at least one of the parties to the proceedings is resident outside the Netherlands or is a company established abroad or incorporated under foreign law, or is a subsidiary of such a company. A particular matter would also qualify as an international dispute when foreign law is applicable or when the dispute involves legally relevant facts or legal acts outside the Netherlands, such as a transfer of property or collateralisation of assets that occurs under the laws of any foreign jurisdiction.[54] Compared with the Brussels I Regulation (recast) and the Hague Choice of Court Convention, one could argue that the criteria to qualify a case as 'international' are different under Article 30r(1) of the DCCP in conjunction with Article 1.3.1(b) of the NCC Rules. According to Article 1(2) of the Hague Choice of Court Convention, a case is international unless the parties are resident in the same Contracting State and the relationship of the parties and all other elements relevant to the dispute, regardless of the location of the chosen court, are connected only with that State.[55] The sole criterion of the applicability of foreign law (cf. Explanatory Notes to Article 1.3.1(b), NCC Rules) will therefore not render a case international under the Hague

[53] Explanatory Notes to Article 1.3.1(b) of the NCC Rules, p. 32.

[54] Surprisingly, the Explanatory Notes to Article 1.3.1(b) of the NCC Rules, p. 32 indicate that a dispute which arises from an agreement prepared in a language other than Dutch also qualifies as an international dispute. This raises the question whether the NCC will also have jurisdiction in purely domestic cases. That would, however, contradict the Explanatory Notes to Article 1.3.1(b) of the NCC Rules, p. 32: 'NCC proceedings are available for international disputes, so that it will not be appropriate for NCC to deal with a matter that is solely national in scope.' See also Kuijpers (2019, pp. 9–10).

[55] The Brussels I Regulation (recast) does not contain a definition of the international aspect of a dispute, but it is nevertheless clear that the Brussels I Regulation (recast) will not apply to purely domestic cases. See also recital 5 of the Brussels I Regulation (recast) and the Jenard Report to the Brussels Convention, OJ 1979, C 59/8:

> It alters the rules of jurisdiction in force in each Contracting State only where an international element is involved. It does not define this concept, since the international element in a legal relationship may depend on the particular facts of the proceedings of which the court is seised. Proceedings instituted in the courts of a Contracting State which involve only persons domiciled in that State will not normally be affected by the Convention; Article 2 simply refers matters back to the rules of jurisdiction in force in that State. [Cf. Antonopoulou (2018, p. 745 et seq)].

Choice of Court Convention. Would it not be preferable to align the criteria of the various instruments?[56]

3.2.3 International Competence of the Amsterdam District Court (Article 1.3.1(c), NCC Rules)

The third condition under Article 1.3.1(c) in conjunction with Article 30r(1) of the DCCP—the international jurisdiction of the NCC—is satisfied if the Amsterdam District Court is qualified to hear the case on the basis of the ordinary rules of Dutch international procedural law, e.g. the domicile of the defendant or a choice-of-court-agreement.[57] Such a choice-of-court-agreement may be made before or after the dispute has arisen. It is to be expected that in most of the cases brought before the NCC, the litigating parties will have already opted for the jurisdiction of the NCC by way of a jurisdiction clause.[58] As clarified in the Explanatory Notes to Article 1.3.1(c), a choice-of-court agreement may also be made in proceedings pending at another Dutch court. If the proceedings were initiated before a court other than the Amsterdam District Court, that other court may, upon request or with the parties' consent, refer the case to the Amsterdam District Court for further proceedings and judgment by the NCC District Court. This referral is binding on the NCC District Court. If the requirements of Article 1.3.1 of the NCC Rules are not satisfied, the NCC District Court will refer the case to an ordinary chamber in the Amsterdam District Court (cf. Article 18 of the DCCP).[59]

Jurisdiction clauses in favour of the NCC will generally fall under the scope of either Article 25 of the Brussels I Regulation (recast) or Articles 3 and 5 of the Hague Choice of Court Convention. These provisions read as follows:

---

[56]For a discussion and critical reflections on the internationality criterion in the NCC Rules, the Brussels I Regulation (recast), and the Hague Choice of Court Convention, see Antonopoulou (2018, p. 744 et seq).

[57]Explanatory Notes to Article 1.3.1(c) of the NCC Rules, p. 33. See the Brussels I Regulation (recast), the Hague Choice of Court Convention, and the Articles 1-14 of the DCCP (Jurisdiction of Dutch courts).

[58]For some observations on the connection between a choice-of-court agreement (e.g. jurisdiction of the NCC) and the applicable law to the case (e.g. Dutch law), *inter alia*, see: Neekilappillai (2017), Schelhaas (2017), Bauw (2016, p 98), Tjittes (2014).

[59]A motion contesting jurisdiction before the NCC may (also) be made after the statement of defence is filed, if the occasion for raising it only arose later, such as where a claim is amended. See the Explanatory Notes to Article 1.3.1(c) of the NCC Rules, p. 33. Cf. Article 30r(2) of the DCCP:

> In derogation from Article 30i, section 4, anyone wishing to raise a preliminary defence contesting jurisdiction or other defences to the effect that the case should not be dealt with by the International Commercial Chamber of the Amsterdam District Court or the Amsterdam Court of Appeal, may raise such preliminary defences until such time as a decision is taken on these defences.

Article 25 Brussels I Regulation (recast):

1. If the parties, regardless of their domicile, have agreed that a court or the courts of a Member State are to have jurisdiction to settle any disputes which have arisen or which may arise in connection with a particular legal relationship, that court or those courts shall have jurisdiction, unless the agreement is null and void as to its substantive validity under the law of that Member State. Such jurisdiction shall be exclusive unless the parties have agreed otherwise. The agreement conferring jurisdiction shall be either:
   (a) in writing or evidenced in writing;
   (b) in a form which accords with practices which the parties have established between themselves; or
   (c) in international trade or commerce, in a form which accords with a usage of which the parties are or ought to have been aware and which in such trade or commerce is widely known to, and regularly observed by, parties to contracts of the type involved in the particular trade or commerce concerned.
2. Any communication by electronic means which provides a durable record of the agreement shall be equivalent to 'writing'.

   ...

5. An agreement conferring jurisdiction which forms part of a contract shall be treated as an agreement independent of the other terms of the contract. The validity of the agreement conferring jurisdiction cannot be contested solely on the ground that the contract is not valid.

Article 3 Hague Choice of Court Convention:
For the purposes of this Convention —

(a) 'exclusive choice of court agreement' means an agreement concluded by two or more parties that meets the requirements of paragraph c) and designates, for the purpose of deciding disputes which have arisen or may arise in connection with a particular legal relationship, the courts of one Contracting State or one or more specific courts of one Contracting State to the exclusion of the jurisdiction of any other courts;
(b) a choice of court agreement which designates the courts of one Contracting State or one or more specific courts of one Contracting State shall be deemed to be exclusive unless the parties have expressly provided otherwise;
(c) an exclusive choice of court agreement must be concluded or documented —
   (i) in writing; or
   (ii) by any other means of communication which renders information accessible so as to be usable for subsequent reference;
(d) an exclusive choice of court agreement that forms part of a contract shall be treated as an agreement independent of the other terms of the contract. The validity of the exclusive choice of court agreement cannot be contested solely on the ground that the contract is not valid.

Article 5 Hague Choice of Court Convention:

(1) The court or courts of a Contracting State designated in an exclusive choice of court agreement shall have jurisdiction to decide a dispute to which the agreement applies, unless the agreement is null and void under the law of that State.

(2) …

Based on the results of comparison, one can conclude that the three provisions show a considerable degree of coherence.[60] After all, in both the Brussels I Regulation (recast) and the Hague Choice of Court Convention, real consent between the contracting parties is implicitly ensured by the term 'agreement' and by the satisfaction of certain formal requirements (e.g. 'in writing').[61]

In its judgment of 7 July 2016, case 222/15 (*Höszig v Alstom Power Thermal Services*) the European Court of Justice (ECJ) ruled that as regards a situation in which a jurisdiction clause covered by Article 23 of the Brussels I Regulation (currently Article 25, Brussels I Regulation (recast)) is stipulated in general terms and conditions, such a clause is lawful where the text of the contract signed by both parties itself contains an express reference to the general terms and conditions which include the jurisdiction clause. According to the ECJ, this applies, however, only in case of an explicit reference which can be controlled by a party applying normal diligence and where it is established that the general terms and conditions containing the jurisdiction clause were actually communicated to the other contracting party.[62]

If there is a conflict of rules with regard to jurisdiction between the Brussels I Regulation (recast) and the Hague Choice of Court Convention, the Brussels I Regulation (recast) will prevail over the Hague Choice of Court Convention where none of the parties is resident in a Contracting State that is not an EU Member State (Article 26(6), Hague Choice of Court Convention). Where one or more of the parties is resident in a Contracting State that is not an EU Member State, the Hague Choice of Court Convention will prevail. Thus, for example, if a Mexican company[63] and a French company choose the Amsterdam District Court to be exclusively competent to hear the case, the Hague Choice of Court Convention (Article 5) will prevail. If, on

[60]Cf., *inter alia*, Weller (2017).

[61]With regard to Article 23 of the Brussels I Regulation (the predecessor of Article 25 of the Brussels I Regulation (recast)) see, for example, ECJ 7 July 2016, case 222/15, ECLI:EU:C:2016:525 (*Höszig v Alstom Power Thermal Services*), paragraph 37, http://curia.europa.eu/juris/document/document.jsf;jsessionid=99AAA0AF04DF24C343CF4A8D8A46E821?text=&docid=181461&pageIndex=0&doclang=EN&mode=lst&dir=&occ=first&part=1&cid=10391360 (hereafter '*Höszig v Alstom Power Thermal Services*'). See also ECJ 8 March 2018, case C-64/17, ECLI:EU:C:2018:173 (*Saey Home & Garden v Lusavouga*), paragraph 25, http://curia.europa.eu/juris/document/document.jsf;jsessionid=593358D2CF08E54A8C579B2CDE22CFD2?text=&docid=200063&pageIndex=0&doclang=EN&mode=lst&dir=&occ=first&part=1&cid=10514025 (hereafter '*Saey Home & Garden v Lusavouga*'). Cf. Hartley and Dogauchi (2005), paragraph 94 et seq.

[62]*Höszig v Alstom Power Thermal Services*, paragraphs 39–40. Confirmed by the ECJ in its ruling of *Saey Home & Garden v Lusavouga*, paragraph 27.

[63]Mexico is a Contracting State to the Hague Choice of Court Convention but is not an EU Member State.

the other hand, a German company and an Italian company choose the Amsterdam District Court as the exclusive forum, the Brussels I Regulation (recast) (Article 25) will prevail.[64]

In Annex II of the NCC Rules, a choice-of-court clause and agreement for proceedings to be conducted in English before the NCC has been included. This model clause—intended as a practical tool—reads as follows:

> All disputes arising out of or in connection with this agreement will be resolved by the Amsterdam District Court following proceedings in English before the Chamber for International Commercial Matters ('Netherlands Commercial Court' or 'NCC'). An action for interim measures, including protective measures, available under Dutch law may be brought in the NCC's Court in Summary Proceedings ('CSP') in proceedings in English.

In brief, the criteria for a valid choice-of-court agreement in favour of the NCC are four-fold: (a) the litigating parties have designated the Amsterdam District Court to hear their case; (b) the parties to the proceedings have expressly agreed for proceedings to be held before the NCC District Court; (c) the litigating parties have expressly agreed that the proceedings will be conducted in the English language; and (d) the choice-of-court agreement must be denoted in writing (see below).

3.2.4 Express Agreement (Article 1.3.1(d), NCC Rules)

Litigation before the NCC shall take place on a voluntary basis only. According to Article 1.3.1(d) of the NCC Rules, the parties to the proceedings must expressly agree in writing that: (a) the proceedings will be before the NCC, and (b) such proceedings will be held in English. See also Article 30r(1) of the DCCP:

> … and it is expressly so agreed, the parties' proceedings may be in English and before the International Commercial Chamber of that district court ('Netherlands Commercial Court') or that appeal court ('Netherlands Commercial Court of Appeal'). … An agreement as referred to in the first sentence is evidenced in writing. A written document containing such a clause or referring to general terms and conditions containing such a clause is sufficient for this purpose, provided that the specific clause has been expressly accepted by or on behalf of the counterparty.

As clarified in the Explanatory Notes to Article 1.3.1(d) of the NCC Rules[65] and the Explanatory Memorandum to Article 30r(1) of the DCCP,[66] an agreement in which the designation of the NCC is included in a party's general terms and conditions and is accepted *tacitly* by the other party, does *not* satisfy the requirement of an express agreement.[67] In such an event, therefore the NCC's designation has no legal effect unless, at the time the agreement was concluded or at a later time, there was express acceptance by the litigating parties in writing of the clause in the general terms and

[64] See Hartley and Dogauchi (2005), paragraph 26.

[65] Explanatory Notes to Article 1.3.1(d) of the NCC Rules, p. 33.

[66] Tweede Kamer, vergaderjaar 2016–2017, 34761, no. 3, p. 11.

[67] The same reasoning will apply to choice-of-court agreements that have been incorporated in company statutes. See Eerste Kamer, vergaderjaar 2017–2018, 34761, B, pp. 9–10.

conditions showing agreement for the proceedings to be held before the NCC in English.[68]

However, in light of the case law of the ECJ (see Sect. 3.2.3 above), this assertion seems to be debatable, since the case law of the ECJ seems to be less strict in this respect. In my view, an alignment between the case law of the ECJ and the (Dutch) legislator's perspective at this particular point would have been preferable. Moreover, do the Brussels I Regulation (recast) and the case law of the ECJ allow (national) legislators to set stricter requirements than those prescribed under the Brussels I Regulation (recast) and provided by the case law of the ECJ? In my opinion, this seems highly unlikely.

3.3 Other Striking Characteristics of the NCC and Its Proceedings

The NCC judges are impartial, independent, and experienced in complex international business matters and are selected for their fluency in the English language. According to Article 3.5.1 of the NCC Rules, the NCC District Court cases are generally heard and disposed of by a three-judge chamber. Matters such as: (a) an application for preparatory witness hearings, or (b) where the Court in Summary Proceedings (CSP) in the NCC District Court has subject matter, jurisdiction may be assigned to a single-judge chamber. Cases in the NCCA (the NCC Court of Appeal) are also heard by a three-judge panel.[69] The NCC's website promises 24/7 availability: 'in exceptionally urgent cases, the court is authorised to hear and decide cases anytime, anywhere.'[70]

The NCC applies Dutch procedural law (cf. Article 1.2, NCC Rules) that is generally recognised for being efficient,[71] pragmatic[72] and cost-effective.[73] As explained in Sect. 3.1 above, the NCC's mode of procedure is regulated by the NCC Rules. These rules consist of 12 Sections and four Annexes.[74] The NCC Rules are an innovative mixture of Dutch procedural law, elements of litigation practice at existing commercial courts, and the International Bar Association (IBA) Rules on the Taking

[68] Where the NCC's designation has no legal effect, it is unclear whether this will affect the choice-of-court agreement as such or only as far as it concerns the (specific) designation of the NCC, leaving the (general) designation of the Amsterdam District Court intact.

[69] See Explanatory Notes to Article 3.5.1 of the NCC Rules, p. 36.

[70] See https://www.rechtspraak.nl/English/NCC/Pages/key-features-NCC.aspx.

[71] The disposition time of Dutch courts in first instance in civil and commercial litigious cases was 121 days (overall average number: 233 days) in 2016. See European Commission for the Efficiency of Justice (CEPEJ) (2018), Table 5.8, p. 250.

[72] For instance, under Dutch procedural law an evidentiary agreement is allowed (Article 153, DCCP).

[73] See Raad voor de rechtspraak (2015, p. 6).

[74] For the content of the NCC Rules, see: https://www.rechtspraak.nl/SiteCollectionDocuments/ncc-procesreglement-en.pdf. For some critical reflection, see Hoefnagel and Welling (2018).

of Evidence in International Arbitration (IBA Rules) (29 May 2010),[75] thus representing a compromise between the rules of procedural law in both common law and civil law systems.[76] The NCC Rules govern proceedings in the NCC District Court and the NCCA. They also apply to proceedings in the CSP, except where the provision or the Dutch Code of Civil Procedure or other legislation indicates otherwise, or should a provision not be appropriate in summary proceedings. As indicated by Article 1.1.3, the NCC Rules focus on actions by claim (*vorderingsprocedure*), but also apply, where appropriate, to actions by application (*verzoekprocedure*).

Except where the DCCP provides otherwise, a party in NCC proceedings may not act *pro se* but must be represented by its lawyer, who must be a member of the Dutch Bar (*advocaat*). Acts of process, such as the submission of a claim or defence, must be carried out by a member of the Dutch Bar. Visiting lawyers as referred to in Article 16b of the Dutch Advocates Act (*Advocatenwet*), i.e. members of the bars in EU Member States, the European Economic Area (EEA) or Switzerland, may not carry out acts of process but may act for a party in other ways in accordance with Article 16e of the Dutch Advocates Act (in cooperation with a member of the Dutch Bar). Other visiting lawyers may not act for a party, but the NCC District Court or NCCA may allow them to speak at any hearing.[77]

Communication and exchange of documents will be facilitated by a (digital) web portal—the so-called 'eNCC'—that is specially designed for the NCC.[78] Section 4 of the NCC Rules (Initiating an action) contains two provisions (Articles 4.1–4.2) in which the rules for initiating an action before the NCC are explained. Such action is initiated by submitting an originating document.[79] According to Article 4.1.1 of the NCC Rules, the originating document must specify:

(a) the claim and its grounds;
(b) the defences asserted by the defendant, the grounds for those defences, and the claimant's reply;
(c) the exhibits available to the claimant and the witnesses whose testimony the originating document relies on to substantiate the disputed grounds;
(d) the designation of the court hearing the matter: 'the Amsterdam District Court (NCC District Court)' or 'the Amsterdam Court of Appeal (NCC Court of Appeal)';

---

[75] See https://www.ibanet.org/ENews_Archive/IBA_30June_2010_Enews_Taking_of_Evidence_new_rules.aspx.

[76] Cf. Kuijpers (2019, p. 36), Dorsman (2016, p. 311).

[77] See Articles 3.1.1-3.1.2, NCC Rules. Cf. Kuijpers (2019, pp. 61–62).

[78] See Article 3.2 of the NCC Rules and Annex IV of the NCC Rules: eNCC Rules. The eNCC is not yet fully implemented. See also: https://www.rechtspraak.nl/English/NCC/Pages/initiating-an-action.aspx; Eerste Kamer, vergaderjaar 2017–2018, 34761, B, p. 1. Except where the court directs otherwise, eNCC is the only means of communication with the court and must be used for all purposes, including the submission of statements, exhibits and correspondence with the court.

[79] For a concise roadmap of NCC proceedings, see: https://www.rechtspraak.nl/English/NCC/Pages/initiating-an-action.aspx.

(e) the confirmation that the conditions of Article 1.3.1 of the NCC Rules[80] have been satisfied and in particular that the parties have agreed for proceedings to be held before the NCC District Court or the NCC Court of Appeal in English;
(f) the business address and the e-mail address of the claimant's lawyer;
(g) if available, the name and the e-mail address of the lawyer of each defendant; and
(h) where applicable: the name, office address and e-mail address of a party's foreign counsel.

The general point of departure of each NCC dispute is a so-called 'case management conference' which will be a hearing of an informal and practical nature. A case management conference may be held at the parties' request whenever it is mutually convenient.[81] The purpose of a case management conference is to enable parties to influence how the proceedings will be conducted—to discuss issues, motions, fact-finding, a timetable—and to make clear what is expected from them.

NCC proceedings are not confidential. A hearing that has been ordered by the NCC is open to the public. The court, however, may direct that the hearing in whole or in part be held in private or that only certain persons be allowed to attend in the interest of public policy, accepted norms of morality or national security, or to protect the interests of minors or the parties' privacy, or to prevent a substantial adverse impact on the sound administration of justice (Article 7.5, NCC Rules).[82] Also, the NCC's judgments will be given in public (Article 9.4, NCC Rules).[83] According to Article 9.5 of the NCC Rules, the court may direct that the decision be published on the website of the Dutch Courts (www.rechtspraak.nl). The basic rule of redaction guidance, as adopted by the Dutch Courts, however, is that all information which directly identifies a natural person will be edited.[84]

The NCC's rules of evidence are codified in Section 8 (Evidence). The design and content of Section 8 have been clearly influenced by the above-mentioned IBA Rules. Under Article 8 of the IBA Rules, witnesses and experts may be heard by way of cross-examination, while under Article 179 of the DCCP, witnesses and experts are heard by the court.[85] Article 8.5.4 of the NCC Rules, however, states that 'parties and their lawyers may examine the witnesses' and that at 'a party's request or of its own initiative, the court may confront a witness with other witnesses or with one or more parties.' The provision also says that the 'court will generally allow specific modes of witness examination where the parties have so agreed, provided the agreement satisfies the provisions under Article 8.3 and there is no adverse impact

[80] See Sects. 3.1 and 3.2 above.

[81] Cf. Article 7.1 of the NCC Rules.

[82] See also Article 27 of the DCCP.

[83] Cf. Article 6, section 1 (Right to a fair trial) of the European Convention for the Protection of Human Rights and Fundamental Freedoms. See also footnote 92 below.

[84] See the Explanatory Notes to Article 9.5 of the NCC Rules, p. 39.

[85] Thus reflecting the differences between the so-called 'adversarial' and 'inquisitorial' systems of justice. In the adversarial system, the judge presides over the trial (his role is largely passive) while in the inquisitorial system, the judge is an investigating magistrate who is largely active.

on due process or sound case management.' Moreover, according to Article 7.7.2 of the NCC Rules, the court may direct that an audio or video recording be made by or on behalf of the court with regard to the court hearing and/or a witness's testimony (Article 8.5.6, NCC Rules).[86] Article 7.7.3 of the NCC Rules allows each party to instruct a so-called 'court reporter' to prepare a verbatim transcript of what is said at the hearing. The court reporter's involvement in the proceedings is however at the party's expense.

While the common law systems are, generally speaking, focused on the process of fact-finding through the procedure of disclosure or discovery, where the litigating parties are required to search for all relevant documents, under Dutch procedural law expensive and time-consuming (pre-trial) disclosure or discovery phases are non-existent and the so-called 'fishing expeditions' are not allowed (cf. Article 843a, DCCP).[87] In line with Article 843a of the DCCP (obligation to produce documents), Article 8.4.6 of the NCC Rules states that:

> Where a party has a legitimate interest, it may make a motion seeking the inspection or production of a copy or extract of specific documents that pertain to a legal relationship which involves that party or its legal predecessors. The order may be given to a person or an entity which has custody or control of the documents, but such person or entity is not required to comply with the order if justified by compelling reasons or if the court determines that it can be reasonably assumed that the sound administration of justice is also assured without the inspection or production of the documents. …

In most civil law jurisdictions, the courts control what is taken into evidence, thus perpetuating the inquisitorial traditions.[88]

As set out in Sect. 3.1 above, the Act for the establishment of the Netherlands Commercial Court inserted a new Article 9a in the Dutch Act on Court Fees in Civil Proceedings (*Wet griffierechten burgerlijke zaken*), with special rules on such fees for the NCC.[89] Every party is charged a court fee (Article 10.1, NCC Rules). Since the NCC must be financially self-supporting,[90] the NCC court fees are higher than those of other Dutch courts. In the Annex to the Dutch Act on Court Fees in Civil Proceedings, a flat court fee is set for all NCC cases at EUR 15,000 (NCC District Court); EUR 20,000 (NCCA); EUR 7500 (CSP in first instance); and EUR10,000 (CSP in appeal).[91] According to Article 10.2 of the NCC Rules, the litigating parties

---

[86] Cf. Article 8 of the IBA Rules.

[87] See also the Commentary on the revised text of the 2010 IBA Rules, p. 7:

> Expansive American- or English-style discovery is generally inappropriate in international arbitration. Rather, requests for documents to be produced should be carefully tailored to issues that are relevant and material to the determination of the case.

[88] Cf. Brouwer and Butijn (2018), p. 168 et seq.

[89] See: https://wetten.overheid.nl/BWBR0028899/2019-01-01.

[90] Cf. Tweede Kamer, vergaderjaar 2016–2017, 34761, no. 3, p. 8.

[91] See: https://wetten.overheid.nl/BWBR0028899/2019-01-01; https://www.rechtspraak.nl/English/NCC/Pages/costs.aspx.

may make agreements they consider appropriate in respect to costs of the proceedings, including court fee and costs for lawyers, service or delivery, translation or interpretation, court reporters, and witnesses' or experts' fees and expenses. Where no agreement is made or conveyed to the court in time, the court will apply Dutch law with respect to costs of proceedings in civil and commercial matters, whereas according to Article 10.3 of the NCC Rules, the unsuccessful party will bear the costs of the proceedings. However, costs incurred by the successful party may not be apportioned to the unsuccessful party other than lawyers' fees and expenses that fall within the scope of Articles 237 et seq. of the DCCP. As a rule, the court will assess lawyers' fees according to the rates stated in Annex III of the NCC Rules (EUR 1000–EUR 12,000 for each act of process). The court may nevertheless order that each party bears its own costs or that certain costs incurred by a party without sufficient cause must be borne by that party (Article 10.3, NCC Rules).

All NCC judgments will be presented in public (Article 9.4, NCC Rules).[92] The court will set the date for giving judgment and notify all parties concerned (Article 9.1, NCC Rules). The court's judgment includes a decision on every part of the claim or application. The court examines and decides the case only on the grounds brought forward by the parties in support of their claim, application or defence, except where the law provides otherwise. The court offers alternative legal bases on its own initiative and may not refuse to issue a decision (Article 9.2, NCC Rules). According to Article 9.3 of the NCC Rules, the judgment must state the decision as well as the facts and reasons it is based on. The rulings of the NCC District Court will be open to appeal to the NCCA and subsequently to appeal in cassation before the Dutch Supreme Court (*Hoge Raad der Nederlanden*). Moreover, the NCC District Court and the NCCA will be able to refer questions to the Dutch Supreme Court (see Article 392 et seq., DCCP) and to the European Court of Justice (see Article 267, Treaty on the Functioning of the European Union (TFEU)) for a so-called 'preliminary ruling'.[93]

---

[92] See Article 6, section 1 (Right to a fair trial) of the European Convention for the Protection of Human Rights and Fundamental Freedoms:

> … Judgment shall be pronounced publicly but the press and public may be excluded from all or part of the trial in the interests of morals, public order or national security in a democratic society, where the interests of juveniles or the protection of the private life of the parties so require, or to the extent strictly necessary in the opinion of the court in special circumstances where publicity would prejudice the interests of justice.

[93] According to Article 267 of the TFEU, the ECJ shall have jurisdiction to give preliminary rulings concerning: (a) the interpretation of the Treaties and (b) the validity and interpretation of acts of the institutions, bodies, offices or agencies of the Union. See: https://eur-lex.europa.eu/legal-content/EN/TXT/PDF/?uri=CELEX:12012E/TXT&from=EN.

4 The NCC's Challenges...

The NCC's features—or, if you prefer, 'unique selling points'—are at the same time the NCC's challenges. A first challenging point of interest might be the composition of the court. All NCC judges will be Dutch nationals.[94] The assignment of judges of foreign nationalities to Dutch courts is not allowed under Dutch law. In this regard, the NCC will differ from the Singapore International Commercial Court that does, indeed, include foreign judges from various jurisdictions (both common law and civil law), such as the UK, the United States, Australia, Canada, Hong Kong, Japan and France.[95] The same goes for the DIFC Courts in Dubai that include judges from Malaysia, Singapore and the UK.[96] In order to boost the NCC's international reputation and prestige while satisfying the strong need for high-profile and tailored decisions, we might have to reconsider the 'monocultural' composition of the NCC, given the fact that the court will not only render decisions based upon the application and interpretation of Dutch law, but also on the application of foreign law.[97] Moreover, there is no doubt that the NCC will hear cases where domain-specific knowledge is required, such as an in-depth knowledge of information and communications technology. For these reasons, a first and intermediate step in shifting the composition of the NCC could be the deployment of deputy or lay judges drawn from legal practice, academia and industry.[98]

Another appealing issue relates to litigation costs. In his March 2018 publicly-defended and thoroughly researched PhD thesis 'The Great Race of Courts: Civil Justice System Competition in the European Union', Erlis Themeli (Erasmus University Rotterdam) shows that, while costs in general are not a primary factor in making a court unattractive, for England and Wales they are.[99] As one of the survey respondents pointed out: '... the costs of English proceedings is horrendous.'[100] These data could boost the NCC's attractiveness. Studies carried out by the Boston Consulting Group and the Dutch Council for the Judiciary show that the average costs of legal proceedings before the London Commercial Court are three to five times higher than litigation costs before the NCC.[101] While the size of court fees

[94] See Article 4 of the Dutch Judiciary Act (*Wet rechtspositie rechterlijke ambtenaren*), https://wetten.overheid.nl/BWBR0008365/2019-01-01.

[95] See: https://www.sicc.gov.sg/about-the-sicc/judges. Cf. Yip (2016).

[96] See: https://www.difccourts.ae/court-structure/judges/.

[97] Cf. Kuipers (2018, pp. 127–128), The Boston Consulting Group (2015, p. 14), Hermans (2015, pp. 194–195).

[98] The Enterprise Division of the Amsterdam Court of Appeal could serve as an example. The Enterprise Division has 5 members: 3 professional judges and 2 experts. See Article 66, section 2 of the Dutch Judiciary Organisation Act (*Wet op de Rechterlijke Organisatie*), https://wetten.overheid.nl/BWBR0001830/2019-01-01. Cf. Oranje (2016, p. 125).

[99] Themeli (2018, p. 303).

[100] Themeli (2018, p. 302).

[101] Raad voor de rechtspraak (2015, p. 17), The Boston Consulting Group (2015, pp. 5 and 15).

between the LCC and the NCC are nearly comparable,[102] the rates charged by London law firms are much higher, including the costs of submitting evidence through the procedure of disclosure. Moreover, the English 'cost-shifting rule'—wherein the losing party is required to pay all of the winning party's costs, including lawyers' fees—is non-existent under Dutch procedural law. The losing party is required to pay the winning party's costs on the basis of a court-approved scale (see Article 10.3 and Annex III, NCC Rules). The court may, however, order that each party bear its own costs.

According to Article 30r(1) of the DCCP, 'the parties' proceedings may be in English'. English—the language of global business—is the NCC's language. Both the proceedings before the NCC and its judgments will be conducted in English. As Article 30r(4) of the DCCP clearly states:

> In cases as meant in section 1, first sentence, and section 3, the court gives its judgment in English, unless the proceedings were in Dutch at the parties' request. The defence that the case must not be dealt with by the International Commercial Camber of the Amsterdam District Court or the Amsterdam Court of Appeal, but by another court, may be raised in the Dutch language. The court gives its decision on the defence in the Dutch language.[103]

According to Article 2.1.1 of the NCC Rules, the court may direct that Dutch will be the language of part or all of the proceedings, if the parties to the proceedings unanimously so request after the originating document is filed. The parties must notify the court of such request as soon as practicable. If, however, the law provides that the NCC's ruling in English must be registered in a Dutch public register, the registerable parts of the judgment shall also be rendered in the Dutch language (Article 30r(5), DCCP). Article 30r(6) of the DCCP requires a certified translation in Dutch (at the applicant's own expense) if the enforceable parts of the judgment are in English and a copy of the judgment is to be delivered in the Netherlands to a third party for the purpose of enforcement.[104]

There is no Act or statutory rule that warrants Dutch as the official language of court proceedings in the Netherlands, but it is generally assumed that Dutch court

---

[102] For the rates of the NCC court fees, see Sect. 3.3 of this Chapter. The rates of the LCC court fees are as follow: value of the claim GBP 10,000 to GBP 200,000 = court fee of 5% of the amount; value of the claim > GBP 200,000 = court fee of GBP 10,000 (EUR 11,422).

[103] The official and original Dutch text reads as follows:

> In zaken als bedoeld in het eerste lid, eerste volzin, en het derde lid doet de rechter uitspraak in de Engelse taal, tenzij op verzoek van partijen de procedure in de Nederlandse taal is gevoerd. Het verweer dat de zaak niet door de internationale handelskamer van de rechtbank of van het gerechtshof Amsterdam moet worden behandeld, maar door een andere rechter, mag worden gevoerd in de Nederlandse taal. Een uitspraak over dit verweer doet de rechter in de Nederlandse taal. (See: https://wetten.overheid.nl/BWBR0001827/2019-01-01#BoekEerste.

[104] Article 2.2 of the NCC Rules contains a regulatory framework on language and third parties that are added in an action pending in the NCC or are involved in a closely connected action. See also Kuijpers (2019, pp. 57–60).

decisions are rendered in Dutch.[105] In its judgment of 15 January 2016, the Dutch Supreme Court ruled that in Dutch court proceedings, translations are not required for documents that were drafted in a foreign language. However, the court may require a translation when it thinks that this would be appropriate out of respect for the court proceedings or the counterparties' legitimate interests.[106] The use of English as the NCC's official language has some major advantages. It will not only save (high) translation costs, but it will also enhance the accessibility of the NCC to foreign parties and improve communication during court proceedings.[107]

The members of the NCC, including their support staff, are expected to have excellent written and verbal communication skills, with a strong command of the English language. A working group of editors, translators and judges has been set up to implement the English-language litigation before the NCC and to standardise the English translations of Dutch legal concepts.[108] But will the NCC's level of English-language proficiency be sufficient enough to secure precise and solid rulings? Will the NCC actually succeed in standardising the English translations of Dutch legal concepts? Or would it have been preferable—in the interest of legal certainty—for authentic versions of the NCC's rulings to be officially rendered in both English and Dutch?[109] Similarly, this question of language could also apply to proceedings before the Dutch Supreme Court, which will hear appeals (in cassation) against the decisions of the NCCA.[110] As set out in the Explanatory Notes to Article 2.1 of the NCC Rules, the Dutch Supreme Court is not bound by the choice of English as the language of the proceedings. In view of the specific nature of the cassation procedure, proceedings before the Dutch Supreme Court must be conducted in the Dutch language.[111] However, the Dutch Supreme Court has indicated that it will decide cases on the basis of documents that have been submitted to the NCC District

---

[105] Cf. Cobussen et al. (2018, p. 51), Oranje (2016, p. 123).

[106] Cf. Dutch Supreme Court 15 January 2016, ECLI:NL:HR:2016:65, paragraph 3.4.4, https://uitspraken.rechtspraak.nl/inziendocument?id=ECLI:NL:HR:2016:65.

[107] See Eerste Kamer, vergaderjaar 2017–2018, 34761, B, p. 4.

[108] See Oranje (2016, p. 123).

[109] Cf. Eerste Kamer, vergaderjaar 2017–2018, 34761, B, p. 7; Cobussen et al. (2018, p. 60), Hoefnagel and Welling (2018, p. 38), Dumoulin (2016, p. 326), Houthoff Buruma (2017, p. 8). In its reaction on the legislative proposal regarding the establishment of a Netherlands Commercial Court, the Dutch law firm Houthoff (formerly Houthoff Buruma) points out the risk of discrepancies between, *inter alia*, the NCC's English judgment on the one hand and the grounds for cassation (*cassatiemiddelen*) that need to be formulated in the Dutch language on the other hand.

[110] Moreover, Article 398 of the DCCP allows for a so-called 'leapfrog appeal' in which appeals in civil cases against first instance decisions of District Courts, such as the NCC District Court, are made directly to the Dutch Supreme Court.

[111] See Explanatory Notes to Article 2.1 of the NCC Rules, p. 34. The cassation procedure is limited to questions of law (cf. Article 79, Dutch Judiciary Organisation Act). Moreover, the Dutch Supreme Court rulings have precedential effect. Since the proceedings before the Dutch Supreme Court must be conducted in the Dutch language, this raises the question whether this could lead to discussions about the interpretation of the NCC's English judgments, thus challenging the NCC's statement of reasons.

Court or to the NCCA in English.[112] Preliminary referrals to the Supreme Court under Article 392 et seq. of the DCCP must, however, be submitted in Dutch by both the NCC District Court and the NCCA. In my opinion, given these circumstances and the fact that the Dutch Supreme Court secures the uniformity of the law and advances the development of the law, the need for an official English translation of the authentic Dutch version of the Supreme Court's judgments seems to me to be quite obvious.[113]

5 … and Its Perspectives, Followed by Some Concluding Reflections

Is the Netherlands Commercial Court doomed to failure, or will it be a successful and innovative legal concept? Brexit or no Brexit, the NCC's judgments for now will be well positioned in view of their recognition and enforcement. Mutual trust is one of the cornerstones of the Brussels I Regulation (recast),[114] which is applicable throughout the EU:

> Mutual trust in the administration of justice in the Union justifies the principle that judgments given in a Member State should be recognised in all Member States without the need for any special procedure. In addition, the aim of making cross-border litigation less time-consuming and costly justifies the abolition of the declaration of enforceability prior to enforcement in the Member State addressed. As a result, a judgment given by the courts of a Member State should be treated as if it had been given in the Member State addressed.[115]

Every decision rendered in civil and commercial matters (cf. Article 1(1), Brussels I Regulation (recast)) by courts of any EU Member State—such as the Netherlands Commercial Court—will enjoy the benefit of full faith and credit in other Member States.[116] Moreover, the 2007 Lugano Convention will extend the recognition and enforcement regime of the NCC judgments to three of the European Free Trade Association (EFTA) Member States, namely Iceland, Norway and Switzerland.[117]

---

[112] See also Tweede Kamer, vergaderjaar 2016–2017, 34761, no. 3, p. 7.

[113] Cf. Drion (2018), Kuipers (2018), paragraph 8.18; van Rhee (2016, p. 120), Ernste and Vermeulen (2016, p. 132). The Dutch Minister for Legal Protection has indicated that cassation proceedings in English might be not feasible at the present but might be in the future. See Eerste Kamer, vergaderjaar 2017–2018, 34761, B, p. 7.

[114] See Sect. 3.1 and footnote 48 above.

[115] Preamble to the Brussels I Regulation (recast), recital 26.

[116] See Article 36(1) of the Brussels I Regulation (recast): 'A judgment given in a Member State shall be recognised in the other Member States without any special procedure being required.' See also Article 39 of the Brussels I Regulation (recast): 'A judgment given in a Member State which is enforceable in that Member State shall be enforceable in the other Member States without any declaration of enforceability being required'.

[117] Convention on jurisdiction and the recognition and enforcement of judgments in civil and commercial matters, 30 October 2007, OJ 2007, L 339/3, https://eur-lex.europa.eu/legal-content/EN/TXT/PDF/?uri=CELEX:22007A1221(03)&from=EN. Similar to the Brussels I Regulation (recast),

Together with the Contracting Parties (other than the EU Member States) to the Hague Choice of Court Convention[118]—Mexico, Singapore, and recently Montenegro (since 1 August 2018)—, the 1971 Hague Convention on the Recognition and Enforcement of Foreign Judgments in Civil and Commercial Matters,[119] as well as certain bilateral treaties,[120] this will result in nearly 40 jurisdictions where NCC judgments are easily recognised and enforceable.

Will the upcoming Brexit affect, in a wider sense, the NCC's becoming an attractive alternative to UK forums? No, I don't believe so. It is to be expected that the government of the United Kingdom will continue to honour the Brussels regime of mutual recognition and enforcement of judgments.[121] Therefore, in my opinion, the implications of Brexit on the attractiveness of the NCC as an alternative forum must not be overestimated.[122] We should be modest in our expectations with regard to the NCC's success rate. Given the NCC's future status of becoming a trustworthy and judicially-experienced commercial court that can resolve international trade disputes within a reasonable time and in a cost-effective way, it is to be expected that the NCC will become a new hub for Dutch multinational companies and foreign companies operating in the Netherlands.

Nevertheless, there is still a lot of work that needs to be done. The NCC should not only be promoted but, more importantly, present a good first impression which is vital for its existence. In short, a good start is half the battle. Moreover, as the proceedings before the NCC will be conducted in English, it seems advisable that

---

the Lugano Convention 2007 is also a 'double instrument' which contains both rules of international judicial competence and rules on the recognition and enforcement of judgments. The Lugano Convention 2007 is binding upon 31 States: the (at present) 28 EU Member States and the 3 Member States of the EFTA: Iceland, Norway and Switzerland.

[118] See Sect. 3.1 as well as footnote 49 above.

[119] Convention on the recognition and enforcement of foreign judgments in civil and commercial matters, 1 February 1971, https://assets.hcch.net/docs/bacf7323-9337-48df-9b9a-ef33e62b43be.pdf. The 1971 Convention has 5 Contracting Parties: Albania, Cyprus, Kuwait, the Netherlands and Portugal. The Brussels I Regulation (recast) takes precedence over the 1971 Convention as far as it concerns the EU Member States of Cyprus, Portugal and the Netherlands (see Article 69, Brussels I Regulation (recast)).

[120] The Netherlands has bilateral treaties with Belgium (1925) (https://wetten.overheid.nl/BWBV0006117/1929-09-01); Italy (1959); Germany (1962); Austria (1963) (https://wetten.overheid.nl/BWBV0004290/1966-04-30); the UK (1967) (https://wetten.overheid.nl/BWBV0004295/1969-09-21); and Suriname (1976) (https://wetten.overheid.nl/BWBV0001018/1979-01-10). As far as it concerns the EU Member States of Austria, Belgium, Germany, Italy, the Netherlands and the UK, the Brussels I Regulation (recast) takes precedence.

[121] See the UK Government Response to the House of Commons Justice Committee report 'Implications of Brexit for the justice system' (22 March 2017), https://publications.parliament.uk/pa/cm201719/cmselect/cmjust/651/65102.htm. See also the recently published (13 September 2018) UK Government Guidance 'Handling civil legal cases that involve EU countries if there's no Brexit deal', https://www.gov.uk/government/publications/handling-civil-legal-cases-that-involve-eu-countries-if-theres-no-brexit-deal/handling-civil-legal-cases-that-involve-eu-countries-if-theres-no-brexit-deal.

[122] As of 1 April 2019, the UK will participate in the Hague Choice of Court Convention as a non-EU Member State. See footnote 49 above.

leading Dutch case law, literature, and relevant Dutch legislation be translated into the English language.[123] Most of all, the success of the NCC will depend on the level of quality of the NCC judges and their support staff. In one of his latest publications, the former President of the UK Supreme Court, the Rt Hon. Lord Phillips of Worth Matravers, underlines the important position of international commercial courts:

> If you get to the Supreme Court you are likely to find yourself before judges who started their careers in the Commercial Court. It is the seed bed of the higher judiciary.[124]

Acknowledgements This Chapter is largely based on the author's keynote address at the Conference on 'Dispute Resolution in Asia and Beyond: Progress and Trends' that was held at the City University of Hong Kong on 17–18 May 2018. The author would like to thank Steven Gilbert, Hilde Wagemaker, Jan-Michiel Hebly and Patricia uit de Bos for their support—in their own special ways—during the writing of this Chapter. The research has been concluded on 17 March 2019. Later developments have not been taken into consideration.

References

Antonopoulou G (2018) Defining international disputes—reflections on the Netherlands Commercial Court proposal. Nederlands Internationaal Privaatrecht 36:740–755

Bauw E (2016) Ondernemerschap in de rechtspleging. Over de kansen van een Netherlands Commercial Court. Ars Aequi 65:93–98

Bauw E (2018) Een Netherlands Commercial Court vanuit rechtsplegingsperspectief. In: Bauw E, Koster H, Kruisinga SA (eds) De kansen voor een Netherlands Commercial Court. Boom juridisch, Den Haag, pp 9–22

Brouwer CJE, Butijn JL (2018) The Netherlands Commercial Court: an international perspective. In: Bauw E, Koster H, Kruisinga SA (eds) De kansen voor een Netherlands Commercial Court. Boom juridisch, Den Haag, pp 155–185

Burrough A, Machon S, Oranje D, Frakes L, Visser W (eds) (2018) Code of civil procedure: selected sections and the NCC rules. Eleven International Publishing, Den Haag

Cobussen RAB, van Kogelenberg M, Kruisinga SA (2018) Taal in de rechtszaal. In: Bauw E, Koster H, Kruisinga SA (eds) De kansen voor een Netherlands Commercial Court. Boom juridisch, Den Haag, pp 49–68

Dickinson A, Lein E (eds) (2015) The Brussels I regulation recast. Oxford University Press, Oxford

Dorsman AAE (2016) Netherlands Commercial Court. In: Holtzer M, Strik D, Oranje DJ (eds) Geschriften vanwege de Vereniging Corporate Litigation 2015–2016 (Serie vanwege het Van der Heijden Instituut), vol 134. Wolters Kluwer, Deventer, pp 305–318

Drion E (2018) De Netherlands Commercial Court (of Appeal), bijna een feit. Nederlands Juristenblad 93:3173

Dumoulin SHMA (2016) Het Netherlands Commercial Court vanuit de onderneming bezien. In: Holtzer M, Strik D, Oranje DJ (eds) Geschriften vanwege de Vereniging Corporate Litigation 2015–2016 (Serie vanwege het Van der Heijden Instituut), vol 134. Wolters Kluwer, Deventer, pp 319–331

Ernste PE, Vermeulen FE (2016) The Netherlands Commercial Court—an attractive venue for international commercial disputes? Tijdschrift voor Civiele Rechtspleging 24:127–137

[123]Cf. Ernste and Vermeulen (2016, p. 132).

[124]Lord Phillips of Worth Matravers (2016, p. 139).

European Commission for the Efficiency of Justice (CEPEJ) of the Council of Europe (2018) European judicial systems. Efficiency and quality of justice. CEPEJ Studies No. 26, 2018 Edition (2016 data). https://rm.coe.int/rapport-avec-couv-18-09-2018-en/16808def9c

European Parliamentary Research Service (EPRS) (author: Tatjana Evas) (2018) Expedited settlement of commercial disputes in the European Union. European Added Value Assessment accompanying the European Parliament's legislative initiative report. http://www.europarl.europa.eu/RegData/etudes/STUD/2018/627120/EPRS_STU(2018)627120_EN.pdf

Hartley T, Dogauchi H (2005) Explanatory report convention of 30 June 2005 on choice of court agreements. https://assets.hcch.net/upload/expl37final.pdf

Hermans R (2015) Een Netherlands Commercial Court. In: Makkink GC, Nieuwe Weme MP, van Wees AJ (eds) Ik ben niet overtuigd (Liber amicorum P. Ingelse), Prinsengrachtreeks. Ars Aequi, Nijmegen, pp 187–196

Hoefnagel JBJ, Welling TM (2018) Processuele aspecten van de Netherlands Commercial Court. Tijdschrift voor de Procespraktijk, pp 36–42

Houthoff Buruma (2017) Reactie op de consultatieversie van het wetsvoorstel Netherlands Commercial Court. https://www.internetconsultatie.nl/ncc/reacties

Jeuland E (2016) The International Division of the Paris Commercial Court. Tijdschrift voor Civiele Rechtspleging 24:143–144

Kuijpers M (2019) The Netherlands Commercial Court. Ars Aequi Libri, Nijmegen

Kuipers P (2018) Bedrijf, jurist en de Netherlands Commercial Court. In: Bauw E, Koster H, Kruisinga SA (eds) De kansen voor een Netherlands Commercial Court. Boom juridisch, Den Haag, pp 119–143

Lord Phillips of Worth Matravers (2016) The English Commercial Court. Tijdschrift voor Civiele Rechtspleging 24:138–139

Magnus U, Mankowski P (eds) (2016) Brussels Ibis Regulation—Commentary. European Commentaries on Private International Law, vol I. Verlag Dr. Otto Schmidt, Köln

Neekilappillai M (2017) Netherlands Commercial Court. Regelgevingsconcurrentie op de markt voor geschilbeslechting. Nederlands Juristenblad 92:1594–1601

O'Toole MJ, Kelly CN (2016) The State of Delaware: a preeminent forum to resolve business disputes. Tijdschrift voor Civiele Rechtspleging 24:154–157

Oranje DJ (2016) The coming into being of the Netherlands Commercial Court. Tijdschrift voor Civiele Rechtspleging 24:122–126

Raad voor de rechtspraak (2015) Plan tot oprichting van de Netherlands Commercial Court. Inclusief kosten-batenanalyse. https://www.rechtspraak.nl/SiteCollectionDocuments/plan-netherlands-commercial-court.pdf

Report of the Singapore International Commercial Court Committee (2013). https://www.mlaw.gov.sg/content/dam/minlaw/corp/News/Annex%20A%20-%20SICC%20Committee%20Report.pdf

Requejo Isidro M (2019) International Commercial Courts in the litigation market. Max Planck Institute Luxembourg for Procedural Law Research Paper Series, No. 2019(2), pp 1–33. https://www.mpi.lu/research/working-paper-series/2019/wp-2019-2/

Schelhaas HN (2017) De markt op met de Nederlandse rechtsorde? Nederlands Tijdschrift voor Burgerlijk Recht 34:73–75

Snijders HJ (2018) NCC en arbitrage. Tijdschrift voor Arbitrage: 1–8

The Boston Consulting Group (2015) Marktverkenning Netherlands Commercial Court, Commissioned by the Dutch Council for the Judiciary (Raad voor de rechtspraak). https://www.rechtspraak.nl/SiteCollectionDocuments/marktverkenning-ncc.pdf

Themeli E (2018) The great race of courts. Civil Justice system competition in the European Union (PhD thesis Erasmus University Rotterdam). Eleven International Publishing, Den Haag

Tjittes R-J (2014) Een Netherlands Commercial Court vereist reclame voor Nederlands recht. Rechtsgeleerd Magazijn Themis 176:261–262

Tjittes R-J (2018) Commercieel Contractenrecht. Boom juridisch, Den Haag

van Bochove L, Haentjens M (2019) Brexit and the courts of London, or how England scrambles to remain a relevant jurisdiction. https://leidenlawblog.nl/articles/brexit-and-the-courts-of-london

van Rhee CH (2016) The Netherlands Commercial Court in an international context. Tijdschrift voor Civiele Rechtspleging 24:120–121
Wagner G (2017) Rechtsstandort Deutschland im Wettbewerb. Impulse für Justiz und Schiedsgerichtbarkeit. Verlag C.H. Beck, München
Weller M (2017) Choice of Court agreements under Brussels Ia and under the Hague convention: coherences and clashes. J Private Int Law 13:91–129
Wetenschappelijke Raad voor het Regeringsbeleid (2003) Nederland handelsland. Het perspectief van de transactiekosten. SDU Uitgevers, Den Haag
World Economic Forum (2017–2018) Judicial independence ranking. http://reports.weforum.org/pdf/gci-2017-2018-scorecard/WEF_GCI_2017_2018_Scorecard_EOSQ144.pdf
World Economic Forum (2018) The global competitiveness report 2018. http://reports.weforum.org/global-competitiveness-report-2018/
World Justice Project (2018) Rule of law index 2017–2018. https://worldjusticeproject.org/sites/default/files/documents/WJP-ROLI-2018-June-Online-Edition_0.pdf
Yee Leong C (2016) The Singapore International Commercial Court. Tijdschrift voor Civiele Rechtspleging 24:148–153
Yip M (2016) The resolution of disputes before the Singapore International Commercial Court. Int Comp Law Q 65:439–473

Jeroen A. van der Weide is counsellor at law and Associate Professor of Private Law at the Institute for Private Law, Leiden Law School, the Netherlands. He holds a Ph.D. in the field of the law of personal property and private international law. Van der Weide regularly advises (global) law firms, courts and legal counsellors in complex cross-border transactions. He is editor-in-chief of one of the leading Dutch law journals.

Further Developments in International Commercial Arbitration

The Efficient Conduct of the Arbitration Proceedings and the 'New' Role of Arbitrators: A Challenging Journey Through Promises and Expectations

Paolo Marzolini

Abstract The debate surrounding the efficiency of arbitration has led international arbitration rules and guidelines to empower arbitrators to conduct the proceedings in a more robust way. Criticism has been recently levelled against the arbitrators' tendency to conduct the arbitral process in a manner which is perceived as excessively adversarial. That criticism has led to the launch in December 2018 of the 'Rules on the Efficient Conduct of Proceedings' (Prague Rules). The Prague Rules are stated to promote the inquisitorial approach to litigation typical of the civil law legal tradition. The present Chapter discusses this trend in international arbitration by pointing out that confining the debate on the efficiency of arbitration to the clash of different legal traditions is unsatisfactory. Arbitrators, parties and institutions alike share the responsibility to render the arbitral process more efficient. Arbitrators, in particular, should rediscover the importance of flexibility in finding proper procedural solutions to concrete issues which may arise in the cases before them.

1 Introduction

This Chapter deals with the widely-debated question of the role arbitrators should play in the course of the proceedings in order to achieve efficiency.

At one end of the spectrum are those who take the view that proactive arbitrators would better serve efficiency because—by taking control of the case and, in particular, by firmly handling the taking of the evidence phase—they would reduce the scope for counsel's and parties' dilatory tactics and streamline the issues arising for determination.

At the other end of the spectrum are those who look with scepticism at any inquisitorial role taken over by arbitrators and who therefore are of the opinion that arbitration still is—and must remain—an adversarial process left mostly in the hands of the parties.

P. Marzolini (✉)
Patocchi & Marzolini, Geneva, Switzerland
e-mail: marzolini@patocchimarzolini.com

L. Chen and A. Janssen (eds.), *Dispute Resolution in China, Europe and World*, Ius Gentium: Comparative Perspectives on Law and Justice 79,
https://doi.org/10.1007/978-3-030-42974-4_5

Many of the textbooks on which generations of arbitration practitioners were formed make no exception to the general proposition that party autonomy is the cornerstone upon which arbitration lies.[1] The principle stated in those textbooks is that party autonomy could shape the arbitration from the formation of the consensus to arbitrate to the choice of law applicable to the merits of the dispute and the place of arbitration; from the selection of the arbitrators to the rules applicable to the proceedings.

One of the most tangible consequences of the acclaimed primacy of party autonomy is that arbitrators have traditionally been very reluctant to overrule agreements—in particular agreements of procedural nature—made by the parties before or in the course of the arbitration. Over the years, such approach has produced some discomfort amongst arbitrators who sometimes feel 'trapped' by procedural agreements to which they would not necessarily adhere but which they feel bound to accept in order to avoid putting the award in peril.[2]

In recent years, the parties' discomfort has been added to the arbitrators'. International surveys conducted amongst in-house counsel have revealed that, while arbitration remains the parties' preferred method for resolving international disputes, end-users are unhappy with what has been perceived as the growing inefficiency of the proceedings due to the manner in which arbitrators often handle the cases before them.[3]

As odd as it may seem, such discomfort has produced a number of amendments to institutional arbitration rules and international guidelines which, at least on paper, are intended to increase the powers of arbitrators. This trend seems to support the idea that, in order to be more efficient, arbitration should be less adversarial and more inquisitorial.

In this Chapter, the author expresses the idea that reducing the debate on the efficiency of arbitration to a battle between supporters of adversarial and inquisitorial proceedings, or, worse, between the common law and the civil law legal traditions, is an oversimplification.

In the author's view, the correct way to address the issue of inefficiency of arbitration is to be found elsewhere.

[1] Fouchard et al. (1996, pp. 34–36), Blackaby et al. (2015, pp. 16, 71, 187, 355), Born (2014a, pp. 84–86).

[2] Weiller (2018, pp. 214–215), Bizikova (2017, pp. 594, 596), Queen Mary University of London and White & Case LLP (2015, p. 2), Polkinghorne and Gill (2017, pp. 935–936), Berger and Jensen (2016, pp. 419–420), Huleatt-James and Gould (1999, p. 69).

[3] Queen Mary University of London and White & Case LLP (2018, pp. 3, 26–27), (2015, pp. 2, 7, 10); see also amongst commentators Berger and Jensen (2016, p. 416), Tercier (2016, p. 1054), Pfisterer (2013, p. 649), Vidak-Gojkovic et al. (2016, pp. 61–62), Greenwood (2011, pp. 199–200).

2 The Arbitrators' 'New' Role in the International Arbitration Rules

Even a cursory survey of recent revisions of international arbitration rules will show a trend towards broadening the rights, powers and duties of arbitrators.

Until a few years ago there was consensus within the arbitration community around the idea that the arbitrators' ultimate task lay mainly—if not exclusively—in the decision of the parties' dispute.[4] While this idea is certainly still valid today, the tendency has been to reshape the manner in which the fundamental task of deciding a dispute may or should be performed by arbitrators.

The quest for efficiency has gradually brought international arbitration institutions to place greater emphasis on the scope of the arbitrators' powers.[5] The analysis of these rules leads to the conclusion that the institutions have reacted to the perceived growing inefficiency of the arbitral process mainly by adding new provisions intended to increase the arbitrators' powers to stir and control the proceedings. The result is that arbitrators are no longer viewed simply as 'adjudicators'; they are now expected to act as 'dispute managers'.[6]

In such role arbitrators may be called upon to deal with, and possibly exercise, multiple tasks such as:

(i) the early determination of procedural and/or substantive issues at stake in the dispute[7];
(ii) the decision of frivolous claims in a summary manner[8];

---

[4]Pfisterer (2013, p. 651), Born (2014b, p. 1986).

[5]Arts. 17.1 and 17.2 of the United Nations Commission on International Trade Law Arbitration Rules of 2013 (UNCITRAL Rules); Art. 22.1 of the International Chamber of Commerce Arbitration Rules of 2017 (ICC Rules); Arts. 14.4(ii) and 22.1(ii) of the London Court of International Arbitration Rules of 2014 (LCIA Rules); Rules 19.1, 19.3, 19.4 and 19.7 of the Singapore International Arbitration Centre Arbitration Rules of 2016 (SIAC Rules); Art. 17.1 of the Permanent Court of Arbitration Rules of 2012 (PCA Rules); Arts. 13.1 and 13.5 of the Hong Kong International Arbitration Centre Arbitration Rules of 2018 (HKIAC Rules); R-21(b), R-23, R-32(b) and R-32(c) of the American Arbitration Association Commercial Arbitration Rules and Mediation Procedures of 2013 (AAA Rules); Art. 17.1 of the Chartered Institute of Arbitrators Arbitration Rules of 2015 (CIArb Rules); Arts. 15.1 and 15.8 of the Swiss Rules of International Arbitration of 2012 (Swiss Rules); Art. 25.3 of the Milan Chamber of Arbitration Rules of 2019 (CAM Rules); Art. 17.7 of the Cairo Regional Centre for International Commercial Arbitration of 2011 (CRCICA Rules); Art. 21.2 of the Australian Centre for International Commercial Arbitration Rules of 2016 (ACICA Rules).

[6]Berger and Jensen (2016, p. 416), Redfern (2015, p. 46), Marzolini (2016).

[7]Letters b and c of Appendix IV, ICC Rules.

[8]Rule 29, SIAC Rules; Art. 39, Arbitration Rules of the Arbitration Institute of the Stockholm Chamber of Commerce of 2017 (SCC Rules); ICC, Note to Parties and Arbitral Tribunals on the Conduct of the Arbitration Under the ICC Rules of Arbitration (2019), https://cdn.iccwbo.org/content/uploads/sites/3/2017/03/icc-note-to-parties-and-arbitral-tribunals-on-the-conduct-of-arbitration.pdf (accessed 5 March 2019), paras 74–79; see also amongst commentators Chong and Primrose (2017), Ryan and Dharmananda (2018).

(iii) the (pro)active role in the gathering of evidence[9];
(iv) the refusal to approve any intended change or addition to the party's legal representatives where such change or addition could compromise the independence and impartiality of the arbitral tribunal[10];
(v) the call for the recognition of arbitrator's power to sanction unethical behaviour of parties' counsel[11]; and
(vi) the involvement in the settlement of the dispute before the final award is rendered.[12]

Arguably, most of the tasks mentioned above have always been part and parcel of the arbitrator's set of prerogatives, duties or powers. However, the fact that institutions are now feeling the need expressly to set out these prerogatives, duties and powers in their rules is a trend which is worth stressing.[13]

3 IBA Rules *v* Prague Rules or Adversarial *v* Inquisitorial Approach to Litigation

This Chapter was originally written in the wake of the launch in December 2018 of the Rules on the Efficient Conduct of Proceedings in International Arbitration (Prague Rules). The Prague Rules are said to be born out of the dissatisfaction of a portion of the arbitration community with the widely-spread and well-known International Bar Association (IBA) Rules on the Taking of Evidence in International Arbitration of 2010 (IBA Rules).[14]

The dissatisfaction described above was openly pointed out by the drafters of the Prague Rules in a passage of the *Note from the Working Group* contained in the draft

[9] Arbitration rules almost invariably provide that arbitrators may, at any time, order a party to produce documents or give evidence: Art. 27.3, UNCITRAL Rules; Art. 25.5, ICC Rules; Art. 15.6, LCIA Rules; Rule 27(h), SIAC Rules; Art. 27.3, PCA Rules; Art. 22.3, HKIAC Rules; Art. 27.3, CIArb Rules; Art. 24.3, Swiss Rules; Art. 43, CIETAC Rules; Art. 27.3, DIAC Rules; Art. 27.3, CRCICA Rules; Art. 26 of the Korean Commercial Arbitration Board Rules of 2016 (KCAB Rules); Art. 27.3 of the Asian International Arbitration Centre Rules of 2018 (AIAC Rules).

[10] Art. 18.3, LCIA Rules.

[11] Art. 18.6, LCIA Rules; see also amongst commentators Wilske (2015), Florescu (2015).

[12] Art. 5 of the Centre for Effective Dispute Resolution Rules of the Facilitation of Settlement in International Arbitration of 2009 (CEDR Rules); Art. 15.8, Swiss Rules; Art. 47, CIETAC Rules; Art. 25.3, CAM Rules; Art. 21.3, ACICA Rules; Art. 26 of the German Arbitration Institute Arbitration Rules of 2018 (DIS Rules); Letter h(ii) of Appendix IV, ICC Rules; see also amongst commentators Stutzer (2017, pp. 589–608), Marzolini (2016, pp. 99–119), Harris (2016, pp. 89–98).

[13] Stutzer (2017, p. 590), Marzolini (2016, p. 99).

[14] Tevendale (2019), Amaral (2018a, b), Henriques (2018, p. 352), McIlwrath (2018), Khvalei (2018a, b).

dated 1 September 2018 (Prague Rules, Draft, 1 September 2018).[15] This passage reads as follows:

> [t]he drafters of the IBA Rules […] bridged a gap between the common law and civil law traditions of taking evidence. The IBA Rules were very successful in developing a nearly standardized procedure in international arbitration, at least for proceedings involving Parties from different legal traditions and those with significant amounts at stake. However, from a civil law perspective, the IBA Rules are still closer to common law traditions, as they follow a more adversarial approach regarding document production, fact witnesses and Party-appointed experts. In addition, the parties' entitlement to cross-examine witnesses is almost being taken for granted. These factors contribute greatly to the costs of arbitration, while their efficiency is sometimes rather questionable.[16]

The criticism against the IBA Rules levelled by the Working Group of the Prague Rules focuses, on the one hand, on the argument that the IBA Rules are mostly the product of the adversarial, common law legal tradition and, on the other hand, that the procedural solutions adopted by the IBA Rules sometimes result in higher costs and inefficient proceedings. The passage quoted above, which did not find its way into the final version of the Prague Rules, reintroduces the quite trite notion of the divide between civil law and common law legal traditions. According to their drafters, the Prague Rules reply to the IBA Rules by encouraging 'a more active role for arbitral tribunals in managing proceedings'.[17]

Once again, the Prague Rules seem to stand by the assumption that, in order to increase the overall efficiency of arbitration proceedings, more power should be given to arbitrators to intervene in the management of the proceedings and, in particular, in the taking of the evidence. Briefly put, the inquisitorial approach of the civil law legal tradition is regarded as a viable cure to the inefficiency affecting the conduct of arbitration proceedings.[18]

The approach taken by the Prague Rules is not new; in fact, it echoes the choices made some twenty years ago by the English legislator with the adoption of the Civil Procedure Rules in 1998 (CPR).[19] In his *Access to Justice Final Report*, Lord Woolf defined the 'judicial case management as crucial to the changes which are necessary in our civil judicial system'[20]; he then also added that the '[u]ltimate responsibility for the control of litigation must move from the litigants and their legal advisers to the court'.[21] This was quite a bold statement to be made in a jurisdiction such as England and Wales which has been based for centuries on the adversarial system. Concerns

[15] Rules on the Efficient Conduct of Proceedings in International Arbitration (Prague Rules), Draft, 1 September 2018, https://praguerules.com/upload/medialibrary/b2e/b2e26123ac310b644b26d4cd11dc67d8.pdf (accessed 4 March 2019), p. 2.

[16] Prague Rules, Draft, 1 September 2018, p. 2.

[17] Prague Rules, Final, https://praguerules.com/upload/medialibrary/9dc/9dc31ba7799e26473d92961d926948c9.pdf (accessed 4 March 2019), p. 3.

[18] For an overview of the two legal traditions, see Rubinstein (2004).

[19] The full text of these Rules is available at https://www.legislation.gov.uk/uksi/1998/3132/contents/made (accessed 15 January 2020).

[20] Lord Woolf (1996), Section II, Chapter I, para 1.

[21] Lord Woolf (1996), Section II, Chapter I, para 1.

were raised in that jurisdiction in this respect, to which Lord Woolf answered by stating that:

> the responsibility of the parties and the legal profession for handling cases will remain. The legal profession will, however, be performing its traditional adversarial role in a managed environment governed by the courts and by the rules which will focus effort on the key issues rather than allowing every issue to be pursued regardless of expense and time, as at present.[22]

Rule 1.4(2) of the CPR titled 'Court's Duty to Manage the Cases' contains a non-exhaustive list of 'active case management' tools and objectives such as:

(i) encouraging the parties to co-operate with each other in the conduct of the proceedings;
(ii) identifying the issues at an early stage;
(iii) deciding promptly which issues need full investigation and trial and accordingly disposing summarily of the others;
(iv) deciding the order in which issues are to be resolved;
(v) encouraging the parties to use an alternative dispute resolution procedure if the court considers that appropriate and facilitating the use of such procedure;
(vi) helping the parties to settle the whole or part of the case;
(vii) considering whether the likely benefits of taking a particular step justify the cost of taking it;
(viii) dealing with as many aspects of the case as [the court] can on the same occasion;
(ix) dealing with the case without the parties needing to attend at court;
(x) making use of technology; and
(xi) giving directions to ensure that the trial of a case proceeds quickly and efficiently.

Arguably, all of the tools and objectives set out in Rule 1.4(2) of the CPR are nowadays considered to represent the arbitrators' duties and prerogatives when it comes to managing the arbitral process proactively. It is, in any event, remarkable that the recent trend in arbitration, which favours the inquisitorial role of arbitrators, seems to mirror what had been done years ago outside the arbitration world and within the framework of a ground-breaking civil justice reform in a common law jurisdiction (i.e. England and Wales).

The question to be answered is whether the whole debate about the lack of efficiency of the arbitral process can be reduced to the issue whether arbitrators should have 'new' or greater powers and whether the distinction between the adversarial and the inquisitorial approach is material at all to the issue of how arbitrators should run their proceedings efficiently.

The present author takes the view that the mere attribution of new powers to arbitrators—while, in principle, potentially useful—does not *per se* solve the issue of the perceived inefficiency of arbitration. It is quite obvious, in fact, that one thing is to confer certain prerogatives, duties and powers on arbitrators and a completely

[22] Lord Woolf (1996), Section II, Chapter I, para 3.

different thing is how these prerogatives, duties and powers will actually be exercised. Each case is different from another; similarly, each arbitrator is different from another. It is, therefore, quite simplistic to take the view that a set of guidelines, no matter how carefully drafted, could provide a one-fits-all solution to every issue which may arise in the course of the proceedings.

Let us take the following case as an example. Art. 4.2 of the Prague Rules provides that '[g]enerally, the arbitral tribunal and the parties are encouraged to avoid any form of document production, including e-discovery'.

This general and broad provision, which is admittedly aimed at discouraging American-style, far-reaching requests for production of documents, is somehow tempered by Art. 4.3 which reads as follows:

> [h]owever, if a party believes that it would need to request certain documents from the other party, it should indicate this to the arbitral tribunal at the case management conference and explain the reasons why the document production may be needed in this particular case. If the arbitral tribunal is satisfied that the document production may be needed, it should decide on a procedure for document production and make an appropriate provision for it in the procedural timetable.

The two provisions set out above illustrate powers which on paper may well produce efficient results in terms of saving time and costs but which will need to be tested against the particulars of the case before the arbitrators. The proposition that arbitral tribunals and parties alike are 'encouraged to avoid any form of document production, including e-discovery' appears to ignore those cases in which a phase dedicated to the document production is nothing less than the 'necessary evil' in order to protect one party's right to put its case before the arbitrators. This is the case, for instance, of the shareholder who alleges in the arbitration to have been defrauded by other shareholders and, consequently, seeks an order by the arbitrator to be provided with the account of the company (also a party to the arbitration). Or, the case of the sub-contractor which, in order to put forward its case for delay against the contractor, will need to access sooner rather than later the Primavera programme in source code in possession of the said contractor.

Far-reaching and general statements like the one contained in Art. 4.2 of the Prague Rules might ultimately lead to opposite results to those they were intended to fulfil. This has nothing to do with the so-called 'due process paranoia' well-known in the arbitration practice and literature.[23] To curtail one party's right to put its case before the arbitrators based only on a statement of principle like the one contained in Art. 4.2 of the Prague Rules would amount to a real breach of due process possibly likely to jeopardise the final award on the merits. It is fair to assume that no arbitrator would ever act in such a way.

If that assumption is correct, why would anyone want to have such a general statement incorporated into the specific procedural rules applicable to her/his case? Asking the question is providing the answer.

---

[23] Berger and Jensen (2016, p. 420), Reed (2017, pp. 372–373), Queen Mary University of London and White & Case LLP (2015, pp. 2, 10).

Art. 4.3 of the Prague Rules further calls for the following remark. The idea underpinning this provision is that at the case management conference (viz. the very first time in the proceedings the parties and the arbitrators meet either in person or via teleconference) one party should be able to plead in full its case in support of document production. Upon hearing the party's application for production of documents and, one would assume, the other party's answer, the arbitrators should assess whether they are 'satisfied that the document production may be needed'. Again, while this course of action may appear (very) efficient on paper, in most arbitrations the initial submissions (viz. request/notice of arbitration and answer to the request/notice of arbitration) are very basic documents; their purpose is mainly to kick-start the arbitration and proceed with the constitution of the arbitral tribunal. None of the major international arbitration rules require the parties to set out their case in full in their first written briefs.[24] As a consequence, arbitrators will almost never have a clear view as to the extent and the merits of the dispute before them at the case management conference. To recommend or even urge arbitrators to make up their minds on one party's case on production of documents at the very beginning of the arbitration seems to ignore how a case normally unfolds.

Art. 4.4 of the Prague Rules is designed to temper the provision in Art. 4.3 in that:

> [a] party can request the arbitral tribunal to order document production *at a later stage* of the arbitration *only in exceptional circumstances*. Such a request should be granted *only if the arbitral tribunal is satisfied that the party could not have made such a request at the case management conference* [emphasis added].

The issue with this provision is that it seems to cover exclusively the case of requests for the production of documents made *after* the case management conference because those requests could not have been made beforehand. However, Art. 4.4 does not provide much assistance in cases like the one described above with respect to Art. 4.3 of the Prague Rules (viz. requests for production of documents which, according to those rules, must be dealt with at the case management conference in the absence of guidelines regarding the drafting of the parties' introductory written submissions).

The remark made above illustrates how general provisions on the manner in which proceedings should be conducted cannot be applied in a vacuum. Quite to the opposite, arbitrators (and the parties) should therefore be better off not forgetting the very basic principle according to which general provisions must always be applied with caution and by taking into account the context within which they are intended to operate. A provision such as Art. 4.3 of the Prague Rules could only work well if, at the very least, the claimant is willing to take it upon itself to file a detailed request for arbitration. This is just a practical observation which, on its face, has nothing to do with the divide existing between the adversarial and inquisitorial approach to litigation.

---

[24] Arts. 3.3 and 4.1, UNCITRAL Rules; Arts. 4.3 and 5.1, ICC Rules; Arts. 1.1 and 2.1, LCIA Rules; Rules 3.1 and 4.1, SIAC Rules; Arts. 3.3 and 4.1, PCA Rules; Arts. 4.3 and 5.1, HKIAC Rules; R-4(e) AAA Rules; Arts. 3.3 and 4.1, CIArb Rules; Arts. 3.3 and 3.7, Swiss Rules; Arts. 10.2 and 11.2, CAM Rules; Arts. 4.1 and 5.1, DIAC Rules; Arts. 3.3 and 4.1, CRCICA Rules; Arts. 5.3 and 6.2, ACICA Rules; Arts. 8.3 and 9.1, KCAB Rules; Arts. 3.3 and 4.1, AIAC Rules.

The disputes that end up in international arbitration most of the times do not involve counsel or parties coming from similar legal backgrounds and they are adjudicated by arbitrators often coming from different jurisdictions. The simple idea of finding proper procedural solutions only in one legal tradition is tantamount to providing a simplistic and surely incomplete answer to a difficult and complex question.

4 Party Autonomy *v* Arbitrators' Duty to Conduct the Proceedings Efficiently

The title to this section may seem odd. It is intended to emphasise long-standing misconceptions surrounding arbitration. The traditional idea is that arbitration is the realm of the parties.[25] When it comes to procedural solutions and rules to be applied in a given case, the traditional approach has been that the parties are entitled to dictate the choices agreed upon to arbitrators who would have no business and no right to disregard or depart from the parties' procedural agreements.

The trend towards the recognition of more powers to arbitrators in the management of the case described above in this Chapter seems to suggest that party autonomy is no longer as paramount as it used to be or was believed to be. In this respect, it is not difficult to imagine situations in which the exercise of the arbitrators' power to act as proactive case managers may conflict with agreements reached by the parties as to the manner in which the proceedings should be conducted.

The arbitrators' 'new' role as it emerges from international arbitration rules and guidelines must, therefore, be tested against party autonomy.[26] This test is crucial, in particular, if one takes into account that the foundation upon which arbitration rests is the parties' consent. Arbitrators' jurisdiction and powers presuppose the existence of an arbitration agreement which may in turn refer to institutional arbitration rules providing for such powers/prerogatives or a separate *ad hoc* agreement entered into between the parties prior to or during the proceedings.

Party autonomy in matters of procedure is recognised in a number of international instruments such as the Geneva Protocol on Arbitration Clauses of 1923,[27] the Geneva Convention on the Execution of Foreign Arbitral Awards of 1927,[28] the New York Convention on the Recognition and Enforcement of Foreign Arbitral Awards of 1958 (New York Convention)[29] and the European Convention on International Arbitration of 1961.[30]

[25] Veeder (2014a, p. 87), Radicati di Brozolo (2012, p. 49).

[26] Patocchi (2013).

[27] Art. 2 of the Geneva Protocol on Arbitration Clauses of 1923.

[28] Art. 1(c) of the Geneva Convention on the Execution of Foreign Arbitral Awards of 1927.

[29] Art. V.1(d), New York Convention.

[30] Art. IV of the European Convention on International Arbitration of 1961.

These procedural agreements are stated to be binding on the arbitrators.[31] The key question to be answered is whether the party autonomy expressed through procedural agreements applicable to the arbitration proceedings should always prevail over divergent solutions envisaged by arbitrators.[32]

A possible answer to the question set out above is contained in Art. 19 of the United Nations Commission on International Trade Law (UNCITRAL) Model Law on International Arbitration of 1985 (UNCITRAL Model Law). That provision deals with the 'Determination of Rules of Procedure' and reads as follows:

(1) Subject to the provisions of this Law, the parties are free to agree on the procedure to be followed by the arbitral tribunal in conducting the proceedings.
(2) Failing such agreement, the arbitral tribunal may, subject to the provisions of this Law, conduct the arbitration in such manner as it considers appropriate. The power conferred upon the arbitral tribunal includes the power to determine the admissibility, relevance, materiality and weight of any evidence.

Arts. 19 and 18 on the equal treatment of the parties are so crucial within the framework of the Model Law that they are referred to as the 'Magna Carta of arbitral procedure'.[33]

This, however, does not mean that party autonomy is not subject to any limitations. According to Art. 19(1) of the Model Law, the parties' freedom to agree on the procedure of the arbitration is '[s]ubject to the provisions of this Law …'. The reference to the 'provisions of the Law' is to be read as a reference to the mandatory provisions contained in the Model Law.[34]

Further limitations on party autonomy when it comes to procedural agreements may be found in national laws. Art. 816*bis* of the Italian Code of Civil Procedure provides that procedural agreements made by the parties *prior* to the constitution of the arbitral tribunal are, in principle, binding on the tribunal, provided that they are contained in the arbitration agreement or made in writing. Italian legal commentators share the view that procedural agreements made *after* the constitution of the arbitral tribunal would also be binding on the arbitrators provided that the arbitrators agree with those procedural arrangements.[35] The arbitrators would always be free to resign in case of disagreement.[36]

---

[31] Patocchi (2013, p. 132), Kaufmann-Kohler and Rigozzi (2015, p. 315).

[32] Born (2014b, pp. 2140–2142), Patocchi (2013).

[33] Binder (2010, p. 280); referring to United Nations Commission on International Trade Law, International Commercial Arbitration: Analytical Commentary on Draft Text of a Model Law on International Commercial Arbitration (1985), A/CN.9/264, https://www.mcgill.ca/arbitration/files/arbitration/Commentaireanalytique-en.pdf (accessed 5 March 2019), p. 44, Holtzmann and Neuhaus (1994, p. 564).

[34] Binder (2010, p. 282), Holtzmann and Neuhaus (1994, p. 564).

[35] Fabbi (2017, p. 229), Salvaneschi (2014, p. 394).

[36] Fabbi (2017, p. 229).

In other jurisdictions, limitations on party autonomy with respect to procedure stem from the fact that their arbitration laws are based on the Model Law. This is the case, for instance, of Australia,[37] South Korea[38] and Germany.[39]

Some countries provide for additional limitations, such as the principle set out in the arbitration law of Saudi Arabia according to which the parties are free to agree on the rules of procedure as far as these procedural agreements do not contravene the principles of *Shari'a*.[40]

As to institutional arbitration rules, Art. 15(1) of the Swiss Rules of International Arbitration of 2012 (Swiss Rules) provides that '[s]ubject to these Rules, the arbitral tribunal may conduct the arbitration in such manner as it considers appropriate, provided that it ensures equal treatment of the parties and their right to be heard'.

Similarly worded provisions are also contained in the Australian Centre for International Commercial Arbitration Rules of 2016 (ACICA Rules) (Art. 21(1)), the Cairo Regional Centre for International Commercial Arbitration Rules of 2011 (CRCICA Rules) (Art. 17(1)), and the Korean Commercial Arbitration Board Rules of 2016 (KCAB Rules) (Art. 16(1)).

From a general standpoint, boundaries to the parties' freedom to agree on procedural rules applicable to the arbitration proceedings may be found in mandatory rules (e.g. the protection of the parties' equal treatment before arbitrators and/or the parties' right to put their case before the arbitrators).[41]

In this respect, the arbitrators' duty to conduct the proceedings efficiently arguably belongs to the category of primary norms which are expressly designed to protect mandatory rules such as the parties' right to present their case. The arbitrators' duty, in fact, operates as a fundamental guarantee against distortions of the proceedings. Those distortions may well be the result of procedural agreements reached by the parties which may ultimately result in compressions, if not clear breaches, of one party's right to present its case. In those circumstances, arbitrators must be entitled to comply with their duty by overruling procedural agreements between the parties without the risk of jeopardising the award as such and its enforceability.

Some practical examples may illustrate the point made above.

- **Example No. 1: Inefficient Provisional Timetable Agreed upon between the Parties.** Before the case management conference, the parties may agree on a leisurely timeline based on the appearance of the complexity of the factual and legal issues arising for determination. While the tribunal may be inclined to accept the various stages set out in the timetable agreed upon by the parties, it might be disinclined to follow the timeline and the generous time limits agreed upon.
- **Example No. 2: Agreed Duration of the Evidentiary Hearing.** Before the case management conference, the parties agree that the hearing should last five weeks.

[37] Art. 19(1) of Schedule 2 of the International Arbitration Act 1974 (Cth).

[38] Art. 20(1) of the Arbitration Act of Korea of 1999.

[39] Section 1042(3) of the German Code of Civil Procedure (ZPO).

[40] Art. 25(1) of the Kingdom of Saudi Arabia Law of Arbitration.

[41] Blackaby et al. (2015, p. 156), Born (2014b, pp. 2142–2143); Patocchi (2013, pp. 133–134); e.g. Art. 18, UNCITRAL Model Law; Art. 17.1, UNCITRAL Rules; Art. 22.4, ICC Rules.

The arbitrators are disinclined to follow such approach and provide directions to streamline the taking of oral evidence and shorten the length of the hearing.

- **Example No. 3: the Parties' Agreement to Refuse the Bifurcation of the Proceedings Suggested by the Sole Arbitrator.** The parties to a consolidated arbitration comprising three original arbitrations have a dispute relating to three similar building contracts. The respondent contends that all claims are barred by limitation under the applicable law. The sole arbitrator suggests that the issue of limitation be heard first, but the parties agree that there should be no bifurcation. The sole arbitrator decides that the limitation defence should be heard in phase 1 of the proceedings as a preliminary matter.
- **Example No. 4: Agreed Bifurcation of the Proceedings Combined with a Short Timetable.** The parties to a joint venture agreement are in dispute as to the breach of the agreement, *quantum* of damages and the termination of that agreement. The dispute involves allegations of fraud and corruption. Prior to the case management conference, the parties agree that the tribunal should declare that the joint venture agreement has come to an end and that should be done in a matter of a few months' time. The sole arbitrator is disinclined to bifurcate the proceedings and expresses his/her preference to hear the full case before rendering his/her final award.
- **Example No. 5: Agreement by the Parties According to which Experts Should Be Examined by Experts.** During the case management conference in a post-acquisition dispute, the parties agree that the examination of experts at the hearing shall be conducted by the party-appointed experts instead of counsel. The sole arbitrator is disinclined to follow such agreement and rules that experts should be entitled only to sit in the hearing room while the other experts are examined. Counsel should be in charge of running the experts' examination.
- **Example No. 6: Agreement Reached between the Parties as to the Procedure to Be Followed for Production of Documents.** The parties agree during the discussion for the finalisation of procedural order No. 1 containing the specific procedural rules applicable to the arbitration that their requests for production of documents will have to be inserted directly in their first exchange of submissions on the merits. The sole arbitrator is disinclined to follow the parties' agreement since he/she will not be in a position to rule on the relevance and materiality of the documents sought in the absence of detailed introductory briefs filed by the parties.

In most cases, conflicts between the parties' procedural arrangements and the arbitrators' duty to conduct the proceedings efficiently are resolved without any need for the arbitrators to make a ruling. To the extent possible, this is, indeed, the preferred course of action.

In this respect, some practical suggestions may be given to arbitrators in order to assist them in dealing with potential conflicts with the parties.

Firstly, arbitrators should be ready to familiarise themselves with the case as soon as possible upon receipt of the file from the administering institution or the parties, as the case may be.[42] The case management conference or the organisational meetings which are held at the beginning of the proceedings should be considered as a key moment to define tailor-made rules applicable to the proceedings.[43] The arbitrators and the parties should never underestimate the importance of these meetings during which the foundations for a smooth conduct of the arbitration are laid.

Secondly, arbitrators should encourage dialogue with the parties. Experience shows that compromise solutions are often found; in particular, if the arbitrators are willing to invest time to explain to the parties the reasons why they are not willing to follow the parties' procedural agreement.

Thirdly, arbitrators should be ready to ask questions in order to probe the parties' agreement and before reaching any conclusion as to whether such agreement is acceptable.

Fourthly, arbitrators should think proactively about alternative procedural solutions; in other words they must be creative and flexible. While useful sometimes in order to save time, models and/or standardised solutions shall not become the norm in the discussion with the parties on the procedural arrangements for the case. The downside of models which are based on arbitrators' past cases is to convey the impression that each case can be treated in the same way. The purpose of this Chapter is precisely to show that this approach may lead to mistakes which must be avoided.

Finally, arbitrators should be ready to follow the case as the arbitration proceeds. This is the only way to ensure that every issue touching upon the merits or procedure will be taken care of and resolved as soon as it arises. In this respect, arbitrators should, for instance, be ready to hold case management conferences during the course of the proceedings and not only at the beginning of the arbitration. This will ensure that the dialogue with the parties remains open and that interventions aimed at keeping the arbitration under control are made in a timely fashion.

5 Conclusion

Efficiency is an objective which may be difficult to achieve in certain cases. It may be affected by the parties' conduct, the particulars of the case or even the dynamics within the arbitral tribunal. Asking arbitrators to exercise their powers and prerogatives in a more robust manner is not entirely convincing as this addresses only one side of the equation. The other side of the equation is the complexity of each case. Experience shows that arbitrations in certain industry sectors have a tendency to become increasingly complex. Complexity relates not only to the issues arising for determination but also to the vast amount of documents which arbitrators are called upon to read and understand.[44]

---

[42] van den Berg (2014, pp. 419–421).

[43] van den Berg (2014, p. 422), Patocchi and Briner (2014, pp. 285–286).

[44] Risse (2019, pp. 291–307).

The exercise of inquisitorial powers and prerogatives by arbitrators could only work to the extent that the case concerned and the parties involved are receptive to this approach and arbitrators are sufficiently equipped to make good use of those powers.

Arbitration has always been praised for its flexibility[45]; in recent years, flexibility has been partly replaced by a somewhat standardised way to conduct the proceedings. In this respect, arbitration rules and guidelines have contributed to a crystallisation of certain practices. Arbitrators must re-discover the importance of flexibility when they manage their cases. Complexity can hardly be efficiently handled by resorting to standardised norms; in particular, if those norms have been originally conceived to be applied to relatively straightforward cases.

The pursuit of efficiency will be successful only if arbitrators, parties and institutions alike will accept to share their respective burden. The shares of the arbitration are owned by the parties; however, the parties do not enjoy a monopoly over those shares; arbitrators and institutions own shares too.

Parties, arbitrators and institutions need to realise that only from their proactive co-operation will come viable and effective answers to the criticisms of arbitration recently raised. Only from such co-operation will arbitration successfully overcome the challenges reserved to it by the future.

Acknwledgements The author wishes to thank Dr. Daniel Durante (Senior Associate) of the law firm Patocchi & Marzolini as well as Mrs Elisabeth Zoe Everson and Ms Emilie Theintz for the assistance in conducting the research for this Chapter.

References

Abramson HI (1999) Protocols for international arbitrators who dare to settle cases. Am Rev Int Arbitr 10(1):1–17

Altenkirch M, Boussihmad M (2018) The prague rules—inquisitorial rules on the taking of evidence in international arbitration. https://globalarbitrationnews.com/the-prague-rules-inquisitorial-rules-on-the-taking-of-evidence-in-international-arbitration/. Accessed 15 Jan 2020

Amaral G R (2018a) Prague rules v. IBA rules and the taking of evidence in international arbitration: tilting at windmills—part I. http://arbitrationblog.kluwerarbitration.com/2018/07/05/prague-rules-v-iba-rules-taking-evidence-international-arbitration-tilting-windmills-part. Accessed 4 Mar 2019

Amaral GR (2018b) Prague rules v. IBA rules and the taking of evidence in international arbitration: tilting at windmills—part II. http://arbitrationblog.kluwerarbitration.com/2018/07/06/prague-rules-v-iba-rules-taking-evidence-international-arbitration-tilting-windmills-part-ii. Accessed 4 Mar 2019

Andersen MB, Ryssdal A, Lindskog S (2011) Achieving efficiency in international arbitration: some strategic suggestions for arbitral tribunals in ICC proceedings. ICC Bull 22(2):5–13

[45]Born (2014a, p. 84), Buchanan (1988, p. 512), Hanotiau (2014, p. 644), Blackaby et al. (2015, p. 30), Polkinghorne and Gill (2017, pp. 935–936), Berger and Jensen (2016, p. 419), Vidak-Gojkovic et al. (2016, p. 61).

Argerich S (2019) A comparison of the IBA and prague rules: comparing two of the same. http://arbitrationblog.kluwerarbitration.com/2019/03/02/a-comparison-of-the-iba-and-prague-rules-comparing-two-of-the-same/. Accessed 15 Jan 2020

Ballantyne J, Ross A (2019) Keeping it civil—the launch of the prague rules. GAR Magazine 14(1):14–24

Baysal P, Çevik BK (2018) Document production in international arbitration: the good or the evil? http://arbitrationblog.kluwerarbitration.com/2018/12/09/document-production-in-international-arbitration-the-good-or-the-evil/. Accessed 16 Jan 2020

Berger KP (2018) The direct involvement of the arbitrator in the amicable settlement of the dispute: offering preliminary views, discussion settlement options, suggesting solutions Caucusing. J Int Arbitr 35(5):501–516

Berger KP (2019) Common law civil law v. in international arbitration the beginning or the end? J Int Arbitr 36(3):295–313

Berger KP, Jensen JO (2016) Due process paranoia and the procedural judgement rule: a safe harbour for procedural management decisions by international arbitrators. Arbitr Int 32(3):415–435

Berger KP, Jensen JO (2017) The arbitrator's mandate to facilitate settlement. Fordham Int Law J 40:887–917

Bernd Ehle (2010) The Arbitrator As Settlement Facilitator. In: Caprasse O (ed) Walking a thin line—what an arbitrator can do, must do or must not do, recent developments and trends, colloquium CEPANI40. Bruylant, Bruxelles, pp 77–95

Binder P (2010) International commercial arbitration and conciliation in UNCITRAL model law jurisdictions, 3rd edn. Sweet & Maxwell, London

Bizikova L (2017) Overcoming due process Paranoia: expeditiousness as a new principle of international arbitration. Les Cahiers de l'Arbitrage 4:593–612

Blackaby N, Partasides C, Redfern A, Hunter M (2015) Redfern and hunter on international arbitration, 6th edn. Oxford University Press, Oxford

Boog C, Raneda J (2016) The 2016 SIAC rules: a state-of-the art rules revision ensuring an even more efficient process. ASA Bull 34(3):584–605

Boog C, Wimalasena P (2018) The 2018 DIS rules: new rules for a renewed institution. ASA Bull 36(1):10–30

Born G B (2014a) International Commercial Arbitration, vol 1, 2nd edn. Wolters Kluwer, Alphen aan den Rijn

Born GB (2014b) International commercial arbitration, vol 2, 2nd edn. Wolters Kluwer, Alphen aan den Rijn

Buchanan MA (1988) Public policy and international commercial arbitration. Am Bus Law J 26(3):511–531

Chong P, Primrose B (2017) Summary judgement in international arbitrations seated in England. Arbitr Int 33(1):63–79

Costa e Silva P (2018) Arbitration, jurisdiction and culture: apropos the rules of prague. http://arbitrationblog.kluwerarbitration.com/2018/07/16/arbitration-jurisdiction-culture-apropos-rules-prague-part/. Accessed 15 Jan 2020

Cremades BM (1998) Overcoming the clash of legal cultures: the role of interactive arbitration. Arbitr Int 14(2):157–172

Cymrot MA (2019) Prague rules: common law and civil law advocates talking past each other. Mealey's Int Arbitr Rep 34(2):1–3

Darwazeh N (2017) Is efficiency an arbitrator's duty or simply a character trait? In: Shaughnessy P, Tund S (eds) The powers and duties of an arbitrator: Liber Amicorum Pierre A. Karrer. Wolters Kluwer, Alphen aan den Rijn, pp 57–63

Dong A, Mayberry D (2018) What's all the fuss about the prague rules?. https://www.chinalawvision.com/2018/09/arbitration-and-litigation/whats-fuss-prague-rules/. Accessed 14 Jan 2020

Doudko A, Golovtchouk O (2018) Introducing the young contender—the prague rules. The Ukrainian Journal of Business Law, pp 20–22

Doudko A, Golovtchouk O (2019) Introducing the young contender—the prague rules on the efficient conduct of proceedings in international arbitration—(the prague rules). Revista Română de Arbitraj 13(2):15–21
Dubovský M, Sanderson B, O'Sullivan N (2019) The Prague rules: "Civil" war on the evidence in international arbitration. https://www.dlapiper.com/en/uk/insights/publications/2019/01/the-prague-rules/. Accessed 15 January 2019
Dubovský M, Trchalíková P (2019) Adverse inferences drawn in international arbitration under the prague rules. Revista Română de Arbitraj 13(2):22–37
Elsing SH (2011) Procedural efficiency in international arbitration: choosing the best of both legal worlds. SchiedsVZ 3:114–123
Fabbi A (2017) Art. 816*bis*. In: Benedettelli M, Consolo C, Radicati di Brozolo LG (eds) Commentario breve al diritto dell'arbitrato nazionale ed internazionale. Wolters Kluwer Cedam, Milano, pp 225–244
Florescu CI (2015) Arbitral tribunal power to disqualify Unethical Counsel. Paper presented at the International Conference on Economic Sciences and Business Administration (ICESBA 2015), Procedia of Economics and Business Administration, Bucharest, 20–21 Nov 2015, pp 78–86
Florescu CI (2019) In pursuit of the cherished notion of efficiency through the new prague rules. Revista Română de Arbitraj 13(2):38–63
Fouchard P, Gaillard E, Goldman B (1996) Traité de l'arbitrage commercial international. Litec, Paris
Giaretta B (2019) Prague rules OK?. The Resolver, pp 8–10
Głuszko E (2018) Will the prague rules on the taking of evidence change anything in international arbitration?. https://www.garrigues.com/en_GB/new/will-prague-rules-taking-evidence-change-anything-international-arbitration. Accessed 15 Jan 2020
Greenwood L (2011) A window of opportunity? building a short period of time into arbitral rules in order for parties to explore settlement. Arbitr Int 27(2):199–210
Hanotiau B (2014) The conduct of the hearings. In: Newman LW, Hill RD (eds) The leading arbitrators' guide to international arbitration, 3rd edn. Juris, New York, pp 633–653
Harris C (2016) Arbitrators and settlement—a common law perspective. In: Baizeau D, Spoorenberg F (eds) The arbitrators' initiative: when, why and how should it be used?, ASA special series no. 45. Juris, New York, pp 89–98
Henriques DG (2018) The prague rules: competitor, alternative or addition to the IBA rules on the taking of evidence in international arbitration? ASA Bull 36(2):351–363
Henriques DG (2019) The prague rules on the efficient conduct of proceedings in international arbitration. Revista Română de Arbitraj 13(2):11–12
Henry M (2019) Les prague rules: ou comment le vent d'est pourrait insuffler une dynamique vertueuse à l'arbitrage. Revue de l'arbitrage 1:315–328
Holtzmann HM, Neuhaus JE (1994) A guide to the UNCITRAL model law on international commercial arbitration: legislative history and commentary. Kluwer, The Hague
Horvath GJ (2017) The angelic arbitrator versus the rogue arbitrator: what should an arbitrator strive to be? In: Shaughnessy P, Tund S (eds) The powers and duties of an arbitrator: Liber Amicorum Pierre A. Karrer. Wolters Kluwer, Alphen aan den Rijn, pp 143–151
Huleatt-James M, Gould N (1999) International commercial arbitration: a handbook, 2nd edn. LLP, London
Javin-Fisher R, Saluzzo E (2019) Prague rules on evidence in international arbitration: a viable alternative to the IBA rules?. https://www.humphrieskerstetter.com/wp-content/uploads/2019/01/Prague_Rules_on_evidence_in_international_arbitration_25.01.19.pdf. Accessed 15 Jan 2020
Jun JW (2019) A critical look at the Prague rules: rules on the efficient conduct of proceedings in international arbitration. Journal of Arbitration Studies 29(3):53–73
Kaufmann-Kohler G, Rigozzi A (2015) International arbitration: law and practice in Switzerland. Oxford University Press, Oxford

Khan S, Winter H (2018) New effort to control time and cost in arbitration—the prague rules. https://www.hlarbitrationlaw.com/2018/11/new-effort-to-control-time-and-cost-in-arbitration-the-prague-rules/. Accessed 15 Jan 2020

Khvalei V (2018a) Join GAR for launch of prague rules this friday. https://globalarbitrationreview.com/article/1177783/join-gar-for-launch-of-prague-rules-this-friday. Accessed 4 Mar 2019

Khvalei V (2018b) The prague rules—dispelling misconceptions. https://globalarbitrationreview.com/article/1177181/the-prague-rules-%E2%80%93-dispelling-misconceptions. Accessed 22 Mar 2019

Khvalei V, Teder M, Nica A, Ponty L, Pizarro JPV (2019) Compatibility, novelty, practical corollary? a collective analysis of the Prague Rules. http://arbitrationblog.kluwerarbitration.com/2019/05/22/compatibility-novelty-practical-corollary-a-collective-analysis-of-the-prague-rules/. Accessed 16 Jan 2020

Kirby J (2017) How far should an arbitrator go to get it right? In: Shaughnessy P, Tund S (eds) The powers and duties of an arbitrator: Liber Amicorum Pierre A. Karrer. Wolters Kluwer, Alphen aan den Rijn, pp 193–199

Kocur M (2018) Why lawyers from civil law jurisdictions do not need the prague rules. http://arbitrationblog.kluwerarbitration.com/2018/08/19/why-lawyers-from-civil-law-jurisdictions-do-not-need-the-prague-rules/. Accessed 15 Jan 2020

Kopecky L, Pernt V (2016) A Bid for Strong Arbitrators. http://arbitrationblog.kluwerarbitration.com/2016/04/15/a-bid-for-strong-arbitrators/. Accessed 15 January 2020

Kröll S (2017) Promoting Settlements in Arbitration: The Role of the Arbitrator. In: Shaughnessy P, Tund S (eds) The powers and duties of an arbitrator: Liber Amicorum Pierre A. Karrer. Wolters Kluwer, Alphen aan den Rijn, pp 209–224

Lissner B (2019) The prague rules: the new kid on the block. Young Arbitr Rev 8(34):15–19

Lord Woolf HK (1996) Access to justice final report. https://webarchive.nationalarchives.gov.uk/20060213223540; http://www.dca.gov.uk/civil/final/contents.htm. Accessed 4 Mar 2019

Marzolini P (2016) The arbitrator as a dispute manager—the exercise of the arbitrator's powers to act as settlement facilitator. In: Baizeau D, Spoorenberg F (eds) The arbitrators' initiative: when, why and how should it be used?. ASA special series no. 45. Juris, New York, pp 99–119

Marzolini P (2019) Switching hats or the complex relation between the roles of arbitrator and mediator seen through the prism of a successful case. New York Dispute Resolut Lawyer 12(2):37–40

McCall T, Doll EC (2018) From Russia with new evidentiary rules. https://www.lexology.com/library/detail.aspx?g=c2fb413a-e0e3-4541-9a06-8a9505f6c0e5. Accessed 15 Jan 2020

McIlwrath M (2018) The prague rules: the real cultural war isn't over civil vs common law. http://arbitrationblog.kluwerarbitration.com/2018/12/12/the-prague-rules-the-real-cultural-war-isnt-over-civil-vs-common-law. Accessed 4 Mar 2019

Mnookin RH (1994) Creating value through process design. J Int Arbitr 11(1):125–131

Moser M (2017) The pre-hearing checklist protocol: a tool for organizing efficient arbitration hearings. In: Shaughnessy P, Tund S (eds) The powers and duties of an arbitrator: Liber Amicorum Pierre A Karrer. Wolters Kluwer, Alphen aan den Rijn, pp 229–238

Newman LW, Zaslowsky D (2018) The Russians are coming, and they want to change how we conduct international arbitration. https://www.law.com/newyorklawjournal/2018/05/23/the-russians-are-coming-and-they-want-to-change-how-we-conduct-international-arbitration/. Accessed 14 Jan 2020

Oliva R (2019) The prague rules: minimal notes from an italian perspective. Revista Română de Arbitraj 13(2):64–79

Panov A (2018) Why the prague rules may be needed?. http://arbitrationblog.practicallaw.com/why-the-prague-rules-may-be-needed/. Accessed 15 Jan 2020

Panov A, Khrapoutski A (2018) The prague rules—an alternative way of conducting international arbitration? Russian Arbitr Assoc J 1:41–46

Park WW (2017) Arbitration and fine dining: two faces of efficiency. In: Shaughnessy P, Tund S (eds) The powers and duties of an arbitrator: Liber Amicorum Pierre A. Karrer. Wolters Kluwer, Alphen aan den Rijn, pp 251–267

Patocchi PM (2013) Party autonomy vs. case management in international arbitration. Banka ve Ticaret Hukuku Dergisi XXIX(2):127–163

Patocchi PM, Briner R (2014) The role of the president of the arbitral tribunal. In: Newman LW, Hill RD (eds) The leading arbitrators' guide to international arbitration, 3rd edn. Juris, New York, pp 281–304

Patocchi PM (to be published) The prague rules on the efficient conduct of proceedings in international arbitration: a step forward?. Paper presented at the international arbitration symposium, Ankara, Yıldırım Beyazıt Law Review, 25–26 Apr 2019

Peter N (2019) The prague rules as choice architecture. Revista Română de Arbitraj 13(2):80–86

Pettibone PJ (2019) The prague rules on the efficient conduct of proceedings in international arbitration: are they an alternative to the iba rules on the taking of evidence in international arbitration? Asian Dispute Rev 21(1):13–17

Pfisterer S (2013) The arbitrator as settlement facilitator. Am Rev Int Arbitr 24(4):649–679

Polkinghorne M, Gill BA (2017) Due process paranoia: need we be cruel to be kind. J Int Arbitr 34(6):935–946

Queen Mary University of London and White & Case LLP (2015) 2015 international arbitration survey: improvements and innovations in international arbitration. http://www.arbitration.qmul.ac.uk/media/arbitration/docs/2015_International_Arbitration_Survey.pdf. Accessed 4 Mar 2019

Queen Mary University of London and White & Case LLP (2018) 2018 international arbitration survey: the evolution of international arbitration. http://www.arbitration.qmul.ac.uk/media/arbitration/docs/2018-International-Arbitration-Survey—The-Evolution-of-International-Arbitration-(2).PDF. Accessed 4 Mar 2019

Radicati di Brozolo LG (2012) mandatory rules and international arbitration. Am Rev Int Arbitr 23(1):49–74

Redfern A (2015) The changing world of international arbitration. In: Caron DD, Schill SW, Cohen Smutny A, Triantafilou EE (eds) Practising virtue: inside international arbitration. Oxford University Press, Oxford, pp 45–51

Reed L (2017) Ab(use) of due process: sword vs shield. Arbitr Int 33(3):361–377

Reeg A (2017) Should an international arbitral tribunal engage in settlement facilitation? In: Shaughnessy P, Tund S (eds) The powers and duties of an arbitrator: Liber Amicorum Pierre A. Karrer. Wolters Kluwer, Alphen aan den Rijn, pp 269–277

Rees P (2017) Arbitration—elastic or arthritic? Asian Dispute Rev 19(3):104–111

Respondek A (2014) Five proposals to further increase the efficiency of international arbitration proceedings. J Int Arbitr 31(4):507–513

Respondek A (2017) How civil law principles could help to make international arbitration proceedings more time and cost effective. Singapore Law Gazette, pp 33–37

Respondek A, Koetter E (2019) New frontiers in international arbitration?—the prague rules. https://lawgazette.com.sg/feature/new-frontiers-in-international-arbitration-the-prague-rules/. Accessed 16 Jan 2020

Risse J (2013) Ten drastic proposals for saving time and costs in arbitral proceedings. Arbitr Int 29(3):453–466

Risse J (2019) An inconvenient truth: the complexity problem and limits to justice. Arbitr Int 35(3):291–307

Rombach A, Shalbanava H (2019) The prague rules: a new era of procedure in arbitration or much ado about nothing? SchiedsVZ 2:53–60

Rubinstein JH (2004) International commercial arbitration: reflections at the crossroads of the common law and civil law traditions. Chicago J Int Law 5(1):303–310

Ryan D, Dharmananda K (2018) Summary disposal in arbitration: still fair or agreed to be fair. J Int Arbitr 35(1):31–57

Salvaneschi L (2014) Arbitrato. Zanichelli, Bologna

Schläpfer A-V, Paralika M (2015) Striking the right balance: the roles of arbitral institutions, parties and tribunals in achieving efficiency in international arbitration. BCDR Int Arbitr Rev 2:329–341
Sessler A, Stein M (2019) The prague rules: problem detected, but imperfectly solved. Alternatives 5:67–69
Stampa G (2019) The prague rules. Arbitr Int 35(2):221–244
Stutzer H (2017) Settlement facilitation: does the arbitrator have a role? the 'referenteaudienz'—the 'zurich-way' of settling the case. ASA Bull 35(3):589–608
Tan J, Choo I (2019) The prague rules: a soft law solution to due process paranoia?. http://arbitrationblog.kluwerarbitration.com/2019/06/29/the-prague-rules-a-soft-law-solution-to-due-process-paranoia/. Accessed 15 Jan 2020
Tercier P (2016) Entre nous à propos des relations entre arbitres. Revue de l'Arbitrage 4:1053–1078
Tevendale C (2019) Are the prague rules the answer?. https://globalarbitrationreview.com/article/1178803/are-the-prague-rules-the-answer. Accessed 22 Mar 2019
van den Berg AJ (2014) Organizing an international arbitration: practice pointers. In: Newman LW, Hill RD (eds) The leading arbitrators' guide to international arbitration, 3rd edn. Juris, New York, pp 415–436
Veeder VV (2014a) Whose arbitration is it anyway—the parties' or the arbitration tribunal's? In: Newman LW, Hill RD (eds) The leading arbitrators' guide to international arbitration, 3rd edn. Juris, New York, pp 87–107
Veeder VV (2014b) Le nouveau règlement 2014 de la LCIA: quelques nouveautés. Revue de l'Arbitrage 1:49–73
Vidak-Gojkovic E, Greenwood L, McIlwrath M (2016) Puppies or kittens? how to better match arbitrators to party expectations. In: Klausegger C, Klein P, Kremslehner F, Petsche A, Pitkowitz N, Power J, Welser I, Zeiler G (eds) Austrian yearbook on international arbitration. Manz, Vienna, C.H. Beck, Munich, Stämpfli, Berne, pp 61–74
Weiller L (2018) Retour sur la liberté de choix des parties à l'épreuve de l'office de l'arbitre. Les Cahiers de l'Arbitrage 2:205–218
Weiss AJ, Klisch EE, Profaizer JR (2017) Techniques and tradeoffs for incorporating cost- and time-saving measures into international arbitration agreements. J Int Arbitr 34(2):257–273
Wilske S (2015) Sanctions against counsel in international arbitration—possible, desirable or conceptual confusion? Contemp Asia Arbitr J 8(2):141–184
Wilske (2017) Work ethics of the international arbitrator, or: the distinction between rendering a service to the parties and being the parties' slave. In: Shaughnessy P, Tund S (eds) The powers and duties of an arbitrator: Liber Amicorum Pierre A. Karrer. Wolters Kluwer, Alphen aan den Rijn, pp 417–424

Paolo Marzolini is a partner of Patocchi & Marzolini (Geneva). He acts as counsel and sits as arbitrator in Switzerland and a number of other jurisdictions under various sets of arbitration rules. He has been involved in several major international arbitrations and his field of expertise includes construction disputes, IP disputes, turnkey contracts, licensing in the pharma industry, State contracts, contracts in the aviation industry, post-M&A disputes, gas price review disputes and banking and finance disputes. He completed his graduate and post-graduate studies in Geneva, Zurich, Pavia and Paris. Marzolini is listed amongst leading arbitration practitioners in various international directories such as Who's Who Legal and Chambers and Partners.

Reflections on the Key Ingredients for Successful Reform of International Commercial Arbitration in the Asia Pacific

Weixia Gu

Abstract Many states have recognised the economic importance of being 'arbitration-friendly', and many have naturally advertised themselves as such. Beyond the catch-phrase lie these questions: What arbitration regimes are sufficiently 'arbitration-friendly'? Looking into the past, is there a standard pathway of arbitration reform in the Asia Pacific? Or are there divergent modes of development? To what degree have political, legal, social, cultural, and other factors influenced a jurisdiction's ability to replicate successful reform patterns? This Chapter looks into the development of arbitration regimes across the Asia Pacific, and aims to reflect on key ingredients for successful arbitration reform in the East. Among the Asia Pacific jurisdictions, some have reached greater success and have attracted many more commercial disputes within and outside the region. Others have been less successful, even with efforts to substantially reform the arbitration laws and institutions. To examine arbitration reform efforts and outcomes of Asia Pacific jurisdictions, this Chapter relies on a hypothetical model of arbitration reform. This model is then tested against the reform pathways undertaken by 12 Asia Pacific jurisdictions for accuracy as a 'formula' for arbitration reform in the region.

1 Introduction

International commercial arbitration has become an important part of modern commerce. Both developed and developing economies in the Asia Pacific are increasingly reliant on and supportive of cross-border arbitration in resolving disputes. States have established laws and institutions regulating arbitration to create a stable arbitration-friendly commercial environment and attract foreign direct investment (FDI), which in turn is expected to promote economic growth. Such an environment typically involves an impartial judiciary that supervises arbitral awards made in its

W. Gu (✉)
Faculty of Law, The University of Hong Kong, Hong Kong Special Administrative Region, Hong Kong, People's Republic of China
e-mail: guweixia@hku.hk

L. Chen and A. Janssen (eds.), *Dispute Resolution in China, Europe and World*,
Ius Gentium: Comparative Perspectives on Law and Justice 79,
https://doi.org/10.1007/978-3-030-42974-4_6

jurisdiction and decides when to recognise and enforce awards from another state.[1] An arbitration-friendly environment would also see the proliferation of arbitration institutions, with market competition promoting further institutional development to attract foreign users.

Efforts by Asia Pacific states to improve their pro-arbitration environment have not been futile. Since 2008, the number of international arbitrations handled by major institutions across the Asia Pacific has overtaken that in the West.[2] Institutions have established themselves in every corner of the region: the Korean Commercial Arbitration Board (KCAB) in Northeast Asia, the Singapore International Arbitration Centre (SIAC) and the Kuala Lumpur Regional Centre for Arbitration (KLRCA) in Southeast Asia, the Australian Centre for International Commercial Arbitration in the Pacific and the China International Economic and Trade Arbitration Commission (CIETAC) in China. The emerging trend of establishing commercial courts, such as those in Singapore and China, shows that states are not only relying on innovation on the part of arbitration institutions; the states are also setting up new institutions with an international bench to better serve the demand of international arbitration, in the areas of arbitral procedural supervision and award recognition and enforcement.

Many states have recognised the economic importance of being 'arbitration-friendly', and many have naturally advertised themselves as such. Beyond the catch-phrase lie these questions: What arbitration regimes are sufficiently 'arbitration-friendly'? Looking into the past, is there a standard pathway of arbitration reform in the Asia Pacific, or are there divergent modes of development? To what degree have political, legal, social, cultural, and other factors influenced a state's ability to replicate successful reform patterns? And looking into the future, how should Asia Pacific jurisdictions compete in the arbitration market among themselves and against leading Western jurisdictions with more established arbitration institutions and jurisdictions (such as London, New York, Paris, Geneva, and Stockholm)? How will the adoption of the United Nations Commission on International Trade Law (UNCITRAL) Model Law on International Commercial Arbitration (hereafter "UNCITRAL Model Law' or 'Model Law') influence the future development of arbitration in the Asia Pacific? To what extent is a pro-arbitration judiciary needed for an arbitration reform to be successful? These questions are what this Chapter tries to explore.

This Chapter looks into the development of arbitration regimes across the Asia Pacific, and aims to reflect on key ingredients for successful arbitration reform in the East. Indeed, the arbitration development paths are different in each jurisdiction, given the diverse economic development across jurisdictions in the Asia Pacific. Some have reached greater success and have attracted many more commercial disputes within and outside the region. Others have been less successful, even with efforts to substantially reform the arbitration laws and institutions.

---

[1]This Chapter uses 'state' in the private international law sense. Thus, the word refers not only to a country (e.g., China or Australia), but also the individual states, provinces or administrative regions making up a country (e.g., the Hong Kong Special Administrative Region of the People's Republic of China or the state of New South Wales of Australia).

[2]Pradhan (2013, p. 407).

To examine arbitration reform efforts and outcomes of Asia Pacific states, this Chapter relies on a hypothetical model of arbitration reform. As will be detailed in Sect. 3 of the Chapter, the model comprises six steps which involve the necessary but by no means sufficient elements of a viable arbitration reform. This model is then tested against the reform pathways undertaken by 12 Asia Pacific jurisdictions for accuracy as a 'formula' for arbitration reform in the region.

These 12 states are: (1) China, (2) Hong Kong, (3) Taiwan, (4) Japan and (5) the Republic of Korea in Northeast Asia; (6) Malaysia, (7) Singapore, (8) the Philippines, (9) Indonesia, (10) Vietnam and (11) India in South and Southeast Asia; and (12) Australia in the Pacific. The role of these states in regional arbitration development is not the only factor of consideration; their importance in regional and global economic development are also accounted for. Indonesia, for example, is economically significant in the Asia Pacific even though it is not active in the development of arbitration.[3] A succinct overview of the arbitration status quo in these 12 states are provided in Sect. 2 below.

2 A Succinct Overview of the States

Despite market reforms in the 1980s, the Chinese government still closely controls China's governance and state-led market economy. Since ad hoc arbitrations are unlawful, all arbitrations (including international commercial arbitrations with a Chinese seat) are administered by arbitral institutions authorised by the Chinese government. In recent years, China's largest arbitration institution, CIETAC, has grown into a remarkable player in the international arbitration market. Much of its success came from Chinese domestic commercial demand and CIETAC's willingness to update institutional rules constantly in line with international standards. City-based arbitration institutions have also flourished, with the Beijing Arbitration Commission (BAC) in Beijing and Shenzhen Court of International Arbitration (SCIA) in Shenzhen becoming flagship institutions nationally and regionally. BAC and SCIA have also pioneered many arbitration innovations by taking advantage of their best local advantages. For example, BAC has been able to assemble the high-profile legal academics from leading law schools in Beijing. On the other hand, SCIA is best known for its international strategy by involving widest-degree of participation in SCIA cases of common law legal professionals in Hong Kong.

Within China is the Hong Kong Special Administrative Region, a semi-autonomous territory. Under the 'One Country, Two Systems' principle, Hong Kong has a capitalist economy and a high degree of autonomy. Hong Kong enjoys extensive legislative powers independent of the Chinese Central Government in Beijing and follows a common law legal tradition. Hong Kong markets itself as a hub for international dispute resolution, especially in relation to commercial or financial disputes. Both ad hoc and institutional arbitrations are available under the Hong Kong

[3]Most of the jurisdictions here are active in arbitration and economic developments.

International Arbitration Centre (HKIAC). With a reputable common law system and rule of law tradition, Hong Kong is always regarded as one of the best arbitral seats in the Far East. Hong Kong's leading arbitration institution, the HKIAC, has earned herself reputation as one of the best in the Asia Pacific.

Officially known as the 'Republic of China', Taiwan is regarded by the Chinese government as part of China. Since most countries do not recognise Taiwan as a sovereign state, while it can adopt entirely or part of the UNCITRAL Model Law into its arbitration regulations, Taiwan cannot accede to the New York Convention on the Recognition and Enforcement of Foreign Arbitral Awards (New York Convention). Taiwan can only incorporate the principles of the New York Convention into its domestic laws. This limits the international accessibility of Taiwan as a favourable arbitral seat.

Japan has a highly-developed economy and is a civil law jurisdiction. Japanese businesses are reputable internationally and are very active in the international commercial scene. However, arbitration is not popular when it comes to resolving cross-border commercial disputes in Japan. Arbitration has remained unpopular despite Japan's adoption of the UNCITRAL Model Law and accession to the New York Convention.

The Republic of Korea (more often referred to as 'South Korea') follows the civil law tradition. An UNCITRAL Model Law jurisdiction and a party to the New York Convention, South Korea has recently revised its laws to make them even more arbitration-friendly and competitive. The KCAB has also had a strong presence in the arbitration market in the Asia Pacific, particularly with respect to commercial disputes involving Korean businesses.

Malaysia, like Hong Kong and Singapore, is a common law jurisdiction. It applies the UNCITRAL Model Law and is a party to the New York Convention. Its government has lately been embroiled in a series of political scandals which have led many to view its politicians as corrupt. Despite the political embeddedness, Malaysia has recently renamed its leading arbitration institution, the KLRCA to the more iconic Asian International Arbitration Center (AIAC) to attract more arbitration businesses.

Singapore is a multi-cultural and multi-racial city-state. Same as Hong Kong, Singapore is a common law jurisdiction. The Singaporean government emphasises the country's political and economic stability. Singapore's economy depends largely on providing services (including dispute resolution services) to businesses from abroad. An UNCITRAL Model Law jurisdiction and a member state to the New York Convention, Singapore's service-reliant economy makes her arbitration system well developed. Singapore's leading arbitration institution, the SIAC, similar to the HKIAC in Hong Kong, is deemed as one of the best in the arbitration market in the Asia Pacific.

The Philippines has a mixed civil and common law system. Even though it signed the New York Convention early on, international commercial arbitration has been slow to develop within the jurisdiction.

Indonesia is strong in its economic development and commercial transactions recently. It is the biggest state in the Association of South East Asian Nations (ASEAN) and is the fourth most populous country in the world. Incompatible with its importance in economic status in the Asia Pacific, however, Indonesia is notorious for its difficulty in enforcing an arbitration award within Indonesia, despite being a party to the New York Convention for quite some years.

India was the seventh state to ratify the New York Convention and adopted the Model Law early on. However, international commercial arbitration has developed slowly. The perception has been that, until recently, Indian courts have been too prone to interfere in arbitration and to refuse to recognise or enforce arbitral awards. There are also long delays in the hearing of cases by the courts, suspected judicial corruption and a lack of judges and lawyers knowledgeable of arbitration. Furthermore, almost all arbitrations in India are ad hoc. There is an absence of established arbitration institutions and professionals specialising in arbitration. Recently, the Indian judiciary has become more arbitration-friendly, and the Indian Parliament has passed a new legislation to streamline the arbitration process.

Vietnam is similarly known for its difficulty when it comes to enforcing foreign arbitral awards. There have been complaints by foreign governments that Vietnam is not meeting its international obligations under the New York Convention. More recently, though, the Vietnamese Ministry of Justice, the Supreme People's Court and the Supreme People's Procuracy have sought to improve the country's track record in relation to the recognition and enforcement of foreign arbitral awards.

Finally, Australia is a federal common law jurisdiction. It is geographically distant from the major finance centres of Asia, Europe and the United States. Australia's International Arbitration Act 1974 has recently been amended to incorporate the 2006 amendments to the UNCITRAL Model Law, which made arbitration procedures more efficient.

3 The Hypothetical Model of Arbitration Reform

The hypothetical model details the steps in which a jurisdiction might follow to transform itself into an arbitration-friendly jurisdiction or a dispute resolution hub in the Asia Pacific.

Step 1: To accede to the New York Convention. Legislation is passed to implement different regimes governing domestic and international arbitration.
Step 2: To adopt the Model Law in its original 1985 version or, more preferably, in its current 2006 amended version (or as much of the latter as a jurisdiction believes it can adopt).
Step 3: To set up national institutions and international centres to administer arbitrations, provide domestic arbitration venues and to ensure that the rules of the arbitration institutions and centres are up to date (and compliant) with international best practices.
Step 4: To establish a corps of judges familiar with arbitration practice to ensure that courts enforce arbitration agreements, do not unduly interfere with the conduct of

arbitrations and enforce arbitral awards in accordance with best practices under the Model Law and the New York Convention.
Step 5: To participate in capacity-building activities (such as workshops, seminars and conferences) to ensure that all stakeholders in the arbitration industry (in-house and external counsels, judges and business persons) are familiar with and supportive of arbitration as a means of dispute resolution.
Step 6: To review consistently legislations relating to arbitration and to review consistently rules of arbitration institutions, so that the jurisdiction remains competitive within the dispute resolution industry.

This 6-step model places emphasis on the adoption of international instruments in the field such as the New York Convention and the UNCITRAL Model Law. Reasons are straightforward. The New York Convention allows a contracting state to recognise and enforce an arbitral award made in another contracting state. While the Convention had only ten signatories in 1958 when it was promulgated, it has now 159 signatories today,[4] making international arbitration a truly global means of dispute resolution.

4 Data and Findings

For Step 1, among the 12 states investigated, as listed in column one in Table 1, all except Taiwan are parties to the New York Convention. Since most states do not recognise Taiwan's sovereignty, Taiwan cannot accede to the New York Convention. Despite this, Taiwanese courts have adhered to the New York Convention principles when it is dealing with the recognition and enforcement of foreign arbitration agreements and foreign arbitral awards.[5] As such, all the 12 states show that acceding to the New York Convention is essential to successful arbitration reform. This is expected, as award enforcement would be difficult outside a jurisdiction without relying on the Convention.

Findings for steps 2–6 are summarised in Table 1.

For column two in Table 1, in spite that only eight of the 12 states have adopted the UNCITRAL Model Law, some are nonetheless heavily influenced by the Model Law. China and Taiwan are two such examples, with their arbitration legislations making substantial reference to the 1985 Model Law provisions. The other two non-Model Law jurisdictions, Indonesia and Vietnam, have divergent positions on the Model Law. Indonesia has no immediate plans to legislate on basis of the Model Law to improve its arbitration regime, but Vietnam is improving its support of international commercial arbitration at the governmental, judicial, institutional and practitioner levels. From the author's perspective, Model Law adoption, in full or in part, actually or in spirit, is not an essential element of arbitration reform, but is nevertheless an

[4] A full list of the 159 contracting states of the New York Convention is available at UNCITRAL (2019).

[5] Li Nigel et al. (2018, pp. 78–79).

Table 1 Arbitration Variables in the Asia Pacific

Jurisdiction (1)	Model law (2)	Institution/centre (3)	Judicial support (4)	Capacity-building (5)	Latest major legislation (6)	Rule of law index 2017–2018[a] (7)	FDI as % of GDP 2017[b] (8)	Kearney FDI confidence index 2018[c] (9)	Ease of doing business 2019[d] (10)	GDP/Capital (US$) 2017[e] (11)
China	No[f]	Yes	Yes	Yes	1995	0.50/75 (41)[g]	1.4	1.76	73.64/46	8827.0
Hong Kong	Yes	Yes	Yes	Yes	2017	0.77/16 (77)	35.8	N/A	84.22/4	46,193.6
Taiwan	No[h]	Yes	Yes[i]	Yes	1998	N/A (63)	2.8[j]	1.5 (2016)	80.90/13	24,318.0 [k]
Japan	Yes	Yes[l]	Yes	Improving[m]	2004	0.79/14 (73)	0.4	1.72	75.65/39	38,428.1
Republic of Korea	Yes	Yes	Yes	Yes	2017	0.72/20 (54)	1.1	1.46	84.14/5	29,742.8
Singapore	Yes	Yes	Yes	Yes	2010	0.80/13 (84)	19.6	1.53	85.24/2	57,714.3
Malaysia	Yes	Yes	Yes	Yes	2005	0.54/53 (47)	3.0	1.65 (2014)	80.60/15	9944.9
Philippines	No	Yes	Yes	Improving[n]	2004[o]	0.47/88 (34)	3.2	N/A	57.68/124	2989.0
Indonesia	No	Yes	No	No	1999	0.52/63 (37)	2.1	1.6 (2014)	67.96/73	3846.9
Vietnam	Yes	Yes	Improving	Improving[p]	2010	0.50/74 (35)	6.3	1.38 (2012)	68.36/69	2343.1

(continued)

Table 1 (continued)

Jurisdiction (1)	Model law (2)	Institution/centre (3)	Judicial support (4)	Capacity-building (5)	Latest major legislation (6)	Rule of law index 2017–2018[a] (7)	FDI as % of GDP 2017[b] (8)	Kearney FDI confidence index 2018[c] (9)	Ease of doing business 2019[d] (10)	GDP/Capital (US$) 2017[e] (11)
India	Yes	No[q]	Improving	Improving[r]	2015	0.52/62 (40)	1.5	1.56	67.23/77	1939.6
Australia	Yes	Yes	Yes	Yes	2010	0.81/10 (77)	3.4	1.66	80.13/18	53,799.9

[a] World Justice Project (2018). The first number is the jurisdiction's overall score, and the second number is its overall ranking
[b] The World Bank (2019b)
[c] Laudicina et al. (2018)
[d] The World Bank (2019a). The first number is the jurisdiction's ease of doing business score, and the second number is its overall ranking. The ease of doing business score indicates 'an economy's position to the best regulatory practice'. It is previously known as the 'distance to frontier' score
[e] The World Bank (2019c)
[f] The Model Law is however used as a guiding reference to modernise the Chinese arbitration regime
[g] The number in brackets is the jurisdiction's score in the Corruption Perception Index for 2017: Transparency International (2018)
[h] Many provisions of the 1998 Arbitration Act are influenced by the Model Law despite the latter's non-adoption
[i] But as a result of the distinction between *zhi xing li* (enforceability) and *ji pan li* (*res judicata*) drawn by the Supreme Court, mainland China awards may not be recognised as giving rise to *res judicata* in Taiwan and may be subject to substantive scrutiny by courts
[j] FDI inward flow as percentage of gross fixed capital formation. See UNCTAD (2018)
[k] Directorate-General of Budget, Accounting and Statistics, Executive Yuan, Republic of China (2018)
[l] The caseload of Japanese arbitration institutions remains low
[m] Despite some efforts to build capacity, public awareness of arbitration remains limited
[n] Public awareness of arbitration remains limited, and arbitration practitioners need to be better trained to mitigate the effect of a litigious culture
[o] Implementing Rules and Regulations issued by the Department of Justice in 2009
[p] Capacity-building is still lacking among judges and lawyers
[q] There are very few arbitration institutions and arbitration in India are mainly ad hoc
[r] Capacity-building is significantly lacking among judges and lawyers

important one. It has a signalling effect, which allows outsiders to observe that a state is considering internationalisation of its regulatory framework by using the Model Law as a legislative guide.

The third column in Table 1 indicates whether arbitration institutions or centres have been established in a given state. Except India, where the vast majority of arbitration cases are ad hoc, all the other jurisdictions have developed either arbitration institutions or centres or both. 'Yes' and 'no' tells only part of the story. China has over 200 arbitration institutions, and on the other hand, excludes ad hoc arbitration practice exception those taking place in the Free Trade Zone and arising between wholly foreign-owned enterprises.[6] The high number of institutions, however, suggests also a mixed bag of arbitral quality and market competitiveness. Only leading Chinese arbitration institutions such as CIETAC, BAC, SCIA and Shanghai International Arbitration Center (SHIAC) have gained international recognition and garnered a sizeable international arbitration caseload. Outside China, the HKIAC in Hong Kong and the SIAC in Singapore have been very successful in attracting international cases, even outside the Asia Pacific. The KCAB in South Korea is picking up quickly these years too. Others, such as the Japan Commercial Arbitration Association (JCAA) in Tokyo, have been less successful.

The comparative analysis in column three in Table 1 shows that establishing at least one leading national arbitration institution or centre is essential. It has been pointed out that 'ad hoc arbitration [should] become the exception rather than the rule in India' for arbitration to thrive.[7] The role of institutions is crucial to arbitration developments as they develop rules governing the conduct of arbitrations, offer training for potential arbitrators and improve the quality of existing arbitrators. Institutions also provide a platform on which private sector initiatives at reforming arbitration can be coordinated, partially through manipulating market competition. This is evident in larger states, such as China, where market demand and competition are driving much of China's arbitration reforms.[8]

The fourth column in Table 1 looks at the judiciary. Except Indonesia, where award enforcement is usually slow and difficult, all other jurisdictions have varying degrees of supportive judiciaries. Some states such as China and Vietnam create separate judicial procedures to review arbitration cases and are seen as in the active progress of providing a pro-arbitration judicial environment, particularly with respect to the recognition and enforcement of foreign awards. This step is thus universally seen as essential to a successful arbitration reform.

Efforts to build arbitration capacity is the focus of the fifth column in Table 1. While arbitration institutions and other non-state organisations in all 12 investigated states hold conferences or run workshops regularly, efforts in Japan, Philippines, Vietnam and India could be increased with regard to the public awareness of arbitration as a popular means of resolving disputes, especially cross-border disputes.

---

[6]Gu (2018b, p. 665).

[7]Aragaki (2018, pp. 221–250).

[8]Gu (2017, pp. 809–810).

Japan, which has one of the world's most developed business communities, is surprisingly found to be very deficient in the arbitration capacity-building within its own nation. It is expected that Japan should significantly enhance its efforts in the field. Since this aspect is widespread across the 12 Asia Pacific states, capacity-building is arguably classified as a highly recommended element to a successful arbitration reform.

The sixth column in Table 1 lists the year the latest major arbitration legislation was passed or reformed. In the last decade, only six states have had a significant legislative reform in arbitration. Some of these states (Hong Kong, South Korea, Singapore and Australia) are few of the most active and arbitration-friendly jurisdictions in the Asia Pacific. Vietnam and India, which also had recent amendments to their arbitration laws, are actively improving their support of arbitration. China, on the other hand, has a flourishing arbitration market, despite having an arbitration law that has not been substantively amended since 1995. The same is observed in Malaysia and Taiwan. As such, active amendment of arbitration laws seems not to be an essential element of arbitration reform, but states that do periodically review their arbitration legislation, such as Hong Kong, Singapore, South Korea and Australia, remain most competitive at the arbitration development forefront and are able to attract most of the foreign users of arbitration outside their own jurisdiction. Ensuring that arbitration legislation is up to date is therefore a highly recommended element of successful arbitration reform.

The seventh column in Table 1 sets out the Rule of Law Index (ROLI) score of the 12 states for 2017–2018. The World Justice Project (WJP) does not define 'rule of law', but instead relies on substantive measures such as governance accountability, respect for fundamental rights and access to justice. The higher a state's ROLI score, the more likely the state adheres to the rule of law. The ROLI score is checked against the state's 2017 score in the Corruption Perception Index (CPI). The higher the score, the less corrupt a country is perceived to be. States with a strong international arbitration culture show divergent scores in ROLI and CPI. Singapore has the highest score (ROLI: 0.80; CPI: 84), while China has the lowest (ROLI: 0.50; CPI: 41). Japan has a high score (ROLI: 0.79; CPI: 73), similar to that of Hong Kong (ROLI: 0.77; CPI: 77), but Japan does not have a strong culture of international commercial arbitration and is much deficient in capacity building of arbitration.

Interestingly, weak rule of law does not seem to prevent a jurisdiction from developing a vibrant international commercial arbitration scene, as what has been manifested by China. It seems that what is crucial is rather the support of a judiciary that consistently recognises and enforces arbitration agreements and awards. However, judicial corruption may motivate the establishment of specialist courts and judges to deal with international commercial arbitration cases to mitigate the effect of corruption within the judicial ranks.[9] China and Vietnam have both developed themselves in the track of specialist judicial procedures and judges to cater to arbitration cases.

Lastly, the eighth column in Table 1 shows the FDI in a state as a percentage of Gross Domestic Product (GDP) in 2017. At the time of writing this Chapter, these

[9]Reyes and Gu (2018, p. 288).

are the most recent figures available from the World Bank. The ninth column sets out a state's score on the 2018 Kearney FDI Confidence Index, which is 'an annual survey of global business executives that ranks which markets are likely to attract the most investment in the next three years'. These figures show no clear pattern. Indeed, it is difficult to draw a causal link relationship between proportion of FDI to GDP and the arbitration caseload a jurisdiction receives from foreign entities. The same can be said of ease of doing business and GDP per capita, simply due to the numerous factors that may influence these indicators. There is also difficulty in preventing reverse causality between arbitration activity and economic indicators.

5 Pathways of Reform

Asia Pacific jurisdictions have adopted multiple pathways of reforming their arbitration regimes. This section concludes whether there is discernible pattern among these reforms. A typical reform pathway is set out as follows:

Stage 1: The provisions of the Model Law are considered, and parts of the Model Law may be implemented as part of the national arbitration law. The judiciary is also likely to actively intervene in arbitral processes when enforcing the new national arbitration law. This step also sees early establishment of private arbitration institutions, with capacity-building activities such as workshops and seminars on arbitration. These early institutions will only see a small caseload.
Stage 2: The judiciary will exercise greater restraint and intervene less in arbitral processes. In the private market, the number of arbitration institutions and their caseload will continue to grow, with more refined capacity-building activities and more developed institutional rules.
Stage 3: The regimes governing domestic and international arbitration become more similar, and more of the 2006 version of the Model Law is incorporated into arbitration legislation. The judiciary will establish regional reputation for enforcing arbitral agreements and recognising and enforcing arbitral awards. Domestic competition between arbitral institutions get more intensive amid greater caseloads. Capacity-building activities are accentuated and offered to those outside of the jurisdiction.
Stage 4: More elements to streamline the arbitration process, such as emergency arbitration and third party funding, are introduced, often to address market demand. These elements will make arbitration within the jurisdiction more attractive compared to other jurisdictions. Inter-jurisdiction competition is now stressed, as opposed to intra-jurisdiction competition in previous stages. Judicial friendliness towards arbitration is maintained, and capacity-building extends towards jurisdictions with a less entrenched arbitration culture.

On basis of the hypothetical model proposed in Sect. 3, and of the pathway discerned above, arbitration development in the 12 states are classified and summarised as follows:

- Indonesia is at Stage 1;
- Vietnam is transitioning from Stage 1 to 2;
- The Philippines and India are at Stage 2;
- China (though not competitive from a legislative viewpoint), Japan (though not competitive in terms of arbitral institutions and culture) and Taiwan (though neither competitive from a legislative nor an institutional viewpoint) are in transition from Stage 2 to 3;
- South Korea, Malaysia, and Australia are at Stage 3 (albeit South Korea is in active transition from Stage 3 to 4; and Malaysia is close to the active transition from Stage 3 to 4);
- Hong Kong and Singapore are in Stage 4.

5.1 China

Despite market reforms in the 1980s, the Chinese government still closely controls China's governance and state-led market economy. However, local arbitration institutions have grown rapidly in the 1990s.[10] Ad hoc awards are enforced, but only if they were made outside mainland China.[11] Consequently, all arbitrations (including international commercial arbitrations with a Chinese seat) are administered by arbitral institutions authorised by the Chinese government. Foreign awards are enforced. The unique 'pre-reporting system' set up by the Supreme People's Court (SPC) in effect debars lower court from refusing to recognise or enforce foreign or foreign-related awards without the confirmation of the SPC.[12]

Much of the driving force behind China's arbitration reform is top-down. An example of this is the requirement that arbitrations be institutional. However, in recent years, China's CIETAC has grown into a remarkable player in the international arbitration market. Much of its success came from its commercial demand and institutional rules that are constantly in development to attract more cases. City-based arbitration institutions have also flourished, with the BAC and SCIA becoming flagship institutions nationally and regionally. The synthesis of top-down control and bottom-up market competition-driven arbitration reforms allows both political ideology and economic forces to contribute to Chinese international commercial arbitration development. Indeed, bottom-up market forces have overtaken top-down regulation in the arbitration reform.

---

[10] Gu (2018a, p. 21).

[11] Including Hong Kong, Macau, and Taiwan awards.

[12] Gu (2017, p. 807).

5.2 *Hong Kong and Singapore*

Both Hong Kong and Singapore's economy depends largely on providing services (including dispute resolution services) to businesses from abroad. Strict control of arbitration reform, such as that in China, may well not be suitable in Hong Kong and Singapore, as it will drive businesses away from these financial hubs. Rather, both jurisdictions have adopted a liberal, open and market-based pathway to arbitration reform. They are proactive in adopting international instruments like the New York Convention and the Model Law. The Singapore and Hong Kong governments have encouraged arbitration by all parties, including those that have little or no connection with the jurisdictions. The respective judiciaries are open to all forms of arbitration, ad hoc or institutional, and consistently recognise and enforce awards. Cases for the recognition and enforcement of arbitral awards go to a single court, to be dealt with by specialist judge(s) who oversee arbitration cases.

Almost everything is possible in relation to arbitration in Hong Kong and Singapore, subject to issues of due process and save for the rare case when a question of public policy arises. The regulatory frameworks in both jurisdictions are kept minimalist to stay as close with international standards as possible. Other items are left to be dealt with in accordance with the principle of party autonomy.

Despite the stark similarities, Singapore's reform pathway has taken a top-down approach, with the government taking a leading role while being conscious of the views of the business sector and practitioners.[13] Hong Kong's reform pathway is largely bottom-up and driven by the business and financial community.[14] Regardless, the approach to reform does not seem to have made a significant difference to the impressions on Hong Kong and Singapore as leading dispute resolution centres in the Asia Pacific.

5.3 *Republic of Korea (South Korea)*

A 2006 Model Law jurisdiction and a party to the New York Convention, South Korea has recently revised its laws to make them even more arbitration-friendly. Reforms in South Korea have made sure that its leading arbitration institution, the KCAB is, and is perceived to be, separate from the South Korean government and the judiciary. The Arbitration Industry Promotion Act (AIPA) was also recently passed to develop the human resources and facilities to move South Korea towards becoming a preferred seat of international arbitration.[15]

The approach towards reform taken by South Korea was much similar to that of Singapore. It adopted a top-down approach while accounting for the views of the

[13]Chan (2018, p. 159).

[14]Ali (2018, p. 55).

[15]Kim (2018, p. 118).

judiciary, the legislature and 'key stakeholders'.[16] While South Korea and Singapore are on the advanced stages of arbitration reform in the Asia Pacific and have both adopted a top-down approach to reforms, it is premature to conclude from this that the top-down approach is the most preferred way to move Asia Pacific jurisdictions into more advanced stages of arbitration development.

5.4 Malaysia

Arbitration reform in Malaysia has been described as 'both top-down and bottom-up'.[17] Both the government and institutions have been developing arbitration. The AIAC[18] has been particularly innovative. This is largely attributable to Datuk Professor Sundra Rajoo, the previous director of the AIAC, who was described to be 'the man responsible for re-branding KLRCA and putting it on the global map'.[19] This not only demonstrates the role of institutions in Malaysia, but also shows that arbitration in a jurisdiction can be galvanised through the dynamism of an individual.

Despite being a jurisdiction with a majority of Muslim population, religion generally and Islam in particular have not majorly affected the development of commercial arbitration. Where Islam seems to be relevant is the i-Arbitration Rules created and administered by the AIAC, which is a modified version of the UNCITRAL Arbitration Rules that is sharia-compliant and thereby appropriate for the resolution of commercial disputes in accordance with Islamic principles.[20]

Surprisingly, Malaysia's low scores on corruption have not prevented the AIAC from building its reputation as a regional and international arbitration hub. It is not yet on par with HKIAC and SIAC, but it is making great strides. The Malaysian judiciary has recently been less willing to intervene in arbitral proceedings and are more willing to uphold party autonomy and recognising and enforcing foreign awards.[21] Evaluating the effect of corruption and the perception of corruption requires more nuance. For example, where the judiciary is not tainted by corruption and the perception of corruption is limited, arbitration reforms may still not be successful. Where judicial corruption exists (as in Indonesia and India), arbitration reform may be more problematic.

---

[16]Kim (2018, p. 120).

[17]Lam (2018, p. 139).

[18]The KLRCA was renamed in 2018 into the AIAC.

[19]Lam (2018, p. 125).

[20]Reyes and Gu (2018, p. 289).

[21]Lam (2018, pp. 129–138).

5.5 *Taiwan, Japan and Australia*

Despite putting much effort into reforming arbitration laws and institutions, Taiwan, Japan and Australia seem to be less successful in marketing their arbitration internationally, for this or that reason.

In Taiwan, the Legislative Yuan is active in making Taiwan arbitration-friendly. For instance, the Arbitration Act of 1998 was recently amended to clarify that foreign arbitral awards are binding and should therefore be enforceable and enjoy *res judicata* effect. Taiwan's impediment in arbitration reform is political. Since most countries do not recognise Taiwan as a sovereign state, while it can adopt entirely or part of the Model Law and New York Convention into its arbitration regulations, Taiwan cannot accede to the New York Convention. The non-accession of the New York Convention thus poses actual obstacles.

More subtly, Taiwan courts run to the problem of how to treat awards from mainland China. Foreign awards are recognised consistently under the Arbitration Act 1998. Awards from Hong Kong and Macau are governed by the Laws and Regulations Regarding Hong Kong & Macau Affairs (LRR), which allows Hong Kong and Macau awards to be recognised in the same way foreign arbitral awards are recognised under the Arbitration Act (i.e. having the same effect as Taiwanese judgments). Mainland Chinese awards are governed by the Act Governing Relations between the People of the Taiwan Area and the Mainland Area (AGR), but such awards are not enjoying *res judicata* effect in Taiwan. Any legislative efforts to allow mainland Chinese awards to be recognised in the same treatment as foreign arbitral awards (or Hong Kong and Macau awards) will be subject to political considerations. Perhaps the commercial pressure brought on by the increasing number of joint ventures between Taiwanese and mainland Chinese entities will lower the barrier for legislative action.

Japan has a highly-developed economy. However, arbitration has remained unpopular despite Japan's adoption of the Model Law, accession to the New York Convention and arbitration-friendly judiciary. Japan is thus a case study demonstrating that mere institutional and legislative reforms are necessary or highly recommended but insufficient elements of arbitration reform; cultural attitudes and capacity-building efforts must also be seriously counted. Japan is adjudication-adverse.[22] It is part of the Japanese culture that disputes be resolved as amicably as possible, and where adjudication is necessary, litigation is preferred over arbitration as the former is inexpensive, efficient and reliable. Arbitration in Japan also suffers from the lack of experienced Japanese arbitrators.

It has further been suggested that the issue here lies with the lack of capacity-building in Japan's arbitration community. Japan's leading arbitration institution, the JCAA, tends to be more hands off and lay-back in reaching out for arbitration cases. JCAA is reluctant in seeking new directions in the market, and would rather follow the footsteps of arbitration developments in other jurisdictions.[23]

---

[22]Teramura and Nottage (2018, p. 104).

[23]Teramura and Nottage (2018, p. 100).

Australia follows Japan in that it lacks 'traction'.[24] Australia is a federal common law jurisdiction. The Australia International Arbitration Act 1974 has recently been amended to incorporate the 2006 amendments to the Model Law, which made arbitration procedures more efficient. The country is geographically distant from the major finance centres of Asia, Europe and the United States, but its geographical isolation is unlikely to be the sole reason for its relatively less successful arbitration developments as compared to Hong Kong, Singapore, and even South Korea. Federal and state governments are consistently supportive of arbitration.[25]

What might be the cause of Australia's lack of arbitration caseload? Some have argued about the over-judicialisation of arbitration, but Trakman dismissed this as overstated.[26] However, there is nonetheless a perception of judicialisation in Australia. Arbitrations too often try to replicate court processes and reflect the issues normally associated with litigation. Beyond perception, however, Trakman suggested that the confidentiality of arbitration and the neutrality of arbitrators have been challenged in court, and these have limited the development of arbitration.[27] The cost and time involved in enforcing awards in domestic jurisdictions have also harmed the reputation of arbitration in Australia.[28] Counsels advising corporate clients are generally more familiar with litigation and are unaware of the savings in cost and time of arbitration compared to litigation.[29]

5.6 *Indonesia, the Philippines, India and Vietnam*

These four jurisdictions, out of the 12 under investigation, have the lowest GDP per capita and the lowest scores in the ROLI. The ease of doing business scores of the four jurisdictions are also low. Despite this, these jurisdictions score well in terms of the Kearney FDI Confidence Index compared to the rest of the group. FDI as a percentage of GDP also indicates that the four jurisdictions fare well in the area of FDI confidence.

Indonesia is strong in its economic development and commercial transactions. Despite having a large Muslim population, religion has little effect on arbitration in Indonesia. Indonesia is notorious for recognition and enforcement of a foreign arbitral award, despite being a party to the New York Convention. However, Indonesia is only at Stage 1 of the reform pathway. It is unlikely, according to leading scholars, that Indonesia will move on to higher stages in the near future. Procedures for the recognition and enforcement of awards remain cumbersome, and 'public policy' may

[24]Teramura and Nottage (2018, p. 108).

[25]Trakman (2018, p. 276).

[26]Trakman (2018, pp. 276–277).

[27]Trakman (2018, p. 276).

[28]Trakman (2018, p. 276).

[29]Trakman (2018, p. 277).

have to be defined in a very rigid Indonesian-oriented manner.[30] Regional competition coming from Singapore and other proximate jurisdictions such as Malaysia is also undermining local developments. 'A poor reputation for competence and integrity'[31] on the part of the judiciary also disincentivises foreign and Indonesia businesses from engaging in arbitration in Indonesia. This does not only concern judicial support of arbitration, but also the perception of impartiality and competence of the judiciary itself as a state institution.

A mixed civil and common law jurisdiction, the Philippines' majority Roman Catholic population does not have a significant effect on how arbitration is received and used in the country. The main challenge the Philippines faces is corruption. Despite the institutional support for arbitration, any progress to a more advanced stage of arbitration reform cannot exist without arbitration being 'insulated from any form of corruption'.[32] Philippine's leading arbitration scholar, Professor Arthur Autea, is cautiously optimistic, noting that cases that have reached the Supreme Court so far have not been involved in corruption.[33] The primary motivation for arbitration to flourish in the Philippines is to alleviate the case backlog of courts. However, lawyers in the Philippines tend to recommend their clients to litigate rather than to arbitrate, which lawyers are unfamiliar with. It is evident that more training and capacity-building work is needed for arbitration to become popular in the Philippines.

India was the seventh state to ratify the New York Convention and adopted the Model Law early on. One of the major problems for arbitration development in India is an absence of established arbitration institutions and professionals specialising in arbitration. Perhaps more urgent is that arbitration institutions should be established to concentrate efforts for capacity-building and training of arbitrators. Most recently, the Indian judiciary has become more arbitration-friendly, and the Indian Parliament has passed a new legislation to streamline the arbitration process. More efforts are needed to increase the public's awareness of arbitration as a means of dispute resolution. Capacity-building is required not only to introduce competition but also to eradicate corruption. It has been noted that as many as 20–50% of Indian judges have received bribes',[34] and it can be reasonably speculated that corruption affects arbitration as well given that retired judges constitute a sizeable number of ad hoc arbitrators.[35] Judicialisation of arbitration is also an issue in India, but the focus is on the attitude with which one approaches arbitration. Arbitration is often thought of in India as a war to achieve victory in one's case or to exhaust the other party's resources by pursuing a hefty remedy.

Vietnam is similarly known for its difficulty when it comes to enforcing foreign arbitral awards. There have been complaints by foreign governments that Vietnam is not meeting its international obligations under the New York Convention. Most

---

[30] Butt (2018, pp. 197–202).

[31] Butt (2018, p. 193).

[32] Autea (2018, p. 187).

[33] Autea (2018, p. 187).

[34] Aragaki (2018, p. 242).

[35] Aragaki (2018, p. 242).

recently, though, the Vietnamese Ministry of Justice, the Supreme People's Court and the Supreme People's Procuracy in Vietnam have sought to improve the country's track record in relation to the recognition and enforcement of foreign arbitral awards. Many awards were being set aside by courts before 2015, but the courts have not set aside any award in 2015.[36] The 2010 Law on Commercial Arbitration (LCA) has also increased the caseload at the Vietnam International Arbitration Center (VIAC). While Vietnam has not adopted the Model Law, the LCA clearly took inspiration from the Model Law. There have been clear efforts in making Vietnam more arbitration-friendly, but it remains to be seen how judges in Vietnam will decide when to recognise and enforce foreign awards. Interestingly, political factors have not played much role in Vietnam. Being a socialist state, although it is ideologically similar to China, Vietnam has not adopted a controlled approach to arbitration reform as witnessed in China. Ad hoc arbitration, for example, is recognised. This might suggest that China can loosen its grip over ad hoc arbitration, and that whether ad hoc arbitration is recognised has little or no bearing on exercising political control over the arbitration market.

5.7 *Elements of Reform*

The particulars and challenges of the 12 jurisdictions are examined above. It appears that there are a few essential elements for arbitration reform to succeed.

First, a jurisdiction must accede to the New York Convention, thus allowing its arbitration awards to be recognised and enforced in foreign jurisdictions.

Second, a jurisdiction must have an arbitration-friendly judiciary with judges who are well versed in the best practices of the Model Law and the New York Convention.

Third, an arbitration community consisting of arbitrators, legal practitioners, business people and academics familiar with domestic and international arbitration is needed. Even for jurisdictions that adopt a top-down approach to reform, such as Singapore, consultation of the arbitration community is indispensable.

Other elements are not essential, but nonetheless highly recommended. To name a few, a jurisdiction must first have a sufficient volume of commercial activity that involves capacity-building, training workshops and conferences. This commercial activity should also be able to justify the expenses incurred in establishing new arbitration infrastructure.

Adopting the Model Law is not strictly necessary, but many jurisdictions tend to adopt legislation that reflects the principles of the Model Law or at least contemplate the Model Law as legislative guide during its drafting process. The most successful arbitral jurisdiction in the Asia Pacific, i.e. Hong Kong and Singapore, have closely and carefully mirrored the Model Law development.

[36]Dang (2018, pp. 213–214).

Establishing at least one national institution to administer arbitrations is also highly recommended, but the institution must be dynamic and innovative, especially if the jurisdiction aims to advance to Stage 4 from Stage 3 of the reform pathway. The rule of law is also highly recommended.

It is also observed that other factors do not have much effect on the development of arbitration. Indonesia, Malaysia and the Philippines have demonstrated that religion plays minimal role in affecting how a commercial arbitration regime is to be designed. Federal or unitary state system also plays little to no role, as Australia has shown. Cultural and ethnic diversity also probably plays no role.

Political considerations are significant in Taiwan and China, where ideology has limited the mode of and tools available for reform. However, Vietnam shows that ideology *can* co-exist with arbitration reform by playing minimal role in the latter. Perception of corruption is also a factor, especially when the judiciary is implicated in corruption (see the Philippines and India, but contrast with Malaysia).

Lastly, the national characteristics and cultural attitudes towards arbitration also affect arbitration reforms. Tendencies to judicialise arbitration are seen in Australia, India and the Philippines, and Japan has a tendency to avoid adjudicative means of dispute resolution and within the adjudicative means to prefer litigation.

6 Conclusion and Prospects

The more successful Asia Pacific jurisdictions (that is, Hong Kong, Singapore, South Korea, Malaysia and Australia) have followed similar pathways in their arbitration reforms. A reason for this is that they have learnt from each other and from Western jurisdictions that have long established institutions, laws and a culture of international commercial arbitration.

While much has been achieved through mimicry, Asia Pacific jurisdictions are yet to have developed services catered for specialised arbitrations, such as specialised financial, investor-state, anti-monopoly, maritime, construction and labour disputes. Competition within the region would require further development and capacity building in these niches. There are emerging products from Hong Kong, Singapore, South Korea, Malaysia, Australia and China, but they have yet to be competitive in the region or internationally.

The Model Law is also popular among the 12 jurisdictions studied. No doubt the Model Law has contributed to the success of the more successful jurisdictions, and the adoption of which is a highly recommended element in arbitration reform. But how and how much of the Model Law is to be utilised is a matter of debate between 'globalised localism' and 'localised globalism'. The former refers to the phenomenon where local norms are made into global norms and are applied outside of their originating jurisdictions as global norms; the latter refers to the case when global norms are adopted, selectively adopted or adapted to make those norms more compatible with the local context.

While Hong Kong, Singapore, South Korea and Malaysia have adopted the Model Law nearly wholesale, other jurisdictions have a varying degree of adoption. Indonesia, for example, has only limited adoption of the Model Law. Avoiding Indonesia arbitration laws might be one of the reasons Indonesian businesses prefer to arbitrate in other jurisdictions. These seem to be cases of localised globalism. The 12 jurisdictions have selectively implemented the Model Law into their arbitration laws. It seems that limited degrees of localised globalism are not detrimental to arbitration reform. In fact, localised adoption of the Model Law is more beneficial to a jurisdiction than largely ignoring the Model Law in the legislative process.

Beyond legislative reform, judicial support to arbitration and fostering an arbitration community are also crucial to reform success. They are complementary. The former ensures that the judiciary are less eager to intervene in the arbitral process or to actively seek to frustrate the enforcement of awards. The latter ensures that practitioners observe due process standards, thus preventing unneeded judicial supervision. Capacity-building activities ensure that such a community is established and maintained. As we have seen in jurisdictions in more advanced stages of reform, an active arbitration community of scholars and practitioners allow local arbitration norms to influence those of other jurisdictions, which increases competitiveness in the regional commercial arbitration market.

Arbitration reform is always a work in progress. Jurisdictions where an arbitration culture is entrenched and private and public institutions are strong in their support of arbitration serve as role models for other developing jurisdictions in the earlier stages of arbitration development. Arbitration regimes can be improved, or reinforced, in some Asia Pacific jurisdictions to a greater extent than might be required in others, but reform on the whole will change for the better. Ultimately, arbitration reform is a development to which Asia Pacific jurisdictions at whatever stage of economic development can and should aspire.

Acknowledgements The comparative study of ingredients for successful arbitration reform in the Asia Pacific has been financially supported by the Hong Kong Government Research Grants Council General Research Fund (Project Codes 17602218 and 17609419), as well as the Outstanding Young Researcher Award Scheme of The University of Hong Kong. Some of the research leading to this Chapter has been published in Anselmo Reyes and Weixia Gu, The Developing World of Arbitration: A Comparative Study of Arbitration Reform in the Asia Pacific (Oxford: Hart Publishing, an imprint of Bloomsbury Publishing Plc., 2018), pp. 279–300. I thank Professors Lei Chen and Andre Janssen at the City University of Hong Kong for kindly inviting me to this wonderful book project. Jack Lau and Wilson Lui are acknowledged for helpful research assistance. The usual disclaimer applies.

References

Ali S (2018) Balancing procedural and substantive arbitration reforms: advancing international arbitration practice in Hong Kong. In: Reyes A, Gu W (eds) The developing world of arbitration: a comparative study of arbitration reform in the Asia Pacific. Hart Publishing, Oxford, Portland, Oregon, pp 39–66

Aragaki HN (2018) Arbitration reform in India: challenges and opportunities. In: Reyes A, Gu W (eds) The developing world of arbitration: a comparative study of arbitration reform in the Asia Pacific. Hart Publishing, Oxford, Portland, Oregon, pp 221–250

Autea AP (2018) Philippine arbitration reform: fresh breathing space from congested litigation. In: Reyes A, Gu W (eds) The developing world of arbitration: a comparative study of arbitration reform in the Asia Pacific. Hart Publishing, Oxford, Portland, Oregon, pp 163–188

Butt S (2018) Arbitration in Indonesia: largely dependable recognition and enforcement. In: Reyes A, Gu W (eds) The developing world of arbitration: a comparative study of arbitration reform in the Asia Pacific. Hart Publishing, Oxford, Portland, Oregon, pp 189–204

Chan LS (2018) Making arbitration work in Singapore. In: Reyes A, Gu W (eds) The developing world of arbitration: a comparative study of arbitration reform in the Asia Pacific. Hart Publishing, Oxford, Portland, Oregon, pp 143–162

Dang XH (2018) Arbitration law and practice in Vietnam: fundamental changes over the past 20 years and potential for the future. In: Reyes A, Gu W (eds) The developing world of arbitration: a comparative study of arbitration reform in the Asia Pacific. Hart Publishing, Oxford, Portland, Oregon, pp 205–220

Directorate-General of Budget (2018), Accounting and Statistics, Executive Yuan, Republic of China (2018) Statistical yearbook of the Republic of China 2017. https://eng.stat.gov.tw/public/data/dgbas03/bs2/yearbook_eng/Yearbook2017.pdf

Gu W (2017) Piercing the veil of arbitration reform in China: promises, pitfalls, patterns, prognoses and prospects. Am J Comp Law 65(4):799–840

Gu W (2018a) China's arbitration modernisation under judicial efforts and marketisation waves. In: Reyes A, Gu W (eds) The developing world of arbitration: a comparative study of arbitration reform in the Asia Pacific. Hart Publishing, Oxford, Portland, Oregon, pp 17–38

Gu W (2018b) Issues of extra-territorial arbitration in non-foreign-related disputes [无涉外因素争议的域外仲裁问题]. Peking Univ Law J [中外法学] 30(3):651–670

Kim J (2018) Arbitration reform in Korea: at the threshold of a new era. In: Reyes A, Gu W (eds) The developing world of arbitration: a comparative study of arbitration reform in the Asia Pacific. Hart Publishing, Oxford, Portland, Oregon, pp 109–122

Lam KL (2018) Arbitration reform in Malaysia: adopting the model law. In: Reyes A, Gu W (eds) The developing world of arbitration: a comparative study of arbitration reform in the Asia Pacific. Hart Publishing, Oxford, Portland, Oregon, pp 123–142

Laudicina PA, Peterson ER, McCaffrey CR (2018) Investing in a localized world: The 2018 A.T. Kearney Foreign Direct Investment Confidence Index. https://www.atkearney.com/foreign-direct-investment-confidence-index/full-report

Li Nigel NT, Lin AY, Li JCF (2018) Cautious optimism for arbitration reform in Taiwan. In: Reyes A, Gu W (eds) The developing world of arbitration: a comparative study of arbitration reform in the Asia Pacific. Hart Publishing, Oxford, Portland, Oregon, pp 67–82

Pradhan V (2013) The continuing growth of international arbitration in Asia. Arbitration 79(4):407–412

Reyes A, Gu W (eds) (2018) The developing world of arbitration: a comparative study of arbitration reform in the Asia Pacific. Hart Publishing, Oxford, Portland, Oregon

Teramura N, Nottage L (2018) Arbitration reform in Japan: reluctant legislature and institutional challenges. In: Reyes A, Gu W (eds) The developing world of arbitration: a comparative study of arbitration reform in the Asia Pacific. Hart Publishing, Oxford, Portland, Oregon, pp 83–108

The World Bank (2019a) Doing business 2019: Training for reform. http://www.worldbank.org/content/dam/doingBusiness/media/Annual-Reports/English/DB2019-report_web-version.pdf

The World Bank (2019b) Foreign direct investment, net inflows (BoP, current US$). https://data.worldbank.org/indicator/BX.KLT.DINV.WD.GD.ZS

The World Bank (2019c) GDP per capita (current US$). https://data.worldbank.org/indicator/NY.GDP.PCAP.CD

Trakman L (2018) The reform of commercial arbitration in Australia: recent and prospective developments. In: Reyes A, Gu W (eds) The developing world of arbitration: a comparative study of arbitration reform in the Asia Pacific. Hart Publishing, Oxford, Portland, Oregon, pp 251–278
Transparency International (2018) Corruption Perceptions Index 2017. https://www.transparency.org/news/feature/corruption_perceptions_index_2017#table
UNCITRAL (2019) Status: convention on the recognition and enforcement of foreign arbitral awards (New York, 1958). http://www.uncitral.org/uncitral/en/uncitral_texts/arbitration/NYConvention_status.html
UNCTAD (2018) UNCTAD World Investment Report 2018: country fact sheet: Taiwan, Province of China. https://unctad.org/sections/dite_dir/docs/wir2018/wir18_fs_tw_en.pdf
World Justice Project (2018) The World Justice Project Rule of Law Index 2017–2018. https://worldjusticeproject.org/sites/default/files/documents/WJP-ROLI-2018-June-Online-Edition_0.pdf

Weixia Gu is an Associate Professor at the Faculty of Law, The University of Hong Kong. Gu's research interests are in international arbitration and private international law. She is the author, editor of three books and the author of more than 50 referred journal articles and book chapters. Her works have been cited by the Taxes Supreme Court, Hong Kong High Court, and Singapore Law Gazette. Gu is an elected Co-Chair of Law in the Pacific Rim Region Interest Group of the American Society of International Law, an Executive Council Member of the China Society of Private International Law, a Member of the Chartered Institute of Arbitrators, and an Associate of the American Arbitration Association International Center for Dispute Resolution.

Interim Remedies in the People's Republic of China

Fang Zhao and Han Ma

Abstract Despite an absence of a specific definition of interim remedy, the law of the People's Republic of China (PRC) provides for measures similar to interim remedies under English law through a wide range of legislation. This Chapter offers an introduction to the interim measures under PRC law and their respective challenges in practice. Currently, a major problem with the interim measures under PRC law is that the legislation does not provide clear enough guidance on the conditions for granting interim measures. This gives courts significant discretion in deciding whether or not and under what circumstances the application for interim measures should be granted. This results in practices that put the respondents in a relatively disadvantageous position. On the one hand, it is relatively easy for applicants to secure interim measures as long as guarantees are provided; on the other hand, the law does not provide respondents with sufficient remedies for interim measures that are taken wrongfully. In terms of the interim measures' relation to arbitration, PRC law does not empower arbitral tribunals to take interim measures. Any application for interim measures in the process of arbitration must be directed to and reviewed by the PRC court, whereas the court is not necessarily best suited to deciding it. In terms of enforcement of interim measures, a foreign interim measure order, rendered by either a foreign court or a foreign arbitral tribunal, is generally not enforceable in the PRC.

Interim remedy is a common law concept which embodies a variety of orders. The remedies are available to a litigant in the course of litigation, a procedure which enables a party to apply to the court for temporary measures against the other party in advance of a final judgment. If and when granted, an interim remedy will have a mandatory effect, requiring the respondent to comply with the measures as stipulated in the court order. Interim remedies are generally regarded as a powerful tool in civil

F. Zhao (✉) · H. Ma
Hui Zhong Law Firm, Shanghai, People's Republic of China
e-mail: zhaofang@huizhonglaw.com

H. Ma
e-mail: mahan@huizhonglaw.com

L. Chen and A. Janssen (eds.), *Dispute Resolution in China, Europe and World*,
Ius Gentium: Comparative Perspectives on Law and Justice 79,
https://doi.org/10.1007/978-3-030-42974-4_7

litigation proceedings since they substantially impact on the rights and obligations of the parties prior to substantive resolution of the dispute. As such, they act as a strong incentive for early settlement.

Due to its rapid economic development, China is an increasingly important participant in international business transactions. Unavoidably, disputes involving Chinese elements and law are on the rise. It follows that the availability of remedies equivalent to interim remedies under the law of the People's Republic of China (PRC) is of relevance to foreign businessmen and practitioners alike. Further, in so far as such remedy is available in principle, the next question which arises is in what circumstances it is likely to be granted and enforced.

This article is intended to give a concise introduction to the regime of interim remedies under PRC law and their respective challenges in practice.

1 General Categories of Interim Remedies Under Current PRC Law

Under English law, interim remedies cover a wide range of measures such as interim injunction, order for detention or preservation of property, freezing injunction, order for disclosure of information, etc.[1] Despite that PRC law does not have a specific definition of interim remedy, it does indeed provide measures similar to interim remedies under English law through a wide range of legislation.

The concept of interim remedies under PRC law is similar but not altogether the same since it has its own peculiarities. In and of itself the term 'interim remedy' does not appear in Chinese legislation, nor does the legislation contain a clear and unified definition of interim remedies. However, PRC courts have at their disposal recourse to a variety of court orders with similar effects.

Specifically, interim remedies available under the current PRC law can be roughly divided into three categories:

(1) Evidence preservation: Evidence preservation is an order by which the court takes control of certain evidence that might be useful at later stages of the litigation proceeding, for fear that the evidence might be lost as time passes. Evidence preservation is provided under Article 81 of the PRC Civil Procedure Law:

> The parties may apply for the preservation of evidence, and the court may proactively make evidence preservation in the circumstance where it is possible that the evidence would be lost or difficult to acquire in the future.

(2) Property preservation: Property preservation is an order by which the court takes control of the defendant's property or freezes its bank account, in circumstances where the court finds that enforcement of the judgment might become difficult in the future.

[1] Fontaine et al. (2016, p. 702).

(3) Specific performance preservation: Specific performance preservation is an order by which the court mandates that the defendant take or refrain from taking certain actions. Both the property preservation and specific performance preservation are provided under Article 100 of the Civil Procedure Law:

> In the event that enforcement of the judgment would become difficult, or a party might suffer other damages, as a result of the conduct of the other party or other reasons, the court is entitled to preserve the other party's property or order it to take or refrain from taking certain action upon application …

The evidence preservation and property preservation are also made available in arbitration proceedings through the PRC Arbitration Law, under its Article 28 and Article 46 respectively.

Additionally, Article 81 and Article 101 of the Civil Procedure Law provide for circumstances where these remedies can be sought and ordered before litigation or arbitration is commenced. According to Article 81 and Article 101, in the event of emergency and if failure to take interim measures would cause irreparable harm to the applicant, a party may apply for evidence preservation, property preservation or specific performance preservation despite that the litigation or arbitration proceeding has not been commenced. If a pre-litigation or pre-arbitration interim remedy is granted, the applicant would be required to commence litigation in a timely manner, or otherwise the interim remedies would become expired.

The intellectual property laws and maritime laws in PRC provide for more specific rules on the application of these interim measures in their respective fields:

(1) For instance, Article 66 of the Patent Law essentially reiterates the definition of 'specific performance preservation' in patent law disputes context; and
(2) The Special Maritime Procedure Law sets out a chapter for 'maritime injunction', through which courts may force parties to take or refrain from taking certain actions in the event of an emergency when the other party might suffer irreparable harm as a result of a contractual breach or violation of law.

The Civil Procedure Law provides for other interim remedies, such as interim payment order, order for disclosure, etc., but evidence preservation, property preservation and specific performance preservation are the most widely applied interim remedies in the PRC legal system. They constitute the major body of interim remedies system under the PRC law.

2 Historical Developments of Interim Remedies Under PRC Law

The development of interim remedies system under the PRC law expanded over the past decades. Many important mechanisms that exist in the current legislation were not introduced when the Civil Procedure Law was first enacted. They were added brick by brick into the system through subsequent amendments to the Civil Procedure Law and enactment of new legislations.

The first legislation in PRC laws that provided for interim remedies was the Civil Procedure Law (Trial Version), which was enacted in 1982. The law provided for evidence preservation, property preservation and interim payment only, whereas, notably, specific performance preservation was not provided therein. The evidence preservation and property preservation were available only in the process of litigation, and there was not a provision similar to Article 81 or Article 100 of the current Civil Procedure Law that allowed parties to seek these preservations before the commencement of litigation.

The Civil Procedure Law (Trial Version) was in effect for nine years until the formal Civil Procedure Law was enacted in 1991. The Civil Procedure Law (1991) introduced pre-litigation property preservation, while specific performance preservation was still missing and evidence preservation remained available only in the process of, rather than before, litigation.

Specific performance preservation first appeared in the special laws. In 1999, the Special Maritime Procedure Law was enacted, which provided for maritime injunction that allowed courts to order that a party take or refrain from taking specific actions. Similarly, major intellectual property laws, including the PRC Patent Law, Trademark Law and Copyright Law, introduced property preservation and specific performance preservation in their respective fields when they were respectively amended in 2000 and 2001. These amendments were resulted from China's commitments in joining the Agreement on Trade-related Aspects of Intellectual Property Rights (TRIPS).

Specific performance preservation as a general interim measure was introduced by a major amendment to the Civil Procedure Law in 2012. The amendment provided that both evidence preservation and specific performance preservation were available to parties before commencement of litigation. It could be said that the foundation of the current framework of interim remedies in PRC has been formed since the 2012 amendment to the Civil Procedure Law.

3 Challenges of Interim Measures in General

3.1 Ambiguity of the Law

A major problem with the interim measures under the PRC law is that the legislation does not provide enough guidance, to either the parties or the court, on the conditions for granting interim measures.

In terms of evidence preservation, the Civil Procedure Law only requires that evidence preservation may be granted where 'it is possible that the evidence would be lost or difficult to acquire in the future'. The law does not specify under what circumstance should the court find that there is such a possibility, nor does it clarify what evidence would be sufficient to prove this possibility. Similarly, in terms of property preservation and specific performance preservation, the Civil Procedure Law provides only that these interim measures may be taken if the court finds that 'enforcement of the judgment would be difficult in the future'. Again, the law does not specify under what circumstance would future enforcement of judgment be made difficult and what evidence would be sufficient to prove such difficulty.

The similar situation is also associated with pre-litigation and pre-arbitration interim remedies, where the law requires that orders for pre-litigation and pre-arbitration preservations may be taken under emergent situations where failure to take these orders would cause irreparable harm to the applicant, but does not specify what would constitute such an emergency and on what basis should the courts find that irreparable harm would be caused if no interim measure is taken.

The generality and abstractness of the law give courts significant discretion in deciding whether or not and under what circumstances the application for interim measures should be granted.[2] Applicants for these interim measures are left with confusion as they do not know what would satisfy the courts' requirements. More importantly, in deciding whether interim measures should be taken, the law itself only requires courts to take into consideration the interest of the applicant of the interim measures, whereas courts are not required to balance the interest of the respondent. On its surface, in deciding whether interim measures should be ordered, courts need not take into consideration whether these interim measures would cause harm to the respondent's business operation.

As will be introduced in the following paragraphs, if the interim measures taken by the court is wrongful and causes harm to the respondent, the respondent's remedy comes only after the litigation is over. The respondent would be entitled to commence an independent litigation against the applicant for its loss. As a result, before taking interim measures, most courts would require the applicant to provide a guarantee to ensure that the respondent would be compensated if the interim measures are wrongful. The guarantee can be in the form of deposit of funds into the court's account, which is generally required to be equivalent to 30% of the value of the preserved property, or an insurance where the insurance company agrees to compensate for the potential damages caused by the property preservation. Collaterals such as real estates are also acceptable.[3]

The problem is that, in reality, so long as the requested guarantees are provided, most courts would unconditionally sustain applications for property preservation without venture to review whether there is indeed a perceived difficulty in enforcement in the future or whether an emergency indeed exists,[4] which are the substantive conditions for interim remedies provided by the law. This is especially prevalent in property preservations. When receiving an application for property reservation, most PRC courts would make only formality review, and whether or not the property preservation is to be granted often entirely depends on whether guarantee is provided.

[2]Sun (2014, p. 121).

[3]Chen (2017, p. 48).

[4]Yang et al. (2013, p. 48).

In many cases, courts have refused to grant property preservation on the sole basis that the applicant failed to provide guarantee.

Based on a research on cases involving interim measures in Wenzhou courts, during January 2010 and September 2012, there were 7275 cases in which the courts granted preservation orders. In 97.71% of these cases, the applicants provided guarantees for their applications upon the courts' requests.[5] However, under Article 100 of the Civil Procedure Law, guarantee is not a mandatory requirement for property preservation in the process of litigation.

One of the few restraints that courts are obliged to take into consideration to balance the respondent's interest is provided in the Supreme People's Court's Regulations on Several Issues Concerning the People's Court's Adjudication of Property Preservation Cases, which is a judicial interpretation announced by the Supreme People's Court in November 2016. Article 13 of the judicial interpretation provides that, in the event that the respondent has multiple properties, the court should choose to preserve the property that has the least impact on the respondent's production and business, provided that the purpose of property preservation would still be achieved. On its surface, however, Article 13 apparently does not require courts to refrain from ordering property preservation even if such order might adversely affect the respondent's production and business. Moreover, if Article 13 is read conversely, its implication would seem to be that, if the respondent has only one property available for preservation, then it should be preserved regardless of whether the respondent's business operation would be affected.

Another disadvantageous aspect on the part of the respondent is that of counter-guarantee. Under Article 104 of the Civil Procedure Law, if the respondent provides counter-guarantee to the court, then the court should release the preserved property. However, there is a contrast between the availability of guarantees to applicants and the availability of counter-guarantees to respondents. As mentioned in the foregoing paragraphs, when the applicant applies for property preservation, it is usually required to provide guarantee equivalent to about 30% of the preserved property's value, and if the applicant does not have sufficient funds or property, it has the option of engaging an insurance company and have the insurance company provide the guarantee instead. However, in the case of the respondent, in order to release its preserved property, it is generally required that the counter-guarantee shall be equivalent to 100% of the preserved property's value, and insurance companies generally do not provide counter-guarantee. As a result, the respondent's cost for financing is substantially higher than the applicant.

As a result of the foregoing practice, for applicants that are capable of providing guarantees, property preservation has in many cases become a litigation/arbitration strategy available for plaintiffs and claimants to exert pressure on the respondents.[6] Respondents of less economic power thus fall in a disadvantageous situation, as the applicants could readily secure an order to freeze an amount of fund in their bank accounts that is equivalent to the value in dispute at the expense of providing the

[5] Xu and Li (2013, p. 67).

[6] Yang et al. (2013, p. 47).

guarantee. The respondent could suffer years of shortage of funds for as long as the litigation or arbitration continues. It has thus been observed by judges that, as a result of the pressure caused by property preservation, settlement rates are substantially higher (over 85%) in cases where property preservations are successful.[7]

On the other hand, applicants that cannot afford offering their own money and property as guarantee or get a guarantee from a third party would find it difficult to secure property preservation orders against uncooperative respondents, as most courts would become reluctant to take interim measures in the absence of guarantee. In our opinion, the measures adopted by the courts are inconsistent with the original intent of the law, and it is obvious that the rules offered by the Civil Procedure Law neither provide enough guidance to the parties and the courts, nor take sufficient consideration to balance the interests of the parties.

Similar problems caused by the ambiguity of the laws also appear in performance preservation orders, as property preservation and performance preservation share the same statutory basis, namely Article 100 of the Civil Procedure Law. However, the recent years have seen courts taking steady steps to make improvements on these problems, at least in the field of intellectual property rights where the need for interim remedies is substantial. In intellectual property disputes, the courts have gradually established a more systematic and balanced approach to review interim measure applications.

Eli Lilly and Company and Lilly China Research and Development Co., Ltd. v *Huang*,[8] decided in 2013, was the first case that a PRC court has ordered specific performance preservation since it was introduced into the Civil Procedure Law through the amendment in 2012.[9] The case concerned the defendant's alleged infringement of the plaintiff's trade secrets, and the plaintiff filed an application for an order that the defendant shall refrain from further infringing the plaintiff's trade secret rights.

It appeared that the rules in the Civil Procedure Law regarding performance preservation order were considered inadequate since the very beginning. Despite that Article 100 of the Civil Procedure Law does not require the courts to take into consideration the defendant's interest, in deciding on the performance preservation, the court nonetheless took the balanced approach and considered various factors in its ruling, which were not specified by Article 100. Though the court's reasoning was not made explicit in the judgment itself, the judge in charge of the case commented later in an article that, in deciding to take specific performance preservation, he balanced the following five factors: (1) the merits of the applicant's case; (2) whether or not the applicant would suffer irreparable harm if the court fails to grant an interim measure; (3) the balance between the potential damage to the applicant if the application is not granted and the potential damage to the respondent if an interim measure is ordered; (4) the application should be sufficiently specific to be enforceable; and (5) the interim measure sought does not offend public interest.[10]

[7] Wang (2018, para 8).

[8] (2013) Hu Yi Zhong Min Wu (Zhi) Chu Zi No. 119.

[9] China Court (2014).

[10] Tang and Lv (2013, pp. 48–50).

In other cases, the courts were more explicit in advancing its own understanding of the law. For instance, in the case of *Novartis (China) Biomedical Research Co. v He Feng*,[11] the court interpreted Article 101 of the Civil Procedure Law and divided it into a four-steps test: (1) whether the applicant has presented a serious case with reasonable grounds; (2) whether damage caused by the infringement would be irreparable; (3) whether the preservation would cause imbalance of the parties' interest; and (4) whether the application is urgent. As can be seen from the above two cases, the tests adopted by the PRC courts are similar to the common law principle applied in the leading case of *American Cyanamid*.[12]

These lines of practice eventually led the Supreme People's Court to announce a new judicial interpretation. On 12 December 2018, the Supreme People's Court announced the Regulation on the Various Issues Concerning the Application of Laws regarding the Specific Performance Perseveration Order in Intellectual Property Disputes, which provides detailed rules for specific performance preservation in intellectual property disputes. The Regulation made notable expansion to the ambiguous terms in the Civil Procedure Law, by providing for more detailed definition of 'emergency' and 'irreparable harm' referred to in Article 101 of the Civil Procedure Law.[13]

Article 7 of the Regulation further requires that courts must take into consideration the respondent's interest in granting specific performance preservation, as well as other various factors, which reflects the reasoning in *Lily v Huang* and *Novartis v He Feng*:

In reviewing an application for specific performance preservation, the courts should take into consideration the following aspects:

(1) Whether the applicant's application has a factual and legal basis, including whether the validity of the intellectual property right for which it seeks protection is stable;
(2) Whether failure to take the specific performance preservation would cause irreparable harm to the applicant or result in difficulty in enforcement of the judgment;
(3) Whether the damage to the applicant that would be caused by not taking specific performance preservation would exceed the damage to the respondent that would be caused by taking the specific performance preservation; and
(4) Whether the specific performance preservation would offend public interest.

In PRC, the Supreme People's Court's judicial interpretation has binding force on lower courts, which means the Regulation is applicable in all intellectual property dispute cases. It is obvious that parties would benefit significantly from the Regulation as it makes the result of specific performance preservation more predictable, and the courts would now be required to balance the respondent's interest, which is also an improvement.

---

[11](2014) Hu Yi Zhong Min Bao Zi No. 1.

[12]*American Cyanamid v Ethicon* [1975] AC 396.

[13]See Article 6 and Article 10 of the Regulation.

However, it should be noted that the Regulation applies to specific performance preservation in intellectual property disputes only.[14] Theoretically, this does not change the difficulties that the parties would encounter in regular contractual and tort disputes, nor does it change the rules concerning evidence and property preservation. Nonetheless, the insight of the Regulation should have a positive impact on the courts' adjudication in other cases.

3.2 Insufficient Remedies

Under PRC laws, there are generally two remedies in connection with interim measures, one for the court's decision to grant or refrain from granting an interim order, the other for damages caused by wrongfully ordered interim measure, which is mentioned in the foregoing paragraphs. However, each of them has its own deficiencies.

The first remedy is that, in the case of property preservation and specific performance preservation, the Civil Procedure Law requires that the court's decision take the form of a written ruling. If either party is unsatisfied with the decision in the ruling, it may file an application for reconsideration of the decision. This is provided under Article 108 of the Civil Procedure Law.

However, while it is clear that Article 108 applies to property preservation and specific performance preservation, the Civil Procedure Law does not make it explicit that Article 108 applies to evidence preservation as well. In practice, many courts found that they did not have to issue any ruling in either granting or rejecting an application for evidence preservation. The decision is usually recorded in the transcript of a hearing. In the absence of a written ruling, the parties would have difficulty in appealing against the courts' decisions.

Even if reconsideration was available, as is the case with property preservation and specific performance preservation, in practice, the likelihood of overturning the original ruling is relatively low if not at all impossible, because the court that is to review the application for reconsideration would be the same court that rendered the original decision, which is required by a relevant judicial interpretation issued by the Supreme People's Court. Once the court decides to accept or reject an application for interim remedy, the possibility of successfully challenging the decision is usually minimal.

This arrangement might seem rigid, but it is not impossible to understand from a different perspective. In any event, the effect of interim measures is temporary and their purpose is to facilitate the litigation proceeding. Allowing parties to appeal the decision before a higher court might result in collateral and satellite litigation, which is at the cost of efficiency, while efficiency is a value that PRC courts hold in high regard.

[14] See Article 1 of the Regulation. For the purpose of the Regulation, 'intellectual property disputes' refers to the intellectual property and competition disputes as set forth in the Provisions on Causes of Action of Civil Cases.

The second remedy is that, in the event that a preservation order is made wrongfully, and the respondent suffers damage from it, then the respondent may file an independent action against the applicant for the damage. This is provided under Article 105 of the Civil Procedure Law. The problem with this remedy is that, the PRC judicial practice is rather protective of the applicant of the preservation, and it is relatively difficult for the respondent to prove the monetary amount of loss it suffered.

In practice, for instance, claims based on wrongful property preservation are treated as regular tort claims, which means the applicant for property preservation would not be held liable unless it can be proven that the applicant was at fault.[15] According to the Supreme People's Court's judgments in various cases, fault was held in a rather high standard.

For instance, in the case of *Chen Yinggui & Fujian Dongquan Construction Engineering Co. v Ninghua Yonglong Real Estate Development Co.*,[16] Chen Yinggui applied for and secured property preservation against Yonglong Co. in the amount of 16 million RMB, whereas eventually only five million of his claim was sustained by the court. Yonglong Co. sued Chen Yinggui for damages caused by the property preservation. The Supreme People's Court held in the retrial judgment that the fact that the plaintiff's claim is not sustained is not sufficient ground to find that the plaintiff is at fault, and that finding of fault requires it be proven that the plaintiff applied for wrongful property preservation intentionally or with gross negligence. Specifically, the Supreme People's Court held:

> In terms of its legislative purpose, Article 105 of the Civil Procedure Law of the People's Republic of China serves to prevent a party from abusing its litigation rights and unjustly causing harm to the others' legitimate rights and interests. In judicial practice, it is not uncommon that there might be a difference between the applicant's evaluation of its own rights and the People's Court's final judgment, and it is not uncommon that claims that the party finds reasonable are not eventually sustained by the People's Court. To interpret the foregoing laws as providing for strict liability under Article 7 of the Tort Liability Law of the People's Republic of China, meaning that the applicant's losing its lawsuit should in and of itself constitute 'wrongful application' and requiring the applicant to assume liability for compensation for wrongful property preservation under any circumstance, is not consistent with the legislative intent of Article 105 of the Civil Procedure Law of the People's Republic of China. Therefore, 'wrongful application' under the said provision should be understood as referring to not only a difference between the People's Court's judgment and the applicant's litigation claims, which is the objective aspect ..., but also the subjective aspect that the applicant has acted intentionally or with gross negligence.

Therefore, even if assuming the plaintiff loses its entire case and the defendant suffers damage as a result of the interim measures, there is no guarantee under Article 105 that the plaintiff would be compensated.

On the other hand, losses caused by wrongful preservation are difficult to prove. As mentioned above, one of the major concerns on the abuse of interim measures is that freezing the respondent's funds or properties might unjustly affect its production and business operation. Losses of this kind are often circumstantial in their

[15]Xiao and Zhang (2016, p. 40).

[16](2015) Min Shen Zi No. 1147.

nature. For instance, a natural consequence of funds shortage is that the company might encounter difficulty in producing products, signing new deals or keeping its employees, or that the company would have to borrow money from a third party. However, the respondent would find it difficult to prove, on a level of certainty, the extent to which it could have benefited from the unproduced products and new deals, the impact caused by the leaving employees or that the money was borrowed on a justifiable interest rate. For instance, in the case of *Jiangsu Huaian Kangbaite Carpet Co. v Xu Zanyou*,[17] Kanbaite Co. claimed that Xu Zanyou wrongfully applied for property preservation and froze 2.4 million RMB in its bank account, as a result it borrowed money at one per cent monthly interest rate from a third party. The High Court of Jiangsu Province rejected this claim on the basis that the one per cent interest rate was higher than the bank interest rate of the same period, and that Kangbaite Co. has failed to prove that 'the personal loan at an interest rate that was twice the bank loan interest rate was Kangbaite's only way of financing itself', which was a rather substantial burden of proof.

As mentioned in the foregoing paragraphs, in PRC judicial practice, application for property preservation is generally easy. Most courts take only formality review and would sustain the application once guarantee is provided, which puts the respondents in a relatively disadvantageous situation. The element of fault and the difficulties to prove actual loss in wrongful preservation disputes further add to the risk on the respondents' economic well-being. As a result, the respondents' interests are comparatively easy to be affected but difficult to remedy.

In our opinion, the parties' interests would be more balanced if the courts either conduct a more prudent review in deciding whether interim measures should be taken or make it less difficult for respondents to claim for their losses. The current approach shows that courts lay more emphasis on ensuring the plaintiffs' access to the interim remedies and to avoid suppressing litigation.

4 Challenges of Interim Measures in Connection with Arbitration

4.1 Arbitral Tribunals Do Not Have Power to Take Interim Measures

In general, PRC laws are silent on the power of arbitral tribunals to take interim measures. None of the interim measures mentioned above are expressly made available to arbitral tribunals where the seat of the arbitration is the PRC.

On the contrary, the Civil Procedure Law and the Arbitration Law provide that where a party has filed an application for property or evidence preservation in connection with an arbitration, the arbitration institution must transfer the application

[17](2008) Su Min San Zhong Zi No. 0071.

and supporting documents to the relevant court, and whether or not the application will be granted is a matter for that court only. The arbitration institution and tribunal's role in this process is that of merely an emissary. Therefore, where the *lex arbitri* is PRC law, strictly speaking, the tribunal has no power to grant an interim measure that is not supported by the court in accordance with the Civil Procedure Law and the Arbitration Law.

This causes several problems. Compared with the courts, in arbitration cases, the arbitral tribunals are in a better position to decide whether interim measures should be taken, as they obviously have more knowledge of the factual and legal issues of the cases concerned, whereas the courts, being less aware of the merits of the cases, are not necessarily capable of rendering decisions that fit the parties' best interests. On the other hand, one of the most important reasons that parties resort to arbitration is confidentiality, whereas decisions made by PRC courts on property preservation are required to be made public by the law.

From another practical point of view, in PRC judicial practice, communication between arbitral tribunals and the relevant courts is relatively inefficient. The First Intermediate Court of Beijing observed that it usually takes about ten days for an arbitral tribunal to forward an application for interim measures to the relevant court and then for the court to distribute the case to a designated judge.[18] According to Article 100 and Article 101 of the Civil Procedure Law, in emergent situations, interim measures are expected to be taken within 48 h upon the parties filing an application. In cases where parties seek emergent interim orders, they sometimes find themselves better off if they could hand deliver the applications directly to the court rather than through the arbitral institutions.

In terms of enforcement of interim measures, giving the arbitral tribunals power to take interim measures would also benefit the parties, as some jurisdictions, such as Hong Kong, have legislated to allow enforcement of interim measures ordered by foreign arbitral tribunals.[19] This saves the parties from both the procedural burdens of applying for an independent interim order at the place of enforcement. On the other hand, the likelihood of enforcement of an interim order taken by a foreign court is significantly lower.

The PRC courts' and legislators' reluctance to give arbitral tribunals power to order interim remedies is closely connected with their perception of the nature of interim remedies. In the eyes of the PRC courts generally, interim remedies are associated with the idea of 'judicial sovereignty', and the PRC courts' jurisdiction over interim remedies is a matter of public interest. This attitude can be seen in the famous case of *Hemofarm DD, MAG International Trade Holding DD, Suram Media Ltd. v Jinan Yongning Pharmaceutical Co. Ltd.*[20] The case involved an International Chamber of Commerce (ICC) arbitral award that held, among others, that Yongning Co. had breached an arbitration agreement by submitting an application for property preservation before a PRC court, and the arbitral tribunal further held that Yongning

[18]The First Intermediate Court of Beijing (2018).

[19]See Section 61(1) of Hong Kong Arbitration Ordinance (Cap. 609).

[20](2008) Min Si Ta Zi No. 11.

Co. shall be responsible for the losses suffered by the opposing party. The High Court of Shandong Province refused to recognize and enforce the arbitral award, holding that the PRC court had jurisdiction over the property preservation. It is important that the refusal was grounded not only on the basis that the arbitral award was beyond the scope of the arbitration agreement, but also on the basis of public policy violation. The court held that the right to apply for property preservation is one of the most fundamental litigation rights of citizens and legal persons, and that the arbitral award infringed the court's jurisdiction to review the party's application for property preservation, which infringed the judicial sovereignty of China. Specifically, it held that:

> According to Article 5(2)(b) of the New York Convention, the recognition or enforcement of an arbitral award may be refused if the competent authority in the country where the recognition and enforcement is sought finds that the recognition or enforcement of the award would be contrary to the public policy of that country.
>
> First, the arbitral award in this case infringed the People's Court's judicial jurisdiction, and thus damaged the judicial sovereignty of China. Specifically, *(1) the arbitral award adjudicated and decided on the legitimacy of Yongning's application for property preservation to the People's Court, which infringed the People's Court's power to adjudicate the party's application for property preservation*; …
>
> …
>
> Third, recognition and enforcement of the arbitral award is in violation of the fundamental civil procedure legal system of PRC. The Civil Procedure Law is one of the basic laws of our nation, and property preservation is a basic litigation mechanism established by the Civil Procedure Law. In the event that a legitimate civil right or interest is infringed, the citizen or legal person is entitled to bring litigation and apply for property preservation. *The right to apply for property preservation is one of the most fundamental litigation rights of citizens and legal persons.* However, the arbitral award in this case held that Yongning Co.'s application and securing of the property preservation order constituted a breach of contract and was even illegal. This in essence denied a citizen and legal person's right to apply for property preservation. Recognition and enforcement of the award would necessarily cause parties to form the following idea: the People's Court's review of the parties' application for property preservation is not final. Even if the court grants the application for preservation, the arbitral tribunal still has the power to hold that the application for property preservation is illegal, and that the arbitral tribunal has the power to hold the applicant for the property preservation granted by the People's Court liable for compensation. If this would happen, then the property preservation system in our civil procedure will be fundamentally affected.

The rationale applied by the Shandong High Court was controversial, but the decision was later affirmed by the Supreme People's Court, which also determined that the arbitral award violated PRC's judicial sovereignty and should not be enforced. Though this is by far the only case where PRC courts have explicitly connected property preservation order with public interest, *Hemofarm v Yongning* has a significant influence on the interpretation of what constitutes public policy in PRC legal system.

On the other hand, some PRC arbitration institutions have announced arbitrations rules that allow the arbitral tribunal to take interim awards according to foreign laws. For instance:

(1) Article 23 of the Arbitration Rules of China International Economic and Trade Arbitration Commission allows the arbitral tribunal to award interim measures

in accordance with the relevant applicable law or by agreement of the parties. Article 62 of the Arbitration Rules of Beijing Arbitration Commission contains similar provisions.

(2) Articles 18 to 24 of the China (Shanghai) Pilot Free Trade Zone Arbitration Rules, published by Shanghai International Arbitration Center, provides that the arbitral tribunal may take interim measures according to the law of the place where enforcement of the interim measures would be sought.

In cases where PRC is not the seat of arbitration, meaning the proceedings are governed by a foreign law, these rules would effectively circumvent the PRC Civil Procedure Law and the Arbitration Law that require the application for interim measures be transferred to the courts, allowing parties to seek interim orders directly from the tribunals.[21] The presumption is that the parties would seek enforcement of the interim measures in jurisdictions other than the PRC. This is particularly true where the parties have agreed that the Chinese arbitral tribunals conduct arbitration proceedings seated at foreign jurisdictions.

However, in the event that PRC is the seat of arbitration, as is in most cases, it is unclear whether or not the relevant arbitral tribunals would nonetheless have the power to apply a foreign law (the law at the place where enforcement of the interim measures is to be sought) and take interim measures according to the foregoing institutional rules. Since the PRC is the seat of arbitration, the arbitration proceeding is still governed by PRC Civil Procedure Law and the Arbitration Law, which do not give arbitral tribunals power to take interim measures.

4.2 Foreign Interim Measures Cannot Be Enforced in PRC

Notwithstanding that the equivalent of interim remedies exists in PRC legislation and that applications for an interim measure have in practice been granted in a variety of industries, it is not altogether common practice for the PRC court to enforce foreign interim orders. The court's position does not change regardless of whether the interim measure was rendered by a foreign court or by a foreign arbitral tribunal. Two main concerns stand in the way of such enforcement.

The procedural obstacle is that the enforcement of any interim measure ordered by a foreign court is governed by Article 282 of the Civil Procedure Law. Under this Article, a judgment or order of a foreign court can only be enforced pursuant to a relevant provision of international law or a treaty. In the absence of either, the parties would have to rely on the principle of reciprocity. To date, no provision of international law or a treaty entered into by the PRC requires the PRC court to enforce foreign interim measures.

With regard to the enforcement of interim measures ordered by a foreign arbitral tribunal, the New York Convention presents a similar problem. PRC courts' prevailing

[21] Yang (2017, p. 62).

understanding of the New York Convention is that its recognition and enforcement requirements are limited to final awards. Given the temporary effect and duration of interim measures, it follows that they fall outside of the outer limit of the New York Convention.

In addition to the above, PRC courts are also reluctant to enforce foreign interim measures because of the difficult jurisdictional issues such enforcement gives rise to.

Article 533 of the Supreme People's Court's Interpretation of the Civil Procedure Law takes a rather conservative stance in terms of parallel lawsuits. It allows the PRC courts to exercise jurisdiction over a case regardless of whether or not a foreign court has seized jurisdiction over the same case. This makes it particularly difficult to convince PRC courts to enforce a foreign anti-suit injunction, which de facto would prevent them from exercising jurisdiction over the case. This position is integral to Chinese jurisprudence and is explicit in the recent leading case of *Huatai Insurance Co. Ltd. v Clipper Chartering SA*.[22]

Huatai v Clipper concerned a bill of lading dispute, in which Clipper obtained an anti-suit injunction from the Hong Kong High Court. Upon Huatai's application, on 21 July 2017, the Wuhan Maritime Court issued an 'anti-anti-suit injunction' ordering Clipper to withdraw the anti-suit injunction from the Hong Kong High Court on the basis that the maritime court had full jurisdiction over the case.

However, the position as set out above does not foreclose other avenues. In the face of judicial reluctance to enforce a foreign anti-suit injunction, parties seeking to prevent parallel proceedings may elect to follow an alternative route, that is raising a jurisdictional challenge based on other grounds but with similar effects.

PRC courts have historically applied the *forum non vonveniens* doctrine as a ground on which to decline the exercise of their own jurisdiction over foreign-related cases. As early as 2005, the Supreme People's Court published the Meeting Minutes on the Second National Conference on Adjudication of Foreign-related Commercial and Maritime Cases, of which Article 11 provides that courts may refuse to hear a plaintiff's claim based on the doctrine of *forum non vonveniens*. The Meeting Minutes sets out the factors to be considered by the court when deciding whether or not to do so. These include whether the major facts of the case took place on PRC territory, and whether it is more appropriate for a foreign court to hear the case. The *forum non conveniens* argument has been successful in quite a few cases. Essentially, if a defendant's jurisdictional challenge based on *forum non conveniens* succeeds, the effect will be the same as that of an anti-suit injunction. The doctrine of *forum non conveniens* and anti-suit injunctions, though different, in this context operate like two sides of the same coin.

Despite that the current legislation does not offer an explicit path for recognizing and enforcing foreign interim orders, and that in some circumstances even mechanisms for enforcing foreign judgments have seemed insufficient, one should not feel overly pessimistic. In recent years, PRC courts have demonstrated increased

[22](2017) E No. 72 Xing Bao No. 3.

willingness to recognize and enforce foreign judgments, especially judgments from common law jurisdictions.

In 2016, the Intermediate Court of Nanjing sustained a claim for recognition and enforcement of a judgment rendered by the Singapore High Court in 2015, on the basis of reciprocity, i.e. on the basis that the Singapore High Court had enforced a PRC judgment earlier in 2014.[23] This was the first time that a PRC court has enforced a commercial judgment made by a Singapore court. Similarly, in 2017 and 2018, two Intermediate Courts from Wuhan[24] and Shanghai[25] respectively recognized and enforced two commercial judgments rendered in the United States of America, which were also on the basis of reciprocity principle.

In terms of bilateral treaties, on 31 August 2018, the Supreme People's Court of PRC and the Supreme Court of Singapore executed a Memorandum of Guidance on Recognition and Enforcement of Money Judgments in Commercial Cases, where the highest judicial organs of the two countries agreed in principle on the measures to mutually enforce money judgments rendered in the other jurisdiction.

Though these measures might still be far away from the day when a foreign interim order is recognized and enforced under a PRC legislation, but the trend, as demonstrated in the aforementioned developments on the judicial front, has certainly been toward more openness and acceptance.

5 Conclusion

In conclusion, PRC law does provide for measures that are similar to common law interim remedies. However, there are several problems with interim measures under the PRC law.

First, the legislation does not provide enough guidance on the conditions for taking interim measures, and as a result the court has substantial discretion in deciding whether to grant interim remedies. In practice, this results in an imbalance between the applicant's and the respondent's interest. However, we see in recent years that the courts have been taking steps to balance the respondent's interest in intellectual property disputes.

Second, the legislation does not provide for sufficient remedy against wrongful interim measures. To hold the applicant liable for damages caused by wrongful interim measures, the law requires that it be proven that the applicant had acted intentionally or with gross negligence, and it is difficult for respondents to prove their actual loss. These further add to the risk on the respondents' economic well-being.

Third, arbitral tribunals do not have the power to take interim measures under the PRC law, whereas they are generally considered to be in a more well-informed

---

[23] *Kolmar Group AG v Jiangsu Textile Industry (Group) Import and Export Co., Ltd.* (2016) Su No. 1 Xie Wai Ren No. 3.

[24] *Liu Li v Tao Li and Tong Wu* (2015) E Wu Han Zhong Min Shang Wai Chu Zi No. 00026.

[25] Shanghai Political Science and Law (2018).

position than the court to make these decisions. The arbitration rules of PRC arbitral institutions have made attempts to give tribunals power to take interim measures under foreign laws, however these changes do not affect arbitration cases seated in PRC.

Fourth, the PRC law does not allow enforcement of foreign interim orders, though PRC courts have demonstrated increased willingness to recognize and enforce foreign judgments, especially judgments from common law jurisdictions, and enforcement of foreign interim measures can be all but a matter of time.

References

Chen H (2017) Research report on introducing liability insurance guarantee mechanism in property preservation. People's Judicature (Appl) 13:48–53

China Court (2014) Eli Lilly and Company's business secret infringement dispute. https://www.chinacourt.org/article/detail/2014/04/id/1281655.shtml

Fontaine JJB et al. (eds) (2016) The white book, civil procedure, vol I. Sweet & Maxwell

Shanghai Political Science and Law (2018) Shanghai No. 1 Intermediate People's Court recognizes and enforces a US civil and commercial judgment at the first time based on the principle of reciprocity. http://gov.eastday.com/node2/zzb/shzfzz2013/zfsd/fy/u1ai1364933.html

Sun C (2014) China's pre-litigation injunction: issues and resolution. Hebei Law Science 32(8):114–124

Tang Z, Lv C (2013) Application of specific performance preservation in trade secret infringement lawsuits. The People's Judicature (Cases) 22:48–50

The First Intermediate Court of Beijing (2018) The First Intermediate Court of Beijing handling property preservation application online. http://www.chinapeace.gov.cn/zixun/2018-11/30/content_11496766.htm

Wang L (2018) No.2 Civil tribunal's analysis of the impact of interim measures on the rate of settlement in commercial cases. http://qdsbqfy.sdcourt.gov.cn/qdsbqfy/404774/404834/3016549/index.html

Xiao J, Zhang B (2016) Discussion on imputation principles of infringement liability arising from wrongly property preservation. J Law Appl 1:39–45

Xu J, Li D (2013) Practice and thoughts on the guarantee of civil interim measures. J Law Appl 10:67–70

Yang H, Luo B, Leng H (2013) The exploration and research about the issues related to the court's handling of property preservation involving enterprises. People's Judicature (Appl) 9:47–50

Yang N (2017) Research on the enforcement of interim measures at foreign jurisdictions in international arbitration. Mod Bus 30:62–64

Fang Zhao is a founding partner of Hui Zhong Law Firm. She holds an LL.B degree of Fudan University and a GDL diploma of City University of London. She has been practicing law in the PRC for over 16 years, and she qualifies as a barrister of England and Wales. Fang has sit as an arbitrator of the China International Economic and Trade Arbitration Commission and Hong Kong International Arbitration Centre. Before Zhong was established, she had been a partner of Beijing Jun He Law Offices.

Han Ma is a senior associate of Hui Zhong Law Firm. He holds an LL.B degree of East China University of Political Science and Law, and an LL.M degree of New York University.

Anti-suit Injunctions in Support of Arbitration and EU Law

Pietro Ortolani

Abstract The Chapter assesses the compatibility of anti-suit injunctions issued in support of arbitration with European Union (EU) law and, in particular, with the Brussels regime. First of all, the Chapter describes the nature of anti-suit injunctions, and their use in the practice of English courts. Against this background, the chapter then provides a critical analysis of the case-law of the Court of Justice of the EU on this topic, and the subsequent reception of that case-law in the Member States. The final part of the Chapter evaluates the relevance of the innovations brought about by the Brussels I *bis* Regulation, and discusses the distinction between injunctions issued by a Member State court and injunctions issued by an arbitral tribunal in the form of an award. The potential impact of Brexit on the current state of the law is also considered.

1 Introduction

The effectiveness of arbitration as a mechanism of dispute resolution hinges, to a large extent, on the binding nature of the parties' agreement to arbitrate. By entering into this agreement, the parties generally[1] waive their right to access state

[1] It must be acknowledged that the parties can theoretically enter into a non-exclusive arbitration agreement, which enables them to commence arbitration (thus binding the respondent, if the claimant starts arbitral proceedings) but does not prevent access to state courts: *Benihana of Tokyo, LLC v. Benihana, Inc.*, 2014 U.S. Dist. LEXIS 99933 (S.D.N.Y. July 22, 2014). This type of clause, however, does not seem to be widely used in practice, as it not afford the parties any certainty as to the forum where future disputes will be resolved.

P. Ortolani (✉)
Radboud University, Nijmegen, The Netherlands
e-mail: p.ortolani@jur.ru.nl

L. Chen and A. Janssen (eds.), *Dispute Resolution in China, Europe and World*,
Ius Gentium: Comparative Perspectives on Law and Justice 79,
https://doi.org/10.1007/978-3-030-42974-4_8

courts[2] and consent to resolve a specific dispute or category of disputes through this particular form of private adjudication. Were the parties left free to unilaterally[3] disregard the arbitration agreement they previously concluded, the reliability of arbitration would be radically undermined. In other words, this exclusionary effect of arbitration agreements *vis-à-vis* court litigation plays a crucial role in establishing arbitration as a 'one-stop shop' for cross-border dispute resolution.[4] It is for this reason that, throughout the history of arbitration, legal devices have been put in place to prevent the parties from escaping the effects of their agreement to arbitrate.

The provision that most evidently ensures the enforcement of agreements to arbitrate is Article II of the New York Convention. Pursuant to it, when the court of a state party to the Convention is 'seized of an action in a matter in respect of which the parties' have agreed to arbitrate, that court is obliged at the request of one of the parties to refer the case to arbitration (the so-called *exceptio compromissi*), unless the agreement is 'null and void, inoperative or incapable of being performed'. Given the widespread success of the Convention as an instrument of international law, it would seem that Article II constitutes a sufficient protection against a disputant's attempts to circumvent the effects of an arbitration clause by seizing a state court. Such a conclusion is apparently reinforced by the circumstance that, in prominent jurisdictions (such as France), the competence-competence doctrine is interpreted in a particularly arbitration-friendly fashion, and the seized court will normally decline jurisdiction whenever an objection based on the existence of an arbitration agreement is raised, unless no arbitral tribunal is constituted yet and the exception is manifestly without merits (so-called 'negative effect').[5]

Despite the unquestionably central role of Article II in the enforcement of agreements to arbitrate, exclusive reliance on the dismissal of jurisdiction on the part of the seized state court may sometimes be regarded as insufficient. From this point of view, three main factors should be taken into account: first, local bias and corruption risks may endanger the functioning of Article II in practice, with state courts disregarding the parties' agreement and retaining jurisdiction on the basis of idiosyncratic and unforeseeable lines of reasoning. When a state party to the Convention violates its obligations under Article II, it may be difficult for the disputant seeking

---

[2]See, in this respect, the case-law of the European Court of Human Rights: *Deweer v Belgium*, Application no. 6903/75, 27 February 1980; *Lithgow and others v the United Kingdom*, Application no. 9006/80; 9262/81; 9263/81; 9265/81; 9266/81; 9313/81; 9405/81, 8 July 1986; *Pastore v Italy*, Application no. 46483/99, 25 May 1999; *Transado—Transportes Fluviais do Sado, S.A. v Portugal*, Application no. 35943/02, 16 December 2003; *Eiffage S.A. and others v Switzerland*, Application no. 1742/05, 15 September 2009; *Tabbane v Switzerland*, Application no. 41069/12, 1 March 2016.

[3]The parties, of course, remain free to disregard the agreement to arbitrate, if all of them agree to do so; this is implicit in Article II of the New York Convention, which does not require the court seized in violation of an agreement to arbitrate to decline jurisdiction *ex officio*, in the absence of any objection as to the jurisdiction of the court.

[4]Born (2014, pp. 1270–1306).

[5]See Article 1448(1) of the French Code of Civil Procedure: '*Lorsqu'un litige relevant d'une convention d'arbitrage est porté devant une juridiction de l'Etat, celle-ci se déclare incompétente sauf si le tribunal arbitral n'est pas encore saisi et si la convention d'arbitrage est manifestement nulle ou manifestement inapplicable*'.

the enforcement of the agreement to obtain adequate redress, considering *inter alia* the numerous pitfalls that any attempt to indirectly obtain protection through inter-state dispute settlement would likely entail.[6] Second, even assuming that Article II (and similar provisions in other instruments of international and domestic arbitration law) would be applied in a correct and comparable fashion across all jurisdictions potentially involved in a given case, the time necessary for the seized court to dismiss the case can vary significantly. In states where court backlog is a serious problem, the simple commencement of a case before a national court in violation of an arbitration agreement may lead to a situation of prolonged legal uncertainty. Litigants operating in bad faith may use such an uncertainty as a weapon, often referred to as 'Italian torpedo', possibly coercing the counterpart into a settlement or, at the very least, disrupting the dispute resolution procedure by driving its costs up. Third, even in cases where risks of violation of the Convention and judicial backlog may be ruled out, the possibility that an arbitral tribunal and a national court will in good faith reach incompatible conclusions as to the validity and/or scope of an arbitration clause can never be excluded. Given the lack of any type of institutional coordination between court litigation and arbitration, disagreements of this sort remain an unavoidable fact of (dispute resolution) life.

It is exactly to address these problems and ensure that the parties comply with their pre-existing contractual dispute resolution arrangements that the anti-suit injunction has been developed. An anti-suit injunction is, in essence, an order to discontinue a litigation previously commenced in a different forum, in breach of an arbitration[7] agreement. The anti-suit injunction, in other words, aims at anticipating the enforcement of the clause, effectively bypassing the protection that the arbitration clause would otherwise receive through Article II of the New York Convention. It is, as such, a form of pre-emptive protection of the parties' agreement. Let us assume, for instance, that one of the parties commences litigation in the courts of state A, in breach of a valid agreement to arbitrate covering the dispute at hand. The respondent in the court proceedings would normally object to the jurisdiction of the seized court and request it to refer the case to arbitration, as required *inter alia* by Article II of the New York Convention. In addition to that, however, the respondent may also request the court of a different state (B) to issue an anti-suit injunction against the claimant, ordering it to refrain from continuing the litigation pending in state A. If claimant complies with the injunction,[8] the question of whether the seized court in state A

[6]One of the few examples of alleged disregard of an international instrument of private international law escalating to the level of an inter-state dispute concerned not arbitration, but a court judgment circulating under the Lugano Convention: see International Court of Justice (ICJ) case *Jurisdiction and Enforcement of Judgments in Civil and Commercial Matters (Belgium v Switzerland)*, case removed from the ICJ List on 5 April 2011. For an analysis of the role of the New York Convention as an instrument of public international law, see Paulsson (2016).

[7]The same holds true for choice-of-court agreements, as discussed in Sect. 4.1 below. This contribution, however, focuses in particular on the use of anti-suit injunctions as a means of enforcing agreements to arbitrate.

[8]Failure to comply with an anti-suit injunction may have serious consequences, as illustrated in Sects. 4.2 and 5.2 below.

would have applied Article II of the New York Convention correctly (referring the disputants to arbitration) automatically becomes moot, as the dispute is removed from that court before the latter makes any determination in that respect. For the same reason, problems of delay and disagreement between the seized court and the arbitral tribunal are also automatically resolved.

Despite its potential usefulness as a means to protect the effectiveness of an agreement to arbitrate, the anti-suit injunction has raised significant doubts, especially concerning its compatibility with the Brussels I system and, more generally, European Union (EU) law. This contribution scrutinises the problem, especially in the light of the amendments introduced in 2012 with the recast Brussels I Regulation. The remainder of this Chapter proceeds in five parts. First, the nature of the anti-suit injunctions is summarily described. Second, the use of anti-suit injunctions in the specific context of arbitration is scrutinized. Third, the historical development of the relationship between anti-suit injunctions and the Brussels I regime is traced, with specific reference to the landmark cases *Turner* and *West Tankers*. Fourth, the influence of the amendments introduced with the Recast Brussels I Regulation and, in particular, the significance of the new Recital 12 are taken into consideration, especially in the wake of the Court of Justice of the European Union (CJEU) judgment in *Gazprom* and of the opinion rendered by the Advocate General in the same case. Finally, the last section draws some general conclusions on the topic.

2 Nature of the Anti-suit Injunction

The anti-suit injunction is not ubiquitously available: it typically is a common law device, with no direct equivalent in most civil law jurisdictions.[9] This difference between civil and common law systems has its origins in a fundamental divergence as to the way in which these two legal traditions[10] conceive of the arbitration agreement[11] and its effects.

According to a first, 'procedural' theory, the arbitration agreement is an expression of private autonomy that produces its effects in the realm of civil procedure, rather

[9] As mentioned above, some civil law jurisdictions aim to ensure the same high level of protection of the parties' agreement to arbitrate by recognising the negative effect of the *competence-competence* doctrine, whereby any analysis as to the validity and scope of the arbitration clause on the part the seized court is generally pre-empted by the mere fact that one of the parties objects to the jurisdiction of that court and requests that the dispute be referred to arbitration. It is important to acknowledge, however, that this mechanism does not protect the arbitration clause if the 'torpedo' action is brought in another jurisdiction, which does not adopt such an arbitration-friendly interpretation of *competence-competence*.

[10] While the distinction between these two legal 'families' does entail some unavoidable and inaccurate simplification, it is useful for the purposes of this Chapter, to grasp the basic contours of two different approaches as to the nature of the arbitration agreement.

[11] The same observations appear to be largely applicable to choice-of-court clauses which, however, fall outside of the scope of this Chapter.

than in the context of substantive private law.[12] An agreement to arbitrate, hence, serves the purpose of derogating from the jurisdiction of state courts and conversely conferring on the arbitrators the power to assess autonomously whether they have jurisdiction to rule on the merits of the case (*competence-competence*), but it does not create substantive rights for the parties.[13] In other words, each of the parties can rely on the procedural effects of the agreement (which gives the arbitral tribunal jurisdiction and conversely prevents state courts from claiming it). A party, however, cannot request the performance in kind of that agreement, i.e. asking a state court to prevent the filing of an action before a different state court, even if that may amount to a breach of the arbitration agreement. In case litigation is started, it will thus be up to the seized court to decline jurisdiction and refer the parties to arbitration, as required by Article II(3) of the New York Convention. This theory is prevailing in continental Europe.

According to a second, 'contractual' theory, the arbitration agreement is a simple contract between the parties. Therefore, the existence of a valid arbitration agreement empowers the parties to obtain the performance of the agreement in kind, similarly to what would happen with any other type of contract giving rise to obligations that the parties must carry out, and where compensation does not constitute an adequate remedy.[14] From this point of view, when issuing an award containing an anti-suit injunction, a state court essentially orders the enforcement of a contract. This theory, prevailing in the common law, has been criticized in the civil law world, as it construes the arbitration agreement as a substantive contract between the parties, despite the fact that it has no bearing on the parties' substantive rights, but rather produces effects on a different and distinctively procedural level. For this reason, it has been argued that '[j]urisdiction is something that is declared, not something that can be ordered'.[15]

In other words, the anti-suit injunction is only conceivable in legal systems where the arbitration agreement is seen as a contract between the parties, whose performance in kind can be ordered by the arbitrators. By contrast, if the arbitration clause is qualified as a procedural agreement between the parties, an anti-suit injunction should in principle not be available. If this 'procedural' perspective is adopted, arbitrators can claim jurisdiction and state courts must conversely dismiss cases covered by

---

[12]Satta (1931, p. 50).

[13]Lévy (2005, p. 115).

[14]Merkin and Flannery (2014, pp. 187–188):

> The juridical basis of the injunction is the enforcement of both a positive right to have any disputes resolved only by way of the contractually agreed forum (arbitration proceedings), and a closely related but legally distinct and concomitant negative right *not* to be sued in any other forum. When viewed as obligations, the negative-positive dichotomy is reversed, but is still one way of looking at the issue—there is a *positive* obligation to bring proceedings by way of the contractually agreed forum (arbitration), which carries with it the *negative* obligation *not* to bring proceedings in another forum.

[15]Lévy (2005), p. 120. Along similar lines Benedettelli (2014, p. 713) argues that, although the arbitration agreement is a contract, it is predominantly procedural in nature and cannot thus be regulated by ordinary contract law.

a valid agreement, but the latter cannot protect the jurisdiction of the former by enjoining a party to discontinue litigation pending in a different forum, even when a violation of the parties' agreement to arbitrate is likely to have occurred.

3 Anti-suit Injunctions in Support of Arbitration in the Practice of English Courts

The use of anti-suit injunctions in support of arbitration is relatively common in English law, when the seat of arbitration is in England.[16] More specifically, an anti-suit injunction is one of the measures that English courts can issue in support of arbitral proceedings, pursuant *inter alia* to section 44 of the Arbitration Act 1996. Notably, the fact that English courts normally derive the jurisdiction to issue this type of injunction from the existence of a legal link between the arbitral proceedings and the seat also explains why this type of remedy is not structurally compatible with the way in which certain civil law systems, and notably the French one, conceptualize arbitration; an anti-suit injunction, in other words, is only conceivable if arbitration is not seen as an entirely de-localised procedure, existing in a legal order other than the national one.[17]

It is difficult to deny that an anti-suit injunction constitutes an intrusion in the workings of a foreign court, albeit an indirect one: while the measure is formally directed at the party that commenced the litigation in violation of a previous agreement to arbitrate, it does ultimately aim at obtaining a discontinuation of court proceedings pending abroad, before the foreign judge has an opportunity to rule on the *exceptio compromissi* raised by the other party.[18] In the words of Lord Scarman in *British Airways Board v Laker Airways Ltd*,

> an injunction restraining a person within the jurisdiction of the English court from pursuing a remedy in a foreign court where, if he proves the necessary facts, he has a cause of action is, however disguised and indirect, an interference with the process of justice in that foreign court.[19]

This rather serious consequence should inspire a measure of caution in the use of the injunction.[20] English courts, however, stress the fact that an anti-suit injunction in support of arbitration does not offend against comity, for the very fact that it is 'vexatious and oppressive for a party to maintain proceedings in breach of its

[16] *Pena Copper Mines Ltd v Rio Tinto Co Ltd* (1911) 105 LT 846.

[17] Gaillard (2010).

[18] See Briggs (2014, p. 390), according to whom an anti-suit injunction 'looks very much like an act of interference with proceedings before (a) foreign court, and the appearance really does not mislead'; see also Andrews (2013, p. 229): '[a]lthough the respondent is the only party subject to the injunction, it might be perceived that the foreign court is indirectly affected'.

[19] *British Airways Board v Laker Airways Ltd* [1985] A.C. 58, 95.

[20] *Sokana Industries Inc v Freyre & Co Inc* [1994] 2 Lloyd's Rep 57, 66, per Colman J.

agreement not to do so'.[21] For this reason, the Supreme Court of the United Kingdom (UK) concluded in the sense of the availability of an anti-suit injunction aimed at protecting an arbitration agreement[22] even in cases where the arbitral proceedings themselves have not been instituted yet and the party requesting the injunction has expressed no intention to commence them.[23]

4 Anti-suit Injunctions and the Brussels Regime: From *Turner* to *West Tankers*

The tension between anti-suit injunctions on the one hand and the Brussels regime[24] on the other hand came to light for the first time in *Turner*.[25] Although this case does not impact arbitration directly, a brief summary of its contents is necessary to set the stage for the further development of the CJEU case-law with respect to anti-suit injunctions in support of arbitration.

4.1 Turner

The dispute in *Turner* arose out of an employment contract, resulting in parallel litigation before Spanish and English courts. Mr Turner brought an action for unfair dismissal before the Employment Tribunal, in London. The defendants in those proceedings, in turn, initiated litigation in Spain, claiming damages from Mr Turner

[21] *Aggeliki Charis Compania Maritima SA v Pagnan SpA (The Angelic Grace)* [1995] 1 Lloyd's Rep 87. See also Lord Mance in *AES Ust-Kamenogorsk Hydropower Plant LLP v Ust-Kamenogorsk Hydropower Plant JSC* [2013] UKSC 35, para 31, with reference to the preclusive effect of an arbitration agreement in respect of court litigation: 'the negative aspect is as fundamental as the positive. There is no reason why a party to either should be free to engage the other party in a different forum merely because neither party wishes to bring proceedings in the agreed forum'. In the same vein, with reference to exclusive choice-of-court agreements, see *Donohue v Armco Inc* [2001] UKHL 64; [2002] 1 All ER 749.

[22] Agreement governed by English law, indicating London as the seat of arbitration.

[23] *AES Ust-Kamenogorsk Hydropower Plant LLP v Ust-Kamenogorsk Hydropower Plant JSC* [2013] UKSC 35, para 4.

[24] The expression 'Brussels regime' will be used in this Chapter to encompass not only the current Brussels I *bis* Regulation (Regulation (EU) No 1215/2012 of the European Parliament and of the Council of 12 December 2012 on jurisdiction and the recognition and enforcement of judgments in civil and commercial matters), but also the original Brussels I Regulation (Council Regulation (EC) No 44/2001 of 22 December 2000 on jurisdiction and the recognition and enforcement of judgments in civil and commercial matters) and the 1968 Brussels Convention. Unless the Chapter expressly draws a differentiation among these instruments, the observations concerning the 'regime' should be read as applicable to all of these instruments in a comparable fashion.

[25] Case C-159/02, *Gregory Paul Turner v Felix Fareed Ismail Grovit, Harada Ltd and Changepoint SA*, ECLI:EU:C:2004:228 (hereafter '*Turner*').

as compensation allegedly resulting from his professional misconduct. Notably, the parties had not circumscribed the courts' jurisdiction over the case contractually, through either a choice-of-court or an arbitration agreement. Mr Turner asked first the High Court and then the Court of Appeal to issue an injunction, ordering the defendants to discontinue the Spanish proceedings on the basis of the fact that those proceedings appeared to have been initiated in 'bad faith'[26] with the 'purpose of frustrating or obstructing the proceedings in England',[27] thus potentially impacting on the 'legitimate interest of the applicant in the English proceedings'.[28] The Court of Appeal issued the requested anti-suit injunction; the defendants appealed against that decision to the House of Lords. The House of Lords, then, made a reference for a preliminary ruling, asking the European Court of Justice to determine whether a measure such as the one at hand was compatible with the Brussels Convention.

The Court based its reasoning on the premise that, in the Brussels regime, '(e)ach court is entitled to rule only as to its own jurisdiction (…) but not as to the jurisdiction of a court in another (Member) State'.[29] Each Member State court, in other words, is prevented from second-guessing the jurisdiction of any other Member State court. This obligation to assume that all courts will make a correct use of the heads of jurisdiction provided for in the Brussels regime is the essence of the principle of mutual trust in the field of judicial cooperation,[30] which in turn serves to establish a borderless area for the circulation of judgments. According to the Court, the assessment of abuse of process on which the issuance of the anti-suit injunction in *Turner* was predicated necessarily entailed an evaluation of appropriateness as to the exertion of jurisdiction on the part of the seized Spanish court[31]; such an evaluation, the Court reasoned, is not compatible with the principle of mutual trust underlying the allocation of jurisdiction in the Brussels regime.[32] On these grounds, the Court concluded that the Brussels Convention precludes the grant of an anti-suit injunction by a Member State court, prohibiting a party from commencing or continuing legal proceedings before the courts of another Member State.

While *Turner* laid a crucial foundation as to the approach of the CJEU with respect to intra-EU anti-suit injunction in general, the possibility to extend the same line of reasoning to the specific case of anti-suit issued in support of arbitration was far from uncontroversial. More specifically, an important distinguishing element is the fact that arbitration has consistently been excluded from both the Brussels Convention and the two subsequent regulations[33]: the question that arose, then, was whether the

[26] *Turner*, para 19.

[27] *Turner*, para 17.

[28] *Turner*, para 17.

[29] *Turner*, para 20.

[30] *Turner*, para 20.

[31] Turner, para 28.

[32] *Turner*, para 28.

[33] See Article 1(2)(d) of the Brussels I *bis* Regulation, Article 1(2)(d) of the Brussels I Regulation and Article 1(4) of the 1968 Brussels Convention.

Turner rationale would also apply in cases where a Member State court issued an anti-suit injunction to protect the effectiveness of a dispute resolution agreement (namely an arbitration clause) which fell outside of the scope of application of the Brussels regime. The Court was presented with an opportunity to answer this question in *West Tankers*.

4.2 West Tankers

The case in *West Tankers*[34] arose from a collision between the 'Front Comor', a vessel owned by West Tankers and chartered by Erg, and a jetty owned by Erg and located in Siracusa, Italy. The charterparty contained a choice-of-law clause in favour in English law and a clause providing for arbitration in London. Since Erg had entered into insurance contracts that partially covered the damages, it claimed compensation from its insurers up to the limit of the insurance cover, and initiated arbitration against West Tankers for the remainder of the damages. The insurers paid compensation to Erg and subsequently brought a subrogation claim against West Tankers before the first instance court of Siracusa. West Tankers objected to the jurisdiction of the Italian court, arguing that the arbitration agreement contained in the charterparty applied to the insurers as well. In addition, West Tankers also filed an application with the High Court of Justice of England and Wales for an anti-suit injunction, aimed at obtaining the discontinuation of the Italian proceedings. The High Court granted the injunction. On appeal, the House of Lords made a reference for a preliminary ruling to the CJEU, asking whether the court of a EU Member State is prevented from issuing an anti-suit injunction restricting proceedings in another Member State even when the injunction's purpose is the protection of arbitral proceedings which, by definition, fall outside of the scope of application of the Brussels regime.

The Court started by summarizing its previous case-law concerning the relationship between arbitration and litigation in Member State courts, namely *Rich*[35] and *van Uden*.[36] Taken at face value, however, these two precedents did not evince the existence of a univocal approach. *Rich*, on the one hand, originated from court proceedings concerning the appointment of an arbitrator. The Court excluded the applicability of the Brussels Convention to those proceedings, in which the Member State court merely plays an ancillary function of *juge d'appui* in support of arbitration. *Van Uden*, on the other hand, concerned a request for provisional measures lodged before a Member State court by a party to a dispute whose merits were to be decided by an arbitral tribunal. In that case, the CJEU concluded that the existence of

[34]Case C-185/07, *Allianz SpA and Generali Assicurazioni Generali SpA v West Tankers Inc.*, ECLI:EU:C:2009:69 (hereafter '*West Tankers*').

[35]Case C-190/89, *Marc Rich & Co. AG v Società Italiana Impianti PA*, ECLI:EU:C:1991:319 (hereafter '*Rich*').

[36]Case C-391/95, *Van Uden Maritime BV, trading as Van Uden Africa Line v Kommanditgesellschaft in Firma Deco-Line and Another*, ECLI:EU:C:1998:543 (hereafter '*Van Uden*').

a valid agreement to arbitrate did not rule out the possibility for Member State courts to issue provisional measures under Article 24 of the Brussels Convention,[37] as provisional measures aim at offering temporary protection for the parties' substantive rights in dispute and are, therefore, parallel[38] rather than ancillary to arbitration.[39] On the surface, therefore, the two judgments at hand reached opposite conclusions: exclusion of arbitration-related proceedings from the scope of the Brussels regime in *Rich*, inclusion in *van Uden*. Behind that surface, however, the CJEU managed to find a common thread, which proved important for *West Tankers*.

The common thread identified by the CJEU is the criterion of the 'nature of the protected rights'. In order to determine the boundaries of the arbitration exclusion, in other words, it is necessary to look at the main subject-matter of the Member State court proceedings in respect of which the question arises. Indeed, this was arguably the criterion used by the court in both *Rich* and *van Uden*; therefore, any given civil or commercial proceedings pending before a Member State court fall within the scope of the Brussels regime inasmuch as their main subject-matter is the protection of rights that do not directly relate to arbitration (as was the case in *van Uden*, where the seized court was asked to temporarily protect the substantive rights of one of the disputants), while they are caught by the arbitration exclusion if they preserve rights which do directly and primarily concern arbitration (such as the case of ancillary proceedings dealing with the composition of the arbitral tribunal, in *Rich*, which ultimately ensure a party's right to obtain a complete arbitral tribunal).

Although the criterion at hand provided a desirably consistent framework for the understanding of the Court's previous case-law, its application in the case of anti-suit injunctions raised additional questions. On the one hand, the anti-suit injunction in *West Tankers* had the main purpose of protecting arbitral proceedings. On the other hand, however, it did so by restricting civil litigation pending in a Member State court. What was, then, the main subject-matter of the English proceedings that led to the issuance of the anti-suit injunction? To answer this question, the Court focused once again on the nature of the rights protected by the measure, which were in this case intimately related to arbitration and ultimately amounting to an expectation to have all disputes resolved in an arbitral forum, to the exclusion of court litigation. For this reason, the Court acknowledged that the English proceedings could not come within the scope of the Brussels regime.[40] However, the Court highlighted that even proceedings that do not fall within the scope of the Brussels regime 'may nevertheless have consequences which undermine its effectiveness, namely preventing the attainment of the objectives of unification of the rules of conflict of jurisdiction in civil

---

[37] Corresponding to Article 35 of the Brussels I *bis* Regulation.

[38] Notably, the characterization of court-issued provisional measures as legitimately 'parallel' to the arbitral proceedings is consistent with the regulatory approach adopted in many arbitration-friendly legal systems in this respect: see e.g. Article 17 J of the United Nations Commission on International Trade Law (UNCITRAL) Model Law.

[39] *Van Uden*, para 33.

[40] *West Tankers*, para 21.

and commercial matters and the free movement of decisions'.[41] It was precisely this qualification, ultimately based on a concern as to the effectiveness of EU procedural law, that proved decisive in *West Tankers*.

Having foreshadowed the idea that a measure can impact on the Brussels regime even if it is not directly covered by it, the Court proceeded to review the specific circumstances of the case. In this regard it observed that the injunction was aimed at obtaining the discontinuation of proceedings pending in the courts of another Member State, the court of first instance of Siracusa. The litigation pending before the Siracusa court certainly dealt with a subject-matter covered by the Brussels regime, irrespective of the fact that one of the parties had objected to the jurisdiction of that court on the basis of the existence of an agreement to arbitrate in the insurance contracts.[42] Therefore the CJEU concluded that, under the Brussels regime, the court of Siracusa had the power to make an autonomous evaluation as to its own jurisdiction, and an anti-suit injunction such as the one granted by the English High Court would curtail this power by forcing the discontinuation of the Italian litigation. In the words of the CJEU, when a party raises an *exceptio compromissi*, 'it is exclusively for [the seized Member State court] to rule on that objection and on its own jurisdiction'.[43] The CJEU thus concluded that, because an anti-suit injunction such as the one in *West Tankers* effectively strips a Member State court of the power to decide on its own jurisdiction, it is incompatible with the mechanism set forth in the Brussels regime for the allocation of jurisdiction and with the principle of mutual trust underlying it.

4.3 The Aftermath

With its narrow interpretation of the arbitration exclusion contained in the Brussels Regulation, *West Tankers* proved to be a controversial judgment. However, what was perhaps even more controversial was the set of inferences that some Member State courts drew from the judgment. In *The Wadi Sudr*,[44] the English Court of Appeal was faced with a judgment previously rendered by a Spanish court, which declared the invalidity of a clause providing for arbitration in London. The question was whether such a judgment, which only dealt with a preliminary *exceptio compromissi* without deciding the merits of the dispute between the parties, was entitled to recognition pursuant to the Brussels regime. The Court of Appeal observed that the subject-matter of the Spanish proceedings fell within the scope of application of the Brussels regime, and thus concluded that any judgment issued in those proceedings, including

[41] *West Tankers*, para 24.

[42] *West Tankers*, para 26.

[43] *West Tankers*, para 27.

[44] *National Navigation Co v Endesa Generacion SA (The Wadi Sudr)* [2009] EWCA Civ 1397; [2010] 1 Lloyd's Rep 193.

the one concerning the (in)validity of the agreement to arbitrate rather than the merits, was in principle entitled to recognition and enforcement under Brussels I.[45]

The effects of the inference drawn by the English Court of Appeal in *the Wadi Sudr* were probably more far-reaching than the ones of *West Tankers* itself, and potentially disruptive for arbitration in Europe: following the line of reasoning of the Court of Appeal, any Member State court would potentially have the power to trigger a pan-European nullification of an agreement to arbitrate by simply declaring in a judgment the invalidity (or inapplicability *ratione materiae*, depending on the case) of said agreement. In other words, such a judgment would have had preclusive effects not only in the state where it was issued, but throughout the entire EU, binding (once recognised under the Brussels regime) the courts of the place of arbitration as well (if located in a EU Member State). Needless to say, this could have significant consequences on the attractiveness of prominent European arbitration-friendly jurisdictions (such as France or England and Wales) as a seat of arbitration.

In the wake of *West Tankers* and its reception by Member State courts, the need for an amendment of the Brussels I Regulation became increasingly clear. The Commission initially considered a proposal[46] according to which the Brussels regime should partially include arbitration within its scope of application, namely conferring exclusive jurisdiction to rule on the validity of any agreement to arbitrate to the courts of the seat, and requiring any other seized court, when faced with an *exceptio compromissi*, to stay proceedings until the competent court at the seat would issue a ruling on this matter. The proposal at hand would have certainly ruled out the risk of 'torpedo actions', granting the courts of the seat absolute priority as to the evaluation of the validity and scope of the arbitration agreement. The practical feasibility of the proposal, however, was hindered by two significant obstacles.

First, when the parties enter into an agreement to arbitrate, they may fail to select the seat of arbitration immediately. This, in principle, has no effect on the validity of the agreement, but it does have a crucial consequence: the objection to the jurisdiction of the Member State court (seized in violation of the agreement) may in practice be raised at a moment when no arbitral proceedings are pending yet, and no seat has been determined. In this case, the only solution would be for the party raising the objection to simultaneously start arbitral proceedings, presumably requesting negative declaratory relief, at least for the purpose of obtaining a determination of the seat of arbitration (typically in accordance with the default mechanism contained

[45]Interestingly, other Member State courts before the CJEU ruling in *West Tankers* had reached the opposite conclusion: *Legal Department du Ministère de la Justice de la République d'Irak v Sociétés Fincantieri Cantieri Navali Italiani, Finmeccanica et Armamenti e Aerospazio*, 15 June 2006, Paris Court of Appeal (2007) 1 Rev Arb 87:

> Une décision italienne présentée à l'exequatur du juge français, limitée à la seule constatation de l'invalidité de la convention d'arbitrage et exclusive de tout jugement sur le fond de l'affaire, lequel n'est d'ailleurs pas encore aujourd'hui tranché par le juge italien porte sur un litige qui est extérieur au champ d'application de la Convention de Bruxelles.

[46]Hess et al. (2007, pp. 49–70).

in most sets of arbitration rules)[47] and then in turn enabling the competent court at the seat to confirm the validity and/or applicability of the clause. Needless to say, such a solution would be costly and difficult to implement in practice.

Second, even assuming that such a reform would encourage all parties entering into an agreement to arbitrate to abandon the practice of postponing the determination of the seat of arbitration to a stage later than the conclusion of the agreement, it must be acknowledged that the proposed mechanism would not have been entirely compatible with the approach of some legal systems, such as France, which recognise the so-called 'negative effect' of the principle of *competence-competence*. In those jurisdictions, the courts of the seat are generally obliged to refer the parties to arbitration immediately, without performing any type of assessment as to the existence and validity of the clause, apart from the unlikely scenario where the arbitration is not pending yet and the agreement is manifestly null or inapplicable.[48] In these legal systems, thus, the arbitral tribunal is normally the only adjudicative body having the power to rule on the validity and scope of the agreement; needless to say, this would have constituted an important obstacle to the implementation of the proposed reform, according to which it would be up to the competent state court at the seat (the *juge d'appui*) to effectively preserve the effects of the clause by confirming its validity and/or applicability.[49]

Because of these practical hurdles, and also in light of the concerns that it raised within the arbitration community, the proposal was eventually not retained. However, a recital was included in the recast Brussels I Regulation, with the purpose of clarifying the interplay between court litigation and arbitration in the EU. In the following section, an analysis of said Recital will provide a background against which the relevance and consequences of the *Gazprom* judgment will be assessed.

---

[47] See e.g. Article 18 of the UNCITRAL Arbitration Rules, entrusting the task of determining the place of arbitration to the tribunal, or Article 18 of the 2017 International Chamber of Commerce (ICC) Rules, giving that power to the administering institution itself.

[48] See Article 1448(1) of the French Code of Civil Procedure.

[49] In theory, a possible corrective would be to allow each Member State to determine whether the ruling as to the validity and scope of the clause should be made by the competent *juge d'appui* or by the tribunal itself. This, however, would in practice mean delegating a decision which has effects on the jurisdiction of a Member State court (namely, the court seized in alleged violation of the agreement to arbitrate) to an adjudicative body which—according to the case law of the CJEU from *Nordsee* (case C-102/81, *Nordsee Deutsche Hochseefischerei GmbH v Reederei Mond Hochseefischerei Nordstern AG & Co. KG and Reederei Friedrich Busse Hochseefischerei Nordstern AG & Co. KG*, ECLI:EU:C:1982:107) to *Achmea* (case C-284/16, *Slowakische Republik v Achmea BV*, ECLI:EU:C:2018:158)—is not bound by the obligation of mutual trust. Furthermore, such a solution may jeopardise the effectiveness of EU law, inasmuch as the same legal provision would receive two significantly different types of application in different Member States, depending on the approach that each single Member State adopts regarding the doctrine of *competence-competence*.

5 Anti-suit Injunctions and the Brussels I Recast Regulation: *Gazprom*, Brexit and Beyond

5.1 The Recast

After it became clear that no consensus could be achieved regarding a partial inclusion of arbitration within the scope of the Brussels regime, a compromise solution was adopted: the arbitration exclusion would be maintained, but its precise contours would be clarified in a Recital. Recital 12 of the Brussels I *bis* Regulation, hence, has the role of ruling out some doubts concerning the relationship between arbitration and court litigation in Europe, overcoming some of the issues that arose out of *West Tankers* and the subsequent interpretation of that judgment by the courts of the Member States.

Recital 12 proceeds in four paragraphs. The first paragraph contains a relatively uncontroversial clarification: the Regulation does not apply to arbitration and does not prevent the courts of the Member States from referring the parties to arbitration, in accordance with their obligations arising *inter alia* out of Article II(3) of the New York Convention.

The second paragraph is probably the most relevant clarification offered by the EU lawmakers, directly tackling the *Wadi Sudr* problem. The paragraphs expressly states that, whenever a EU Member State court issues a judgment deciding whether an arbitration agreement is null and void, inoperative or incapable of being performed, that judgment is not entitled to recognition and enforcement under the Brussels regime. In other words, applying this rule in the *Wadi Sudr* scenario, the Spanish judgment would not be entitled to produce any effect in the UK, so that UK courts (and, *a fortiori*, arbitral tribunals seated in England) would not be bound by it. Notably, it is irrelevant whether the ruling concerning the arbitration agreement was issued to address an incidental question, or whether the issue of the validity of the clause constituted the main subject-matter of the litigation.

The third paragraph addresses the obvious consequences of the lack of coordination between arbitration and litigation, namely the possibility that a Member State court and an arbitral tribunal will reach incompatible conclusions as to the existence and validity of an agreement to arbitrate. More specifically, there is an inherent risk that the seized Member State court will retain jurisdiction, having deemed the agreement null and void, inoperable or incapable of being performed, while the arbitral tribunal will consider the agreement valid and proceed to adjudicate the merits of the same case. In this case, there is a concrete risk of conflict between the judgment issued by the Member State courts on the substance of the case and the final award rendered by the arbitral tribunal.

The Regulation addresses the problem at hand by clarifying that, in principle, the Member State court judgment on the merits (unlike the one on the arbitration agreement, if any) is entitled to recognition and enforcement under the Regulation. In other words, the fact that the Member State court had to dismiss an *exceptio compromissi* and declare the agreement to arbitrate invalid, before dealing with the merits of the case, is irrelevant as far as the intra-EU circulation of the judgment on the merits is concerned. At the same time, however, Paragraph 3 of Recital 12 also specifies that this rule is 'without prejudice to the competence of the courts of the Member States to decide on the recognition and enforcement of arbitral awards in accordance with [the New York Convention], which takes precedence over [the] Regulation'. In a nutshell, this means that a Member State court cannot invoke its obligations to recognise and enforce the court judgments on the merits under Articles 36 and 39 of the Regulation to escape its obligation to recognise and enforce an arbitral award covering the same subject-matter under Article III of the New York Convention. The risk of inconsistent outcomes, hence, is expressly accepted and somewhat 'codified' in Recital 12.

The inherently imperfect nature of the compromise that Recital 12(3) constitutes begs the question of whether a Member State court could potentially refuse the recognition and enforcement of a judgment issued by another Member State court, based on the fact that the same case has already been decided by an arbitral tribunal, and the award produces binding effects in the requested State.[50] Although the Regulation does not contain any express answer to this question, two provisions could potentially be used to address this issue: Article 45(1)(a) and Article 45(1)(d).

The first provision recognises the possibility for the requested Member State court to decline recognition and enforcement on public policy grounds. While the notion of public policy is not entirely[51] harmonized at the EU level, and it is therefore impossible to reach a consistent answer in this respect, a comparative analysis suggests that national provisions on *res judicata* are, at least in some Member States, regarded as fundamental enough to amount to public policy.[52] It could therefore be argued that, inasmuch as the award already produces binding effects in the requested State at the time when the recognition of the incompatible judgment is sought, the latter may be refused on public policy grounds.

The second provision concerns the existence of an earlier judgment given either in another EU Member State or third States, involving the same cause of action and between the same parties, provided that that earlier judgment fulfils the conditions necessary for recognition: in this case, once again, recognition of a later Member State court judgment may be denied. The provision at hand does not expressly mention arbitral awards; however, it is undeniable that the notion of 'judgment' relevant for the purposes of Article 45(1)(d) is not the same as the one enshrined in Article 2(a) of the Regulation, as the former (unlike the latter) also covers judgment given by courts of a non-EU Member State. In other words, the main concern of the Regulation seems to be the avoidance of any direct conflict of *res judicata*, irrespective of whether those effects emanate from a Member State court or not. In light of this, it would not be illogical to argue that the same provision should apply to an arbitral award as well,

---

[50] It does not seem to be relevant whether the source of these binding effects lies in the fact that the arbitration was seated in the requested State itself, or whether the award (made in a third EU or non-EU Member State) has been recognized in the State that is now requested to recognize the incompatible court judgment.

[51] See however for the potential public policy relevance of some areas of EU law case C-126/97, *Eco Swiss China Time Ltd v Benetton International NV*, ECLI:EU:C:1999:269.

[52] Ortolani (2015).

inasmuch as that award has been issued before the incompatible judgment and is indeed capable of producing *res judicata* effects in the requested state.

Finally, the last paragraph of Recital 12 addresses those court proceedings that are directly ancillary to arbitration, like the ones for the appointment of arbitrators that the CJEU had already dealt with in *Rich*.[53] In this respect, the Recital unsurprisingly confirms the non-applicability of the Regulation.

5.2 Anti-suit Injunctions Issued by an Arbitral Tribunal: Gazprom

The problem of the incompatibility of anti-suit injunctions with the Brussels regime initially arose with regard to injunctions issued by Member State courts against proceedings pending in the courts of a different Member State. In 2015, however, *Gazprom*[54] provided the CJEU with the opportunity to revisit this issue from a different perspective: the one of an anti-suit injunction issued by an arbitral tribunal.

Indeed, court-issued anti-suit injunctions are not the only type of procedural device that can be used to protect the effectiveness of an agreement to arbitrate: pursuant to many national arbitration statutes,[55] arbitral tribunals also have the power to grant this type of measure. The issuance of such a measure provided the backdrop for *Gazprom*: the case arose out of a shareholders agreement that Gazprom and the Republic of Lithuania had entered into, and which contained an Stockholm Chamber of Commerce (SCC) arbitration clause. The Republic of Lithuania initiated proceedings against Gazprom before Lithuanian courts, and Gazprom objected to the jurisdiction of those courts, arguing that the dispute fell within the scope of the aforementioned arbitration clause. In addition to that, Gazprom also initiated arbitration proceedings against the Republic of Lithuania, not regarding the merits of the dispute, but simply requesting the tribunal to issue an award ordering the discontinuation of the Lithuanian court proceedings. The tribunal indeed issued such an award, which did in substance amount to an anti-suit injunction.[56] The question then arose whether the courts of Lithuania were prevented from recognising and enforcing the award, in order to preserve their power to assess their own jurisdiction under the Regulation.

AG Wathelet issued an opinion that was largely based on the effects of Recital 12 on the interpretation of the Regulation. This choice fails to convince entirely, as the Brussels I *bis* Regulation was not applicable to the *Gazprom* case *ratione temporis*;

---

[53] *Rich*.

[54] Case C-536/13, '*Gazprom*' *OAO v Lietuvos Respublika*, ECLI:EU:C:2015:316 (hereafter '*Gazprom* (2015)').

[55] Notably, this is the case for the UNCITRAL Model Law, as a result of the 2006 revision: see Article 17(2)(b), empowering the tribunal to order a party to 'take action that would prevent, or refrain from taking action that is likely to cause, current or imminent harm or prejudice to the arbitral process itself'. See Ortolani (2019).

[56] *Gazprom* (2015), para 18.

the Advocate General, however, argued that Recital 12 operated 'somewhat in the manner of a retroactive interpretative law',[57] thus covering Regulation 44/2001 as well. According to the Advocate General, Recital 12 had the effect of effectively overruling *West Tankers*, by specifying that only a judgment on the substance of a dispute, and not one dealing with the preliminary question of the validity of the agreement to arbitrate, is entitled to circulate under the Brussels regime.[58] This clarification, according to the Advocate General, had the following implication: even if an anti-suit injunction could have the effect of preventing a Member State court from issuing a ruling on its own jurisdiction, this would have no impact on the effectiveness of the Regulation, as the jurisdictional ruling at hand would not be entitled to circulation under the Regulation in the first place.

The Court did not follow the opinion of the Advocate General. Such an outcome was not particularly surprising since (apart from the significant issue of chronological inapplicability of Recital 12 to the case) the inapplicability of the Regulation to anti-suit injunctions issued in support of arbitration was never the main point of contention, and *West Tankers* itself clearly acknowledged this very point.[59] The reasoning of the Advocate General seemed to proceed on the basis of the fallacious assumption that, since a Member State court judgment dealing exclusively with an *exceptio compromissi* (and hence with the jurisdiction of the court itself) would not be entitled to recognition and enforcement under the Regulation, then a measure aimed at curtailing the court's ability to issue that judgment could not possibly limit the effectiveness of the Regulation. Such an assumption runs counter not only to the broader principle of mutual trust underlying the instrument, but also to the nature of *traité double* that the Regulation inherits from the 1968 Brussels Convention. In other words, the Regulation has two distinct and equally important goals: not only the implementation of a regime for the intra-EU recognition and enforcement of Member State court judgments, but also the creation of a harmonised set of rules for the allocation of jurisdiction in civil and commercial matters among those courts. The rules set forth by the Regulation with respect to jurisdiction—which are not ancillary to the ones on recognition and enforcement, but independent from them and equally important—presuppose that each Member State court will have an equal power to assess its own jurisdiction, subject only to the supervisory role and guidance offered by the CJEU through the preliminary reference mechanism of Article 267 of the Treaty on the Functioning of the European Union. A measure can therefore constrain the effectiveness of the Regulation not only if it hinders the circulation of Member State court judgments, but also if it prevents a Member State court from freely evaluating its own jurisdiction.

Rather than overruling *West Tankers*, the CJEU distinguished it in *Gazprom*, on the basis of two important differences between the two cases. First the CJEU observed that, because arbitral tribunals do not form part of the court system of the Member States, they are not bound by the principle of mutual trust, and hence they do not

[57] ECLI:EU:C:2014:2414 (hereafter '*Gazprom* (AG)'), para 91.

[58] *Gazprom* (AG), para 136.

[59] *West Tankers*, para 23.

infringe EU law by second-guessing whether a EU Member State court has jurisdiction under the Regulation.[60] Second, an anti-suit injunction issued in the form of an arbitral award by a tribunal has very different consequences, as compared with a court-ordered injunction.[61] Indeed, one of the concerns raised by the CJEU in *West Tankers* with respect to court-issued anti-suit injunction regarded precisely the serious consequences faced by a party that fails to comply with the injunction. The Court noted in particular how, under English law, 'non-compliance with an anti-suit injunction is contempt of court, for which penalties can be imposed, including imprisonment or seizure of assets'.[62] For these reasons the CJEU concluded that no incompatibility existed between the Brussels regime and anti-suit injunctions issued by an arbitral tribunal, while at the same time confirming *West Tankers* with respect of court-issued injunctions.[63]

The assessment made by the CJEU in *Gazprom* with respect to the prospects for enforceability of an injunction issued by an arbitral tribunal is perhaps reductive: while it is clear that non-compliance with such a measure may not result in contempt of court, an arbitral tribunal may (depending on the applicable law) award damages for breach of the agreement to arbitrate.[64] This type of damages (which, notably, were not at issue in *Gazprom*) could be seen as a form of *astreinte*, indirectly forcing compliance by attaching negative economic consequences to the failure to conform to the interpretation of the arbitration agreement given by the tribunal. Apart from this aspect, however, the *Gazprom* judgment comes across as a (partial) clarification concerning the legal status of anti-suit injunctions in the area of freedom, security and justice.

5.3 *The Brexit Spectre Haunting Europe*

It is finally necessary to mention what could potentially happen in the near future, if the UK ceased to be a Member State of the EU. In the event of a 'hard Brexit', determining the immediate inapplicability of the entire legal framework of European procedural law, English courts would in principle be free to issue anti-suit injunctions again, ordering the discontinuation of civil or commercial proceedings pending before the courts of any EU Member State court. This could potentially enhance the attractiveness of London as a place of arbitration; it should however be noted that a court-issued anti-suit injunction is not the only mechanism through which an agreement to arbitrate may be protected, and that an order made by the arbitral tribunal itself (coupled, of course, with the international obligations arising out of Article II(3)

---

[60] *Gazprom* (AG), paras 36–37.

[61] *Gazprom* (AG), para 40.

[62] *West Tankers*, para 20.

[63] *Gazprom* (AG), para 33.

[64] Betancourt (2018).

of the New York Convention) could in practice be as effective, and more respectful of the arbitrators' jurisdiction to rule on the validity and scope of the clause.

6 Conclusions

This Chapter has offered an overview of the interplay between anti-suit injunctions issued in support of arbitration and the Brussels regime, governing civil and commercial litigation in the EU. Having clarified the nature of the anti-suit injunction as an order to perform an agreement to arbitrate, the Chapter has described the scope of availability of the measure at hand in the practice of English courts. Against this background, the Chapter has followed the evolution of the case-law of the CJEU on these matters, from *Turner* to the differentiation between court- and arbitrator-issued injunctions made by the Court in *Gazprom*.

In light of its very nature, the anti-suit injunction is bound to remain a controversial measure, especially when it is meant to have effects *vis-à-vis* the courts of a continental European legal system, where this type of measure is not typically available. Yet, in the absence of any type of inclusion of arbitration within the scope of the Brussels regime, the case-law of the CJEU and the insertion of Recital 12 in the Brussels I *bis* Regulation undoubtedly help to clarify the issue at hand.

References

Andrews N (2013) Andrews on civil processes. Intersentia, Cambridge

Benedettelli MV (2014) Le anti-suit injunctions nell'arbitrato internazionale: questioni di legittimità e opportunità. Rivista dell'Arbitrato 4:701–740

Betancourt JC (2018) Damages for breach of an international arbitration agreement under english arbitration law. Arbitr Int 34(4):511–532

Born G (2014) International commercial arbitration. Kluwer, Deventer

Briggs A (2014) Private international law in english courts. Oxford University Press, Oxford

Gaillard E (2010) Legal theory of international arbitration. Martinus Nijhoff, Leiden

Hess B, Pfeiffer T and Schlosser P (2007) Study JLS/C4/2005/03, report on the application of regulation brussels I in the Member States. Heidelberg University

Lévy L (2005) Anti-suit injunctions issued by arbitrators. In: Gaillard E (ed) Anti-suit injunctions in international arbitration. JURIS, Huntington, p 115

Merkin R, Flannery L (2014) arbitration act 1996. Informa, Colchester

Ortolani P (2015) The recast brussels i regulation and arbitration. In: Cadiet L, Hess B, Requejo M (eds) Procedural science at the crossroads of different generations. Nomos, Baden-Baden, p 125

Ortolani P (2019) Article 17. In: Bantekas I, Ortolani P, Ali S, Gomez M, Polkinghorne M (eds) The UNCITRAL model law on international commercial arbitration: a commentary. Cambridge University Press, Cambridge

Paulsson M (2016) The New York convention as an instrument of international law. In: Paulsson M (ed) The 1958 New York convention in action. Kluwer, Deventer, p 31

Satta S (1931) Contributo alla dottrina dell'arbitrato. Vita e Pensiero, Milan

Pietro Ortolani is an Assistant Professor at Radboud University. He specializes in international arbitration. Pietro holds a Ph.D. in arbitration from LUISS Guido Carli University, Rome. Before joining Radboud University, he was a Senior Research Fellow at the Max Planck Institute Luxembourg for Procedural Law and a Law Research Associate at Queen Mary, University of London. Pietro is admitted to the Bar in Italy. He has experience in both ad hoc and institutional arbitration. He has acted as an expert for the European Parliament and the European Commission. In 2016 Pietro won the James Crawford Prize.

Overseas Recognition and Enforcement of China's Arbitral Awards—From the Perspective of the Enforcement of SCIA Arbitral Awards in Hong Kong

Xiaochun Liu and Xiongfeng Li

Abstract This Chapter reviews the early history of overseas enforcement of Chinese arbitral awards and re-examines the issues in a milestone case that brought before the courts of Hong Kong decades ago, followed by an illustration on the current state of overseas recognition and enforcement of mainland China's arbitral awards from the perspective of Hong Kong. It also discusses the potential practical issues of significance to the future interaction between the New York Convention and China's international arbitration practices.

1 Background

Sixty years ago in 1958, the Convention on the Recognition and Enforcement of Foreign Arbitral Awards (New York Convention) was adopted at a United Nations conference in New York. To date, it has 159 contracting states which include the major trading nations of the world,[1] making it one of the most successful international conventions.

Forty years ago in 1978, China[2] unveiled its reform and opening-up policy.[3] Two years later, China's first special economic zone was created in Shenzhen. From 1982,

[1]United Nations Commission on International Trade Law (2019).

[2]For the purpose of this Chapter, 'China' refers to the 'People's Republic of China', 'Hong Kong' refers to the 'Hong Kong Special Administrative Region (HKSAR) of the People's Republic of China' and 'mainland China' refers to the mainland of the People's Republic of China excluding the HKSAR, the Macao Special Administrative Region and Taiwan region.

[3]The reform and opening-up policy of China was officially announced at the Third Plenary Session of the Eleventh Central Committee of the Communist Party of China in 1978, for more information, see People's Daily Online (2019).

X. Liu · X. Li (✉)
Shenzhen Court of International Arbitration, Shenzhen, People's Republic of China
e-mail: lixiongfeng@scia.com.cn

X. Liu
e-mail: liuxiaochun@scia.com.cn

L. Chen and A. Janssen (eds.), *Dispute Resolution in China, Europe and World*,
Ius Gentium: Comparative Perspectives on Law and Justice 79,
https://doi.org/10.1007/978-3-030-42974-4_9

the Shenzhen Special Economic Zone (SEZ) started the planning for an international arbitration institution based on international practices to boost China's reform and opening up, the development of SEZ, and the cooperation in the Guangdong-Hong Kong-Macao region. On 19 April 1983, the Shenzhen Court of International Arbitration (i.e. South China International Economic and Trade Arbitration Commission, formerly known as China International Economic and Trade Arbitration Commission Shenzhen Sub-commission and China International Economic and Trade Arbitration Commission South China Sub-commission; hereinafter the 'SCIA') was established as the first arbitration institution in the Guangdong-Hong Kong-Macao Greater Bay Area.

The following sections will begin with reviewing the early history of overseas enforcement of Chinese arbitral awards, discuss the current state of recognition and enforcement of SCIA arbitral awards in Hong Kong, and then provide an outlook on the future interaction between the New York Convention and China's international arbitration practices.

2 Relation Between the New York Convention and SEZ's International Arbitration Practices: Starting with China's First Overseas Enforced Award

On 2 December 1986, the Standing Committee of the National People's Congress (NPC) of China adopted a decision on China's accession to the New York Convention[4]; on the following 22nd of April, the New York Convention became officially binding on China.[5] On 12 July 1988, SCIA delivered an arbitral award,[6] which was later enforced by the High Court of Hong Kong (HKHC) on 29 June 1989, setting a precedent for the enforcement of Chinese awards in a foreign jurisdiction as per the New York Convention.[7]

This landmark arbitration case relates to a dispute over a sales contract between a Chinese company based in Guangdong province (the 'Claimant') and a Hong Kong-based company (the 'Respondent'). The Claimant, as the seller, exported a certain quantity of calculators to a Hong Kong-based trading company, as the original buyer, as agreed in the contract (the 'Original Contract'). After the Original Contract was

[4]Decision of the Standing Committee of the NPC on China's Accession to the Convention on the Recognition and Enforcement of Foreign Arbitral Awards [全国人大常委委员会关于我国加入《承认及执行外国仲裁裁决公约》的决定] (passed on 2 December 1986), http://www.npc.gov.cn/wxzl/gongbao/2000-12/16/content_5001874.htm.

[5]On 22 January 1987, China submitted its instrument of ratification and made declarations of reciprocal and commercial reservations in respect of the New York Convention. Three months later, on 22 April 1987, the New York Convention entered into force for China. See United Nations Commission on International Trade Law (2019).

[6]No. 216 [1988] of SCIA Arbitral Award.

[7]At that time, the sovereignty of Hong Kong had not been returned to China. China resumed its sovereignty over Hong Kong from the United Kingdom since 1 July 1997.

executed, the original buyer, the seller and the Respondent entered into an assignment agreement under which the original buyer assigned its rights and obligations under the Original Contract to the Respondent. Those obligations were later incorporated into a new sales contract between the Claimant and the Respondent but not honored. As a result, the Claimant filed a complaint against the Respondent with SCIA. According to an arbitration agreement entered into between the Claimant and the Respondent on 1 November 1986, SCIA accepted the case in May 1987.[8] The Claimant appointed Mr. Luo Zhendong as an arbitrator; SCIA appointed Mr. Dong Yougan as an arbitrator on behalf of the Respondent; Mr. Luo and Mr. Dong jointly appointed Mr. Zhou Huandong as the presiding arbitrator of the case. The arbitral tribunal held four hearings in Shenzhen—each on 17 August 1987, 9 September 1987, 29 February 1988, and 27 June 1988—and rendered an award on 12 July 1988.[9] Afterwards, the Claimant, acting as the plaintiff, sought leave to enforce the arbitral award before the HKHC and the defendants (two individuals who were formerly trading as the Respondent) opposed the enforcement on two grounds. The presiding judge, the Hon. Mr. Justice G.P. Nazareth, delivered a judgment in favor of the Claimant,[10] which found that the two grounds of opposition raised by the defendants were groundless. He held that the arbitral award rendered by the SCIA was a New York Convention award as defined by the Arbitration Ordinance (Cap. 341) of Hong Kong (HKAO)[11] as then in effect, and ruled that the arbitral award should be enforced.

This case set two precedents: It was not only China's first arbitral award enforced overseas pursuant to the New York Convention, but also the first foreign arbitral award enforced by the courts of Hong Kong in accordance with the New York Convention. By dismissing the defendants' two grounds for opposition, the HKHC provided an illustrative and valuable answer to resolving the common problems encountered in cross-border recognition and enforcement of arbitral awards. The unequivocal analysis and determination of the Court on the issues of the changes in the name of the arbitration institution and the place of origin of the arbitral award remain significant till this day in stabilizing market entities' expectations, understanding the spirit and implications of the New York Convention, and promoting cross-border recognition and enforcement of arbitral awards.

---

[8]No. 216 [1988] of SCIA Arbitral Award.

[9]No. 216 [1988] of SCIA Arbitral Award.

[10]MP 1221/1989. The case was heard under the Miscellaneous Proceedings by the High Court in the then Supreme Court of Hong Kong.

[11]The Arbitration Ordinance (Cap. 341) of Hong Kong was originally enacted in 1963 and amended in 1982 and 1990 and was based on a split regime—a regime for international arbitrations, formulated on the basis of the United Nations Commission on International Trade Law (UNCITRAL) Model Law on International Commercial Arbitration 1985, and a domestic regime based on the English Arbitration Act 1950. It has now been replaced by the Hong Kong Arbitration Ordinance (Cap. 609 of the Laws of Hong Kong) effective from 1 June 2011. See, Weeramantry (2017).

2.1 *First Issue in Dispute: Change in the Name of the Arbitration Institution*

In their first ground for opposing the enforcement, the defendants contended that:

> The award was not made by the arbitrators provided for in the relevant agreement, and should therefore be refused under Section 44(2)(e) of the Arbitration Ordinance (Cap. 341) which provides that enforcement may be refused if the composition of the arbitral authority was not in accordance with the agreement.[12]

Justice Nazareth found that the underlying issue here is in the change in the name of the agreed arbitration institution: When the parties agreed upon SCIA as the arbitration institution in their arbitration agreement, the former name of SCIA was still in use; while after accepting the case, SCIA rendered the arbitral award in its new name. However, the arbitral award was in fact made by the same arbitration institution; the only change was its name. The judge held that the defendants' first ground cannot be justified as the arbitral award was rendered by the same arbitration institution as agreed upon by the parties, even though the name had since been changed, which meant the argument that 'the composition of the arbitral authority … was not in accordance with the agreement' based on a name change of the agreed arbitration institution was without merit.

It should be noted that the Judiciary of Hong Kong subsequently took the same position as Justice Nazareth regarding the change in the name of an arbitration institution, i.e., a change in name does not mean a change of the arbitration institution—a position that has been reflected in the statistics provided by the Judiciary of Hong Kong on the recognition and enforcement of arbitral awards over the years.[13] Specifically, in these published data, the Judiciary of Hong Kong has consistently noted the current and former names of a particular arbitration institution both of which refer to the same arbitral institution. Taking SCIA as an example, SCIA has changed its name several times over the years.[14] In the Hong Kong Judiciary's statistics over the years on the number of awards enforced in Hong Kong, the former Chinese and English names of SCIA have always been given notice to refer to the same arbitral institution.

---

[12] MP 1221/1989.

[13] The Judiciary of Hong Kong constantly publishes statistics on the recognition and enforcement of arbitral awards. See, Hong Kong International Arbitration Centre (2017).

[14] SCIA is the abbreviation for Shenzhen Court of International Arbitration and it is also known as the South China International Economic and Trade Arbitration Commission and the Shenzhen Arbitration Commission. It is formerly known as the China International Economic and Trade Arbitration Commission Shenzhen Sub-commission and the China International Economic and Trade Arbitration Commission South China Sub-commission.

2.2 *Second Issue in Dispute: Nationality of the Arbitral Award*

In their second ground for opposing the enforcement, the defendants argued that Sect. 2 of the HKAO defines a 'Convention award'[15] as 'an award made in pursuance of an arbitration agreement in a State or territory, other than Hong Kong, which is a party to the New York Convention'. The words 'in a State or territory' qualify 'arbitration agreement' instead of 'an award'. In other words, an award would not be a 'Convention award' as defined in Sect. 2 of the HKAO, if the country of origin of the award had not been a party to the New York Convention when the arbitration agreement was entered into, regardless of whether such country later became such a party when the award was made.

The Court listed the key facts of this case: The parties entered into the arbitration agreement on 1 November 1986; the New York Convention became binding on China in April 1987; and the arbitral award was rendered by the arbitral tribunal on 12 July 1988. The defendants pointed out that when the arbitration agreement was concluded, China was not a party to the New York Convention, and therefore the arbitral award was not a 'Convention award' as defined under Sect. 2 of the HKAO even if the New York Convention had become binding upon China at the time when the arbitral award was made; and if construed to the contrary, the HKAO would have retrospective operation in a sense that it would cover awards that would not have been within the definition of 'Convention award'. In view of the above, the defendants asserted that the arbitral award in question should not be enforced by the Court.

Justice Nazareth went on dismissing the defendants' argument for the following three reasons: First, in the definition of 'Convention award' in Sect. 2 of the HKAO, the words 'in a State or territory' qualify 'an award' rather than 'arbitration agreement'. The sections of the HKAO relating to enforcement of a 'Convention award' are procedural and have an effect only on the enforcement procedure for the arbitral award after China became a party to the New York Convention. The determination that the words 'in a State or territory' qualify 'an award' would not cause the HKAO to have a retrospective operation to cover awards that would not have been so covered by the definition of 'Convention award'. Second, the Court's approach of construction, as compared to that of the defendants, is more in line with the purpose of the HKAO as a whole. When it comes to the New York Convention, 'it is the award that is material, rather than the agreement'.[16] Third, even if the Court's approach of construction indeed gives retrospective operation (which the Court has repeatedly said 'no') to the HKAO, such approach is 'clear upon the words and arises by necessary implication'.[17]

[15] 'Convention' refers to the New York Convention.

[16] MP 1221/1989.

[17] MP 1221/1989.

3 Subsequent Enforcement of China's Arbitral Awards in Hong Kong: From the Perspective of the SCIA

This landmark case has made 'Shenzhen plus Hong Kong' a 'special channel' for the implementation of the New York Convention in China. Since then, mainland China and Hong Kong have been highly cooperative in the mutual recognition and enforcement of arbitral awards according to the New York Convention. Statistics show that from 1989 till the return of Hong Kong to China in 1997, more than 150 arbitral awards made in mainland China had been enforced by the HKHC—only two of them were refused for enforcement due to procedural issues; and the courts in mainland China had, before Hong Kong's return to China, accepted 26 applications for enforcement of Hong Kong's arbitral awards in accordance with the New York Convention, about 50% of which had been enforced.[18]

After the return of Hong Kong to China on 1 July 1997, the recognition and enforcement of arbitral awards between Hong Kong and mainland China has become an issue between two different jurisdictions within a sovereign nation, to which the New York Convention no longer applies. In *Ng Fung Hong Limited v ABC*,[19] the arbitral award made in mainland China was no longer recognized by the courts of Hong Kong as a 'Convention award', nor as a 'domestic award' of Hong Kong, resulting in the uncertainty of the nature of the laws governing the award. As anticipated by arbitration practitioners and scholars in mainland China and Hong Kong, the Supreme People's Court of China and the Hong Kong Special Administrative Region (HKSAR) Government signed a Memorandum of Understanding on the 'Arrangement Concerning Mutual Enforcement of Arbitral Awards Between the Mainland and the Hong Kong Special Administrative Region'[20] (Arrangement) in Shenzhen on 21 June 1999. Mr. Shen Deyong, the then Vice Chief Justice of the Supreme People's Court, and Ms. Elsie Leung, the then Secretary for Justice of Hong Kong (currently a Council Member of the SCIA), signed the Memorandum of Understanding on the Arrangement on behalf of the Supreme People's Court and the HKSAR Government respectively. The SEZ witnessed the judicial assistance in arbitration between the two jurisdictions back on track and enter into a new historical stage.

The Arrangement was drafted in the spirit of the New York Convention to maintain the continuity and stability of the mutual enforcement of arbitral awards between Hong Kong and mainland China. In terms of its content, the Arrangement has also essentially followed the relevant parts of the New York Convention; especially with

[18] Shao and Gao (1999).

[19] [1998] 1 HKLRD 155, 156.

[20] English version of the Arrangement is available at: Department of Justice of the Government of the Hong Kong Special Administrative Region, 'Arrangements Concerning Mutual Enforcement of Arbitral Awards Between the Mainland and the Hong Kong Special Administrative Region', https://www.doj.gov.hk/eng/topical/pdf/mainlandmutual2e.pdf. The Arrangement amounts to a juridical assistance agreement, which was applied in Hong Kong by an amendment to the Arbitration Ordinance in 2000 and was applied in mainland China by the Supreme People's Court's judicial interpretation (Fa Shi [2000] No.3) taking effect on 1 February 2000. See, Brock, Knapton and Kurian (2017).

Table 1 Overview of the enforcement of SCIA arbitral awards in Hong Kong

	Number of enforced Mainland China arbitral awards	Number of SCIA's enforced arbitral awards	Number of not enforced Mainland China arbitral awards	Number of SCIA's not enforced arbitral awards
2012	6	2	0	0
2013	8	2	0	0
2014	13	5	0	0
2015	8	2	2	0
2017	17	7	0	0
Total	52	18	2	0

Note Figures above are formulated based on information pertinent to SCIA through 2012 to 2017, as provided by Hong Kong Judiciary to Hong Kong International Arbitration Centre and published on the latter's website annually

respect to refusing the enforcement of arbitral awards, the two are substantially identical to each other. According to the statistics provided by the Judiciary of Hong Kong,[21] most of the arbitral awards from mainland China have been enforced in accordance with the Arrangement. Since the implementation of the Arrangement, SCIA has been ranked first by the number of awards enforced in Hong Kong, accounting for 31.4% of all awards from mainland China enforced in Hong Kong during 2012–2015 and 31.8% of all awards from arbitration institutions around the world enforced in Hong Kong in 2017 (see Table 1).[22]

Moreover, up until now, never once have courts in Hong Kong refused to enforce an award from SCIA in accordance with the Arrangement, which by and large reflects the 'outstanding quality of Shenzhen in China's international arbitration practices', the pro-arbitration approach of Hong Kong courts, and the unique role of arbitration as the primary method of resolving cross-border dispute resolution, which has much to do with the New York Convention and its underlying principles. To recognize the historic role of 'Shenzhen plus Hong Kong' in the implementation of the New York Convention in China, the United Nations Commission on International Trade Law (UNCITRAL) and the SCIA jointly held an event, in Shenzhen on 15 May 2018, celebrating the 60th anniversary of the New York Convention and the 35th anniversary of SCIA.

[21] Hong Kong International Arbitration Centre (2017).

[22] Hong Kong International Arbitration Centre (2017).

4 Future Interaction Between the New York Convention and China's International Arbitration Practices: Issues and Recommendations

Over the past 35 years, the SCIA has gained extensive experience in the resolution of domestic and foreign economic and trade disputes. As of today, the SCIA has handled arbitration and mediation cases for parties from 118 countries. In December 2016, the SCIA Guidelines for the Administration of Arbitration under the UNCITRAL Arbitration Rules (Guidelines) came into effect. One of the highlights of the Guidelines is its Article 3 which provides that:

> Where the parties have agreed upon the place of arbitration, the parties' agreement shall prevail. Where the parties have not agreed on the place of arbitration, unless otherwise determined by the arbitral tribunal, the place of arbitration shall be Hong Kong.

This arrangement respects the party autonomy and promotes Hong Kong as the place of arbitration, which conforms to market needs in the context of international cooperation under the Belt and Road Initiative. As is widely known, China has become the world's largest trading economy; both Chinese enterprises and investments are going global; and foreign investment in China has also been growing steadily,[23] all of which may significantly increase the number of international commercial disputes and investment controversies.

Based in Shenzhen, a growth engine of the Guangdong-Hong Kong-Macao Greater Bay Area and a bridgehead of the Maritime Silk Road, the SCIA is the first among its domestic peers to converge with internationally accepted rules by formulating the Guidelines. Predictably, an increasing number of parties may elect to have their international commercial disputes resolved through arbitration by SEZ-based SCIA and have Hong Kong or a foreign country as the place of arbitration. Therefore, interaction between the New York Convention and China's international arbitration practices promises to have broad potentials. However, there are some significant and longer-term issues that cast a cloud over the innovation to international arbitration in SEZ. Before presenting these issues, it is necessary to discuss a preliminary question, the answer to which will influence the analysis to these issues.

---

[23] The influence of Chinese foreign investment in global foreign direct investment has continued to expand. The investment flow is second only to the United States (USD 342.27 billion) and Japan (USD160.45 billion), ranking third in the world. From the perspective of two-way investment, China's foreign direct investment flows have been higher than attracting foreign investment for 3 consecutive years. See, Ministry of Commerce, National Bureau of Statistics and State Administration of Foreign Statistics of the People's Republic of China (2017).

4.1 Determining the Nationality of Arbitral Award Under Chinese Law

From the legislative perspective, it seems that the Arbitration Law of the People's Republic of China (China's Arbitration Law)[24] has already given the criterion, expressly or impliedly, by its strong institutional characteristic. The meaning of 'institutional characteristic' is twofold: first, ad hoc was not allowed under China's Arbitration Law, regardless of some recent appeal and endeavors for improvement[25]; and second, the identity of an arbitral award is closely linked to the arbitration institution by which the arbitral award was made. For instances, there is even no mentioning of the concept of 'place of arbitration' in China's Arbitration Law and 'Arbitration Commission(s)'[26] can be found throughout the text. In practice, for the courts of China to exercise their judicial authority over arbitration, it is a prerequisite that the courts will analyze the arbitral award in question because different rules will apply accordingly.[27] Taking the enforcement procedure for example, the courts will normally divide the arbitral awards into the following kinds: (1) China's domestic arbitral awards; (2) China's foreign-related arbitral awards; (3) Foreign arbitral awards; and (4) Arbitral awards from Hong Kong, Macao and Taiwan. The courts will then scrutinize China's domestic and foreign-related arbitral awards against the standards as set out in Articles 237 and 274 of the Civil Procedure Law of the People's Republic of China (China's Civil Procedure Law), foreign arbitral awards against Article 5 of the New York Convention or the principle of reciprocity, and awards from Hong Kong, Macao and Taiwan against the criteria set out in the applicable arrangements (the criteria for non-enforcement listed in these arrangements are essentially the same as Article 5 of the New York Convention). There is no issue about such categorization but what has been left out by the laws is the criterion to determine the nationality of an arbitral award. What is exactly a Chinese arbitral award or a foreign arbitral award? The law is unclear in this regard.

As implied by the institutional feature of China's Arbitration Law and reading together with the chapters related to arbitration in China's Civil Procedure Law,[28]

[24]The Arbitration Law of the People's Republic of China was promulgated by the Standing Committee of the 8th NPC on 31 August 1994, effective on 1 September 1995, and amended in 2009 and 2017. English translation is available at: http://www.law-lib.com/law/law_view.asp?id=10684.

[25]The Supreme People's Court of China issued an Opinion on the Provision of Judicial Safeguards for the Building of Pilot Free Trade Zones (Fa Fa [2016] No.34) to allow for ad hoc arbitration in free-trade zones, but it has a very limited scope of application and does not have a binding force.

[26]'Arbitration Commission(s)' is a term used in China's Arbitration Law and it refers to arbitration institution established in accordance with the China's laws and regulations. Civil Procedure Law of the People's Republic of China (China's Civil Procedure Law) uses 'Arbitration Institution(s)', a more internationally accepted term, to refer to the 'Arbitration Commission(s)' in China's Arbitration Law.

[27]Gao (2017).

[28]China's Civil Procedure Law was promulgated by the Standing Committee of the 7th NPC on 9 April 1991, effective on the same day, and amended in 2007, 2012 and 2017. English translation is available at: http://en.pkulaw.cn/display.aspx?cgid=297379&lib=law.

it was naturally widely believed in China that the legislative intent was to make the nationality of an arbitration institution determine the nationality of an arbitral award it made.[29] Consequently, an arbitral award made by a China's arbitration institution will be regarded as a Chinese arbitral award.[30] The same logic will apply to those arbitral awards made by foreign arbitration institutions or that of Hong Kong, Macao and Taiwan. This approach of interpretation was put into test in a case where the parties submitted their dispute to the International Court of Arbitration of International Chamber of Commerce (ICC Court) for arbitration with Hong Kong as the seat. The Supreme People's Court of China was of the opinion that the New York Convention, rather than the Arrangement, should apply to the recognition and enforcement of the arbitral award in question because the ICC Court is an arbitration institution established in France.[31] However, this analysis contradicted with the internationally accepted rule that the nationality of arbitral award is dependent on the place of arbitration. In addition, as provided in its Article 1, the New York Convention included both the 'territorial criterion'[32] and the 'non-domestic criterion',[33] but neither of which will lead to a conclusion that the nationality of an arbitral award has any bearing on the place of incorporation of an arbitration institution. In 2009, the Supreme People's Court of China changed its view on this question by issuing the Notice on Issues Concerning the Enforcement of Hong Kong Arbitral Awards in the Mainland (Notice)[34] and according to this document:

---

[29]Gao (2017).

[30]On a separate note, at the early stage, only China's foreign-related arbitration institution could accept foreign-related cases, whereas China's domestic arbitration institutions could only hear domestic cases. This division was abolished in 1996 according to Article 3 of the Circular of the General Office of the State Council Regarding Some Problems Which Need to be Clarified for the Implementation of the Arbitration Law of the People's Republic of China, 8 June 1996, Guo Fa Ban [1996] No. 22. Since then China's domestic arbitration institutions can hear foreign-related cases just as its counterparts do, as long as the parties so agreed. Therefore, there is no need to distinguish an arbitral award of a China's domestic arbitration institution from that of a China's foreign-related arbitration institution.

[31]Supreme People's Court of China, Reply of the Supreme People's Court to the Request for the Refusal to Enforce the Final Award of ICC Court 10334/AMW/BWD/TE [最高人民法院关于不予执行国际商会仲裁院10334/AMW/BWD/TE最终裁决一案的请示的复函] (5 June 2004), [2004] Min Si Ta Zi No. 6, http://china.findlaw.cn/info/zhongcai/zcfl/zcfl/360623.html.

[32]See, United Nations Commission on International Trade Law (2016, pp. 18–19). The legal basis for the 'territorial criterion' is the first sentence of Article 1 of the New York Convention which provides that: 'This Convention shall apply to the recognition and enforcement of arbitral awards made in the territory of a State other than the State where the recognition and enforcement of such awards are sought.'

[33]United Nations Commission on International Trade Law (2016, pp. 18–19). The legal basis for the 'non-domestic criterion' is the second sentence of Article 1 of the New York Convention which provides that: 'It shall also apply to arbitral awards not considered as domestic awards in the State where their recognition and enforcement are sought.'

[34]Supreme People's Court of China, *Notice of the Supreme People's Court on Issues concerning the Enforcement of Hong Kong Arbitral Awards in the Mainland*, Supreme People's Court, China [最高人民法院关于香港仲裁裁决在内地执行的有关问题的通知] (30 December 2009), Fa [2009] No. 415, http://www.court.gov.cn/shenpan-xiangqing-117.html.

> Where a party applies to the people's courts for enforcement of an ad hoc arbitral award made in the Hong Kong Special Administrative Region or an arbitral award made in the Hong Kong Special Administrative Region by ICC Court or other foreign arbitration institutions, the people's courts shall conduct a review in accordance with the provisions of the Arrangement. Where there not exist circumstances under Article 7 of the Arrangement, the arbitral award may be enforced in the Mainland.

It is contended that the Notice has clarified the criterion to determine the nationality of an arbitral award is the place of arbitration,[35] and the judicial practice appears to turn into another direction subsequently. In 2016, a court in Nanjing gave a judgment allowing enforcement of an arbitral award made in Hong Kong by a mainland arbitration institution's Hong Kong branch.[36] The case *Ennead Architects International LLP v R&F Nanjing Real Estate Development Co., Ltd* (*Ennead* Case) concerns a dispute between a United States (US) entity and a Chinese entity, and the parties agreed to submit their dispute for arbitration to China International Economic and Trade Arbitration Commission (CIETAC), an arbitration institution incorporated in mainland China, as per its applicable arbitration rules. They further agreed that the place of arbitration is Hong Kong. By virtue of the applicable arbitration rules, where the parties agreed for arbitration in Hong Kong, it is the CIETAC Hong Kong Arbitration Center, an entity incorporated in Hong Kong with liability limited by guarantee, that accepts and administers the relevant case. The CIETAC Hong Kong Arbitration Center later rendered an award and the US claimant applied for enforcement before the Intermediate People's Court of Nanjing. The court eventually held in favor of the claimant based on the Arrangement, meaning that the court regarded the award as a Hong Kong award in light of its place of arbitration and enforced it.[37] This judgment was regarded as a milestone one for it is the first mainland China's judgment that allows the enforcement of an arbitral award of the Hong Kong branch of a mainland China's arbitration institution.[38]

Undoubtedly, the Notice and the *Ennead* Case are welcomed developments for, to some extent, they brought China's judicial practice in line with the internationally acknowledged standards. Nevertheless, this never suggests that the place of arbitration as the criterion to determine the nationality of arbitral award has been well established under Chinese law. The uncertainty lies in two aspects. First, at the legislative level, place of arbitration is still largely in an unchartered waters of Chinese legislation. To make it a nationally applicable rule, it has to be incorporated into the wordings of arbitration legislation, mainly China's Arbitration Law and China's Civil Procedure Law. It will involve systematic amendments to the current arbitration legislation and will take time. What is worth mentioning here is that China's conflict of laws rule, the Law of the People's Republic of China on the Application of Laws

[35]Gao (2017).

[36]*Ennead Architects International LLP v R&F Nanjing Real Estate Development Co., Ltd* with regard to enforcement of arbitral award before the Intermediate People's Court of Nanjing, Jiangsu Province (2016) Su 01 Ren Gang No. 1 (hereafter '*Ennead* Case').

[37]*Ennead* Case.

[38]Gao (2017).

to Foreign-related Civil Relations,[39] mentions the concept of place of arbitration in its Article 16, by designating the law of the place of arbitration one of the laws applicable to determining the validity of foreign-related arbitration agreement. But there is no provision that directly links the place of arbitration and the nationality of arbitral award at the legislative level. This partly explains why the Notice asks the courts to apply the Arrangement without expressly clarifying that the determining factor is the place of arbitration. The Supreme People's Court is a judicial organ and cannot legislate.

Second, the significance of the Notice and the *Ennead* Case might be overstated and the judicial practice hasn't established the principle of the place of arbitration in all aspects. With regard to the scenario which involves a Hong Kong arbitral award (i.e. the place of arbitration is Hong Kong) made by a mainland China's arbitration institution, it is unclear that whether this award will be regarded as a Hong Kong arbitration award. First, as discussed earlier in this section, a perusal of China's Arbitration Law will instead favor the institutional approach, meaning that this award will be viewed as a mainland China's arbitral award. And this is not contrary to the Notice because the Notice only clarified an arbitral award made in Hong Kong by ICC Court or other 'foreign' arbitration institutions will be regarded as a Hong Kong award. Second, will the *Ennead* Case be relied to reverse the institutional approach, as it is believed to be so? The answer is not crystal clear. One key fact of the *Ennead* Case that should be distinguished is that the arbitral award in question is technically not an award made by mainland China's arbitration institution but rather an award made by a Hong Kong arbitration institution, because CIETAC Hong Kong Arbitration Center is an independent entity incorporated in accordance with and under the laws of Hong Kong. The scenario about which the *Ennead* Case concerns is different from that in which a mainland China arbitration institution rendered an arbitral award with Hong Kong as the place of arbitration. Strictly speaking, there is neither legislation nor judicial authority to be relied upon to confirm the award is a Hong Kong award in the latter scenario. These ambiguities of law result in the uncertainties in the development of international arbitration in China. On the other hand, they unintentionally give some advantages to the mainland China's arbitration institutions. The following section will discuss the potential issues in details.

4.2 Issues and Suggestions

First, if the parties have chosen SCIA as the arbitration institution and Hong Kong as the place of arbitration, can they apply to a court in mainland China or Hong Kong for interim measures? This question involves the governing law of the arbitration procedure. According to the general theory and practice of international commercial

[39]Law of the People's Republic of China on the Laws Applicable to Foreign-related Civil Relations was promulgated by the Standing Committee of the 11th NPC on 28 October 2010 and effective on 1 April 2011. English translation is available at: https://wipolex.wipo.int/zh/text/206611.

arbitration, the answer is obvious in a sense that the court in the seat (i.e. the place of arbitration) often possesses such a power to grant interim measures.[40] However, it is worth noting that there is no such concept of place of arbitration under China's Arbitration Law. By contrast, China's Arbitration Law has a strong institutional characteristic, meaning that the identity of an arbitral award is closely linked to the arbitration institution. Therefore, the answer depends on how to identify such arbitral award.

If the arbitration procedure is deemed to be governed by the laws of mainland China, meaning that it is a mainland China arbitration, the courts of Hong Kong will grant interim measures in accordance with Sect. 45 of HKAO,[41] because the place of arbitration is Hong Kong. At the same time, the parties will not be precluded from applying in mainland China for interim measures before and during the arbitration under China's Arbitration Law and China's Civil Procedure Law, on the grounds that such arbitration is deemed as administered by a mainland China's arbitration institution. On the other hand, if the arbitration procedure is deemed to be governed by the laws of Hong Kong, meaning that it is a Hong Kong arbitration, the courts of Hong Kong will certainly grant interim measures in accordance with Sect. 45 of HKAO. But in mainland China, China's Arbitration Law and Civil Procedure Law only allow parties in its domestic or foreign-related arbitration procedure to apply for interim measures, and except for certain maritime cases, courts in mainland China are unable to offer court-ordered interim measures for parties in overseas arbitration, even including those in Hong Kong. The Arrangement is also silent in this regard.

Therefore, it is suggested that, in the interest of the development of the Guangdong-Hong Kong-Macao Greater Bay Area, the legislative and judicial authorities of mainland China may adopt a more positive and flexible view to ensure that the parties to arbitration can successfully apply for interim measures in both mainland China and Hong Kong. On 2 April 2019, the Supreme People's Court of China and the HKSAR Government signed the Arrangement Concerning Mutual Assistance in Court-ordered Interim Measures in Aid of Arbitral Proceedings by the Courts of the Mainland and of the Hong Kong Special Administrative Region[42] (Interim Measures Arrangement) which materializes the industry's expectation. According to this Interim Measures Arrangement, parties in 'arbitral proceedings in Hong Kong' (as defined in Article 2) may apply to the courts in mainland China for interim measures by reference to China's Arbitration Law, China's Civil Procedure Law and related

[40]The 2006 revisions to the UNCITRAL Model Law on International Commercial Arbitration even provide another possibility for the courts outside the seat to grant measures. See, Born (2015, pp. 111–128).

[41]Court-ordered interim measures. See, Article 45 of HKAO.

[42]A courtesy English translation of the Interim Measures Arrangement is available at: Department of Justice of the Government of the Hong Kong Special Administrative Region, 'Arrangements Concerning Mutual Assistance in Court-ordered Interim Measures in Aid of Arbitral Proceedings by the Courts of the Mainland and the Hong Kong Special Administrative Region', http://gia.info.gov.hk/general/201904/02/P2019040200782_307637_1_1554256987961.pdf. Effective date of the Interim Measures Arrangement is to be announced after the authorities of both sides have gone through the relevant procedures.

judicial interpretations. Another feature of the Interim Measures Arrangement is that it reflects the penetration of the concept of place of arbitration into mainland China's judicial practice, though China's Arbitration Law remains intact. When defining the 'arbitral proceedings in Hong Kong', Article 2 of the Interim Measures Arrangement expressly provides that they 'shall be seated in HKSAR'. Undoubtedly, the Interim Measures Arrangement marks new prospects for arbitration in both sides.

Second, if the parties have chosen SCIA as the arbitration institution and Hong Kong as the place of arbitration, can they apply to a court in mainland China or Hong Kong for enforcement of the arbitral award? This question involves the determination of the nationality of the arbitral award. If the arbitral award is deemed as one made in Hong Kong, the parties should apply for its enforcement in accordance with the HKAO in Hong Kong and the Arrangement in mainland China. On the other hand, if the arbitral award is deemed as one made in mainland China, the parties should apply for its enforcement in accordance with the Arrangement in Hong Kong and China's Civil Procedure Law in mainland China.

Third, if the parties have chosen SCIA as the arbitration institution and Hong Kong as the place of arbitration, can they apply to a court in mainland China or Hong Kong for setting aside the arbitral award? This question, like the second one, also involves the nationality of the arbitral award. If the arbitral award is deemed as one rendered in Hong Kong, the courts of Hong Kong should have jurisdiction over whether or not it should be set aside. Conversely, if it is deemed as one rendered in mainland China, the courts in mainland China should have such jurisdiction.

With regard to the second and third issues, the certainty rests on a uniform standard to determine the nationality of the arbitral award. Therefore, it is suggested that legislative and judicial authorities of mainland China should incorporate the principle of place of arbitration or seat of arbitration.[43] Advantages of a uniform standard are manifold. First, it is more consistent with the spirit of the New York Convention. Pursuant to Article 1 of the New York Convention, the arbitral awards to be recognized and enforced should be 'arbitral awards made in the territory of a State other than the State where the recognition and enforcement of such awards are sought', rather than arbitral awards made based on the arbitration institution. Second, it may eliminate the asymmetry in the scope of application of the Arrangement resulted from the different altitudes of courts from both sides. In the preface of the Arrangement, it states that: 'The People's Courts of the Mainland agree to enforce the awards made in the HKSAR pursuant to the Arbitration Ordinance of the HKSAR'. Meanwhile, it also provides that:

> The Courts of the HKSAR agree to enforce the awards made pursuant to the Arbitration Law of the People's Republic of China by the arbitral authorities in the Mainland (the list to be supplied by the Legislative Affairs Office of the State Council through the Hong Kong and Macao Affairs Office the State Council).[44]

---

[43] It means that the identity of an arbitral award should be based on its seat or place of arbitration, instead of the seat or place of the arbitration institution from which the award is rendered.

[44] See the preface of the Arrangement.

There is clearly an issue of asymmetry in terms of the scope of application between courts of Hong Kong and mainland China because the courts of Hong Kong only recognize the arbitral awards rendered by the arbitration institutions in mainland China, rather than arbitral awards made within the physical boundaries of mainland China. If the principle of place of arbitration is established, the courts of mainland China should enforce all arbitral awards which are made in Hong Kong, irrespective of whether they are made by domestic or foreign arbitration institutions, unless they fall within the conditions for non-enforcement. This will provide more certainties than what the *Ennead* Case gave. Mainland arbitration institutions are free to render a Hong Kong arbitral award simply by designating Hong Kong as the place of arbitration without incorporating an entity, either being a branch office or subsidiary.

Fourth, if the parties have chosen to apply the UNCITRAL Arbitration Rules (hereafter 'UNCITRAL Rules'), have arbitrators appointed by SCIA (i.e. SCIA only acts as the appointing authority), and have Hong Kong as the place of arbitration, can they apply to a court in mainland China or Hong Kong for interim measures? This question involves the governing law of an ad hoc arbitration procedure. If 'the place of arbitration' principle is applied, the ad hoc arbitration procedure should be governed by the laws of Hong Kong, and the parties to the ad hoc arbitration will not be precluded from seeking interim measures in Hong Kong, but to do so in mainland China will still face some uncertainties even after the Interim Measures Arrangement became effective. The reason is that the Interim Measures Arrangement does not include ad hoc arbitral proceedings in both mainland China and HKSAR. Article 2 defines 'arbitral proceedings in Hong Kong' as those administered by the stipulated institutions or permanent offices, which adds a second layer requirement in addition to the first layer requirement: seat is Hong Kong. Similarly, Article 6 mentions only the arbitral proceedings administered by a mainland China arbitration institution. On the other hand, if the ad hoc arbitration procedure is governed by the laws of mainland China, the parties will also not be precluded from applying interim measures in Hong Kong as HKAO covers both institutional and ad hoc arbitration; but given that ad hoc arbitration procedures are neither recognized in principle by the laws of mainland China nor covered by the Interim Measures Arrangement, there will be no legal basis for parties in such arbitration to apply for interim measures before courts in mainland China.

Therefore, it is suggested that the legislative and judicial authorities of mainland China adopt a more positive and flexible view to support arbitration institutions in the China (Guangdong) Pilot Free-Trade Zone to explore the use of ad hoc arbitration in the Guangdong-Hong Kong-Macao Greater Bay Area.

Fifth, if the parties have chosen to apply the UNCITRAL Rules, have arbitrators appointed by SCIA (i.e. SCIA only acts as the appointing authority), and have Hong Kong as the place of arbitration, can they apply to a court in mainland China or Hong Kong for enforcement of the arbitral award? This question involves the nationality of the ad hoc arbitral award. If the ad hoc arbitral award is deemed as one made in Hong Kong, the parties should apply for its enforcement in accordance with the HKAO in Hong Kong and the Arrangement in mainland China. On the other hand, if the ad hoc arbitral award is deemed as one made in mainland China, the parties should in theory not apply for its enforcement in accordance with China's Civil Procedure Law in mainland China and the Arrangement in Hong Kong, given that China's Civil Procedure Law does not recognize ad hoc arbitration and the Arrangement only allows courts in Hong Kong to recognize arbitral awards made by arbitration institutions in mainland China.

Therefore, it is suggested that the 'place of arbitration' principle should be adopted according to the spirit of the New York Convention to allow Hong Kong's courts to accept applications for the enforcement of such ad hoc arbitral awards made in mainland China.

Sixth, if the parties have chosen to apply the UNCITRAL Rules, have arbitrators appointed by SCIA (i.e. SCIA only acts as the appointing authority), and have Hong Kong as the place of arbitration, can they apply to a court in mainland China or Hong Kong for setting aside the arbitral award? This question also involves the nationality of the ad hoc arbitral award. If the ad hoc arbitral award is deemed as one made in Hong Kong, the courts in Hong Kong should have jurisdiction over whether or not to set aside the arbitral award. If the ad hoc arbitral award is deemed as one made in mainland China, the courts in mainland China should have such jurisdiction.

It is suggested that the legislative and judicial authorities of the mainland China should incorporate the 'place of arbitration' principle according to the spirit of the New York Convention.

Lastly, if the parties have chosen to apply the UNCITRAL Rules, have arbitrators appointed by SCIA (i.e. SCIA only acts as the appointing authority), and have any other State to the New York Convention as the place of arbitration, when they apply for interim measures, enforcement of the arbitral award or setting aside of the arbitral award, etc., they will also encounter issues as complex as those described above. The suggestions in this paper may provide the starting point to answer these questions.

References

Born G (2015) International arbitration: law and practice, 2nd edn. Kluwer Law International, Alphen aan den Rijn, The Netherlands

Brock D, Knapton S, Kurian A (2017) Recognition and enforcement of the arbitral award. In: Ma G, Brock D (eds) Arbitration in Hong Kong: a practical guide, 4th edn. Thomson Reuters Hong Kong Limited, Hong Kong, pp 664–693

Gao X (2017) Judiciary shall determine the nationality of arbitral award based on the place of arbitration rather than place of the arbitration institution [司法应依仲裁地而非仲裁机构所在地确定仲裁裁决籍属]. People's Justice (Cases) 20:68–74

Hong Kong International Arbitration Centre (2017) Enforcement of awards. http://www.hkiac.org/about-us/statistics/enforcement-awards

Ministry of Commerce, National Bureau of Statistics and State Administration of Foreign Statistics of the People's Republic of China (2017) statistical bulletin of China's outward foreign direct investment. http://images.mofcom.gov.cn/fec/201810/20181029160824080.pdf

People's Daily Online (2019) 40 years of reform and opening-up: into the New Era. http://en.people.cn/102775/414303/index.html

Shao W, Gao S (1999) Understanding and application of the arrangement concerning mutual enforcement of arbitral awards between the Mainland and the Hong Kong special administrative region [关于《内地与香港特别行政区相互执行仲裁裁决的安排》的理解与适用]. People's Justice 10:4–5

United Nations Commission on International Trade Law (2016) UNCITRAL secretariat guide on the convention on the recognition and enforcement of foreign arbitral awards, 2016th edn. United Nations Publication, Vienna

United Nations Commission on International Trade Law (2019) Status of the convention on the recognition and enforcement of foreign arbitral awards. http://www.uncitral.org/uncitral/en/uncitral_texts/arbitration/NYConvention_status.html

Weeramantry R (2017) The arbitration ordinance. In: Ma G, Brock D (eds) Arbitration in Hong Kong: a practical guide, 4th edn. Thomson Reuters Hong Kong Limited, Hong Kong, pp 1–16

Xiaochun Liu is the President of Shenzhen Court of International Arbitration (also known as South China International Economic and Trade Arbitration Commission). He obtained his LLB, MA (Economics), PhD from Peking University and MBA from Roosevelt University (Chicago). Liu is the panel arbitrator of SCIA, SHIAC, HKIAC and KCAB, and panel mediator of China High-Tech Fair and China Import & Export Fair. In 2012, he pushed SCIA to establish China's first international corporate governance structure. In 2015, he resolved the largest Sino-U.S. arbitration dispute as the sole mediator and sole arbitrator. In 2017, Shenzhen Court of International Arbitration and Shenzhen Arbitration Commission merged together, which created a precedent for the merger of China's arbitration institutions.

Xiongfeng Li is the Secretary of the Council, Shenzhen Court of International Arbitration (also known as South China International Economic and Trade Arbitration Commission). He obtained his LLB, LLM from Hunan University and LLM from National University of Singapore. He is qualified to practise Chinese law and his experience includes working at Singapore-based international and local law firms with a focus on cross border banking and finance. His research interests cover international commercial arbitration, competition law and public international law.

Navigating Conflict of Laws in International Commercial Arbitration in China

Patrick Zheng, Charles Qin, and Han Li

Abstract One area where private international law and arbitration interact is to unlock the applicable substantive law. Identification of the substantive law governing contractual claims (*lex contractus*) provides the framework for the formulation of subsequent arguments and strategies, and establishes the source of legal foundation that any discussion on the merits cannot bypass and disregard. Absent choice-of-law agreements, parties often seize the opportunity arguing the laws most favorable on their sides, particularly when a different applicable law will make significant difference on the outcome of the dispute. In the Chinese arbitration practice, arbitrators apply Chinese law in majority cases, resulting in over-generalized perception on conflict of laws. This Chapter seeks to address the approaches employed by arbitrators in international commercial arbitrations seated in China, in the hope of shedding some light on this seemingly extremely complex field.

1 Introduction

Arbitration, recognized as a preferred dispute resolution mechanism, has the capacity to generate conflict of laws questions at least as complex as those in litigation.[1] First, an arbitration agreement or its underlying contract is not always accompanied by choice-of-law arrangement, as a failure to choose the applicable law may result

[1]Born (2014, p. 2617).

P. Zheng (✉) · H. Li
Llinks Law Offices, Beijing, People's Republic of China
e-mail: patrick.zheng@llinkslaw.com

H. Li
e-mail: han.li@llinkslaw.com

C. Qin
Llinks Law Offices, Shanghai, People's Republic of China
e-mail: charles.qin@llinkslaw.com

L. Chen and A. Janssen (eds.), *Dispute Resolution in China, Europe and World*, Ius Gentium: Comparative Perspectives on Law and Justice 79,
https://doi.org/10.1007/978-3-030-42974-4_10

from a number of reasons, e.g. the parties conclude the contract without first consulting lawyers, or they cannot agree on the applicable law, or their choice-of-law is ineffective.[2]

Second, the problem of ascertaining the applicable law is more perplexing in the case of contracts than in almost any other area.[3]

Third, because an arbitral tribunal does not have a *lex fori*, conflict of laws rules applicable in a national court do not necessarily apply to international arbitrators.[4] This blocks the parties from, to a certain extent, better predicting the result of interpretation and application of a certain chosen law.[5] In the words of the Supreme Court of the United States, parties will enter a legal no-man's-land which would imperil the willingness and ability of businessmen to enter into international commercial agreements.[6]

Dealing with conflict of laws issues in arbitration is like navigating in 'swamp'. This is also true in arbitration in China. First, by virtue of the confidential nature of arbitration, arbitrators generally do not have access to cases previously decided for reference purpose. Moreover, it is difficult to seek useful guidance from court judgments since an error on the applicable law is not subject to judicial review.[7]

As a point of departure, conflict of laws issues arise when dealing with cases having a foreign element.[8] Arbitral tribunals not infrequently face with the task of determining the applicable substantive law in foreign-related[9] arbitration cases, as shown by recent data published in 2019 by China International Economic and Trade Arbitration Commission (CIETAC), a leading arbitration institution in China, among which 36 cases involve disputes between both foreign parties.[10]

This Chapter examines different approaches adopted by arbitral tribunals in international commercial arbitrations seated in China when determining the applicable substantive law, with a focus on conflict of laws rules governing contractual disputes where express choice-of-law agreements are lacking. The following four approaches are frequently relied upon by arbitrators in China: (1) conflict of laws rules of arbitral seat; (2) substantive law of arbitral seat; (3) general principles of conflict of laws rules; and (4) default application of *lex mercatoria*.

[2]Giuliano and Lagarde (1980, p. 20).

[3]Torremans (2017, p. 681).

[4]van den Berg (1996, p. 448).

[5]Girsberger and Voser (2016, pp. 340–341).

[6]*Scherk v Alberto-Culver Co.*, 417 U.S. 506, 516–17 (1974).

[7]Art. 58, Arbitration Law of the People's Republic of China (2017 Amendments); Art. 274, Civil Procedure Law of the People's Republic of China (2017 Amendments).

[8]Collins (2012), Ch 3 [1-001].

[9]The term will be defined in the next section of this Chapter.

[10]CIETAC (2019).

2 Determination of Foreign Element

As introduced above, the topic we are dealing with involves cases with foreign elements, namely *foreign-related* as labelled by Chinese law.[11] Because *foreign* under Chinese law is used to mean *jurisdiction-based sovereignty* rather than *territory-based sovereignty*,[12] it follows that cases involving Hong Kong, Macau and Taiwan are also considered *foreign-related*.[13]

Foreign-related cases and domestic cases are subject to different treatments in many aspects. For example, only parties to contracts with foreign elements are allowed to make enforceable choice-of-law arrangements within the Chinese legal framework.[14] By contrast, parties are not entitled to choose foreign laws to govern purely domestic legal relations, and Chinese law directly applies.[15]

Following a series of judicial interpretations,[16] it is established that a foreign-related civil relation is present if:

(1) either party or both parties are foreign citizens, foreign legal persons or other organizations or stateless persons;
(2) the habitual residence of either party or both parties is located outside the territory of the People's Republic of China (PRC);
(3) the subject matter is outside the territory of the PRC;

---

[11] See e.g. Law of the People's Republic of China on the Law Applicable to Foreign-Related Civil Relations (2010).

[12] Zhang (2006, p. 299).

[13] Art. 19, Interpretation of the Supreme People's Court on Several Issues concerning the Application of the 'Law of the People's Republic of China on the Law Applicable to Foreign-Related Civil Relations' (I), Fa Shi [2012] No. 24.

[14] Art. 126(1), Contract Law of the People's Republic of China (1999):

'The parties to a foreign-related contract may choose the laws applicable to the resolution of contractual disputes, unless otherwise prescribed by law. Where the parties to a foreign-related contract make no such choice, the laws of the country that has the closest connection to the contract shall apply.'

[15] Art. 12, General Rules (民法总则) on Civil Law of the People's Republic of China (2017):

'The law of the People's Republic of China shall apply to civil activities within the territory of the People's Republic of China, unless otherwise stipulated by law.'

See also Art. 8, General Principles (民法通则) of Civil Law of the People's Republic of China (2009 Amendments):

'The law of the People's Republic of China shall apply to civil activities within the People's Republic of China, except as otherwise stipulated by law.'

For the avoidance of doubt, the articles cited above are not in conflict and both can be applied. See Shen (2017, p. 1336).

[16] Art. 178, Opinions of the Supreme People's Court on Several Issues concerning the Implementation of the General Principles of Civil Law of the People's Republic of China, Fa [Ban] Fa [1988] No. 6; Art. 1, Interpretation of the Supreme People's Court on Several Issues concerning the Application of the 'Law of the People's Republic of China on the Law Applicable to Foreign-Related Civil Relations' (I), Fa Shi [2012] No. 24; Art. 522, Interpretation of the Supreme People's Court on the Application of the Civil Procedure Law of the People's Republic of China, Fa Shi [2015] No. 5. Note that the provisions cited above are still in force.

(4) the legal fact that leads to establishment, change or termination of civil relation happens outside the territory of the PRC; or
(5) other circumstances under which the civil relation may be determined as foreign-related civil relation.

Besides, it should be noted that peculiarity exists on the classification of arbitration cases. Under the Chinese arbitration regime, *foreign-related* arbitrations refer to those seated in China with foreign element, which are distinct from *foreign* arbitrations, which are seated outside China irrespective of foreign element.[17]

Having set the scene, this Chapter now considers the current legal framework regulating conflict of laws issues in China.

3 Legal Framework of Conflict of Laws Rules in China

3.1 Domestic Law

First and foremost, in the arbitration context, as correctly put by Hayward, domestic law sits at the baseline of the legal framework for regulating conflict of laws.[18] This is also the case in China. Determination of the applicable substantive law in absence of choice is governed by Article 41 of the PRC Law on the Law Applicable to Foreign-Related Civil Relations (PRC Law on the Applicable Law),[19] the codified conflict of laws rules in China, which provides:

> Parties concerned may choose the laws applicable to a contract by agreement. Where the parties have made no such choice, laws of the habitual residence of the party whose performance or obligations best reflects the characteristics of the contract or other laws having the closest connection with the contract shall apply.

It reconciles with identical provisions contemplated in Article 126 of the PRC Contract Law[20] and Article 145 of the General Principles of the PRC Civil Law.[21]

---

[17]Arbitral awards rendered in foreign arbitrations are governed by the New York Convention.

[18]Hayward (2017), p. 51.

[19]For the purpose of this Chapter, the discussion of conflict of laws rules in China does not extend to Taiwan, Hong Kong and Macau.

[20]Art. 126, Contract Law of the People's Republic of China (1999):

'The parties to a foreign-related contract may choose the laws applicable to the resolution of contractual disputes, unless otherwise prescribed by law. Where the parties to a foreign-related contract make no such choice, the laws of the country that have the closest connection to the contract shall apply.'

[21]Art. 145, General Principles of the PRC Civil Law (2009 Amendments):

'The parties to a foreign-related contract may choose the law applicable to settlement of their contractual disputes, except as otherwise stipulated by law. If the parties to a contract involving foreign interests have not made a choice, the law of the country to which the contract is most closely connected shall be applied.'

Although it is unclear whether the legislators intentionally inserted these identical provisions in different set of laws, according to a guideline circulated within the people's court system,[22] the nuances of the wording between Article 126 of the PRC Contract Law and Article 41 of the PRC Law on the Applicable Law do not intend to create any contradiction. Moreover, the contents are substantially identical, and to a certain extent, Article 41 of the PRC Law on the Applicable Law inherited relevant provision under the PRC Contract Law.[23]

Article 41 provides relatively clear instruction for the identification of applicable law, by way of implementing the reasonable and legitimate expectations of the parties to a transaction or occurrence.[24] On the one hand, it upholds party autonomy, so far as party's choice of law is express.[25] On the other hand, it follows an objective test, namely characteristic performance or the closest connection, as the default rule in the absence of express choice of law, although different from the one advocated under English law, which firstly looks into the implied intentions of the parties.[26]

It follows that what the relationship is between the test of the closest connection and characteristic performance in China, and the priority in their applications, if any. First, the closest connection test is the key notion, ranking on top, and does not stand on the same level as characteristic performance.[27] As evidenced in the commentary on the PRC Law on the Applicable Law, Article 41 merely encompasses two rules, namely, party autonomy and the closest connection.[28] In a press conference addressing issues arising from the implementation of laws, the spokesman on behalf of the Supreme People's Court explained that characteristic performance, generally adopted by civil law countries, is a method of applying the closest connection test.[29] Contemporary scholarly works also endorse such view that the domicile of the person exercising characteristic performance is but one aspect of the closest connection test.[30] In this regard, characteristic performance is deemed part of the closest connection test.

---

[22] Section VII, Guidelines of the Jiangsu High People's Court on Deciding Commercial Cases with Foreign Element (2012).

[23] Section VII, Guidelines of the Jiangsu High People's Court on Deciding Commercial Cases with Foreign Element (2012).

[24] Collins (2012), Ch 4 [1-005].

[25] Note that implied choice-of-law is not acknowledged in China, either by way of reference to the parties' conduct at the time of conclusion of the contract or other factors. See the SPC 4th Civil Division (2011, p. 296).

[26] See *Credit Lyonnais v New Hampshire Insurance Co* [1997] 2 Lloyd's Rep 1 at 5, CA. Under the objective proper law approach, the courts have often referred to the parties' intentions, in the sense of the intentions that they would have had if they had considered the matter, or ought to have had as reasonable persons. However, it is considered a subjective approach by way of researching the hypothetical intentions of the parties. See van den Berg (1996, p. 406).

[27] van den Berg (1996, p. 415).

[28] The SPC 4th Civil Division (2011, p. 295).

[29] Transcript of Press Conference on Questions regarding the Implementation of the Provisions of the Supreme People's Court on Certain Issues Concerning the Application of Law in the Trial of Cases Involving Disputes over Foreign-related Civil or Commercial Contracts, 8 August 2007.

[30] van den Berg (1996, p. 415).

Second, the test of characteristic performance alone is not sufficient. It prevails in civil law countries and is largely influenced by the Swiss and German legal traditions.[31] The introduction of characteristic performance is nonetheless accompanied with criticism that, oddly, the law of the place where the 'characteristic performer' is resident or incorporated should be treated as synonymous with, or even just presumed to be, the law which has the 'closest' or 'most significant' connection with a contract.[32] As noted by Jones, the nature of modern international commercial exchanges has developed dramatically with the advent of technology and globalized businesses such that it is not always possible to determine what constitutes the characteristic performance.[33] For example, because of tax and regulatory reasons, business is frequently transacted via companies incorporated in jurisdictions with which they themselves have no connection besides the fact of their incorporation, and which have still less connection to any contract which the company might enter.[34]

Previously, the exercise of the closest connection test was guided by standards too rigid. In 2007, the Supreme People's Court issued a judicial interpretation addressing issues concerning foreign-related contracts,[35] which, however, was repealed after the PRC Law on the Applicable Law came in force. Article 5 of the judicial interpretation enumerated the laws to be applied in frequently used contracts, providing that:

(1) In the case of a purchase and sale contract, the law of the place where the seller is domiciled at the time of the conclusion of the contract shall apply or otherwise, the law of the place where the buyer is domiciled shall apply, if the contract is negotiated and concluded at the place of the domicile of the buyer, or if the contract explicitly specifies that the seller must fulfill the delivery obligation at the place of the domicile of the buyer;
(2) In the case of a contract on processing with supplied materials or assembling with supplied parts, or any other toll processing contract, the law of the place where the processor is domiciled shall apply;
(3) In the case of a contract on supplying complete sets of equipment, the law of the place where the equipment is installed shall apply;
(4) In the case of a contract on the sale, lease, or mortgage of real property, the law of the place where the real property is located shall apply;
(5) In the case of a contract on the lease of movable property, the law of the place where the lessor is domiciled shall apply;
(6) In the case of a contract on the pledge of movable property, the law of the place where the pledgee is domiciled shall apply;
(7) In the case of a loan contract, the law of the place where the lender is domiciled shall apply;

[31] Blessing (1997, p. 52).

[32] Sun and Willems (2015, p. 124).

[33] Jones (2018, p. 309).

[34] Jones (2018, p. 309).

[35] Art. 5, Provisions of the Supreme People's Court on Certain Issues concerning the Application of Law in the Trial of Cases Involving Disputes over Foreign-related Civil or Commercial Contracts, Fa Shi (2007) No. 14.

(8) In the case of an insurance contract, the law of the place where the insurer is domiciled shall apply;
(9) In the case of a financial leasing contract, the law of the place where the lessee is domiciled shall apply;
(10) In the case of a construction project contract, the law of the place where the construction project is located shall apply;
(11) In the case of a warehousing or custody contract, the law of the place where the warehousing or custody service provider is domiciled shall apply;
(12) In the case of a guaranty contract, the law of the place where the guarantor is domiciled shall apply;
(13) In the case of an entrustment contract, the law of the place where the trustee is domiciled shall apply;
(14) In the case of a contract on the issuance, sale, or transfer of bonds, the law of the place where bonds are issued, sold, or transferred shall apply respectively;
(15) In the case of an auction contract, the law of the place where the auction is held shall apply;
(16) The law of the place where the broker is domiciled shall apply in the case of a brokerage contract; and
(17) In the case of an intermediary service contract, the law of the place where the intermediary is domiciled shall apply.

As a result, adjudicators are restrained from considering peculiar factors that may affect the applicable law in individual cases. The promulgation of the PRC Law on the Applicable Law relaxes the closest connection test and empowers adjudicators with broader discretions. Nonetheless, as Greenburg, Kee and Weeramantry observed, it is easy to understand it, but not always an easy test to apply.[36] This is also true in China. As pointed out in the commentary, the people's court should pay close attention to not only the quantum but also the quality of connecting factors involved.[37]

3.2 *Court Practice*

As a national court judge must apply the conflicts rules of the forum,[38] Chinese judges are bound by the closest connection test in their conflict of laws analysis. However, before applying Article 41 of the PRC Law on the Applicable Law, which governs contractual claims, Chinese courts are required to follow a two-step enquiry in the identification of applicable law, namely:

(1) Characterization of the legal relation in question; and
(2) Selection of the proper conflict of laws rules.

---

[36]Greenberg et al. (2011, p. 111).

[37]The SPC 4th Civil Division (2011, pp. 300–301).

[38]Craig et al. (2000, para 17.01).

As noted in the official commentary edited by seasoned judges of the Supreme People's Court, in private international law, characterization (or categorization) is a pre-requisite for selecting the conflict of laws rule.[39] Different results of characterization (or categorization) may lead to different conflict of laws rules, which further direct to different applicable laws.[40] In a more detailed judgment, it was articulated that in private international law, the first stage is to identify the issue in question, i.e. to determine the nature of the legal relation. It is only after such a characterization can the conflict of law rule be selected to determine the substantive laws applicable to the rights and obligations of the parties.[41]

For this purpose, identification of cause of action will determine the nature of the legal relation in question, which further determines characterization. The PRC Law on the Applicable Law envisages six types of legal relations, i.e. capacity and status, matrimonial and family, inheritance, property, obligation and intellectual property, each in a separate chapter. However, such broad classifications do not answer to which kind of dispute belongs to which type of legal relation, for instance, a dispute concerning share transfer may implicate legal relations between a principal and an agent (capacity and status), and proprietary interest (property).

As pointed out in the Notice of the Supreme People's Court on the Revised Provisions on Causes of Action for Civil Cases, cause of action is an indispensable component and requisite for filing a case, and reflects the nature of the legal relation concerned in a dispute, which is a crucial means for case administration work of the people's court.[42]

Under the current Chinese legal regime, there are four levels of causes of action, within which there are ten first-level causes of action (第一级案由),[43] under which are 43 second-level causes of action (第二级案由), under which are 424 third-level causes of action (第三级案由), under which are the fourth-level causes of action (第四级案由).[44] As the level descends, the causes of action expand and become more specific.

Once a judge identifies a dispute fits into any sub-level causes of action under Sect. 4 of the first-level causes of action titled 'contract, *negotiorum gestio* and unjust enrichment', provided that it is a contractual claim, Article 41 of the PRC Law on the Applicable Law will be applied guiding the judge in finding the proper law.

[39]The SPC 4th Civil Division (2011, p. 61).

[40]The SPC 4th Civil Division (2011, p. 61).

[41]*Liangsen Xie v Jiamin Li*, Shenzhen Intermediate People's Court, [2017] Yue 03 Min Zhong No. 3385.

[42]Notice of the Supreme People's Court on the Revised Provisions on Causes of Action for Civil Cases, Fa [2011] No. 42.

[43]The ten first-level causes of action concern legal relations evidenced in disputes relating to: (1) right of personality; (2) matrimonial, family and inheritance; (3) property; (4) contract, *negotiorum gestio* and unjust enrichment; (5) intellectual property and competition; (6) labour; (7) maritime; (8) company, securities, insurance, negotiable instrument; (9) tort; and (10) others.

[44]Notice of the Supreme People's Court on the Revised Provisions on Causes of Action for Civil Cases, Fa [2011] No. 42.

3.3 Arbitration Rules

As far as conflict of laws in the context of arbitration is concerned, the PRC Arbitration Law is silent on the determination of the applicable substantive law in arbitration.[45] Instead, arbitral institutions have addressed the issue by specifying in their arbitration rules,[46] although not all in China have done so, however.[47]

According to the CIETAC Arbitration Rules, the arbitral tribunal shall determine the law applicable to the merits of the dispute in the absence of express choice of law agreement or where such agreement is in conflict with a mandatory provision of the law.[48] The Arbitration Rules of Shenzhen Court of International Arbitration contain an identical provision, which provides that the arbitral tribunal shall determine which law is applicable in the absence of express choice of law agreement or where such agreement is in conflict with a mandatory provision of *the law of the place of arbitration*.[49] Slightly different wording is found in the Beijing Arbitration Commission Arbitration Rules, according to which the arbitral tribunal may determine the applicable law according to *all the relevant circumstances of the case* in the absence of an agreed choice of law.[50] Notably, it further provides that the arbitral tribunal shall take into account the relevant industry practices and trade usages in all cases.[51] It remains unclear whether such provision is an express endorsement on the application of general principles of law, transnational law, international trade law or *lex mercatoria.* In that case, the arbitration rules actually empower the arbitral tribunal to elect 'rules of law' instead of 'the law', the former denotes a wider notion which may not only mean a particular national law.

To sum up, the arbitration rules of arbitral institutions in China have mainly adopted the approach of *voie directe*, also known as the direct application method, meaning to apply whatever law the arbitrator deems appropriate, without having to choose and apply conflict of laws rules first.[52] Contrary to that is the approach of *voie indirecte*, meaning that arbitrators must detour to conflict of laws rules in finding the applicable law.[53] One further note is that, irrespective of whether the conflict rule

[45]Following the 2017 amendments, the PRC Arbitration Law still contains no provision dealing with party autonomy for choice of law, let alone indicating which law is applicable in the absence of an agreement.

[46]Girsberger and Voser (2016, p. 341).

[47]Note the current arbitration rules of Shanghai International Arbitration Center, the main hub of accepting international commercial arbitration cases in the East of China, does not contain any provision determining the law applicable to the substance of dispute.

[48]Art. 49 (2), China International Economic and Trade Arbitration Commission Arbitration Rules (Effective as from 1 January 2015).

[49]Art. 51(2), Shenzhen Court of International Arbitration Arbitration Rules (Effective as from 21 February 2019).

[50]Art. 69 (2), Beijing Arbitration Commission Arbitration Rules (Effective as from 1 April 2015).

[51]Art. 69 (4), Beijing Arbitration Commission Arbitration Rules (Effective as from 1 April 2015).

[52]Schwarz and Konrad (2009, p. 619).

[53]Huser (2015, p. 844).

contained in the *lex arbitri* favors the direct or indirect approach, arbitrators will generally resort to the closest connection test.[54]

The power to determine the applicable law according to the above arbitration rules sometimes is not properly exercised. For example, arbitrators sometimes simply give an answer to what the applicable law is without engaging in lengthy analysis and articulating the process in the award, which is commonly seen in Chinese arbitration. Even in judgments delivered by judges, the reasoning on the applicable law can be sparse. Although none of the arbitration rules above imposes a requirement on the arbitral tribunal to give reasons for the identification of the governing law,[55] it has been acknowledged amongst scholars and practitioners that there is an implicit duty to give reasons for the decision on the applicable law. Berger argued that more attention to the giving of reasons may actually be required.[56] In addition, as noted by Jones, the tribunal has an obligation to give reasons for why the law determined to be applicable is the most appropriate, and it may also be good practice for the tribunal to consider and discuss the implications of different approaches and results depending on the circumstances of the particular case.[57]

One consequence of the broad discretion and potential lack of reasoning is that it is difficult to predict what an arbitrator would do in using the *voie directe* approach.[58] First, even applying the direct approach, it does not necessarily mean that arbitrators will completely disregard conflict of laws rules of either the *lex arbitri*, or potential forum of enforcement. As described by Worthmann, arbitrators are always influenced by certain considerations which amount in reality to de facto conflict of laws considerations.[59] They will certainly apply some notion of private international law, at least for his internal thinking process.[60] Therefore, the direct choice of law often conceals the implicit consideration of certain conflict of laws rule.

Second, even worse is that arbitrators may identify the proper law on the basis of completely different criteria other than a conflict rule, such as the law that the members of the tribunal happen to know best.[61] This deviates from the parties' intention in that, by arbitrating, the parties submit their dispute to a process involving its adjudication according to law. It cannot be within their expectations or intentions that the governing law would be identified on the basis of the arbitrators' personal characteristics rather than the features of their dispute.

---

[54] Berger (2015, p. 518).

[55] Art. 49 (3), CIETAC Arbitration Rules (Effective as from 1 January 2015): 'The arbitral tribunal shall state in the award the claims, the facts of the dispute, the reasons on which the award is based, the result of the award, the allocation of the arbitration costs, and the date on which and the place at which the award is made.' However, this provision merely provides a general obligation of giving reasons on which the award is based.

[56] Berger (1993, p. 502).

[57] Jones (2014, p. 915).

[58] Greenberg (2004, p. 214).

[59] Worthmann (1998, p. 101).

[60] Blessing (1997, p. 55).

[61] Moss (2008, p. 42).

Discussions above over the uncertainties generated in the course of identifying the applicable law show that predictability is still much desired in arbitration. As observed in a study of survey conducted by the School of International Arbitration at Queen Mary University of London, predictability, foreseeability and certainty were among the most frequently given explanations for respondents choosing their most frequently chosen law.[62] Also, as Chinese leadership constantly calls on reinforcing the credibility of arbitration in China,[63] certainty and predictability surely are two main themes that fall into the scope of such ambitious agenda.

Admittedly, sometimes arbitrators are blinded by their own ego, where an arbitrator may rely on his or her own preconceptions and give undue weight to, or even seek out evidence to support these preconceptions, rather than be fully open to the parties' arguments.[64] However, this Chapter does not aim to ascertain arbitrator's subjective state of mind; instead, examining arbitrator's conflict of laws analysis evidenced in the award is preferred for the purpose of case study.

In this regard, this Chapter will now examine some cases evidencing the application of different approaches to resolving conflict of laws issues in arbitration in China.

4 Case Study on Approaches Adopted by Arbitrators

Given that sales law influences the broader law of contract, conflict of laws issues situated in the context of international sales law are particularly illustrative examples.[65] When talking about international sales law, it is not surprising to refer to the United Nations Convention on Contracts for the International Sale of Goods (CISG), a remarkable uniform substantive law initiative.[66] A case study situated in the context of the CISG is informative because of the following two reasons.

First, conflict of laws rules will come into play, requiring the application of certain residual law for matters beyond the scope of the CISG, albeit that the CISG has its own conflict norm on the basis of places of business of the parties to the contracts of sale of goods.[67] It means that, although, the CISG, being a substantive law convention,

---

[62] School of International Arbitration, Queen Mary University of London (2010, pp. 8–9).

[63] Notice concerning Several Opinions on the Improvement of Arbitration System and Credibility of Arbitration, General Office of the Central Committees of the Communist Party of China, General Office of the State Council, 31 December 2018.

[64] Reed (2013, p. 91).

[65] Lando (1990, p. 10).

[66] Paragraph 3 of the Preamble features the CISG as 'uniform rules which govern contracts for the international sale of goods and take into account the different social, economic and legal systems...'.

[67] Art. 1(1), United Nations Convention on Contracts for the International Sale of Goods (Vienna, 11 April 1980). Note that China, a signatory to the CISG, does not apply Art. 1(1)(b) of the CISG as a result of its reservation under Art. 95 of the CISG.

See https://treaties.un.org/Pages/ViewDetails.aspx?src=TREATY&mtdsg_no=X-10&chapter=10&lang=en.

shall generally prevail over domestic laws,[68] there is room for the application of domestic law by virtue of the rules of private international law as supplement to the CISG.[69] As pointed out by Wu, in arbitration practice administered by CIETAC, some tribunals applied both the PRC laws and the CISG in parallel in their awards.[70]

Second, the Albert H. Kritzer CISG Database at Pace University has contributed to the transparency of arbitral awards by disclosing a vast number of awards applying the CISG,[71] in the form of excerpts or summaries deleting pertinent identifying information, thus it provides profitable samples for the study of the topic of this Chapter. Premised on selected cases, this section now analyzes what arbitrators' private international laws are and what approaches may be drawn from the cases.

4.1 Conflict of Laws Rules of Arbitral Seat

Although the view that international arbitration tribunals are assimilated to national courts, and mandatorily required to apply the same conflict of laws rules as national judges, has been almost universally rejected as contrary to the basic premises of international arbitration,[72] some tribunals still endorse the out-of-favor approach that international arbitral tribunals are bound by the procedural law of the arbitral seat, including the seat's conflict of laws rules.

In a case concerning the sale of medical manufacturing equipment between a Chinese buyer and a Swedish seller, despite the application of the CISG, the tribunal was of the view that, 'since this case involves the contract for import of equipment, the law of the place for the installation and operation of the equipment, which is the law of People's Republic of China, is applicable according to the conflict rule of the seat of arbitration, China.'[73] Therefore, the relevant PRC law shall apply to issues not stipulated in the CISG.

Similar to the foregoing mindset, a tribunal seated in China even pinpointed pertinent judicial interpretation of the *lex arbitri* in force at the time,[74] according to which contracts for the international sale of goods shall be governed by the law of the seller's principal place of business when the contract is concluded.[75] In another

---

[68] Wu (2005).

[69] Art. 7(2), United Nations Convention on Contracts for the International Sale of Goods (Vienna, 11 April 1980).

[70] Wu (2005).

[71] CISG case database, Institute of International Commercial Law, Pace Law School http://www.iicl.law.pace.edu/cisg/search/cases.

[72] Born (2014, p. 2631).

[73] CIETAC, Docket No.: CISG/2002/29, http://cisgw3.law.pace.edu/cases/021227c1.html.

[74] CIETAC, Docket No.: CISG/2000/02, http://cisgw3.law.pace.edu/cases/000211c1.html.

[75] Art. 2(6)(1), Answer of the Supreme Court of the People's Republic of China to Some Problems of Application of the Law of the People's Republic of China on Economic Contracts Involving Foreign Elements, Fa [Jing] Fa [1987] No. 27.

CIETAC case, the tribunal specifically based its conflict of laws analysis on the proximate connection principle stipulated in Article 145(2) of the General Principles of the PRC Civil Law and Article 126(1) of the PRC Contract Law.[76]

Moreover, in another case involving disputes over the quality of product, the arbitral tribunal referred to the PRC Law on the Applicable Law and identified PRC law as the applicable substantive law.[77] The tribunal therefore adopted the *voie indirecte* approach, meaning that the arbitrators were guided by certain conflict of laws rules, which are specified under the PRC Law on the Applicable Law,[78] despite that the CIETAC Arbitration Rules require arbitrators to follow a *voie directe* approach.[79]

As opposed to the seeming simplicity and certainty created through the above conflict of laws analysis, applying conflict of laws rules of the arbitral seat is, in fact, obsolete and almost entirely abandoned.[80] As observed by Hayward, requiring application of the seat's conflict rules represents an incursion into the general principle that arbitration is a flexible procedure, and it is difficult to see why conflicts rules should be a particular exception.[81] In the words of a classic summary from modern arbitration commentators, any perceived obligation to apply the choice of law rules of the seat stems from a false comparison of the seat of an arbitral tribunal with a judicial forum.[82]

However, the above criticism may not be utmost objective, as it presumes that *lex arbitri* is the decisive factor, without further considering the interaction with the nationalities of the parties, the convenience of using other applicable law etc. Incidental question also comes across as to if arbitrator's choice of Chinese law is because China is the arbitrator's home jurisdiction. Another possibility lies in that arbitrators may accommodate to the conflict rules of the place of likely enforcement, in order to make sure that the judges in charge of judicial review would feel familiar with the method of finding applicable law as adopted by the arbitral tribunal.

As arbitral case law above has shown that arbitrators are much influenced by conflict of laws rules of the *lex arbitri*, rejecting such approach in its entirety simply because it is a historic view might be an overreaction.[83]

---

[76] CIETAC, Docket No.: CISG/2005/05, http://cisgw3.law.pace.edu/cases/051207c1.html.

[77] Final Award (unpublished), CIETAC South China Sub-Commission, Case [2011] CIETAC Shen Zhong Cai Zi No. 140.

[78] Art. 41, Law of the People's Republic of China on the Law Applicable to Foreign-Related Civil Relations (2010).

[79] Art. 49 (2), China International Economic and Trade Arbitration Commission Arbitration Rules (Effective as from 1 January 2015).

[80] Gaillard and Pinsolle (2004, p. 146).

[81] Hayward (2017, p. 191).

[82] Craig et al. (2000, para 17.01).

[83] Born (2014, p. 2661).

4.2 Substantive Law of Arbitral Seat

A more radical variation is that arbitrators apply the substantive law of arbitral seat. In a case administered by CIETAC concerning the sale of steel products between a Chinese buyer and a Swiss seller, the parties disputed on whether the CISG together with the PRC Contract Law or the law of Switzerland constitute the governing law when determining the nature of Clause 7.2 of the Contract,[84] namely whether it is a penalty clause and, if so, whether it is void or in fact an agreed liquidated damages clause.

In its conflict of laws analysis, the arbitral tribunal surveyed in lengthy contemporary arbitration literature in support of its consideration for the *lex arbitri*, holding that:

> *The curial law/the lex arbitri, i.e. the law of the situs or the site of the arbitration, viz, Chinese Law, determines the powers and duties of the arbitrators. This fact triggers the application of the PRC Contract Law.* After considering all of the submissions that have been made, it is the tribunal's view that the powers and duties of the arbitral tribunal are determined by the curial law of the arbitration which is Chinese law and that in turn triggers, in an appropriate case, the provision of Article 114.[85]

The arbitral tribunal made a dramatic turn and stated in the award that,

> Although the choice of the seat of arbitration does not always amount to the choice of the substantive law of the seat of arbitration, in the case at hand the choice in favor of arbitration administered by the China International Economic and Trade Arbitration Commission with seat in China amounted to an implicit choice of the Chinese law.[86]

Nonetheless, such explanation in essence was making the point that the *lex arbitri* played a decisive role in the identification of applicable law.

4.3 General Principles of Conflict of Laws Rules

Sometimes arbitral tribunals also turn to general private international law rules in identifying the applicable law. In a case published in CIETAC's '2017 Annual Report on International Commercial Arbitration in China',[87] a Singaporean company and a Chinese company agreed in the sales contract that part of the contract will be

---

[84]Clause 7.2 reads:

'If Buyer opens an acceptable Letter of Credit as per the Contract and thereafter the Seller cancels the present contract or fails to deliver the Goods for reasons other than Force Majeure, the Seller shall pay a penalty of USD/MT 2 to the Buyer. The Seller will pay no further claims on this account.'

[85]CIETAC, Docket No.: CISG/2004/07, http://cisgw3.law.pace.edu/cases/040900c1.html.

[86]CIETAC, Arbitral Award n. 0291-1, http://www.unilex.info/case.cfm?id=1441. See also Ferrari and Silberman (2010, footnote 90).

[87]CIETAC Case (2016) Jing Cai Zi No. 0517, cited in CIETAC's 2017 Annual Report on International Commercial Arbitration in China (2017, p. 147).

governed by English law. The issue facing the arbitral tribunal was to determine the applicable substantive law for the rest part of the contract.

The Singaporean company argued that English law shall apply, because the part of the contract governed by English law correlated with the rest of the contract. Therefore, applying English law would ensure consistency on the application of law to the same dispute, and manifest the true intention that the parties in fact did not mean to differentiate the two parts of the contract.

The arbitral tribunal held that express choice of law was only evidenced in part of the contract. For the rest part, the parties failed to come to consensus on the applicable substantive law. Because the parties' places of business are Singapore and China, both contracting States to the CISG, the CISG shall apply to the rest part of the contract. Matters governed by the CISG but not expressly settled in it are to be settled *in conformity with the principle of the closest connection*. In this regard, the arbitral tribunal decided that Chinese law shall apply in the event of lack of clarity under the CISG.

It also provides an illustrative example of *dépeçage*,[88] also known as 'separation of choice of law'. Although Chinese law does not address the issue of *dépeçage*, no restrictions are imposed on the parties concerning the matter.[89] As observed by the judges from the Supreme People's Court, allowing the parties to separate the substance of the contract and apply different laws will greatly facilitate the development of international trade and commerce.[90]

Some tribunals made a step forward by listing the connecting factors in the exercise of the closest connection test. For instance, as observed in an award,

> As the arbitral institution selected by the parties, the domicile of buyer and the installation place of the device are all located in China, *according to the principle of the closest relation in conflict rules of private international law*, matters not provided in the CISG, should be governed by the substantive law of the PRC.[91]

In the PTA powder case, the arbitral tribunal held that, for matters that are not governed by the CISG, Chinese law should be applicable *pursuant to the doctrine of the closest connection*, because both the place of business of the buyer and the place of arbitration are China.[92]

The principle of closest connection seeks to ascertain the law that reasonable persons in the parties' positions would have identified by virtue of the relationship of a tribunal's conflicts analysis to the parties' disputes,[93] and enjoys wide endorsement from the cases we looked into. However, sometimes application of the closest connection test may stem from an implicit choice. In a case between a German seller and

[88] *Dépeçage* is the process of applying rules of different States on the basis of the precise issue involved. The doctrine of *dépeçage* involves the separation of issues and the application of a distinct choice-of-law analysis to each issue.

[89] The SPC 4th Civil Division (2011, p. 297).

[90] The SPC 4th Civil Division (2011, p. 297).

[91] CIETAC, Docket No.: CISG/2007/04, http://cisgw3.law.pace.edu/cases/070630c1.html.

[92] CIETAC, Docket No.: CISG/2008/01, http://cisgw3.law.pace.edu/cases/080418c1.html.

[93] Thomas (1984, p. 142).

a Chinese buyer, the arbitral tribunal directly selected Chinese law after connecting a number of factors, including the place where the contract is executed, the place where the contract is performed and the place of arbitration, seemingly omitting a clear reference to the closest connection test.[94]

Whether the closest connection test is specifically referred to as a source is accompanied with concerns over uncertainty and may trigger questions whether the so-called general principles of conflict of laws do or do not truly exist.[95] Although it is advocated in some literature that the closest connection test is a general principle of conflict of laws,[96] it remains to be seen what the broad 'general principles of conflict of laws' would encompass.

4.4 Default Application of Lex Mercatoria

Lex mercatoria can be defined as those transnational rules and usages applied by merchants in the regulation of international trade,[97] also a key principle not unfamiliar in arbitration,[98] as arbitration rules of leading Chinese arbitral institutions empower arbitrators to consider international practice.[99]

In an arbitration administered by CIETAC, absent the parties' choice of law, the arbitral tribunal decided that Chinese law should apply under the closest connection rule. Further, the tribunal held that the UNIDROIT Principles of International Commercial Contracts (UNIDROIT Principles), as international usages, should be applied only in the absence of relevant provisions in the applicable domestic law.[100] Because in the case at hand the issues at stake were capable of being settled under the applicable law, the UNIDROIT Principles should not be applied.

Although the tribunal in the end declined to apply the UNIDROIT Principles, it cannot be excluded that arbitrators sometimes do seek help from their knowledge of private international law, part of which being *lex mercatoria*.

5 Conclusion

The case study above reveals that many arbitrators are misled by the preconception that they are obligated to apply the conflict of laws rules of arbitral seat. As a result, a mature system resolving conflict of laws issues in international commercial arbitration in China is yet to be established.

---

[94]CIETAC, Docket No.: CISG/2005/24, http://cisgw3.law.pace.edu/cases/051000c1.html.

[95]Hayward (2017, p. 198).

[96]Greenberg et al. (2011, p. 110).

[97]Gaillard and Savage (1999, p. 806).

[98]Born (2014, p. 2664).

[99]Art. 49 (1), China International Economic and Trade Arbitration Commission Arbitration Rules (Effective as from 1 January 2015).

[100]CIETAC, Arbitral Award in 2007, http://www.unilex.info/case.cfm?id=1208.

Arbitrators generally enjoy too wide discretions deciding conflict of laws issues, resulting in lack of uniformity on the proper positions that should be taken. As evidenced in the cases analyzed above, there are mainly four approaches adopted by arbitral tribunals seated in China in the process of finding the appropriate applicable law:

(1) Conflict of laws rules of arbitral seat;
(2) Substantive law of arbitral seat;
(3) General principles of conflict of laws rules; and
(4) Default application of *lex mercatoria*.

With respect to the first approach, applying the seat's conflict of laws rules is yet not obsolete in China. As illustrated earlier, such approach does have the advantage of simplicity, despite that that the function of the seat is to regulate the conduct of the arbitral procedure, rather than to regulate the applicable substantive law.[101]

The strong preference for the seat's conflict rules in international commercial arbitration in China may be because the seat is not just a legal term, but also the place of contractual performance, and the place, in majority of the cases, one party comes from.[102] As a consequence, it seems natural that the seat happens to be the place that the dispute is the most closely connected with.

The second approach is premised on the theory that the parties' choice of the arbitral seat constitutes an implied choice of the substantive law of the seat, nonetheless, such view is emphatically rejected in all developed jurisdictions and has been largely abandoned by most contemporary authorities.[103]

The third approach greatly reflects international consensus as it considers the application of conflict rules sourced from international practice, the fruit developed beyond parochialism. Although tribunal's findings made on the basis of the wider general principles approach have sometimes been criticized as made 'with some audacity',[104] on the bright side, the benefit of adopting this approach is that the concept of 'general principles' per se is quite inclusive and is capable of being interpreted extensively enough for the purpose of helping arbitrators solve troublesome conflict of law issues.

In line with the analysis drawn from the selected cases, the mainstream is to adopt the closest connection test in determining the applicable substantive law. Apart from CIETAC, the Hong Kong International Arbitration Centre (HKIAC) has also endorsed the application of the closest connection test, even though its arbitration rules merely provide that the arbitral tribunal shall apply the *rules of law* which it determines to be appropriate.[105]

---

[101] Hayward (2017, p. 190).

[102] Only 36 out of 552 international arbitration cases concern purely foreign parties (both claimant and respondent are from outside of China). See CIETAC (2019).

[103] Born (2014, p. 2631).

[104] Lando (1986, p. 111).

[105] Art. 36, 2018 HKIAC Administered Arbitration Rules (Effective as from 1 November 2018).

As evidenced in the Q&A section on HKIAC's webpage, HKIAC indicates that if the contract is silent as to its governing law, the tribunal will be required to determine what its governing law is (typically as a preliminary issue). This will be the law of the jurisdiction with which *the contract has the closest connection.*[106] If the contract provides for arbitration in Hong Kong, this may be *a factor* in favor of the tribunal applying Hong Kong law as the governing law of the contract.

However, it is questionable as to where the idea of applying the closest connection comes from, be it a truly generalized international instruments rule or actually the conflict law rule of *lex arbitri*. Premised on the fact that leading arbitral institutions rarely publish their official excerpts of arbitration cases omitting relevant confidential information, the discussion surrounding applicable law against the backdrop of international commercial arbitration in China remains in the mystery box, because circumstances and connecting factors may vary on a case-by-case basis, and the case samples available at hand are very limited.

In addition, a revisit to the closest connection test discloses that it is still open to possible criticism. The closest connection test is largely situated within arbitrator's broad discretion with respect to both the identification of connecting factors, and the assessment of their weight,[107] making the test ultimately under the control of the arbitral tribunal.

In this regard, it remains to be seen how cases involving multi-parties whose subsidiaries incorporated in different jurisdictions all participated in the contractual performance would affect the connecting factors in the way of applying the closest connection test. In the near future, the closest connection test may also be challenged in the following scenarios:

(1) Where parties engage in complex long-term construction contracts, such as turnkey agreements;
(2) Where disputes take place in E-commerce, such as online-shopping and transfer of funds;
(3) Where contractual performance is evenly distributed between subsidiaries of one party, or cases involving joint ventures; and
(4) Other complex contractual settings, such as technology transfers and mining concessions, e.g. determination of the law applicable to the expropriation of a diamond drilling facility directed through an act of state, albeit that the relevant contract and concession are made under a foreign law.

The last approach, which may not be followed, shows the tribunal struggles to balance the competing interests between *lex mercatoria* and state-promulgated substantive law as the law governing merits of the case. In the case analyzed above, the reasoning of the tribunal, in essence, illustrates that it treated international usages as a default mechanism, as supplementary to national laws. Advocating the application of *lex mercatoria* in international commercial arbitration in China may be subject to unpopularity that an arbitrator trained with knowledge of Chinese law may feel reluctant to

---

[106]Question 46 of Hong Kong Arbitration 100 Questions & Answers, http://hkiac.org/arbitration/why-hong-kong/hong-kong-arbitration-faqs.

[107]Burckhardt and Groz (2013, p. 167).

apply 'soft laws', in that they lack binding effects compared with state-promulgated laws.

Overall, the closest connection test stands out from the cases we examined as the optimal and appropriate conflict of laws rule for international commercial arbitration in China. Given that the test itself is objective,[108] it leaves arbitrators fairly limited space to exercise discretion in an arbitrary manner. Not only must justice be done, it must also be seen to be done.[109] To this end, arbitrators must carefully look for the connecting factors spread in the bigger picture of the dispute, and assess the weight of each single factor in an attempt to satisfy parties' expectations.

References

Berger KP (1993) International economic arbitration. Kluwer, The Hague

Berger KP (2015) Private dispute resolution in international business: negotiation, mediation, arbitration, 3rd edn. Kluwer, The Hague

Blessing M (1997) Choice of substantive law in international arbitration. J Int'l Arb 14(2):39–65

Born G (2014) International commercial arbitration, 2nd edn. Kluwer, The Hague

Briggs A (2013) The conflict of laws, 3rd edn. Oxford University Press, Oxford

Burckhardt P, Groz P (2013) The law governing the merits of the dispute and award *ex aequo et bono*. In: Geisinger E, Voser N, Petti A (eds) International arbitration in Switzerland—a handbook for practitioners, 2nd edn. Kluwer, The Hague

CIETAC (2019) 2018 CIETAC work report and 2019 CIETAC work plan. http://www.cietac.org.cn/index.php?m=Article&a=show&id=15803

Collins L (ed) (2012) Dicey, morris and collins on the conflict of laws, 15th edn. Sweet & Maxwell, London

Craig WL, Park WW, Paulsson J (2000) International chamber of commerce arbitration, 3rd edn. Oceana/ICC Publishing, Dobbs Ferry

Ferrari F, Silberman L (2010) The law applicable to the merits of the dispute. Revista Brasileira de Arbitragem 26:73–121

Gaillard E, Pinsolle P (2004) Advocacy in international commercial arbitration: France. In: Bishop R (ed) The art of advocacy in international arbitration. Juris Publishing, New York

Gaillard E, Savage J (eds) (1999) Fouchard, Gaillard, Goldman on international commercial arbitration. The Hague, Kluwer

Girsberger D, Voser N (2016) International arbitration: comparative and Swiss perspectives, 3rd edn. Schulthess Verlag, Zürich

Giuliano M, Lagarde P (1980) Report on the convention on the law applicable to contractual obligations. Off J C 282:1–50

Greenberg S (2004) The law applicable to the merits in international arbitration. Vindobona J Int'l Comm'l Law&Arb 8(2):315–335

Greenberg et al (2011) International commercial arbitration: an Asia-Pacific perspective. Cambridge University Press, Cambridge

Hayward B (2017) Conflict of laws and arbitral discretion: the closest connection test. Oxford University Press, Oxford

Huser D (2015) Determining the relevant limitation period for international sales contracts before international arbitral tribunals. ASA Bulletin 33(4):825–848

[108] Briggs (2013, p. 242).

[109] *R v Sussex Justices* [1924] 1 KB 256, [1923] All ER Rep 233.

Jones D (2014) Choosing the law or rules of law to govern the substantive rights of the parties. Singap Academy Law J 26:911–941
Jones D (2018) The substantive rights of parties in arbitration: *voie directe* and *voie indirecte*. In: Kaplan N, Moser M (eds) Jurisdiction, admissibility and choice of law in international arbitration: Liber Amicorum Michael Pryles. Kluwer, The Hague
Lando O (1986) The law applicable to the merits of the dispute. Arb Int'l 2(2):104–115
Lando O (1990) European Contract Law. In: Šarčević P (ed), International contracts and conflicts of laws-a collection of essays. Graham & Trotman, London
Moss GG (2008) International arbitration and the quest for the applicable law. Glob. Jurist Adv. 8(3) [Article 2]
Reed L (2013) The 2013 Hong Kong international arbitration centre kaplan lecture—arbitral decision-making: art, science or sport. J Int'l Arb 30:85–99
School of International Arbitration, Queen Mary University of London (2010) 2010 international arbitration survey: choices in international arbitration, pp 8–9. http://www.arbitration.qmul.ac.uk/media/arbitration/docs/2010_InternationalArbitrationSurveyReport.pdf
Schwarz FT, Konrad CW (2009) The Vienna rules: a commentary on international arbitration in Austria. Kluwer, The Hague
Shen DY (ed) (2017) Understanding and application of the General Rules on civil law of the People's Republic of China (II). People's Court Press, Beijing
Sun W, Willems M (2015) Arbitration in China. Kluwer, The Hague
The SPC 4th Civil Division (2011) Understanding and application of the Provisions of the Law of the People's Republic of China on application of laws to foreign-related civil relations, China Legal Publishing House, Beijing
Thomas R (1984) Arbitration agreements as a signpost of the proper law. Lloyd's Mar Com L Q, pp 476–488
Torremans P (ed) Cheshire, North & Fawcett private international law, 15th edn. Oxford University Press, Oxford
van den Berg AJ (ed) (1996) Planning efficient arbitration proceedings: the law applicable in international arbitration. Kluwer, The Hague
Worthmann B (1998) Choice of law by arbitrators: the applicable conflicts of laws system. Arb Int'l 14(2):97–114
Wu D (2005) CIETAC's practice on the CISG. http://www.cisg.law.pace.edu/cisg/biblio/wu.html#i
Zhang M (2006) Choice of law in contracts: a Chinese approach. Nw. J. Int'l L. & Bus. 26:289–333

Patrick Zheng is a partner of Llinks Law Offices in Beijing. His practice areas cover international commercial and investment arbitration and cross-border litigation. He has represented numerous high profile cases, such as the Government of Yemen in the ICSID Case No. ARB/14/30, ZTE in its US investigations and etc. Mr. Zheng is a panel arbitrator of CIETAC, HKIAC and other leading arbitration institutions. He is qualified in China and the State of New York.

Charles Qin is a co-founder and senior partner of LIinks Law Offices in Shanghai. Mr. Qin specializes in the study of contract law and commercial law and regularly acts as a PRC law expert in international arbitrations. Mr. Qin is well-regarded for his experience in banking, corporate and dispute resolution by Chambers, Benchmark Litigation, Asialaw and other international publications. Mr. Qin is a panel arbitrator of SHIAC and SCIA, and a member of the Chartered Institute of Arbitrators.

Han Li is an associate of Llinks Law Offices. Mr. Li holds a master degree in international commercial arbitration law from Stockholm University and is a member of Young ICCA, which functions under the auspices of the International Council for Commercial Arbitration.

Developments in International Investment Arbitration

Investor-State Arbitration in China: A Comparative Perspective

Leon E. Trakman, Qiao Liu, and Lei Chen

Abstract Notwithstanding China's endorsement of investor-state arbitration (ISA) more than a decade ago, few investor claims have been initiated against it. These concerns are not peculiar to China. Economically and politically powerful states, not least of all the United States, are less frequently subject to ISA than poorer states for much the same reason. What is increasingly likely is that, China is preparing itself and its investors abroad for investor-state proceedings in the future. This is evident, for example, in China's growing interest in the functioning of the International Center for the Settlement of Investment Disputes (ICSID), among other institutions, in its inclusion of ISA in its Model Bilateral Investment Agreement and in various regional and bilateral agreements it has concluded. China is now one of the biggest recipients of foreign investment in the world, as well as being a key player in outward foreign direct investment. In light of China's rise in the foreign investment sphere and the consequence this may have on its engagement with investment claims, this Chapter has two primary purposes. The first purpose is to examine China's limited experience with ISA under bilateral investment treaties (BITs). The second purpose is to identify how China is likely to develop its investor-state dispute resolution regime through strategic investment alliances with other states without sacrificing its distinctive national interests including those of its investors abroad.

L. E. Trakman (✉)
University of New South Wales, UNSW Law, Sydney, Australia
e-mail: l.trakman@unsw.edu.au

Q. Liu
School of Law, City University of Hong Kong, Kowloon Tong, People's Republic of China
e-mail: q.liu@law.uq.edu.au

L. Chen
School of Law, Hong Kong Special Administrative Region, City University of Hong Kong, Kowloon Tong, People's Republic of China
e-mail: leichen@cityu.edu.hk

L. Chen and A. Janssen (eds.), *Dispute Resolution in China, Europe and World*,
Ius Gentium: Comparative Perspectives on Law and Justice 79,
https://doi.org/10.1007/978-3-030-42974-4_11

1 Introduction

On the world stage, China has emerged as a major importer and exporter of direct investment. China's projected investment is expected to reach close to two trillion US dollars by 2020.[1] China's investments are diverse and global. It is a net importer of, among other products, oil, gas, and coal. It is investing significantly in Africa, Asia and South America, to meet its energy supply needs. Over 85% of its outbound investments are concentrated in less than one dozen destinations including Hong Kong, the United States, Singapore, Netherland and Australia.

For a country that excluded both inbound and outbound investment between 1949 and 1978, China's growth as a foreign direct investment (FDI) importer, and increasingly, exporter, is remarkable.[2] Both inbound and outbound investments continue to grow at an impressive rate.[3] In 1999, China adopted its 'Going Abroad' strategy, followed by its 2001 Outline of the Tenth Five-Year Plan for National Economy and Social Development.[4] China's BITs program thereafter focused increasingly on outbound investment.[5] Notable results following China's 'Going Abroad' strategy was its accession to the International Center for the Settlement of Investment Disputes (ICSID) in 1993; the provision for investor-state arbitration (ISA) in its BITs; and the provision of 'national treatment' to foreign investors in its more recent BITs.[6] As a consequence, China's FDI abroad has been increasing rapidly and steadily in the past two decades (except for 2017, when a fall occurred for the first time due to restrictive policies on capital outflows). This is highlighted by an increase in foreign contract projects, particularly franchising engineering projects (including Build-Operate-Transfer (BOT), Build-Own-Operate (BOO) and Public-Private Partnership (PPP)), investment in countries along the 'Belt and Road' and Merger & Acquisition abroad.[7]

China's pattern of investment practices is: It often negotiates investment treaties on a one to one basis with other countries. It focuses increasingly on investment quality, rather than investment quantity; and it is concerned about outbound not only inbound investments, such as the investments by state-owned enterprises abroad.

As a result, China has one of the largest networks of BITs in place next to Germany, as well as a growing number of free trade agreements (FTAs) containing

[1]UNCTAD (2018b).

[2]Gu et al. (2008), Neumayer and Spess (2005).

[3]On the growth of FDI in China, see the statistics provided by Ministry of Commerce, People's Republic of China (2018) at: http://english.mofcom.gov.cn/article/statistic/foreigninvestment/201812/20181202815485.shtml.

[4]The Outline of this Plan is available at: http://english.gov.cn/official/2005-07/29/content_18334.htm.

[5]See Cai (2006).

[6]See Shan and Gallagher (2009, §§ 1.77–1.82).

[7]Ministry of Commerce, People's Republic of China (2016). On China as a driving force in outward bound investments across the developing world, see Buckley et al. (2007), Kaplinsky and Messner (2008).

detailed investment chapters. To be specific, China has concluded 130 BITs with other countries, including the latest BIT signed with Turkey in 2015 (which is yet to enter into force). Among these are 34 BITs with African countries including among others, Ghana, Tunisia, Egypt, Kenya, South Africa, Mozambique and Mali.[8] China also has BITs with various Western countries, most recently with Canada concluded in 2012. It concluded 23 treaties with investment provisions, including with both Australia and South Korea in 2015.

China is aware that the price of attracting global investment is the prospect that investor claims will inevitably be lodged against it in the future. This is particularly so after the promulgation of the new Foreign Investment Law.[9] The new law intends to ease restrictions on foreign firms' operation in the country by creating a fair, transparent, and predictable investment environment. However, China is also aware that the benefits may well outweigh the costs. After all, China has grown into the second largest economy in the world. It is the second largest recipient of foreign investment. It is third in outward direct foreign investment.[10] It appreciates the economic rationalist reasons for promoting FDI, as well as the risks.

Drawing upon a comparative examination of international norms and practice, and evaluating them from the perspectives of both Chinese and Western scholarship, this Chapter analyses the trends behind improving statutory structures by reviewing China's gradual engagement in ISA. This Chapter has two primary purposes. The first purpose is to examine China's limited experience with ISA under BITs with foreign countries. It addresses evolving case law governing investor-state dispute resolution in China. The second purpose is to identify how China is likely to develop its investor-state dispute resolution regime through strategic investment alliances with other states without sacrificing its distinctive national interests including those of its investors abroad. These trends, though deliberate, showcase China's inexorable drive toward compliance with international investment and trade regimes.

2 Investment Claims and China

China now ranks second only to Germany in the number of BITs it has concluded. These developments are all the more striking considering that China concluded its first BIT in 1982 with Sweden, its second BIT in 1989; and it only ratified the ICSID

---

[8]For a list of China's BITs, see: http://www.unctad.org/sections/dite_pcbb/docs/bits_china.pdf. The text of each BIT is available at: http://www.unctadxi.org/templates/docsearch____779.aspx. On China's investment treaty partners, see: https://icsid.worldbank.org/ICSID/FrontServlet. See also, Kragelund (2009); Bennell (1997); Alden and Davies (2006); Davies (2008); Huliaras and Magliveras (2007).

[9]Foreign Investment Law of the People's Republic of China [中华人民共和国外商投资法], promulgated on 15 March 2019, effective 1 January 2020.

[10]See UNCTAD (2018b).

Convention in 1993.[11] Equally striking is the development of China's three model BITs, the first initiated in the early 1980s, the second developed in the mid-1990s, and the third in 1998. A notable feature of the current Model BIT is in the emphasis it gives to investor protection over market accession; its endorsement of ISA under the ICSID Rules or ad hoc arbitration under the United Nations Commission on International Trade Law (UNCITRAL) Rules; and its sanctioning of umbrella clauses protecting the rights of investors from treaty partner states.[12]

Despite these developments, there are only two decided ICSID cases ISA in which China was the respondent, namely, *Ekran Berhad* and *Ansung Housing*.[13] China did not lose in either of these two cases: *Ekran Berhad* was settled before the proceeding was completed, whereas in *Ansung Housing*, the tribunal found in favour of China on the expiry of limitation period. Aside from these two cases, there is only one investor's ICSID claim pending against China.[14] There are various explanations given for this paucity. First, foreign investors do not want to proceed against China and jeopardize their future dealings there, or risk a run-in with the Chinese legal system, such as happened with the *Stern Hu* case.[15] As a European Union (EU) Report of 7 March 2012 reflects, initiating ISA against China is likely to be the 'last resort'.[16] Second, China is well resourced to defend itself against foreign investors including by engaging in costly, dilatory and fractious ISA proceedings. Thirdly, at least under 'first generation' Chinese BITs, foreign investors could claim compensation, but not that an expropriation has occurred.[17] As a result, any investor claim against a host state would likely fail *ab initio* on grounds that, given the exclusion of a legally determined expropriation, an ISA tribunal would lack jurisdiction to hear the investor's claim. Adding to this absence of ISA jurisdiction are tribunal decisions involving BIT treaty language that has limited compensation claims by investors against other state parties to those BITs.[18]

---

[11] See, e.g. ICSID, 'List of Contracting States and Other Signatories of the Convention', http://icsid.worldbank.org/ICSID/. See also, Willems (2011); Heymann (2008); Schreuer (2001), Chapter 1.

[12] An example of China's endorsement of ISA under the ICSID and UNCITRAL is contained in Articles 5 and 9 of the Germany-China BIT which came into force on 11 December 2005. Article 10(2) of that BIT provides an umbrella clause, providing that each state party shall respect its treaty obligations relating to investors from the other state party. On the provisions in China's Model BIT, see e.g. Cohen and Schneiderman (2017), pp. 10–128.

[13] *Ekran Berhad v People's Republic of China* (ICSID Case No. ARB/11/15) (hereafter '*Ekran Berhad*') and *Ansung Housing Co., Ltd. v People's Republic of China* (ICSID Case No. ARB/14/25).

[14] *Hela Schwarz GmbH v People's Republic of China* (ICSID Case No. ARB/17/19) (hereafter '*Hela Schwarz GmbH*').

[15] Stern Hu, an Australian businessman of Chinese origins, was found guilty in 2010 by a Chinese court of stealing commercial secrets and accepting bribes. See Bath (2010).

[16] See Rubinacci (2012); European Commission (2011).

[17] See Smith (2010).

[18] See *Vladimir and Moise Berschader v Russian Federation*, award in Stockholm under the auspices of the Arbitration Institute of the Stockholm Chamber of Commerce, 21 April 2006, available at: http://italaw.com/cases/documents/142; *RosInvest Co UK Ltd v The Russian Federation*, award in Stockholm under the auspices of the Arbitration Institute of the Stockholm Chamber of Commerce, 12 September 2010, available at: http://italaw.com/documents/RosInvestCoAward.pdf.

Fourth and quite differently, inbound investors benefit more from negotiation or conciliation with China than through ISA. According to this fourth view, foreign investors have less reason to bring ISA against China because China often accords foreign investors better than 'national treatment', offsetting concerns that they receive less than fair and equitable treatment or are subject to indirect expropriations.[19] China has committed itself to recognizing and enforcing arbitration awards, inter alia, as a signatory to the New York Convention on the Recognition and Enforcement of Foreign Arbitration Awards (New York Convention). It has undertaken to submit ISA disputes to the ICSID and acceded to the ICSID Convention.[20] Perhaps most importantly, China also has an image to project, namely, as being 'friendly' towards foreign investors while foreign investors in China have received handsome returns on their investments there.[21] For example, investors have been willing to tolerate losses for the sake of future business. Whatever the criticisms that are directed at this aspiration, China has succeeded in attracting huge amounts of FDI over several decades and is perceived as economically and politically stable in material respects.[22]

The problem is that it is difficult to verify which of these reasons are most likely to account for China's limited experience with ISA to date. The negotiation and conciliation of investor-state disputes prior to filing an ISA claim with an institution like the ICSID is ordinarily done confidentially. Even the general proposition that dispute prevention and resolution measures are secretive in China is subject to different interpretations. Arbitration claims heard by Chinese arbitration institutions such as the China International Economic and Trade Arbitration Commission (CIETAC) are likely to remain confidential, similar to claims brought before international arbitration associations in the United States or Europe.[23] Claims brought by foreign investors before Chinese courts may also be inadequately reported; alternatively, the court judgment may contain little reasoning, not unlike judicial reports in civil law countries more generally, or be unnecessarily complex.[24] Finally, investor claims against China or against Chinese state trading corporations may not be heard by Chinese courts, given that China subscribes to an absolute theory of sovereign immunity.[25]

However, despite the secrecy associated with commercial arbitration proceedings in China as elsewhere, there are a number of indications that Chinese arbitration

---

[19]See Shan et al. (2012); Trakman (2011); Qin (2003), p. 490; Kueh (ed) (1997); Kinnear (2009).

[20]But see Rooney (2007), arguing that even after China's accession to the Washington Convention became effective, it was some years before China provided for ICSID arbitration in early BITs. On the ICSID, see generally, Trakman (2012a).

[21]See Nottage and Weeramantry (2011), p. 25.

[22]On China's shifting position with regard to investment arbitration, see Bath (2011).

[23]Moser (1998).

[24]See e.g. Liu (2019).

[25]See e.g. *Democratic Republic of the Congo v FG Hemisphere Associates LLC* (FACV Nos, 5, 6 & 7 of 2010) in which the Hong Kong Court of Final Appeal, in a judgment regarding the ability of states to claim sovereign immunity before Hong Kong courts, decided by majority that foreign states enjoy absolute immunity from jurisdiction. See generally, Yang Xiaodong (2012) State Immunity in International Law. Cambridge University Press, Cambridge (2012).

institutions strive for arbitral independence and impartiality, similar to the American Arbitration Association (AAA), the International Chamber of Commerce (ICC) or the London Court of International Arbitration (LCIA).[26] For example, the new 2015 Arbitration Rules of the CIETAC provide explicitly that '[U]nder all circumstances, the arbitral tribunal shall act impartially and fairly and shall afford a reasonable opportunity to both parties to present their case'[27] and that '[T]he arbitral tribunal shall independently and impartially render a fair and reasonable arbitral award based on the facts of the case and the terms of the contract, in accordance with the law, and with reference to international practices'.[28] Articles 31 to 33 of the CIETAC Rules stipulate further the procedures for disclosure and, based on such disclosure, challenge to and replacement of an arbitrator if 'justifiable doubts' arise 'as to his/her impartiality or independence'.[29] These rules governing the conduct of arbitrators are comparable to those prescribed by arbitration institutions in the West.[30] There is also at least some record of challenges to arbitration awards, notably through the judicial review of Chinese arbitral decisions. For example, in *Beijing Yingjia Real Estate Development Ltd. v Third Branch of the Beijing Union Construction Group Corporation Ltd.*,[31] a Beijing court held that the failure of a presiding arbitrator to disclose her relationship with the attorney of the defendant in a significant number of prior arbitrations violated 'legal procedure', contrary to Article 32 of the CIETAC Rules then in effect; and set aside the arbitration award.[32] Similarly, the Hong Kong Court of Appeal declined to enforce a CIETAC award on grounds that the Tribunal had deprived the defendant of the right to question the evidence arising from the presiding arbitrator's inspection of a factory in the absence of the other arbitrators, expert witnesses and the defendant,[33] contrary to Article 32 of the CIETAC Rules then in

[26]See CIETAC: http://cietac.org/index.php?m=Page&a=index&id=42&l=en (hereafter 'CIETAC 2015 Arbitration Rules'); International Centre for Dispute Resolution: http://www.adr.org/icdr, International Chamber of Commerce: http://www.iccwbo.org, London Court of International Arbitration: http://www.lcia.org/, Trakman (2006, pp. 1, 19–20), 26–28 (discussing private international commercial arbitration associations). See further, Trakman (2008, pp. 292–305).

[27]CIETAC 2015 Arbitration Rule, Art 35(1).

[28]CIETAC 2015 Arbitration Rule, Art 49(1).

[29]CIETAC 2015 Arbitration Rule, Arts 31(1) and 32(2).

[30]On the rules governing the appointment and conduct of arbitrators internationally, see e.g. Hong Kong Arbitration Ordinance 2000; Article 16, Arbitration Act 1996 of the United Kingdom; Article.12–18, Sweden Arbitration Act; and Chapter 3, Commercial Arbitration Rules of Japan Commercial Arbitration Association 1997. See also, Trakman (2012a).

[31]*Beijing Yingjia Real Estate Development Ltd. v Third Branch of BUCC (Beijing Union Construction Group Corporation) Ltd.*, Beijing Second Intermediate People's Court, 2003, in Lin (ed) (2008), p. 42.

[32]But see *Beijing Longrun Huizhitong Real Estate Developments Ltd Corp. v Beijing Second Construction Projects Ltd Corp*, Beijing Second Intermediate People's Court, 2004 (in which it was held that an arbitrator's failure to disclose that the defendant had nominated that arbitrator to another prior arbitration did not violate the Beijing Arbitration Association Rules. See generally Lin (2018).

[33]*Polytek Engineering Company Ltd v Hebei Import & Export Corporation*, 16 January 1998, High Court of the Hong Kong Special Administrative Region, Court of Appeal, Civil Appeal No. 116 of 1997, in van den Berg (ed) (1998, pp. 666–684).

effect.[34] While the Hong Kong Court of Final Appeal reversed this decision, holding that the respondent had waived its right by not objecting during arbitral proceedings,[35] the scrutiny of the arbitral award by each Hong Kong court is consistent with judicial review for procedural irregularities in commercial arbitration.

Similarly, concerns about Chinese arbitration tribunals defying principles of natural justice are comparable to concerns expressed in other jurisdictions.[36] In *Gao Haiyan* et al. *v Keeneye Holdings Ltd*,[37] a Hong Kong court refused to enforce an arbitral award of the Xi'an Arbitration Commission in mainland China on grounds that the Tribunal had shown 'favoritism and malpractice'[38] towards one party, a lack of impartiality and failed to exercise procedural fairness in conducting a mediation-arbitration. The Hong Kong court refused to enforce the arbitration award, as 'an affront to this Court's sense of justice'.[39] Yet, in 2011, the Court of Appeal overruled this decision and enforced the Xi'an Arbitration Commission's award.[40]

These cases all deal with determinations reached by Chinese tribunals in international commercial arbitration in general, and not investor-state disputes in particular.[41] A more difficult question relates to ISA in which China is a defendant, or Chinese nationals are claimants against foreign host countries under a BIT with China. First, such disputes focus less on the conduct of arbitrators in international commercial arbitration that may include investor claims but not necessarily against a state party, and more on the conduct of state and investor parties. Second, such disputes ordinarily, although not invariably, are brought before specialist investor-state tribunals, such as under the ICSID rules, or the UNCITRAL. Third, there is a need to assess the manner in which ISA proceedings are conducted, given that they are often private and the publication of comprehensive ISA awards is subject

[34] Article 32 of CIETAC Rules:

The arbitration tribunal shall hold oral hearings when examining a case. At the request of the parties or with their consent, oral hearings may be omitted if the arbitration tribunal also deems that oral hearings are unnecessary, and then the arbitration tribunal may examine the case and make an award on the basis of documents only.

Cf Art. 35(2) of the 2015 CIETAC Rules:

The arbitral tribunal shall hold oral hearings when examining the case. However, the arbitral tribunal may examine the case on the basis of documents only if the parties so agree and the arbitral tribunal consents or the arbitral tribunal deems that oral hearings are unnecessary and the parties so agree.

See also, Article 45 of the Chinese Arbitration Association (CAA): 'The evidence should be demonstrated only at the tribunal section, and the parties have the right to question the evidence'.

[35] 9 February 1999, Court of Final Appeal of the Hong Kong Special Administrative Region, FACV No. 10 of 1998, in van den Berg (ed) (1999, pp. 652–677).

[36] See e.g. Han (2000, p. 191).

[37] HCCT, No. 41, 2010.

[38] HCCT, No. 41, 2010, § 30.

[39] HCCT, No. 41, 2010, §§ 92–96.

[40] [2011] HKEC 514.

[41] On similarities and differences between international commercial arbitration and investment arbitration, see Nottage and Miles (2009).

to the consent of the disputing parties.[42] Finally, even the contention that ISA tribunals lack jurisdiction to hear an investor complaint under a 'first generation' BIT that provides only for investor claims to compensation, is not self-evident. In the case of *Tza Yap Shum v The Republic of Peru*, involving a 'first generation' China-Peru FTA, the Tribunal upheld the Chinese investor's claim, despite the challenge to its jurisdiction.[43] Further affirming the jurisdiction of ISA tribunals to determine whether an expropriation has occurred in a 'first generation' BIT are the decisions of at least some ISA tribunals that a Most-Favored-Nation (MFN) clause in a BIT accords the same protection to an investor from a BIT partner state as the protection accorded to a partner state with the MFN protection accorded to its investors. As a result, ISA tribunals may interpret expansively BITs that purport to restrict 'first generation' Chinese BITs to compensation claims by granting investors from those BIT countries the MFN treatment that China accords to investors from a BIT partner state whose investors are more favored.[44] Given the significant number of Chinese BITs that provide for MFN treatment, the scope for investors from any one of those BIT partners to lodge an ISA claim under a MFN clause is all that much greater. This is particularly pertinent with regard to the right of an investor to bring an ISA claim rather than being forced to exhaust local remedies under an ISA restricted BIT.[45]

3 ISA Claims by Chinese Investors Abroad

In purely arithmetic terms, given the geometric increase in investments abroad by Chinese investors including by Chinese state enterprises, it is reasonable to expect a comparable increase in claims brought by Chinese investors against foreign states. The extent to which these observations are borne out in practice is analyzed below.

---

[42]See: *Tza Yap Shum v The Republic of Peru* (hereafter '*Tza Yap Shum*'), Decision on Jurisdiction and Competence, 12 February 2007; Final Award on the Merits, 7 July 2011, summary available at: http://www.italaw.com/documents/TzaYapShumAwardIACLSummary.pdf; *Tza Yap Shum*, Decision on annulment, ICSID Case No ARB/07/6, IIC 677 (2015), despatched 12 February 2015, International Centre for Settlement of Investment Disputes, World Bank. See also Sect. 9 of this Chapter below.

[43]See *Tza Yap Shum*, 19 June 2009. See also, *Renta 4 S.V.S.A. v The Russian Federation*, award on jurisdiction in Stockholm under the auspices of the Arbitration Institute of the Stockholm Chamber of Commerce, 20 March 2009; *Czech Republic v European Media Ventures SA* [2007] EWHC 2851, 5 December 2007.

[44]On such an expansive interpretation of a MFN clause, see e.g. *MTD Equity Sdn Bhd and MTD Chile SA v Republic of Chile* (ICSID Case No. ARB/01/07), Award, 25 May 2004; *Emilio Agustin Maffezini v Kingdom of Spain* (ICSID Case No. ARB/97/7), Decision on Jurisdiction, 25 January 2000 (hereafter '*Emilio Agustin Maffezini*'). On limits placed on the scope of an MFN clause in a BIT, see *Siemens v Republic of Arg.* (ICSID Case No. ARB/02/8), Decision on Jurisdiction, 3 August 2004 (hereafter '*Siemens*'). See generally on controversy associated with the meaning and scope of MFN clauses, Maupin (2011); Banifatemi (2009).

[45]On an expansive interpretation of a MFN clause, see e.g. *Emilio Agustin Maffezini*, [54]–[56]; *Siemens*. But see *Plama Consortium Ltd v Republic of Bulgaria* (ICSID Case No. ARB/03/24), Decision on Jurisdiction, 8 February 2005.

An initial reaction is to avoid overstating the volume of ISA arbitrations in general. For example, the ICSID caseload has grown geometrically, from a single case in 1972 to approximately ten cases in 1990, to 53 new cases filed in 2017.[46] However, despite this growth, the absolute number of ICSID cases is limited compared to international commercial arbitration cases, such as 1,435 claims filed with the CIETAC, 994 cases filed with the International Center for Dispute Resolution (ICDR) of the AAA and 795 cases filed with ICC.[47]

A problem in attempting to draw any definitive conclusions about the application of ISA to claims by outbound Chinese investors against host states and claims by foreign investors against China in particular is the limited number of decided ISA cases upon which to rely. In particular, Chinese foreign investors have brought only a few ISA cases against host states under BITs in which China is the investor's home state.

Included among these cases is the 2011 ICSID decision in the case of *Tza Yap Shum v Peru*.[48] In that case, a Chinese investor, purporting to expand a fish factory in Peru, alleged that the Peruvian taxation authority had breached the expropriation provision in the China-Peru BIT of 1994[49] by investigating his business and levying liens on his firm's bank accounts that 'ended up destroying [his] business operations and economic viability'.[50] He claimed that this constituted an 'indirect expropriation'.[51]

The case raised a jurisdictional issue, namely, whether a Hong Kong national was qualified as an investor under the China-Peru BIT[52]; whether a prescribed waiting period of six months for amicable settlement had taken place[53]; and whether the claimant was required to exhaust local remedies before proceeding to ISA.[54] The Tribunal also considered the significance of a MFN clause in Article 3(2) of the China-Peru BIT, providing that: 'The treatment and protection referred to in Paragraph 1 of this Article [the fair and equitable guarantee] shall not be less favourable than that accorded to investments and activities associated with such investments of investors of a third State'.[55]

Peru lost the case. The Tribunal ruled that the imposition of interim measures by the tax authority of Peru was arbitrary in failing to comply with Peru's own

---

46 See ICSID (2018).

47 ICSID (2018); see also Steingruber (2012).

48 *Tza Yap Shum*, Decision on Jurisdiction and Competence, 12 February 2007; Final Award on the Merits, 7 July 2011 See also Eliasson (2011).

49 Agreement between the Government of the Republic of Peru and the Government of the People's Republic of China Concerning the Encouragement and Reciprocal Protection of Investments done at Beijing on 9 June 1994, entered into force 1 February 1995, 1901 U.N.T.S. 257 (hereafter 'Peru-China BIT'), Art 1(2)(a).

50 *Tza Yap Shum*, § 31.

51 *Tza Yap Shum*, § 31.

52 *Tza Yap Shum*, § 32.

53 Peru-China BIT, Ch 10, Art 126.

54 ICSID Convention, Regulations and Rules, Art 26.

55 Peru-China BIT, Art 3(5). See also Eliasson (2011).

internal procedures.[56] It ruled further that the provision in Article 8(3) of the China-Peru BIT 'involving the amount of compensation for expropriation' included both a determination of the amount of compensation and a determination whether the property was actually expropriated.[57] In its decision on the merits on 7 July 2011, the Tribunal awarded the claimant over USD 700,000 in damages and USD 200,000 in interest.[58] Peru filed to have the award annulled.[59]

A significant aspect of the decision was in holding that the claimant, a resident of Hong Kong, was a national of the People's Republic of China (PRC) for the purpose of bringing a claim under the ICSID. However, that issue is not peculiar to China, other than in affirming the particular legal relationship between a Hong Kong resident and the PRC. What is questionable about the decision is the Tribunal's restrictive construction of the MFN clause in favor of the more specific wording in Article 8(3) which specified when an investor could resort to ISA. This flies in the face of the general applicability of an MFN clause which should entitle investors to the most favorable treatment accorded to investors under any other BIT to which the host state, here Peru, is a signatory.[60]

In the case of *Heilongjiang v Mongolia*,[61] a Chinese investor brought a claim against Mongolia under the China-Mongolia BIT. The issue before the ISA tribunal was to determine whether it had jurisdiction to determine that an expropriation had occurred in a 'first generation' Chinese BIT that did not provide a claim for expropriation, but only for compensation.[62] In another case, Chinese insurer Ping An filed an ICSID claim against Belgium (the *Ping An* case). Ping An, China's second largest insurer, lost approximately USD 3 billion when failed Belgo-Dutch bank Fortis was nationalized and sold during the 2008 financial crisis. The collapse of the price of Fortis Bank and its subsequent sale significantly diminished Ping An's interest in European financial services of the Bank. This is the first mainland Chinese company to file a claim in the ICSID. It is also the first claim by a Chinese national against the government of a developed economy.[63] The claim relied on two BITs: the 1986 BIT between the Belgium-Luxembourg Economic Union (BLEU) and China, and

---

[56] *Tza Yap Shum*, § 218.

[57] *Tza Yap Shum*, § 88.

[58] *Tza Yap Shum*, Final Award on the Merits, 7 July 2011.

[59] *Tza Yap Shum*, Decision on annulment, ICSID Case No ARB/07/6, IIC 677 (2015), despatched 12 February 2015, International Centre for Settlement of Investment Disputes, World Bank.

[60] On the general applicability of an MFN clause, see *Renta 4 S.V.S.A. v The Russian Federation*, SCC Case No. ARB V024/2007, §101; *RosInvestCo UK Ltd v The Russian Federation*, SCC Case No. ARB V079/2005, § 130.

[61] *China Heilongjiang International Economic & Technical Cooperative Corp.*, et al. *v Mongolia*, Permanent Court of Arbitration (PCA) Case (China-Mongolia BIT 1991), http://www.pca-cpa.org/showpage.asp?pag_id=1378.

[62] China-Mongolia BIT, Art 8. See also, China's Model BIT, Art 4(iv).

[63] See *Ping An Life Insurance Company of China, Limited and Ping An Insurance (Group) Company of China, Limited v Kingdom of Belgium* (ICSID Case No. ARB/12/29) (hereafter '*Ping An*'). See also, Agreement between the Government of the People's Republic of China and the Belgian-Luxembourg Economic Union on the Reciprocal Promotion and Protection of Investments done

the 2009 BLEU-China BIT that superseded the earlier one. It is notable that the dispute settlement provision of the 1986 BIT was much more restrictive than that of the 2009 BIT. In particular, the 1986 BIT granted exclusive domestic jurisdiction to 'all disputes': international arbitration could only be invoked to determine the amount of compensation for expropriation. By comparison, the 2009 BIT has a much broader dispute settlement clause, which provides that the investor of one state may choose to submit any legal dispute between it and another state to ICSID for arbitration. Ultimately, the tribunal found that there was nothing in the 2009 BIT to justify an extension to these disputes.[64]

Finally, and most notably, Chinese state-owned enterprise, Beijing Urban Construction Group Co. Ltd. (BUCG) filed an ICSID claim against the Republic of Yemen (*BUCG v Yemen*). BUCG alleged under the 2002 China-Yemen BIT that Yemen unlawfully deprived it of its investment in the construction of a new terminal in Sana's International Airport. The Tribunal rejected Yemen's objection that BUCG was a state agent, having found that in the relevant fact-specific context BUCG acted as a commercial contractor, rather than discharging governmental functions. Yemen also objected to the Tribunal's subject matter jurisdiction based on a narrow interpretation of the dispute settlement clause of the BIT. However, the Tribunal dismissed the objection, considering that the words 'relating to the amount of compensation for expropriation' in the dispute settlement clause must be construed to 'include disputes relating to whether or not an expropriation has occurred' as it promotes the BIT's overall purpose and objective.[65] The parties appeared to have subsequently settled upon the dispute. They consequently filed a request for the discontinuance of the proceeding and on 7 June 2018, the Tribunal issued a procedural order granting the discontinuance of the proceeding pursuant to ICSID Arbitration Rule 43(1).[66]

None of these cases represents a finding that significantly embellishes investment arbitration jurisprudence. None to date involves substantial damages or other remedies. What the cases do demonstrate is the willingness of a few Chinese foreign investors in recent years to mount effective claims against host states. What is further evident is that, on balance, these claims have been modestly successful, albeit involving limited claims. It would be more telling if a Chinese multinational, particularly a state enterprise, were to bring a multimillion dollar claim against a host state focusing on the nature and impact of an expropriation under a treaty based on China's Model BIT. The probability of this occurring presumably will depend somewhat on the prospects of China's BIT partners negotiating with large scale Chinese investors to avoid formal ISA claims against them brought by those investors (as what happened in *BUCG v Yemen*). Both the *Ping An* case and the *BUCG v Yemen*

---

at Brussels on 4 June 1984, entered into force 5 October 1986, 1938 U.N.T.S.305. See generally Neligan (2012).

[64]See *Ping An*.

[65]See *Beijing Urban Construction Group Co. Ltd. v Republic of Yemen* (ICSID Case No. ARB/14/30). See details at: https://www.iisd.org/itn/2017/09/26/a-look-into-chinas-slowly-increasing-appearance-in-isds-cases-dilini-pathirana/.

[66]https://icsid.worldbank.org/en/Pages/cases/casedetail.aspx?CaseNo=ARB/14/30.

case may represent a turning point in China's large companies bringing substantial claims against China's BITs partners.

4 ISA Claims Brought Against China

There are only three registered cases to date against China. The first, being *Ekran Berhad v China*, brought under the Rules of the ICSID Convention.[67] That claim was brought by a Malaysian construction company. In issue was the right of the local government to revoke a license for construction on leasehold property of 90,000 hectares of land in the Hainan Province of China. The Malaysian claimant subsequently withdrew the claim and the case was suspended.[68] Had it proceeded to an award, it would have required consideration of the meaning and significance of a provision in the China-Malaysia BIT, based on China's Model BIT under which an ISA Tribunal is required to follow 'domestic legal procedure' in a direct or indirect expropriation.[69] Much would also have hinged on the Tribunal's determination of the meaning and application of Article 7(4) of the China-Malaysia BIT, particularly in relation to the nature and limits of a compensation claim.[70] If the aborted claim signifies anything, it is that a single foreign investor was willing to initiate a claim against China; China apparently responded aggressively; and the investor apparently withdrew the complaint.[71]

In the second case, *Ansung Housing v China*, China, as a respondent, argued that Ansung's claims were time-barred as the investor initiated arbitration more than three years after acquiring acknowledgment of the loss or damage suffered as a result of China's acts. Ansung therefore invoked the MFN clause of the BIT, pointing to other Chinese BITs that do not provide for a three-year limitation period. However, the Tribunal found that the MFN clause did not extend to a state's consent to arbitrate with investors, or to the temporal limitation period for investor—state arbitration.[72] As a result, the case was closed on this technical ground in favour of China. Most recently, a German-owned investor initiated a claim against China in June 2017, under the China-Germany BIT.[73] The proceedings are still on-going.

Drawing any salutary conclusion from the two concluded cases would be suspect, except to lend credence to the assumption that China is likely to be a tenacious

---

[67] *Ekran Berhad.*

[68] *Ekran Berhad*, proceedings suspended pursuant to the parties' agreement on 22 July 2011. See: http://icsid.worldbank.org.

[69] The provision for an ISA tribunal to adhere to 'domestic legal procedure' is contained in Article 4(ii) of China's Model BIT.

[70] This BIT article is modeled on Article 4(iv) of China's Model BIT providing for compensation.

[71] The terms of any settlement reached by the disputing parties is not publicly known.

[72] https://www.iisd.org/itn/2017/09/26/a-look-into-chinas-slowly-increasing-appearance-in-isds-cases-dilini-pathirana/.

[73] *Hela Schwarz GmbH.*

adversary; and that only a well-financed foreign investor would likely prevail in a potentially protracted and costly dispute with China. However, much would also depend on the nature and terms of the investment treaty in issue and the specific claim and defense. In issue would also be a tension between China's need to demonstrate its willingness to defend the national good from foreign intrusion and its countervailing interest in mollifying skittish foreign investors who might retreat from investing in China to avoid its regulatory regime.

5 Chinese Arbitrators

To date, five Chinese investment arbitrators have been appointed in five different ISA cases.[74] Two arbitrators have served on an annulment committee, while three have served on ISA tribunals.[75] These numbers are sparse. However, they are reasonably offset by the limited number of cases in which China has been a respondent in an ISA dispute, or Chinese investors have proceeded against host countries, or to annulment proceedings.[76] The numbers may well increase, given China's heightened participation in BITs this last decade.[77]

The argument favoring an increased number of Chinese arbitrators appointed to ISA tribunals is not peculiar to China. There is a limited pool of ICSID arbitrators available; a few arbitrators from developed countries repeatedly are appointed to tribunals; and widening the pool of appointed ISA arbitrators is ultimately determined by the disputing parties and the arbitrators they appoint, usually through their nomination to the ICSID or by the Permanent Court of Arbitration.[78] Given that nationals cannot preside over an ISA dispute involving their home or host state, China could not appoint Chinese arbitrators to preside over disputes in which it is a defendant. However, China's wider participation in ICSID and UNCITRAL proceedings is likely to raise its profile in ISA disputes; it could also serve as an inducement to other states and investors to appoint Chinese nationals to preside over their ISA disputes in the complex global arena of political and economic gamesmanship.

[74] See: https://icsid.worldbank.org/ICSID/. See generally UNCTAD (2018a).

[75] An Chen, from mainland China, was appointed to 2 annulment proceedings and to 1 ISDS arbitration tribunal. Teresa Cheng from Hong Kong SAR was appointed to 1 annulment proceeding and 1 ISDS tribunal.

[76] The only annulment procedure to date involving China was Peru seeking an annulment of an ISA award in the case of *Tza Yap Shum*.

[77] See: https://www.bilaterals.org/?-china-.

[78] https://www.bilaterals.org/?-china-.

6 Withdrawing from ISA?

A less likely prospect is that China will withdraw from ISA. It could insist, with regard to inbound FDI, that investor-state claims against it be resolved by Chinese arbitration institutions or by Chinese courts. It could also decline to include ISA provisions in its BITs, impacting on both inbound and outbound investors. It could do so on grounds that ISA favors developed states and their investors; and that international investment law and practice is biased against developing states and their investors.[79]

The prospect of China requiring domestic courts to decide investor-state disputes has some foundation. China could insist that, as a sovereign state, its domestic courts ought to preside over disputes within its territorial jurisdiction; and that its courts have the jurisdiction, legal competence and substantive knowledge to decide investment disputes under Chinese law.[80] China could also modify its BIT practices, by providing for domestic courts to preside over investor-state disputes generally. It could point to other countries, most recently Australia, that have seemingly discarded ISA in favor of domestic courts deciding investment disputes,[81] and the undertaking by others, like South Africa, to do so as well.[82]

China is unlikely to follow Australia's lead. Relying on Chinese courts may well satisfy its domestic public policy interests. However, should it modify its BITs practice by providing for resort to domestic courts generally, it would place its investors abroad at the mercy of the domestic courts of BIT partner states whose courts it would prefer to avoid.[83] China could carve out middle ground. It could provide that domestic courts resolve investor-state disputes involving investors from BIT partner states whose courts it trusts. It could revert to ISA in respect of the other BIT partner states, or to a system requiring exhaustion of domestic remedies first, with a long waiting period before ISA can be initiated. This middle course is conceivable. However, China would need to adopt a two-tier BIT negotiating strategy that could alienate existing and prospective BIT partners, such as the African states with which it has built extensive BIT partnerships more to bolster diplomatic alliances than

---

[79] See, e.g. Latha Jishnu, Secretive Tribunals, Hidden Damages (Interview) (31 January 2012), http://www.downtoearth.org.in/content/secretive-tribunals-hidden-damages. In this interview, van Harten observes that developing countries sometimes are the target of treaties directed at enhancing opportunities for foreign investors from other states and on occasions, leading to significant losses for those target countries. See also, Trakman (2012a).

[80] An assertion of sovereignty would not be exceptional, given the historical practices of states. See e.g. Shan et al. (eds) (2008), Part Four (commenting on the complexity of sovereignty in international investment law); Stumberg (1998, pp. 491, 503–504), 523–525 (discussing sovereignty); Jackson (1990); Jennings and Watts (eds) (1992, p. 927).

[81] See Trakman (2012b).

[82] See Peterson (2012).

[83] There is empirical data confirming such concerns. See Kantor (2011, p. 10), demonstrating that approximately 76% of the cases in which investment treaty awards were rendered up to June 2006 involved states that fell at or below Number 50 on the Transparency International's 2008 Corruption Perception Index. See also, Franck (2007a). The World Bank's Worldwide Governance Indicators demonstrated further that 68% of those States were in the bottom 60% of its Index for the 'rule of law': World Bank (2018).

develop immediate investment opportunities.[84] China would also need to redress its long-standing preference for arbitration where foreign companies are involved, both inside and outside China.[85]

Could China conceivably reject ISA for political or economic reasons? That would seem unlikely, at least at present. However, attacks on ISA institutions and proceedings are not entirely novel.[86] In recent years, a number of countries have challenged the ICSID: Ecuador in 2009,[87] Bolivia shortly afterwards and in 2012, Venezuela. Each country withdrew from the ICSID Convention.[88] The alleged affront, starting with Ecuador, is that the ICSID is a creature of the World Bank,[89] and the United States in particular.[90] The sub-text is historical antagonism towards multinationals, a fear of neo-colonial sublimation, but more specifically, a reaction to adverse ISA determinations.[91]

In contrast, China is unlikely to withdraw from the ICSID, at least not in the immediate future. Certainly, China can identify with the assertion that the ICSID is a creature of the World Bank, while the Bank is a creature of the United States and its allies. In particular, China has endured the ills of colonialism and its subjugation by developed countries. However, China has not had negative experiences with ISA comparable to those of Ecuador, Bolivia and Venezuela. China is also in a global economic growth spurt as both an inbound and an outbound investment destination that distinguishes it from these Latin American countries.[92] In addition, China's bureaucratic and legal apparatus is more sophisticated than almost any other developing country. China also has the capacity to determine the most tactical manner of proceeding to ISA, whether administered by the ICSID, or by such bodies as the Permanent Court of Arbitration administering the UNCITRAL Rules.[93] China is

---

[84] See generally Cotula (2011); Agyemang (1988) (discussing the African signatories, particularly their consent to jurisdiction, their position in the institution, and the appointment of African arbitrators); Johnson (2010) (discussing BITs in relation to African countries).

[85] Cotula (2011), Agyemang (1988), Johnson (2010).

[86] See generally Tzanakopoulos (2011), Krever (2011), Vincentelli (2010).

[87] See e.g. ICSID (2012), Garcia (2012). See generally Appleton (2010).

[88] For commentary on these events, as well as investment arbitration in Latin America generally, see Appleton (2010).

[89] Compare ICSID, List of Contracting States and Other Signatories to the Convention (http://icsid.worldbank.org/ICSID/) with World Bank, Member Countries (http://web.worldbank.org/).

[90] See Bretton Woods Project (2009).

[91] See Trakman and Ranieri (2013) Ch 10 (discussing the consequences of these comments for international investment law, ICSID, and the World Bank). See Krever (2011); UNCTAD (2010b).

[92] For statistics on China's FDI between January and May 2018, see: http://english.mofcom.gov.cn/aarticle/statistic/foreigninvestment/.html.

[93] While the ICSID administers ISA, the UNCITRAL is *not* an administering authority. The UNCITRAL website states: 'UNCITRAL does not administer arbitration or conciliation proceedings, nor does it provide services. in connection with dispute settlement proceedings'. See: http://www.uncitral.org/uncitral/en/uncitral_texts/arbitration_faq.html#dispute. Other institutions, most notably the PCA, administer investor-state disputes under the UNCITRAL Rules.

fully cognizant of the nuances of ISA proceedings and their potential economic and political consequences.[94]

Still, one should never say 'never'. Were China to suffer a significant defeat in ISA proceedings, coupled with a loss of international reputation and investment opportunity, it could reconsider its endorsement of ISA in whole or in part. It is worth noting that on 1 October 2017, the Investment Arbitration Rules of CIETAC (CIETAC IAR Rules) entered into force.[95] This is the first time a Chinese arbitral institution has adopted a set of rules specifically designed for the resolution of international investment disputes. While there is some room for further improvements, two key features of the CIETAC IAR Rules are notable. First, the CIETAC IAR Rules authorise the arbitral tribunal to conduct mediation prior to an investment arbitration. Second, the CIETAC IAR Rules allow public access to hearings and documents submitted in the arbitration, unless otherwise agreed by the parties.[96] The CIETAC IAR Rules highlight China's commitment to transparency, responding specifically to the 'legitimacy crisis' confronted by investment arbitration in recent years. To our knowledge, the Beijing Arbitration Commission has drafted its own investment arbitration rules and these rules are under consultation at the moment.

A salutary caution is not to overstate the extent to which foreign investors triumph over domestic states in ISA proceedings generally, despite the accusation that ISA tends to be investor-centric. For example, the latest 2018 ICSID statistics demonstrate that 62% of the cases filed with the ICSID were decided by arbitration tribunals, while 38% were settled or otherwise discontinued. Of the cases decided by a tribunal, states won ICSID disputes approximately half the time. ICSID tribunals dismissed 52% of the cases, primarily on jurisdictional grounds. They upheld 48% of investor claims in whole or in part.[97] These macro statistics are by no means definitive; however they do suggest that ISA decision-making is more balanced between states and investors than is presumed by ISA detractors; and they do modulate the sometimes summary dismissal of ISA as being drawn more by commercial than public policy considerations.[98]

---

[94]See Shihata (2009, pp. 2–35) (discussing old world views); Franck (2007b) (analyzing different views of the rule of law).

[95]http://www.cietac.org/index.php?m=Page&a=index&id=390&l=en.

[96]CIETAC Investment Rules, Arts 32 and 55.

[97]ICSID (2018).

[98]See Franck (2011). Franck undertakes a quantitative analysis of awards with Latin American countries as parties, and finds that 'on the whole, … ICSID arbitration awards were not statistically different from other arbitral processes, which is preliminary evidence that ICSID arbitration was not necessarily biased or that investment arbitration operated in reasonably equivalent ways across forums'. See also Franck (2011, p. 998). On ICSID's figures, including that foreign investors have won 48% of ICSID/Additional Facility cases, see ICSID (2018).

7 A 'China-Made' Investment Jurisprudence?

Will China recreate investment jurisprudence in its image, permanently transforming the principles and practice of investment law upon which ISA tribunals rely? Given China's formidable growth in inbound and outbound investment, it certainly has the economic stature to influence the development of international investment law and practice in the future. An FDI prognosis that is not beyond the realms of possibility is that a 'new' FDI International Economic Order will evolve in the wake of the seemingly continuing recession of 2008 in which FDI powerful states, now including India, China and other BRIC countries (Brazil, Russia, India, China and South Africa), replicate the FDI 'leadership' previously occupied by the United States and Western European states. These prognoses are difficult to pronounce with any degree of conviction not only because they invite disputation, but also because such a determination depends on the ideological and functional variables that are ascribed to such leadership.[99]

Difficult, too, is predicting how political and economic leadership will translate into the development of international investment law. In question is the validity of the proposition that investment rights ought to be determined by established principles of investment law operating prospectively, rather than by geo-political and economic interests that circumscribe those principles and their prospective application.[100] Under scrutiny, too, is whether arbitration processes that sometimes are closed to public scrutiny and that lead to ad hoc determinations are sufficiently transparent to transcend the political context in which ISA awards are reached and treaty law is made.[101] A less than heartening observation is that ICSID annulment proceedings are 'not designed to bring about consistency in the interpretation and application of international investment law'.[102]

Subject to these observations, China's influence over treaty and customary investment jurisprudence is likely to gain traction over the structural fluidity and arguably,

---

[99]See Stiglitz (2010) (providing an account of these recessionary forces and their global consequences). On the New International Economic Order through the General Assembly of the United States, a Charter of Economic Rights and Duties of States, and a Declaration on the Permanent Sovereignty of States over Natural Resources, see G.A. Res. 3281(xxix), U.N. GAOR, 29th Sess., Supp. No. 3150, UN Doc. A/9631 (12 December 1974) (Charter of Economic Rights and Duties of States); G.A. Res. 3201 (S-VI), U.N. Doc. A/res/S-6/3201 (1 May 1974) (New International Economic Order). See also Trakman (2010, pp. 15–16), 20.

[100]By far the most dominant view is that investment law is based on determinative principles of law. See, e.g. Dolzer and Schreuer (2008), Ch 1. But see Sornarajah (2013), Ch 17 and Appendix (providing a critique of this principled approach).

[101]See generally Yackee and Wong (2010) (discussing transparency in international investment arbitration); Marian (2010) (discussing transparency in international investment arbitration).

[102]See *M.C.I. Power Grp. L.C. & New Turbine, Inc. v Ecuador* (ICSID Case No. ARB/03/6), Annulment Decision, para 24 (19 October 2009); see also *Hochtief AG v Arg.* (ICSID Case No. ARB/07/31), 7 October 2011, (providing different interpretations of a treaty in the same case in the dissent of Christopher Thomas, Q.C.). See generally Puig and Kinnear (2010) (providing a systematic approach towards investment arbitration, through the prism of Chapter 11 of the North American Free Trade Agreement (NAFTA)).

malleability, of an arbitral jurisprudence in which treaty law is inevitably unpredictable in light of the variability among BITs.[103] Just as customary international investment law that developed largely in the West influenced the interpretation of BITs, the proliferation of BITs will increasingly influence the development of customary international law. As a result, the interpretation of new BITs such as emanate from China will be a further source of international investment law.[104] However, much will depend on the kind and variety of Chinese BITs that eventuate, how distinctive they are from other BITs, the extent to which other countries replicate them in whole or in part, and the interpretation that ISA tribunal's accord to them in future cases. Much will also depend on the capacity of treaty drafters, administrative agencies and tribunals that craft this new jurisprudence to develop a unified body of investor-state law based on universal principles, widely endorsed standards of treatment, and pervasive rules of application. Especially difficult for ISA tribunals is determining how to apply common norms of investment law to different kinds of expropriation in investment contexts that are complicated by cultural and ideological differences as they relate to China.[105]

The more likely inference is that, whatever China's influence may be on the development of BITs, a uniform body of investment law will remain elusive. First, investment treaty jurisprudence will necessarily be circumscribed by the words used in different treaties.[106] Second, ISA tribunals will interpret different words in different treaties differently, and even the same words in the same treaties differently. Third, ISA will not subscribe to arbitral precedent.[107] So long as ISA tribunals do not have to agree in interpreting the words of BITs, the unification of BIT jurisprudence, whether led by China or not, is unrealistic.[108] Greater uniformity might stem from the global community of states endorsing a new multilateral investment agreement (MIA), but it is difficult to fathom how such a movement would be led, let alone whether it would lead to global endorsement.[109]

[103] See generally Schill (2009), VI–VII (discussing non-ICSID methods of multilateralization and investment jurisprudence); Hindelang (2004), Salacuse (2007).

[104] On the customary nature of international investment law and its contest with treaty made law, see for example, McLachlan (2008), Schwebel (2005), Dumberry (2010, p. 701) (for a rejection of the proposition that BITs represent customary law).

[105] On the development of such international investment norms, see OECD Investment Committee, Organisation for Economic Co-operation and Development, http://www.oecd.org/daf/inv/oecdinvestmentcommittee.htm. See generally Trakman (2006), von Staden (2011) (discussing how different investment policies can influence investment law).

[106] On different interpretations of words used in BITs, see e.g. Peinhardt and Allee (2011), Weeramantry (2012).

[107] See, e.g. Schreuer and Weiniger (2008, p. 1188) (discussing the absence of binding precedents, at least in principle, in international investment law).

[108] See generally, Dolzer and Schreuer (2008) (investment treaties); Dolzer and Stevens (1995), Schreuer (2001, pp. 89–91).

[109] See generally, Dolzer and Schreuer (2008), Ch 1; Schill (2009), Chs 1–2. See also, Organisation for Economic Co-operation and Development, The Multilateral Agreement on Investment Negotiating Text (24 April 1998), http://italaw.com/documents/MAIDraftText.pdf.

What Chinese BITs may add to investment treaty law in the short term is a layer of ISA jurisprudence to an already multi-layered and sometimes inconsistent body of international investment law.[110] Yet that influence will be hampered by ISA tribunals construing BITs literally and therefore restrictively, more than contextually.[111] Further complicating the development of a uniform ISA jurisprudence will be the accentuated difficulty of construing conflicting conceptions of property law, already diffuse across mainstream legal systems,[112] so as to accommodate China's particular variants of property law.[113]

Added to these challenges will be the need to delineate the scope of 'fair and equitable' treatment accorded to foreign investors in China who may complain that they are being disadvantaged in favor of state-owned enterprises.[114] ISA tribunals will also need to determine the 'legitimate' expectations of foreign investors in relation to China's expropriation practices, in respect of which ISA tribunals are unlikely to agree.[115] These challenges will be compounded in relation to outbound investment from China, such as in deciding upon the application of doctrines like the 'margin of appreciation' to Chinese BITs, for example between China and the EU.[116]

---

[110]For commentaries on selected model BITs, see Brown (2013). On attempts to redress consistencies in international investment arbitration, see Hofmann and Tams (eds) (2011), Paulsson (2007, p. 879).

[111]For concerns that ISA arbitrators who are commercial, not public, lawyers will pay less attention to the public policy consequences of their awards for developing states than to the plain words of treaties devised by dominant treaty, see generally Schill (ed) (2010), van Harten (2007, pp. 122–151). See also, Reinisch (2011) (discussing the restrictive construction of investment agreements).

[112]See, e.g. Dolzer and Schreuer (2008), Ch 1–2 (discussing the alleged foundations of investment law in contract and property.

[113]On such differences, see, e.g. *Salini Costruttori SpA and Italstrade SpA v Kingdom of Morocco* (Decision on Jurisdiction), ICSID Arbitral Tribunal, Case No. ARB/00/4, 23 July 2001; (2003) 42 ILM 609; See also, Sasson (2010) (see especially Chapter Four for a discussion of property in investment treaty context); Garcia-Bolivar (2010) (discussing the requirements that must be met in order to invoke the ICSID's jurisdiction); Schreuer (2001, pp. 90–91) (discussing jurisdictional requirements under Article 25 of the ICSID Convention).

[114]Illustrating these variable conceptions of 'fair and equitable' treatment is a series of cases commencing with the ICSID award in *Maffezini v Kingdom of Spain (Award on the merits)* (ICSID Arbitral Tribunal, Case No ARB/97/7, 13 November 2000), [64]; *MTD Equity Sdn Bhd and MTD Chile S.A. v Republic of Chile* (ICSID Arbitral Tribunal, Case No ARB/01/7, 25 May 2004), [178]; and Laird (2004).

[115]On such 'legitimate expectations', see *Saluka Investments BV (The Netherlands) v The Czech Republic (Partial Award)* (Arbitration under the UNCITRAL Rules, 17 March 2006), [304]; *Waste Management, Inc v The United Mexican States (Final Award)* (ICSID Arbitral Tribunal, Case No ARB(AF)/00/3 (NAFTA), 30 April 2004), [98]; *International Thunderbird Gaming Corporation v The United Mexican States* (Arbitration under the UNCITRAL Rules (NAFTA), 26 January 2006), [147]; *GAMI Investments Inc v The Government of the United Mexican States (Final Award)* (Arbitration under the UNCITRAL Rules, 15 November 2004), [100].

[116]On the 'margin of appreciation' doctrine, see for example, Muhammad (2019), Bakircioglu (2007), Shany (2005).

The result is likely to be an even more varied and inconsistent investment jurisprudence,[117] an issue with which ISA has long contended.[118] These challenges will be accentuated by the proliferation among diverse generations of BITs and different constructions that are accorded to them. Efforts will be made to reign in such proliferation, such as by efforts to sublimate the BITs of Germany, France, Italy and the United Kingdom under the umbrella of a faltering EU.[119] However, it remains to be seen whether these developments, economically and politically motivated, will stem the tide of proliferation. Finally, it is not clear that it is in China's self-interest to lead a new MIA movement, not only because it may falter, but also because investment bilateralism might suit China's global investment agenda best, at least for the immediate future.

8 'Alternative' Dispute Resolution

There is a perceptible global movement towards ISA to resolve investor-state disputes, notably under the rules of the ICSID and the UNCITRAL[120] and limited resort to international commercial arbitration.[121] The extent to which China follows this global development is difficult to determine conclusively.

What is clear, however, is that China's most recent BITs provide predominantly for ISA and notably, a preference for the ICSID.[122] In addition, China has not negotiated BITs that provide for recourse to domestic courts, as Australia provided in April 2011.[123] However, investment disputes with some foreign elements are heard

---

[117]On the varied and inconsistent interpretations of investment treaties, see Kurtz (2010) (Kurtz identifies three different methodologies of interpretation). But see Burke-White and von Staden (2008) (considering the interpretive challenges posed by provisions for non-precluded measures, such as for maintenance of security and public order).

[118]On inconsistent ISA decisions in the *CME/Lauder* cases against the Czech Republic, see *Lauder v Czech Republic (Final Award)*, ad hoc (UNCITRAL Arbitration Rules, 3 September 2001); *CME Czech Republic BV v Czech Republic (Partial Award)*, ad hoc (UNCITRAL Arbitration Rules, 13 September 2001); *CME Czech Republic BV v Czech Republic (Final Award)* (UNCITRAL Arbitration Rules, 14 March 2003); (2003) 62 IIC; See also Franck (2011, pp. 825, 826, 909–914).

[119]The EU is in the process of restricting its member states from concluding BITs on the grounds that the EU represents EU states, see European Commission, EU Regulation Number 1219/2012 (21 September 2012), The New Regulation on Member States BITs. See also Bernasconi-Osterwalder (2012).

[120]The UNCITRAL Rules are a general set of rules that can be applied flexibly to resolve any type of international dispute and are adopted widely globally, including for resolving investor-state disputes. Some of the amendments to the UNCITRAL rules were inspired by the rising use of the Rules in ISA. See: http://www.uncitral.org/pdf/english/texts/arbitration/arb-rules-2013/UNCITRAL-Arbitration-Rules-2013-epdf.

[121]On similarities and differences between international commercial arbitration and investment arbitration, see Nottage and Miles (2009).

[122]On the case for investor-state arbitration, see generally Dugan et al. (2008), Muchlinski et al. (eds) (2008).

[123]See Emerson (2011). See also Trakman (2013), Kurtz (2012), Trakman (2012c).

by domestic courts in China which, in turn, may influence the interpretation and application of BITs in which China is a party. Again, the prospect of Chinese courts and domestic law influencing the evolution of investment treaty law is not peculiar to China. It pervades investment jurisprudence generally.[124]

No doubt, too, concerns are likely to arise about the conduct of ISA proceedings in which China is the respondent, such as China's reluctance to permit third party intervention in proceedings, its possible refusal to hold public hearings or insistence on confidential documentation and unpublished awards.[125] However, the transparency concerns arising from such action is not an indictment peculiar to China. Other states have adopted comparable measures in the past.[126] ISA is initiated with the consent of both direct parties to ISA disputes. Third parties, such as public interest groups, until comparatively recently were not permitted to participate in proceedings, such as under the ICSID, without the consent of the investor-state parties.[127] ISA awards ordinarily could only be published with the consent of the direct investor and state parties.[128] Typically, the Secretary General of the ICSID could publish reports of conciliation commissions or awards rendered by arbitral tribunals in ICSID proceedings, but only 'with the consent of both disputing parties', with a limited added power discussed later.[129] There were also explanations, and not always convincing ones, for limiting the transparency of ISA proceedings and awards. For example, in *Suez Sociedad General de Aguas de Barcelona S.A. and Vivendi Universal S.A. v Republic of Argentina,* the arbitration tribunal acknowledged that the case 'potentially involved matters of public interest and human rights' and that the public access

---

[124]See Vandevelde (2005, p. 172). See also UNCTAD (2018b).

[125]See also Moser (1998).

[126]See generally Yackee and Wong (2010) (discussing transparency in international investment arbitration); Marian (2010) (discussing transparency in international investment arbitration).

[127]*Suez Sociedad General de Aguas de Barcelona S.A. and Vivendi Universal S.A. v the Republic of Argentina (Order in Response to a Petition by Five Non-Governmental Organizations for Permission to Make an Amicus Curiae Submission)* (ICSID Arbitral Tribunal, Case No ARB/03/19, 12 February 2007) (hereafter '*Suez Sociedad General de Aguas de Barcelona S.A. and Vivendi Universal S.A.*'); *(Order in Response to a Petition for Transparency and Participation as* Amicus Curiae*)* (ICSID Arbitral Tribunal, Case No ARB/03/19, May 2005). The petition challenged the decision by the Government of Argentina to accede to the ICSID treaty on grounds that it violates the constitutional guarantees of citizens of Argentina to participate in proceedings. While the government of Argentina was willing to hear the petition, the complainant company was not. However, the Attorney General of Argentina published on the internet the information in his possession on the related cases. See also Alfaro and Lorenti (2005).

[128]See, e.g. *GEA Group Aktiengesellschaft v Ukraine (Award)* (hereafter '*GEA Group Aktiengesellschaft*') (ICSID Arbitral Tribunal, Case No ARB/08/16), March 2011; *Talsud, S.A. v United Mexican States (Award)* (ICSID Arbitral Tribunal, Case No ARB(AF)/04/4), 16 June 2010; *Gemplus, S.A., SLP, S.A. and Gemplus Industrial, S.A. de C.V. v United Mexican States (Award)* (ICSID Arbitral Tribunal, Case No ARB(AF)/04/3, 16 June 2010) (hereafter '*Gemplus*').

[129]See, e.g. *GEA Group Aktiengesellschaft* (ICSID Arbitral Tribunal, Case No. ARB(AF)/04/4), 16 June 2010; *Gemplus. Aguas del Tunari, S.A. v. Republic of Bolivia (Order Taking Note of Discontinuance)* (ICSID Case No ARB/02/3), 28 March 2006. See further Vandevelde (2007) (providing an overview and analysis of the case).

'would have the additional desirable consequence of increasing the transparency of ISA'.[130] It nevertheless declined to permit public participation under the petition.

Much has changed in the last decade in ISA practice, commencing with greater transparency and open hearings under Chapter 11 of the North American Free Trade Agreement (NAFTA), including efforts to redress the economic, social and political costs of protectionism.[131] In 2006, the ICSID revised its rules, adding a new Rule 37 which provides for the admission of third parties to proceedings and the submission of *amicus curiae* briefs.[132] Some of these changes are qualified. For example, provision is made for the publication of ICSID awards.[133] But that is subject to the consent of the direct parties to the ISA dispute.[134] The ICSID Arbitration Rules do state that 'the Centre shall, however, promptly include in its publications excerpts of the legal reasoning of the Tribunal'.[135] A review committee with limited authority, which includes no right to overturn an ICSID award on its merits, continues to be able to review ICSID decisions.[136]

Whether China and/or 'its' state enterprises abroad will deny consent or otherwise resist public interest petitions, *amicus* briefs or other forms of participation by third parties in ISA proceedings, is uncertain. Much will depend on the nature of the dispute, the parties, the anticipated consequences of such action and intervening events.

An equally difficult issue is how ISA tribunals will decide disputes in which foreign investors claim that China has advantaged state-owned enterprises over them. This concern is plausible only when considered in the context of other factors, such as the admission of foreign investment into China and the standard of treatment accorded to foreign investors under the particular BIT regime in issue.[137] Multinational corporations of the West, while legally autonomous, are often more powerful

---

[130] *Order in Response to a Petition for Transparency and Participation as* Amicus Curiae (ICSID Case No ARB/03/19), 19 May 2005, [19] and [22].

[131] On public statements by the NAFTA parties on open hearings, see Foreign Affairs and International Trade Canada (2009). This practice is further reflected in the interpretation of Chapter 11 by the Free Trade Commission, confirming the decision in *Metalclad Corporation v. The United Mexican States* (ICSID Case No. ARB(AF)/97/1), para 103 that '[n]othing in the NAFTA imposes a general duty of confidentiality on the disputing parties to a Chapter Eleven arbitration'.

[132] See Gómez (2012).

[133] ICSID tribunals began to admit third party interventions in 2007, after the ICSID's new rule 37 came into force. See e.g. *Biwater Gauff (Tanzania) Ltd. v United Republic of Tanzania* (ICSID Case No. ARB/05/22), 2 February 2007; *Suez, Sociedad General de Aguas de Barcelona, S.A., and Vivendi Universal S.A.* See International Center for Settlement of Investment Disputes, ICSID Convention, Regulations and Rules 95–96 (2006); Baldwin et al. (2006) (discussing 'tactics' that may be employed in attempts to 'delay' or 'avoid' compliance with ICSID Awards).

[134] See e.g. Antonietti (2006).

[135] See ICSID Rules of Procedure for Arbitration Proceedings, ICSID/15 (April 2006), Art 48(4). cf. ICSID Additional Facility Arbitration Rules, Art 53(3), http://icsid.worldbank.org/ICSID/ICSID/AdditionalFacilityRules.jsp (almost identical text). See also Franck (2004–2005, p. 1616), Maupin (2011, p. 162).

[136] See, e.g. Nathan (2000).

[137] See Bath (2011).

than the liberal states that nurtured them and that usually serve as their supplicants. If the liberalization of international investment law is to be truly evenhanded, it also needs to focus on the functional advantages to such large-scale investors, not only the functional advantages countries like China may give to state-owned enterprises.

A further concern is that China will use conflict prevention and avoidance measures to force inbound investor complainants into submission, or diplomatic measures to intimidate foreign states to submit to claims by outbound Chinese state enterprises. This is not a China-specific criticism. More often than not, states will adopt conflict prevention and avoidance measures based on their capacity to deliver preferred results, such as ensuring that their subjects abroad are treated 'fairly' measured according to 'home' rather than 'host' state standards of treatment.[138] Self-interest is an underlying characteristic of both strictly regulated and liberalized investment markets, wherever that state may happen to be. It is true that China has, and already does, resolve some investor-state disputes through negotiation in a manner that is not public and that may involve bargaining or take-it-or-leave it results. This appears to be what occurred in the only three ISA cases against China, as explained above. Such dispute avoidance methods, pontificated by the United Nations Conference on Trade and Development (UNCTAD),[139] are not peculiar to Chinese arbitration. Nor would one expect investor-state negotiations necessarily to take place on a level playing field, although the latter is probably not what the UNCTAD intended to encourage in promoting conflict prevention and avoidance measures in investor-state disputes.[140] It is therefore perfectly explicable that the Chinese Model BIT urges investor-state parties to first attempt to resolve their differences through negotiation.[141]

China also subscribes to conciliation prior to commencing arbitration, notably in relation to international commercial arbitration.[142] More controversial is its resort to 'mediation during arbitration' or 'med-arb', in relation to commercial arbitration.[143] The conception of arbitrators mediating is controversial, not least of all because it leads to party disclosures during mediation proceedings that would ordinarily not be disclosed during arbitration proceedings before the same tribunal even with the parties' consents.[144] However, this controversy is also not peculiar to China, but rather arises in both institutional and ad hoc arbitration in general.[145]

[138] See, e.g. Brower and Steven (2001, pp. 193–195), Coe (2002), Gantz (2006); But see Dodge (2001) (presenting the case for modeling Chapter 11 on the World Trade Organization appellate process).

[139] UNCTAD (2010a, p. xxiii).

[140] On the UNCTAD's most recent report on investor-state dispute settlement, see UNCTAD (2018a).

[141] See e.g. Art 12(3) of the Singapore-China BIT, providing: 'If a dispute involving the amount of compensation resulting from expropriation, nationalization or other measures having effect equivalent to nationalization or expropriation cannot be settled within six months after resort to negotiation. it may be submitted to an international arbitral tribunal established by both parties'.

[142] See Tang (2005, p. 547).

[143] Schneider (1998, p. 57).

[144] See Qiao (2001), Ali (2011).

[145] See Ali (2011). But see Kaufmann-Kohler and Fan (2008), Nakamura (2009).

9 Conclusion

The sometimes loud trumpet call from the West that China should further liberalize its investment regime is ahistorical at worst and disingenuous at best. Even the process of liberalization in the West which is presented as an example of good practice, has evolved incrementally, unevenly and often, incompletely. Western countries were—and often are—protectionist and reluctant to surrender their sovereignty through treaties with other states.[146] Not only is there a history of reticence in granting foreign states MFN treatment. There is also a history of even greater reluctance to grant foreign investors national treatment.[147] The process of developing BITs in China is not entirely different from that development. Given China's late participation in BITs, its ideological differences from the West, and its developing economy, it is unrealistic to expect it to embrace the liberalization of investment that most Western countries themselves initially did not do either, notwithstanding their liberal traditions.[148]

There has been a significant shift in China's status and ensuing policies from a capital importer to a capital exporter. As a capital importer, China had significant historical reasons to regulate inbound capital including through BITs, domestic laws, administrative regulation, its court system and commercial arbitration. As a capital exporter today, China has equally significant reasons to expand on the BIT protections that it wants its BIT host partner states to accord Chinese investors there.

China's growing interest in concluding FTAs and BITs that enable its investors to profit abroad is entirely consistent with the aspirations of other capital exporters. Nor should one expect otherwise. Investment protectionism is the other side of the investment liberalization coin. It is a coin that liberal states of the West repeatedly flip when it comes to the rights of foreign investors. It is not a coin whose use should be treated as abhorrent because China is increasingly flipping that coin.

At the same time, it would be disingenuous to suggest that China has not continued to adopt a protectionist stance towards vulnerable sectors of its economy, notably its struggling rural sectors. The Supreme Peoples' Court of China has affirmed the virtue of such protectionism as a matter of national interest.[149] The defense of necessity is likely to arise in the interpretation of Chinese BITs or under customary international law in cases in which China is an ISA defendant; and the scope of such a defense globally is significant.[150] However, it would be an overstatement to suggest that

---

[146] On the complexity of sovereignty in international investment law, see Trakman (2018, p. 207).

[147] See e.g. Kurtz (2010). Kurtz relies on the commentary of Joseph Stiglitz to assert that '"all countries engage in some discrimination" against foreign investors', and concedes that 'protectionism is a political temptation that is not confined to any political or legal tradition' (at p. 11). But see Shen (2018, pp. 799–840).

[148] See Mukand (2006).

[149] See, e.g. Wolff (2010, pp. 1001, 1003, 1110–1111) (noting China's protectionism); see also Shen (2010, pp. 183–185) (discussing limits placed on complainants under bilateral investment agreements with China).

[150] On the successful use of the defense of necessity, see e.g. *Continental Casualty Company v Argentine Republic* (ICSID Case No. ARB/03/9), 5 September 2008, para 28. But see *Pope & Talbot* Inc. *v Can.*, Award, part III (10 April 2001) (UNCITRAL Award). See also *Pope & Talbot*

China and its courts are unique in erecting national interest and security barriers to intrusion from foreign investors.[151]

Moreover, ascribing the lack of ISA against China to its failure to liberalize FDI is equally tenuous. The fact that China has expanded the grounds for investor claims in its more recent BITs beyond compensation is a sign of investment liberalization, however much it also benefits Chinese investors in foreign host states. The rarity of investors bringing ISA claims against China is also not exceptional. The United States and many European countries that historically were capital exporters seldom were, or are, targets of ISA claims. Germany has had only one ISA claim brought against it, despite having concluded the largest number of BITs to date. This is not to deny that foreign investors that lodge ISA claims against China may face formidable resistance from a centrally directed economy, and not least of all from China's well-financed and consolidated defense of its national interest. What is contended is that the legitimacy crisis imputed to ISA, in pitting the public interests of states against the private interests of foreign investors, is not distinctive to China.[152] Nor does the absence of mass ISA claims by foreign investors against China infer investor temerity. It may well infer that foreign investors are in fact receiving fair and equitable treatment.

Therefore, the Chinese Model BIT and its various negotiated BITs, arguably, are expected from a developing country that is modifying its investment regime to accommodate its growing stature as a global power and capital exporter.

References

Agyemang AA (1988) African states and ICSID arbitration. CILSA 21:177

Alden C, Davies M (2006) A profile of the operations of Chinese multinationals in Africa. South African J Int'l Aff 13(1):83

Alfaro CE, Lorenti PM (2005) The growing opposition of argentina to ICSID arbitral tribunals: a conflict between international and domestic law? J World Investment Trade 6:417

Ali SF (2011) The Morality of conciliation: an empirical examination of arbitrator 'role moralities' in east asia and the west. harv Negot L Rev 16(1):1

Antonietti A (2006) The 2006 amendments of the ICSID rules and regulations and the additional facility rules. ICSIC Rev—Foreign Investment L J 21: 427

Appleton S (2010) Latin american arbitration: the story behind the headlines. Int Bar Assoc, London, 31 March 2010. http://www.ibanet.org/Article/Detail.aspx?ArticleUid=78296258-3B37-4608-A5EE-3C92D5D0B979

Bakircioglu O (2007) The application of the margin of appreciation doctrine in freedom of expression and public morality cases. German L J 8:711

Baldwin E, Kantor M, Nolan M (2006) Limits to enforcement of ICSID awards. J Int'l Arb 23:1

Inc. v Gov't of Canada, Foreign Affairs & Int'l Trade Canada, http://www.international.gc.ca/trade-agreements-accords-commerciaux/disp-diff/pope.aspx?lang=en.

[151]On governmental bureaucracies faced by foreign investors in Asia, in particular in China and Australia, see Bath (2012).

[152]On the tension between private and public interests in investor-state arbitration with regard to the publication of awards, see Karton (2012). On the public interest rationale for *amicus curiae* interventions, see De Brabandere (2011), Mills (2011).

Banifatemi Y (2009) The emerging jurisprudence on the most favored nation treatment in investment arbitration. In: Bjorklund A, Laird I, Ripinksy S (eds), Investment treaty law: current issues III, remedies in international investment law, emerging jurisprudence of international investment law. british institute of international and comparative law, London, Part II (Chapter 7)
Bath V (2010) The Chinese legal system and the Stern Hu Case. East Asia Forum. http://www.eastasiaforum.org/2010/03/28/the-chinese-legal-system-and-the-stern-hu-case/. 28 Mar 2010
Bath V (2011) The quandary for chinese regulators: controlling the flow of investment into and out of China. In: Bath V, Nottage L (eds), Foreign Investment and Dispute Resolution Law and Practice in Asia. Routledge, New York (Chapter 4)
Bath V (2012) Foreign investment, the national interest and national security: foreign direct investment in Australia and China. Sydney L Rev 34:5
Bennell P (1997) Foreign direct investment in Africa: Rhetoric and reality. SAIS Rev 17(2):127
Bernasconi-Osterwalder N (2012) Analysis of the European commission's draft text on investor-state dispute settlement for EU agreements, Investment Treaty News. IISD. http://www.iisd.org/itn/2012/07/19/analysis-of-the-european-commissions-draft-text-on-investor-state-dispute-settlement-for-eu-agreements/. 19 July 2012
Bretton Woods Project (2009) ICSID in Crisis: straight-jacket or investment protection? http://www.brettonwoodsproject.org/art-564878. 10 July 2009
Brower C, Steven L (2001) NAFTA Chapter 11: Who then Should Judge? Developing the international rule of law under NAFTA Chapter 11. Chicago J Int'l L 2: 193
Brown C (2013) Commentaries on selected model investment treaties (Oxford Commentaries on International Law). Oxford University Press, Oxford
Buckley PJ, Clegg J, Cross AR, Liu X, Voss H, Zheng P (2007) The determinants of Chinese outward foreign direct investment. J Int'l Bus Studies 38(4):499
Burke-White WW, von Staden A (2008) Investment protection in extraordinary times: the interpretation and application of non-precluded measures provisions in bilateral investment treaties. Va J Int'l L 48:307
Cai CY (2006) Outward foreign direct investment protection and the effectiveness of Chinese BIT practice. J World Invest Trade 7:621
Coe JJ (2002) Domestic court control of investment awards: necessary evil or achilles heel within NAFTA and the proposed FTAA. Int'l Arb 19:185
Cohen T, Schneiderman D (2017) The political economy of chinese bilateral investment treaty policy. Chinese J Comparative Law 5(1):10–128. https://doi.org/10.1093/cjcl/cxx011
Cotula L (2011) Law and power in foreign investment in Africa: shades of grey in the shadow of the law. Routledge, London and New York
Davies M (2008) China's developmental model comes to Africa. Rev African Pol Econ 35(1):134
De Brabandere E (2011) NGOs and the 'public interest': the legality and rationale of amicus curiae interventions in international economic and investment disputes. Chi J Int'l L 12:85
Dodge WS (2001) Case report: waste management, Inc v Mexico. Am J Int'l L 95:186
Dolzer R, Stevens M (1995) Bilateral investment treaties. Kluwer Law International, The Hague
Dolzer R, Schreuer C (2008) Principles of international investment law. Oxford University Press, New York
Dugan C, Wallace D, Rubins N, Sabahi B (2008) Investor-state arbitration. Oxford University Press, New York
Dumberry P (2010) Are BITs representing the 'new' customary international law in international investment law? Pa St Int'l L Rev 28:675
Eliasson N (2011) China's investment treaties: a procedural perspective. In: Bath V, Nottage L (eds), Foreign investment and dispute resolution law and practice in Asia. Routledge, New York (Chapter 5)
Emerson C (2011) Trading our way to more jobs and prosperity. Government trade policy statement. http://www.dfat.gov.au/publications/trade/trading-our-way-to-more-jobs-and-prosperity.html#investor-state. 12 April 2011

European Commission (2011) Public consultation on the future relationship between the EU and China. http://trade.ec.europa.eu/consultations/?consul_id=153. 6 July 2011
European Commission (2012) Proposal for a regulation of the european parliament and of the council, establishing a framework for managing financial responsibility linked to investor-state dispute settlement tribunals established by international agreements to which the European Union is party. https://eur-lex.europa.eu/legal-content/EN/TXT/PDF/?uri=CELEX:52012PC0335&from=EN. 21 June 2012
Foreign Affairs and International Trade Canada (2009) NAFTA—Chapter 11—investment settlement of disputes between a party and an investor of another party: transparency. 9 Sept 2009
Franck SD (2004–2005) The legitimacy crisis in investment treaty arbitration: privatizing public international law through inconsistent decisions. Fordham L Rev 73: 1521
Franck SD (2007a) Empirically evaluating claims about investment treaty arbitration. N C L Rev 86:1
Franck SD (2007b) Foreign direct investment, investment treaty arbitration, and the rule of law. Pac McGeorge Global Bus Dev L J 19:337
Franck SD (2011) The ICSID effect? Considering potential variations in arbitration awards. Va J Int'l L 51:977
Gantz DA (2006) An appellate mechanism for review of arbitral decisions in investor-state disputes: prospects and challenges. Vanderbilt J Transnat'l L 39:39
Garcia L B (2012) We have to get out of the ICSID. venezuelanalysis.com. http://venezuelanalysis.com/analysis/6766. 24 Jan 2012
Garcia-Bolivar OE (2010) Protected investments and protected investors: the outer limits of ICSID's reach. Trade Law Development 2:145
Gómez KF (2012) Rethinking the role of amicus curiae in international investment arbitration: how to draw the line favorably for the public interest. Fordham Int'l L J 35:510
Gu J, Humphrey J, Messner D (2008) Global governance and developing countries: the implications of the rise of China. World Dev 36(2):274
Heymann MCE (2008) International law and the settlement of investment disputes relating to China. J Int Econ Law 11(3):507–526
Hindelang S (2004) Bilateral investment treaties, custom and a healthy investment climate: the question of whether BITs influence customary international law revisited. J World Inv Trade 5:789
Hofmann R, Tams C (eds) (2011) International investment law and general international law: from clinical isolation to systematic integration. Nomos, Baden-Baden
Huliaras A, Magliveras K (2007) Truths, lies and misperceptions: United States and European Union reactions to the growing Chinese presence in Africa (paper presented at the Second European Conference on African Studies, University of Leiden)
ICSID (2012) Venezuela submits a notice under article 71 of the ICSID convention, Washington DC. http://icsid.worldbank.org/ICSID/FrontServlet?requestType=CasesRH&actionVal=OpenPage&PageType=AnnouncementsFrame&FromPage=Announcements&pageName=Announcement100. 26 Jan 2012
ICSID (2018) The ICSID caseload—statistics. https://icsid.worldbank.org/en/Documents/resources/ICSID%20Web%20Stats%202018-1(English).pdf (Issue 2018-1)
Jackson RH (1990) Quasi-states: sovereignty, international relations and the third world. Cambridge University Press, Cambridge
Jennings R, Watts A (eds) (1992) Oppenheim's international law. Longman, London
Johnson AR (2010) Comment: rethinking bilateral investment treaties in sub-Saharan Africa. Emory L J 59:919
Kantor M (2011) The transparency agenda for uncitral investment arbitrations: looking in all the wrong places. http://www.iilj.org/research/documents/IF2010-11
Kaplinsky R, Messner D (2008) Introduction: the impact of asian drivers on the developing world. World Dev 36(2):197

Karton JDH (2012) A conflict of interests: seeking a way forward on publication of international arbitral awards. Arb Int'l 28:447–486

Kaufmann-Kohler G, Fan K (2008) Integrating mediation into arbitration: why it works in China. J Int'l Arb 25(4):479–492

Kinnear M (2009) The continuing development of the fair and equitable treatment standard. In: Bjorklund AK, Laird IA, Ripinsky S (eds), Investment treaty law: current issues III. Remedies in international investment. british institute of international and comparative law, London, Part II, Chapter 6

Kragelund P (2009) Knocking on a wide open door: Chinese investments in Africa. Rev African Pol Econ 36(122):479

Krever T (2011) The legal turn in late development theory: the rule of law and the world bank's development model. Harv Int'l L J 52:287

Kueh YY (ed) (1997) The political economy of Sino-American relations: a greater China perspective. Hong Kong University Press, Hong Kong

Kurtz J (2010) Adjudging the exceptional at international investment law: security, public order and financial crisis. Int'l Comp L Q 59:325

Kurtz J (2012) Australia's rejection of investor-state arbitration: causation, omission and implication. ICSIC Rev—Foreign Investment L J 27(1): 65–86

Laird IA (2004) MTD Equity Sdn Bhd and MTD Chile S.A. v. Republic of Chile—recent developments in the fair and equitable treatment standard. Transnational Dispute Management. https://www.transnational-dispute-management.com/article.asp?key=289. 4 Oct 2004

Lin Y (ed) (2008) Newest commercial arbitration and judicial practical cases on specific issues, vol 1. UIBE Press, Beijing

Lin Y (2018) Judicial review of arbitration: law and practice in China. Wolters Kluwer, Leiden

Liu Q (2019) Chinese 'case law' in comparative studies: illusions and complexities. Asian J Comparat Law (forthcoming)

Marian C (2010) Balancing transparency: the value of administrative law and mathews-balancing to investment treaty arbitrations. Pepp Disp Resol L J 10:275

Maupin JA (2011) MFN-based jurisdiction in investor-state arbitration: is there any hope for a consistent approach? J Int'l Econ L 14:157

McLachlan C (2008) Investment treaties and general international law. Int'l Comp L Q 57:361

Mills A (2011) The public-private dualities of international investment law and arbitration. In: Brown C, Miles K (eds) Evolution in investment treaty law and arbitration. Cambridge University Press, Cambridge, pp 97–116

Ministry of Commerce, People's Republic of China (2016) Director's Comments. http://english.mofcom.gov.cn/article/zt_cv/lanmucc/201602/20160201251492.shtml

Ministry of Commerce, People's Republic of China (2018) Statistics of FDI in January–October 2018. http://english.mofcom.gov.cn/aarticle/statistic/foreigninvestment/.html

Moser MJ (1998) CIETAC arbitration: a success story? J Int'l Arb 1:30

Muchlinski P, Ortino F, Schreuer C (eds) (2008) The Oxford handbook of international law. Oxford University Press, Oxford

Muhammad N (2019) A comparative approach to margin of appreciation in international law. Chinese J Comparative Law 7(1) (forthcoming)

Mukand SW (2006) Globalization and the 'confidence game'. J Int'l Econ 70:406

Nakamura T (2009) Brief empirical study on Arb-Med in the JCAA arbitration. JCAA News Lett 22:10–12

Nathan KVSV (2000) ICSID convention: the law of the international centre for settlement of investment disputes. Juris Publishing, Huntington

Neligan M (2012) China insurer ping an files claim for fortis loss. Reuters. http://in.reuters.com/article/2012/09/24/pingan-fortis-idINL5E8KO9V520120924. 24 Sept 2012

Neumayer E, Spess L (2005) Do Bilateral investment treaties increase foreign direct investment to developing countries? World Dev 33(10):1567

Nottage L, Miles K (2009) 'Back to the future' for investor-state arbitrations: revising rules in Australia and Japan to meet public interests. J Int Arbitr 26(1):25–58

Nottage L, Weeramantry R (2011) Investment arbitration in Asia: five perspectives on law and practice. In: Bath V, Nottage L (eds), Foreign investment and dispute resolution law and practice in Asia, Routledge, New York (Chapter 2)

Paulsson J (2007) International arbitration and the generation of legal norms: treaty arbitration and international law. In: van den Berg AJ (ed), International arbitration 2006: back to basics? (International Council for Commercial Arbitration Congress Series No. 13). Kluwer Law International, Alphen aan den Rijn, The Netherlands, p 879

Peinhardt C, Allee T (2011) Devil in the details? The investment effects of dispute settlement variation in BITs. In: Sauvant KP (ed), Yearbook on international investment law & policy 2010–2011. Oxford University Press, Oxford (Chapter 21)

Peterson LE (2012) South Africa pushes phase-out of early bilateral investment treaties after at least two separate brushes with investor-state arbitration. Inv Arb Reporter. http://www.iareporter.com/articles/20120924_1. 23 Sept 2012

Puig S, Kinnear M (2010) NAFTA chapter eleven at fifteen: contributions to a systemic approach in investment arbitration. ICSID L Rev 25:225

Qiao X (2001) The research on arbitration right. Law Press Beijing, China

Qin JY (2003) WTO-plus obligations and their implications for the world trade organization legal system: an appraisal of the China accession protocol. J World Trade 37(3):483

Reinisch A (2011) How narrow are narrow dispute settlement clauses in investment treaties? J Int'l Disp Settlement 2:115

Rooney KM (2007) ICSID and BIT arbitrations and China. J Int'l Arb 24:704

Rubinacci L (2012) EU-China investment relationship, update on state of play. DC trade civil society dialogue. http://trade.ec.europa.eu/doclib/docs/2012/march/tradoc_149185.pdf. 7 Mar 2012

Salacuse JW (2007) The treatification of international investment law. Law Bus Rev Am 13:155

Sasson M (2010) Substantive law in investment treaty arbitration: the unsettled relationship between international and municipal law. Kluwer Law International, The Netherlands

Schill SW (2009) The multilateralization of international investment law. Cambridge University Press, Cambridge

Schill SW (ed) (2010) International investment law and comparative public law. Oxford University Press, Oxford

Schneider M (1998) Combining arbitration with conciliation. In: van den Berg AJ (ed), International dispute resolution: towards an international arbitration culture (ICCA Congress Series No. 8). Kluwer Law International, The Hague, p 57

Schreuer C (2001) The ICSID convention: a commentary. Cambridge University Press, Cambridge

Schreuer C, Weiniger M (2008) A doctrine of precedent? In: Muchlinski P, Ortino F, Schreuer C (eds) The oxford handbook of international investment law. Oxford University Press, Oxford, p 1188

Schwebel S (2005) The influence of bilateral investment treaties on customary international law. Transnat'l Disp Mgmt 2(5):1

Shan W, Simons P, Singh D (eds) (2008) Redefining sovereignty in international economic law. Hart Publishing, Oxford and Portland, OR

Shan W, Gallagher N (2009) Chinese investment treaties: policies and practice. Oxford University Press, Oxford

Shan W, Gallagher N, Zhang S (2012) National treatment for foreign investment in China: a changing landscape. ICSID Rev 27:120

Shany Y (2005) Toward a general margin of appreciation doctrine in international law? Eur J Int'l L 16:907

Shen W (2010) Case note, beyond the scope of 'investor' and 'investment': who can make an arbitration claim under a Chinese BIT? Some implications from a recent ICSID case. Asian Int'l Arb J 6:164

Shen W (2018) Evolution of Non-discriminatory standards in China's BITs in the context of EU-China BIT negotiations. Chinese J Int Law 17(3):799–840. https://doi.org/10.1093/chinesejil/jmy018

Shihata IFI (2009) Towards a greater depoliticization of investment disputes: the roles of ICSID and MIGA. In: Lu KW, Verheyen G, Perera SM (eds) Investing with confidence: understanding political risk management in the 21st Century. World Bank Publications, Washington D C, pp 2–35

Smith G (2010) Chinese bilateral investment treaties restrictions on international arbitration. Arb 76: 58. http://gordonsmithlegal.com.au/resources/Chinese%20BITs%20(GS).pdf

Sornarajah M (2013) The case against an international investment regime. In: Trakman LE, Ranieri N (eds), Regionalism in international investment law. Oxford University Press, Oxford (Chapter 17)

Steingruber AM (2012) Consent in international arbitration. Oxford University Press, Oxford

Stiglitz J (2010) Freefall: America, free markets, and the sinking of the world economy. W W Norton, New York

Stumberg R (1998) Sovereignty by subtraction: the multilateral agreement on investment. Cornell Int'l L J 31:491

Tang H (2005) Combination of arbitration with conciliation: Arb/Med. In: van den Berg AJ (ed), New horizons in international commercial arbitration and beyond (ICCA Congress Series No. 12). Kluwer Law International, The Hague, p 547

Trakman LE (2006) Legal traditions and international commercial arbitration. Am Rev Int'l Arb 17:1

Trakman LE (2008) Arbitrating options: turning a morass into a panacea. UNSW L J 41(1):292–305

Trakman LE (2010) Foreign direct investment: hazard or opportunity? Geo Wash Int'l L Rev 41:1

Trakman LE (2011) Enter the Dragon IV: China's proliferating investment treaty program. In: UNSW Centre for Law, Markets & Regulation. https://clmr.unsw.edu.au/article//enter-the-dragon-iv%3A–china%27s-proliferating-investment-treaty-program

Trakman LE (2012a) The ICSID under Siege. Cornell Int'l L J 45(3):603–665

Trakman LE (2012b) Rejecting investor-state arbitration in favor of domestic courts: the Australian example. J World Trade 46(1):83

Trakman LE (2012c) Investor state arbitration or local courts: will Australia set a new trend? J World Trade 46(1):83–120

Trakman LE (2013) Investor-state arbitration: the Australian case. In: Trakman LE, Ranieri N (eds) Regionalism in international investment law. Oxford University Press, Oxford (Chapter 12)

Trakman LE (2018) Aligning state sovereignty with transnational public policy. Tulane Law Rev 93(2):207

Trakman LE, Ranieri N (2013) Regionalism in international investment law. Oxford University Press, Oxford

Tzanakopoulos A (2011) Denunciation of the ICSID Convention under the General International Law of Treaties. In: Hofmann R, Tams CJ (eds) International investment law and general international law: from clinical isolation to systemic integration. Nomos, Baden-Baden, pp 75–93

UNCTAD (2010a). Investor–state disputes: prevention and alternatives to arbitration. In: UNCTAD series on international investment policies for development, xxiii. http://www.unctad.org/en/docs/diaeia200911_en.pdf. May 2010

UNCTAD (2010b) Denunciation of the ICSID convention and BITS: impact on investor-state claims. IIA Issues Note No. 2. https://unctad.org/en/Docs/webdiaeia20106_en.pdf. Dec 2010

UNCTAD (2018a) Investor-state dispute settlement: review of developments in 2017. IIA Issues Note No. 2. https://unctad.org/en/PublicationsLibrary/diaepcbinf2018d2_en.pdf. June 2018

UNCTAD (2018b) UNCTAD world investment report. https://unctad.org/en/PublicationsLibrary/wir2018_en.pdf. 6 June 2018

van den Berg AJ (ed) (1998) Yearbook commercial arbitration 1998, vol XXIII. Kluwer Law International, The Hague

van den Berg AJ (ed) (1999) Yearbook commercial arbitration 1999, vol XXIV. Kluwer Law International, The Hague

van Harten G (2007) Investment treaty arbitration and public law. Oxford University Press, Oxford
Vandevelde K (2005) A brief history of international investment agreements. UC Davis J Int'l L Pol'y 12:157
Vandevelde KJ (2007) Aguas del Tunari, S.A. v Republic of Bolivia. Am J Int'l L 101:179
Vincentelli IA (2010) The uncertain future of ICSID in Latin America. Law Bus Rev 16:409
von Staden A (2011) Towards greater doctrinal clarity in investor-state arbitration: The CMS, Enron and Sempra annulment decisions. Czech Y B Int'l L 2:207
Weeramantry JR (2012) Treaty interpretation in investment arbitration. Oxford University Press, Oxford
Willems JY (2011) The settlement of investor state disputes and China new developments on ICSID jurisdiction. South Carolina J Int'l Law Business 8:1
Wolff L-C (2010) Pathological foreign investment projects in China: patchwork or trendsetting by the supreme people's court? Int'l Law 44:1001
World Bank (2018) Worldwide governance indicators. http://info.worldbank.org/governance/wgi/index.aspx#home
Yackee JW, Wong J (2010) The 2006 procedural and transparency-related amendments to the ICSID arbitration rules: model intentions, moderate proposals, and modest returns. In: Sauvant KP (ed), Yearbook on international investment law & policy 2009–2010, Oxford University Press, Oxford (Chapter 6)
Yang X (2012) State immunity in international law. Cambridge University Press, Cambridge

Leon F. Trakman is Former Dean of Law at the University of New South Wales, 2002–2007 and is currently a UNSW Professor of Law. He holds both Masters' and Doctorate degrees earned at the Harvard Law School. He is author or editor of 9 books, over 40 book chapters and more than 100 articles published in international law journals. His primary areas of research are international dispute resolution, international investment law and contract law. He is active as an inter-governmental trade adjudicator, frequently appointed since 1993 by the US, Canadian and Mexican Governments under the NAFTA. Trakman has also served as presiding arbitrator or as co-arbitrator in over 120 international commercial arbitration disputes over the past 3 decades.

Qiao Liu is currently an Associate Professor in the School of Law, City University of Hong Kong (People's Republic of China), an Adjunct Professor of Comparative Law at the School of Law of Xi'an Jiaotong University (China) and the Editor-in-Chief of the Chinese Journal of Comparative Law (OUP). He obtained his DPhil in law from the University of Oxford. He teaches and researches in contract law (both Anglo-Australian and Chinese), comparative Chinese law and commercial law (both domestic and international). He has published in leading law journals including the Modern Law Review, American Journal of Comparative Law and the Cambridge Law Journal. He is the author of the book entitled Anticipatory Breach (Hart Publishing Oxford 2011) and co-authored a leading contract text, Contract Law Australian Edition (Palgrave Macmillan 2015), with Professor Ewan McKendrick of the University of Oxford. He was elected a member of the International Academy of Comparative Law early 2013 and a member of a small expert group working with the United Nations Commission on International Trade Law (UNCITRAL) Secretariat on the updating of the Digest on the Convention on Contracts for the International Sale of Goods.

Lei Chen is Associate Professor at School of Law, City University of Hong Kong until June, 2020. He becomes Chair of Chinese Law and co-Director of Centre for Chinese Law and Policy, Durham University, UK since July, 2020. He is also Eastern Scholar Professor of Law at East China University of Political Science and Law. He is on the Law Panel of Hong Kong Research Assessment Exercise 2020. His research areas are Chinese and comparative private laws and dispute resolution. He is a seasoned arbitrator at a number of arbitration institutions in Asia and Europe.

For Whom the Bell Tolls: Any Hope Left for Investment Arbitration After *Achmea*?

André Janssen and Christian Johannes Wahnschaffe

Abstract On 6 March 2018, the European Court of Justice (ECJ) rendered its long-awaited judgment in Case C-284/16, better known as the *Achmea* decision. This judgment addressed the compatibility of the bilateral investment treaty concluded between the Netherlands and the Slovak Republic with European Union (EU) law. The ECJ ultimately held that the treaty's dispute settlement provisions infringe EU law. Although the ECJ only addressed this particular bilateral investment treaty, the judgment is widely considered to be a landmark decision with far-reaching implications. The decision sparked a vivid debate amongst scholars, politicians and practitioners as to the impact of the judgment, focussing in particular on whether *Achmea* puts an End to (intra-EU) Investor-state dispute settlement (ISDS) as a whole. This Chapter outlines the factual background of the *Achmea* decision and analyses its key findings. It then particularly explores the potential impact of the judgment on the status of other intra-EU bilateral investment treaties as well as the enforcement of awards that have already been rendered in ISDS proceedings. The Chapter further discusses the highly controversial question of the *Achmea* decision's impact on bilateral investment treaties between EU Member States and non-EU States as well as its impact on investment treaties the EU itself is a party to, such as the Energy Charter Treaty and the EU-Canada Comprehensive Economic and Trade Agreement. Finally, this Chapter also addresses the potential impact of the *Achmea* decision on commercial arbitration. This Chapter reflects the legal status and scholarly discussion in early 2019. To the extent necessary, further updates have been included regarding the most significant recent developments.

A. Janssen (✉)
Faculty of Law, Radboud University Nijmegen, Nijmegen, The Netherlands
e-mail: a.janssen@jur.ru.nl

C. J. Wahnschaffe
Faculty of Law, University of Münster, Münster, Germany
e-mail: cjwahnschaffe@uni-muenster.de

L. Chen and A. Janssen (eds.), *Dispute Resolution in China, Europe and World*, Ius Gentium: Comparative Perspectives on Law and Justice 79,
https://doi.org/10.1007/978-3-030-42974-4_12

1 General Introduction

In 2018, hardly any other decision of the European Court of Justice (ECJ) has caused as much turmoil amongst scholars and practitioners as the judgment of the ECJ in *Case C-284/16*, better known as the *Achmea* decision.[1] In the aftermath of this decision, the concept of 'Investor-State Dispute Settlement' (ISDS) appears to be under significant pressure.

The *Achmea* decision addresses an issue that has been the subject of a prolonged heated discussion: The compatibility of arbitration provisions in intra-EU Bilateral Investment Treaties (intra-EU BITs) with European Union (EU) law. Reportedly, there were 196 intra-EU BITs in force when the ECJ rendered its decision.[2] Besides, there are approximately 1200 BITs between EU Member States and Non-EU States.[3] Lastly, there are numerous investment treaties in which the EU itself is a party to, for example the Energy Charter Treaty (ECT), the Economic Partnership Agreement with Japan (EPA), the EU-Singapore Free Trade Agreement (EUSFTA), and the Comprehensive Economic and Trade Agreement with Canada (CETA). Whilst the provisions of the treaties just mentioned are of course not identical, there is a considerable consistency regarding their key features. Many investment treaties entitle investors to certain minimum standards of substantive protection. For this reason, they guarantee, for example, a fair and equitable treatment[4] as well as the absence of any discriminatory measures[5] or any measures depriving investors of their investment without compensation.[6] As a matter of procedural protection, investors can regularly seek compensation for breaches of the former guarantees before an arbitral tribunal.[7] The tribunals render final and binding awards.[8] Investors thus do not need to commence proceedings in the domestic courts of the host state.

This not only allows investors to settle disputes before well-suited arbitral tribunals, but also establishes a distinct justice system outside any national court system. In the context of the EU, arbitral tribunals thus—potentially—interpret EU law in a final manner. This final interpretation is, again, potentially only subject to limited review by domestic courts. Yet only the domestic courts are integrated in a uniform, European judicial system under the aegis of the ECJ. In light of this, there was an

---

[1] ECJ, Judgment of the Court in Case C-284/16 (*Achmea*), 6 March 2018 (ECLI:EU:C:2018:158) (hereafter 'ECJ, *Achmea*').

[2] ECJ, Press Release (2018).

[3] For the number, see e.g. Lavranos and Singla (2018, p. 351), and Woolcock (2010, p. 53).

[4] See e.g. Germany-China BIT, Art 3(1); Morocco-Dominican Republic BIT, Art 2(4); Netherlands-Slovakia BIT, Art 3(1).

[5] See e.g. Germany-China BIT, Art 2(3); Morocco-Dominican Republic BIT, Art 2(3); Netherlands-Slovakia BIT, Art 3(1).

[6] See e.g. Germany-China BIT, Art 4(2); Morocco-Dominican Republic BIT, Art 4(2); Netherlands-Slovakia BIT, Art 5.

[7] See e.g. Germany-China BIT, Art 8(2); Morocco-Dominican Republic BIT, Art 8(2); Netherlands-Slovakia BIT, Art 8(2).

[8] See e.g. Germany-China BIT, Art 8(6); Morocco-Dominican Republic BIT, Art 8(5); Netherlands-Slovakia BIT, Art 8(7).

intense debate whether the EU law allows this sort of 'judicial outsourcing' to arbitral tribunals. This is the core issue of the *Achmea* decision. In short, the *Achmea* decision is about the autonomy of EU law. In this regard, the ECJ decided that safeguarding the autonomy of EU law prevails over the arbitration provision in the intra-EU BIT at stake. The latter is thus incompatible with EU law.

This Chapter aims at illustrating the possible consequences for the system of ISDS pursuant to the *Achmea* decision. It firstly establishes the factual background of the *Achmea* decision (Sect. 2). The next section examines the *Achmea* decision and outlines the reasoning of the ECJ (Sect. 3). Subsequently, this contribution lays emphasis on providing an overview of the decision's consequences and of what is left of (investment) arbitration after *Achmea* (Sect. 4). In this regard, the immediate consequences for *Achmea* are the starting point (Sect. 4.1). This contribution will then examine the consequences for intra-EU BITs (Sect. 4.2), the perspectives for pending and future arbitration proceedings (Sect. 4.3) and the enforcement of arbitral awards rendered under intra-EU BITs (Sect. 4.4). As a next step, the future of BITs between EU Member States and third, non-EU States (Sect. 4.5) as well as the future of investment treaties concluded between the EU itself and third, non-EU States (Sect. 4.6) are to be examined. Finally, this Chapter briefly addresses the impact of the *Achmea* decision on commercial arbitration (Sect. 4.7) before concluding some final remarks (Sect. 5).

2 Factual Background of the *Achmea* Decision

In October 2008, the Dutch insurance company *Achmea* commenced arbitration against the Slovak Republic.[9] *Achmea*, previously known as '*Eureko*', claimed damages for the violation of the Agreement on Encouragement and Reciprocal Protection of Investments between the Kingdom of the Netherlands and the Czech and Slovak Federal Republic (Netherlands-Slovakia BIT).[10]

As of 1 January 1993, the Slovak Republic is the Successor State to the Czech and Slovak Federal Republic.[11] The Slovak Republic acceded to the EU on 1 May 2004.[12] In the course of its accession, the government of the Slovak Republic decided to reform the health system. The government particularly opened the health insurance market to private sickness insurance services.[13] In the light of this, *Achmea* set up a Slovak subsidiary that offered private sickness insurance services on the market.

[9]*Achmea B.V. v Slovak Republic*, PCA Case No. 2008–13, Final Award, 7 December 2012, https://www.italaw.com/sites/default/files/case-documents/italaw3206.pdf (hereafter '*Achmea*, PCA Case No. 2008–13 (2012)'), para 12.

[10]*Achmea*, PCA Case No. 2008–13 (2012), para 6.

[11]*Achmea*, PCA Case No. 2008–13 (2012), para 82.

[12]See Art 2(2) of the Treaty of Accession of the Czech Republic, Estonia, Cyprus, Latvia, Lithuania, Hungary, Malta, Poland, Slovenia and Slovakia.

[13]*Achmea*, PCA Case No. 2008–13 (2012), paras 87 et seq.

Shortly thereafter, the government attempted to reverse these reforms. By passing a law on 25 October 2007, the government particularly put a halt to the distribution of profits generated by private sickness insurance services.[14] However, the Constitutional Court of the Slovak Republic found this legislative action to be unlawful in 2011.[15] Following this court ruling, the government of the Slovak Republic permitted the distribution of profits again as of 1 August 2011.[16]

Achmea claimed that the revocation of the reforms violated various provisions of the Netherlands-Slovakia BIT and caused losses. *Achmea* thus invoked proceedings on the grounds of the Slovak Republic's violation of the Netherlands-Slovakia BIT provisions assuring a fair and equitable treatment, non-impairment by discriminatory or unreasonable measures, full protection and security, free transfer of profits and dividends, as well as the provision assuring protection against unlawful indirect expropriation.[17]

The ad hoc arbitral tribunal (seated in Frankfurt am Main, Germany) rendered a final award on 7 December 2012, affirming the Slovak Republic's violation of various provisions of the Netherlands-Slovakia BIT.[18] The arbitral tribunal awarded *Achmea*, *inter alia*, damages in the amount of EUR 22.1 million.[19] In turn, the Slovak Republic filed an application to have the final award set aside before the Oberlandesgericht Frankfurt am Main (Higher Regional Court).[20] The Slovak Republic objected to the jurisdiction of the arbitral tribunal. It based its objection on doubts as to the compatibility of the Netherlands-Slovakia BIT with Articles 18, 267 and 344 of the Treaty on the Functioning of the EU (TFEU).[21] The court dismissed this action with its judgment delivered on 18 December 2014 and rejected the arguments the Slovak Republic brought forward.[22] The Slovak Republic then appealed to the German Bundesgerichtshof (Federal Court of Justice). In its appeal, the Slovak Republic again contested the compatibility of Article 8 of the Netherlands-Slovakia BIT with Articles 18, 267 and 344 of the TFEU.[23] The German Federal Court of Justice expressed a

---

[14] *Achmea*, PCA Case No. 2008–13 (2012), para 96.

[15] *Achmea*, PCA Case No. 2008–13 (2012), para 115.

[16] *Achmea*, PCA Case No. 2008–13 (2012), para 119.

[17] *Achmea*, PCA Case No. 2008–13 (2012), para 7.

[18] *Achmea*, PCA Case No. 2008–13 (2012), paras 278–295.

[19] *Achmea*, PCA Case No. 2008–13 (2012), para 352 lit. (c).

[20] Higher Regional Court, Frankfurt am Main, Germany, Decision in Case 26 Sch 3/13, 18 December 2014 (ECLI:DE:OLGHE:2014:1218.26SCH3.13.0A) (hereafter 'Higher Regional Court, Frankfurt am Main, Germany, Case 26 Sch 3/13 (2014)'). Notably, after an objection to the tribunal's jurisdiction by the Slovak Republic, the tribunal rendered an Award on Jurisdiction, Arbitrability and Suspension on 26 October 2010. The Slovak Republic had already filed an application to have this earlier award on jurisdiction set aside. After the Final Award had been issued, this first proceeding before the Higher Regional Court of Frankfurt am Main was, however, terminated.

[21] Higher Regional Court, Frankfurt am Main, Germany, Case 26 Sch 3/13 (2014), para 29.

[22] Higher Regional Court, Frankfurt am Main, Germany, Case 26 Sch 3/13 (2014), paras 46 et seq.

[23] ECJ, *Achmea*, para 14.

tendency in favour of compatibility of the Netherlands-Slovakia BIT with EU law.[24] Before ruling on the appeal itself, the German Federal Court of Justice nonetheless submitted a reference for a preliminary ruling to the ECJ pursuant to Article 267(3) of the TFEU.[25]

3 The Decision and the Ruling of the ECJ in a Nutshell

Much has already been said about the sense or the drawbacks of the decision of the ECJ and its reasoning, opposing dispute settlement by arbitral tribunals in the context of ISDS.[26] Before analysing the decisions' consequences in detail, this section will briefly examine the ruling of the ECJ and its key findings to facilitate later discussions.

The decisive clause of the Netherlands-Slovakia BIT, Article 8, reads in its relevant parts as follows:

(1) All disputes between one Contracting Party and an investor of the other Contracting Party concerning an investment of the latter shall if possible, be settled amicably.

(2) Each Contracting Party hereby consents to submit a dispute referred to in paragraph (1) of this Article, to an arbitral tribunal, if the dispute has not been settled amicably within a period of six months from the date either party to the dispute requested amicable settlement.

[…]

(5) The arbitration tribunal shall determine its own procedure applying the arbitration rules of the United Nations Commission for International Trade Law (UNCITRAL).

(6) The arbitral tribunal shall decide on the basis of the law, taking into account in particular though not exclusively: the law in force of the Contracting Party concerned; the provisions of this Agreement, and other relevant Agreements between the Contracting Parties; the provisions of special agreements relating to the investment; the general principles of international law.

(7) The tribunal takes its decision by majority of votes; such decision shall be final and binding upon the parties to the dispute.

In the light of this provision, the German Federal Court of Justice referred the following three questions to the ECJ for a preliminary ruling[27]:

---

[24] German Federal Court of Justice, Reference for a Preliminary Ruling in Case I ZB 2/15, 3 March 2016, (ECLI:DE:BGH:2016:030316BIZB2.15.0) (hereafter 'German Federal Court of Justice, Case I ZB 2/15 (2016)'), paras 24 et seq.

[25] German Federal Court of Justice, Case I ZB 2/15 (2016), para 24.

[26] For some of the first analyses of the decision after it had been rendered, see, for example, Hess (2018), Hindelang (2018). For a detailed analysis of the reasoning of the ECJ, see also Hindelang (2019).

[27] ECJ, *Achmea*, para 23.

(1) Does Article 344 of the TFEU preclude the application of a provision in [...] [an] intra-EU BIT under which an investor of a Contracting State, in the event of a dispute concerning investments in the other Contracting States, may bring proceedings against the latter State before one of the Contracting States acceded to the EU but the arbitral proceedings are not to be brought until after that date?

If Question 1 is to be answered in the negative:

(2) Does Article 267 of the TFEU preclude the application of such provision?

If Questions 1 and 2 are to be answered in the negative:

(3) Does the first paragraph of Article 18 TFEU preclude the application of such provision under the circumstances described in Question 1?

In its ruling, the ECJ did not strictly adhere to the standards-based reference of the German Federal Court of Justice. Instead, it first jointly addressed Questions 1 and 2.[28]

A key principle the ECJ relied on is the autonomy of EU law.[29] As a starting point, the ECJ summarised fundamental principles of EU law, as they were relevant to assessing the compatibility of Article 8 of the Netherlands-Slovakia BIT with EU law. First and foremost, the ECJ had emphasised on previous occasions that the 'autonomy of the EU legal system, observance of which is ensured by the Court' is one of the cornerstones of the EU.[30] According to the deciding judges, this is justified by the 'essential characteristics of the EU and its law' as the latter 'stems from an independent source of law, the Treaties', and enjoys primacy over the law of the Member States.[31] Article 344 of the TFEU serves as a safeguard to the said autonomy.[32] The characteristics of EU law led to a 'structured network of principles, rules and mutually interdependent legal relations binding the EU and its Member States reciprocally and binding its Member States to each other'.[33] Such a system builds on common values among the Member States as set out in Article 2 of the Treaty on the European Union (TEU). The system implies mutual trust that those values and the legal order safeguarding those values will be respected. The ECJ then highlighted some of the means that oblige Member States to protect the autonomy of the EU legal system. In this regard, the ECJ referred to the judicial system established by the TEU and the TFEU. This system is meant to ensure consistency and uniformity

[28]ECJ, *Achmea*, paras 31–60.

[29]Amongst others, this finding was shared by Alvarez (2018, p. 151), Bodenheimer and Eller (2018, p. 787), and Glinski (2018, p. 49). Cf. Editorial Board of the Common Law Market Review (2018, p. 1329). For a analysis of the legal concept of the autonomy of EU law and the pitfalls of an extensive interpretation of the concept, see O'Sullivan (2018, p. 1 et seq.). She noted that the interpretation of the autonomous legal order as exercised by the court constitutes an 'expansionism that places the future relevance and viability of the CJEU's jurisprudence at risk' (p. 19).

[30]ECJ, *Achmea*, para 32.

[31]ECJ, *Achmea*, para 33.

[32]Cf. ECJ, *Achmea*, para 32.

[33]ECJ, *Achmea*, para 33.

in the interpretation of the EU law. The judicial system obliges 'national courts and tribunals and the Court of Justice to ensure the full application of EU law in all Member States'.[34] In the context of the judicial system, the preliminary ruling procedure according to Article 267 of the TFEU is a cornerstone in guaranteeing the uniform interpretation and application of the EU law, its full effect and, finally, its autonomy.[35]

Having established these core principles of the EU law, the ECJ then turned to a three-stage examination of the compatibility of the Netherlands-Slovakia BIT with the said principles. As a first step, the ECJ affirmed that arbitral tribunals within the meaning of Article 8 of the Netherlands-Slovakia BIT 'may be called on to interpret or indeed to apply EU law'.[36] The fact that the arbitral tribunals were to rule on violations of the BIT only, was deemed to be irrelevant by the ECJ.[37] Since the scope of Article 8(6) of the Netherlands-Slovakia BIT covers the EU law, which particularly qualifies as part of the law in force in every EU Member State,[38] the decisions of an arbitral tribunal may potentially relate to EU law as well.[39]

In its second step, the Court rejected the stance that arbitral tribunals qualify as courts or tribunals of EU Member States within the meaning of Article 267 of the TFEU.[40] Instead, the 'exceptional nature of [a] tribunal's jurisdiction' is the very reason for their existence.[41] In this regard, the ECJ particularly compared the nature of arbitral tribunals to the role of 'court[s] common to a number of Member States'.[42] In earlier decisions, the ECJ addressed the role of the courts common to a number of Member States.[43] Such courts, for example the Benelux Court of Justice, are closely related to the judicial system of EU Member States: their proceedings form an element of the *domestic* court proceedings.[44] This does, however, not apply to arbitral tribunals. The role of arbitral tribunals is thus different.

As a third and final step, the ECJ concluded that arbitral awards are not subject to sufficient review by courts of EU Member States. It is true that the German Higher Regional Court of Frankfurt and the German Federal Court of Justice scrutinised the final award in the case at hand. However, this was deemed to be merely coincidental

---

[34]ECJ, *Achmea*, para 36.

[35]ECJ, *Achmea*, para 37.

[36]ECJ, *Achmea*, para 42.

[37]ECJ, *Achmea*, para 40.

[38]ECJ, *Achmea*, para 41.

[39]For criticism of this finding, see Wuschka (2018, p. 31), who observed that the ECJ did not further investigate the particular role EU law could play.

[40]ECJ, *Achmea*, paras 43 et seq. Notably, Advocate General Wathelet considered arbitral tribunals to qualify as a court or tribunal of one of the Member States as per Art 267 of the TFEU. See Advocate General Wathelet, Opinion on Case C-284/16 (*Achmea*), 19 September 2017 (ECLI:EU:C:2017:699) (hereafter 'Wathelet (2017)'), para 131.

[41]ECJ, *Achmea*, para 45.

[42]ECJ, *Achmea*, para 49.

[43]See e.g. for the Benelux Court of Justice: ECJ, Judgment of the Court in Case C-337/95 (*Parfums Christian Dior*), 4 November 1997 (ECLI:EU:C:1997:517), para 21.

[44]ECJ, *Achmea*, paras 47 et seq.

by the ECJ. Article 8(5) of the Netherlands-Slovakia BIT allows arbitral tribunals to determine their own procedure, including the choice of the seat of arbitration. The present tribunal chose Frankfurt am Main, Germany, as the seat of arbitration. It was for this reason that German law was applied as *lex arbitri* and was allowed for review by domestic courts.[45] An arbitral tribunal could nonetheless choose a seat outside of the EU, barring a uniform interpretation of the EU law by the ECJ.[46] In view of this, the ECJ held that there is no review mechanism that sufficiently safeguards the primacy of EU law.[47]

As a consequence of the abovementioned, the ECJ found the following:

> [The] Articles 267, 344 TFEU must be interpreted as precluding a provision in an international agreement concluded between Member States, such as Article 8 of the BIT, under which an investor from one of those Member States may, in the event of a dispute concerning investments in the other Member State, bring proceedings against the latter Member State before an arbitral tribunal whose jurisdiction that Member State has undertaken to accept.[48]

In light of this finding, the ECJ did not address the third question.[49]

The present decision has made some other findings that are noteworthy. Firstly, the ECJ profoundly relied on and reaffirmed its prominent Opinion 2/13 on the Accession of the EU to the European Convention for the Protection of Human Rights and Fundamental Freedoms.[50] This decision, *inter alia*, emphasised the paramount importance of the autonomy of the EU law and is thus key in understanding the *Achmea* decision of the ECJ. Secondly, the ECJ neither followed nor mentioned the arguments Advocate General Melchior Wathelet put forward in favour of the compatibility of such an intra-EU BIT with the EU law.[51] Thirdly, despite its potential impact, the judgment is remarkably brief and only encompasses 62 paragraphs.[52]

4 The Aftermath of *Achmea* or: What Is Now Left of (Investment) Arbitration?

As an aftermath, the *Achmea* judgment has stuck heated debate as to its impact on arbitration. However, the exact scope of such impact is yet to be seen. The following

---

[45] ECJ, *Achmea*, paras 52 et seq.

[46] Cf. ECJ, *Achmea*, paras 51 et seq.

[47] ECJ, *Achmea*, paras 50 et seq. For an opposing view, see German Federal Court of Justice, Case I ZB 2/15 (2016), paras 61 et seq.

[48] ECJ, *Achmea*, para 60.

[49] ECJ, *Achmea*, para 61.

[50] ECJ, Opinion 2/13 of the Court, 18 December 2014 (ECLI:EU:C:2014:2454).

[51] For a brief discussion of the arguments of AG Wathelet, see Wuschka (2018, p. 29 et seq.).

[52] See Glinski (2018, p. 49), who noted that the considerations of AG Wathelet were more extensive. Equally, see Wuschka (2018, p. 30), who noted that the 'entire reasoning only spans over 31 paragraphs'.

sections will analyse some of the early reactions to the decision as well as its potential consequences.

4.1 *Immediate Consequences for the Achmea Case Itself*

Firstly, the judgment of the ECJ has immediate consequences for the proceedings between *Achmea* and the Slovak Republic. Under EU law, judgments following a preliminary reference are binding to all courts that are involved in the particular case.[53] As the Slovak Republic appealed to the German Federal Court of Justice, it was for this court to effectuate the judgment of the ECJ.

By its decision on 31 October 2018, the German Federal Court of Justice[54] set the award aside according to Section 1059(2) No. 1 lit. (a) of the German Code of Civil Procedure (German *Zivilprozessordnung*).[55] The German Federal Court of

---

[53]ECJ, Judgment of the Court in Case 52-76 (*Benedetti*), 3 February 1977 (ECLI:EU:C:1977:16), para 26. See also Wuschka (2018, p. 39).

[54]German Federal Court of Justice, Decision in Case I ZB 2/15, 31 October 2018 (ECLI:DE:BGH:2018:311018BIZB2.15.0) (hereafter 'German Federal Court of Justice, Case I ZB 2/15 (2018)').

[55]Section 1059 of the German Code of Civil Procedure (Petition for reversal of an arbitration award):

(1) Only a petition for reversal of the arbitration award by a court pursuant to subsections (2) and (3) may be filed against an arbitration award.
(2) An arbitration award may be reversed only if:

1. The petitioner asserts, and provides reasons for his assertion, that:
   (a) One of the parties concluding an arbitration agreement pursuant to sections 1029 and 1031 did not have the capacity to do so pursuant to the laws that are relevant to such party personally, or that the arbitration agreement is invalid under the laws to which the parties to the dispute have subjected it, or, if the parties to the dispute have not made any determinations in this regard, that it is invalid under German law; or that
   (b) He has not been properly notified of the appointment of an arbitral judge, or of the arbitration proceedings, or that he was unable to assert the means of challenge or defence available to him for other reasons; or that
   (c) The arbitration award concerns a dispute not mentioned in the agreement as to arbitration, or not subject to the provisions of the arbitration clause, or that it contains decisions that are above and beyond the limits of the arbitration agreement; however, where that part of the arbitration award referring to points at issue that were subject to the arbitration proceedings can be separated from the part concerning points at issue that were not subject to the arbitration proceedings, only the latter part of the arbitration award may be reversed; or where the petitioner asserts, and provides reasons for his assertion, that
   (d) The formation of the arbitral tribunal or the arbitration proceedings did not correspond to a provision of this Book or to an admissible agreement between the parties, and that it is to be assumed that this has had an effect on the arbitration award; or if
2. The court determines that
   (a) the subject matter of the dispute is not eligible for arbitration under German law; or
   (b) The recognition or enforcement of the arbitration award will lead to a result contrary to public order.

Justice held that Article 8(2) of the Netherlands-Slovakia BIT is the only article that manifests the intent of the Contracting States to conclude an arbitration agreement.[56] Following the finding of an infringement of EU law, this provision was ruled to be inapplicable.[57] Absent any other proof that the Slovak Republic had intended to resort to arbitration, an arbitration agreement between *Achmea* and the Slovak Republic had not been concluded.[58] According to the German Federal Court of Justice, the absence of an arbitration agreement is equivalent to an arbitration agreement that is void.[59] This allows the award to be set aside pursuant to Section 1059(2) No. 1 lit. (a) of the German Code of Civil Procedure.

The court further rejected *Achmea*'s manifold objections to setting the award aside. In particular, it is immaterial that the arbitral tribunal did not apply EU law in the specific proceedings.[60] It is equally immaterial whether the Netherlands-Slovakia BIT remains valid under Public International Law. At least between EU Member States, the primacy of EU law mandates the inapplicability of the Netherlands-Slovakia BIT.[61] The Slovak Republic is also not barred from relying on the absence of an arbitration agreement by considerations of good faith. This is because the Slovak Republic did not give rise to any legitimate expectation to arbitrate after its accession to the EU[62] and it equally did not act contradictory in this regard.[63] The German Federal Court of Justice did not consider itself obliged to refer the proceedings to the German Federal Constitutional Court (*Bundesverfassungsgericht*).[64] As a last point, the German Federal Court of Justice held that *Achmea* enjoys sufficient legal protection as it may litigate its claims in the domestic courts of an EU Member State, the Slovak Republic.[65]

---

(3) Unless the parties to the dispute agree otherwise, the petition for reversal must be filed with the court within a period of three (3) months. The period begins on the day on which the petitioner has received the arbitration award. In cases in which a petition has been filed pursuant to section 1058, the period shall be extended by at most one (1) month following receipt of the decision regarding this petition. The petition for reversal of the arbitration award may no longer be filed once a German court has declared the arbitration award to be enforceable.

(4) If the reversal has been petitioned, the court may remand the matter to the arbitral tribunal where appropriate, as petitioned by a party, while reversing the arbitration award.

(5) In cases of doubt, the reversal of the arbitration award will result in the arbitration agreement once again entering into force concerning the subject matter of the dispute.

[56] German Federal Court of Justice, Case I ZB 2/15 (2018), para 28.

[57] German Federal Court of Justice, Case I ZB 2/15 (2018), para 25.

[58] German Federal Court of Justice, Case I ZB 2/15 (2018), paras 25–28.

[59] German Federal Court of Justice, Case I ZB 2/15 (2018), para 15.

[60] German Federal Court of Justice, Case I ZB 2/15 (2018), para 32.

[61] German Federal Court of Justice, Case I ZB 2/15 (2018), paras 40 et seq.

[62] German Federal Court of Justice, Case I ZB 2/15 (2018), paras 44–53.

[63] German Federal Court of Justice, Case I ZB 2/15 (2018), paras 54–58.

[64] German Federal Court of Justice, Case I ZB 2/15 (2018), paras 60–71.

[65] German Federal Court of Justice, Case I ZB 2/15 (2018), para 72.

After having its arbitral award set aside, *Achmea* was left in a difficult position. In the course of the year-long proceedings, the company incurred considerable costs.[66] Following the setting aside of the arbitral award, it was left with few options. As proposed by the German Federal Court of Justice,[67] it could file a claim against the Slovak Republic in a domestic state court.[68] Such a claim could lead to questions of state liability that, in turn, might again lead to a reference to the ECJ. Yet even after the annulment of the arbitral award, there is another, albeit improbable, path for *Achmea*: the highly controversial enforcement of the award notwithstanding its annulment at the seat of arbitration in a state outside of the EU.[69]

4.2 The Future of Intra-EU BITs

Intra-EU BITs have been subject to increasing criticism for some time.[70] At first, the criticism was distinctly political and voiced by the European Commission.[71] In view of the recent decision of the ECJ, the criticism expands to a judiciary level that will arguably put an end to the existence of intra-EU BITs.

On 18 June 2015, the European Commission published a press release, asking the EU Member States to terminate their intra-EU BITs.[72] The European Commission confirmed that it had formally requested five EU Member States to terminate intra-EU BITs they concluded among each other. The European Commission issued these requests as the first stage of infringement procedures under the EU law.[73] It emphasised that the intra-EU BITs are regarded as incompatible with the EU law. In this context, the European Commission also announced the initiation of an administrative dialogue with all 21 EU Member States that were party to intra-EU BITs.

---

[66]Achmea B.V. does not only have to bear its own costs but, for example, also the costs of the annulment proceedings, see the operative part of German Federal Court of Justice, Case I ZB 2/15 (2018).

[67]German Federal Court of Justice, Case I ZB 2/15 (2018), para 72.

[68]See De Sadeleer (2018, p. 370), who assumed that 'nothing prevents them [the investors] from invoking their rights before the national courts'. But see also Lavranos and Singla (2018, p. 353), who noted that 'there is no alternative system in place within the EU that can grant effectively the same investment protection and, therefore, because of *Achmea*, all European investors lost a significant benefit without gaining anything in particular'. Finally, see Ohler (2018, p. 517), who observed considerable gaps in the legal protection of investments, particularly in third countries outside the EU.

[69]See Bischoff (2018, p. 591), who suggested that in view of this option, the *Achmea* saga might continue. For a more general discussion on the enforcement of an arbitral award after it had been set aside in their place of origin, see Koch (2009, p. 267 et seq.).

[70]See Glinski (2018, p. 48), who observed that the treaties have 'come under fire in recent years'.

[71]See, for instance, European Commission (2015).

[72]European Commission (2015).

[73]See Art 258 of the TFEU.

The ECJ's decision could now potentially deprive intra-EU BITs from having any significance in the future.[74] It is true that the ECJ decided on one particular intra-EU BIT and found its dispute settlement mechanism to be incompatible with the EU law. Moreover, the ECJ's decision itself does not affect the *general* validity of any intra-EU BIT.[75] The decision equally does not render all clauses providing for dispute settlement by arbitration in other intra-EU BITs immediately void.[76]

These limited effects of the judgment have led to a vivid debate as to the impact of the ECJ's decision on ISDS. On the one hand, numerous scholars forthrightly announced that the judgment would nonetheless have an immediate effect on *all* intra-EU BITs that include arbitration clauses.[77] Or, to put it in more drastic words: 'After *Achmea*, there is no future for BITs concluded between EU Member States'.[78] There are indeed strong indicators that the judgment does not differentiate between the numerous intra-EU BITs. Firstly, the wording of the judgment is distinctly broad and general. The ECJ held that Articles 267 and 344 of the TFEU preclude

> *a* provision in an international agreement concluded between Member States, *such as* Article 8 of the BIT, under which an investor from one of those Member States may [...] bring proceedings against [...] [a] Member State before an arbitral tribunal whose jurisdiction that Member State has undertaken to accept.[79]

Secondly, in view of the rationale of the judgment, it is apparent that the ECJ intended to safeguard the autonomy of the EU law by ruling out arbitration under intra-EU BITs to the largest extent possible.[80] On the other hand, some scholars contemplate possibilities to safeguard intra-EU BITs at least from full termination. In particular, some propose an explicit, strict choice of law provision in intra-EU BITs excluding any application or consideration of the EU law as a potential solution.[81]

Yet *Achmea* not only alarmed the scholars, it also sparked off a debate as to whether Article 351 of the TFEU requires Member States to terminate or at least renegotiate their intra-EU BITs.[82] In the course of this debate, politicians have also responded to the judgment. This is prominently illustrated by the response of the

[74] This presumption inspired scholars to distinctively despondent captions, announcing the decision, for example, to be the 'deathblow' to autonomous ISDS. This term was used by Thym (2018).

[75] See Wuschka (2018, p. 41), who noted that 'intra-EU BITs, for now and until their termination, remain valid as a matter of public international law'. See further Lavranos and Singla (2018, p. 350).

[76] See Lavranos and Singla (2018, p. 350), and further Stöbener de Mora (2018, p. 366). But see also Lang (2018, p. 16 et seq.). Lang emphasised that the binding effect of a ruling in a preliminary reference is not limited to the original case, but extends to comparable cases.

[77] See Glinski (2018, p. 63).

[78] Hess (2018, p. 9).

[79] ECJ, *Achmea*, para 60 (emphasis added).

[80] See Lang (2018, p. 17), Pinna (2018, p. 87).

[81] See e.g. Ohler (2018, p. 515), for a comparable approach. However, see also Hess (2018, p. 10), who stated that such a 'formalistic approach does not correspond to the concerns the ECJ expressed in *Achmea*'. Cf. Bodenheimer and Eller (2018, p. 791).

[82] See Lavranos and Singla (2018, p. 350), who noted that most intra-EU BITs were once concluded as extra-EU BITs in the 1980s and 1990s which '[a]rguably [...] supports the view that Art. 351 TFEU is—at least analogously—applicable to intra-EU BITs'.

Dutch government following the judgment. On 26 April 2018, the Dutch Minister for Foreign Trade and Development Cooperation announced that the judgment left the government with no choice but to terminate the Netherlands-Slovakia BIT.[83] She further announced that the Dutch government intends to terminate 11 other intra-EU BITs that are still in force.[84] According to Article 54 of the Vienna Convention on the Law of Treaties (VCLT), the termination of a treaty requires the consent of all the signatories after consultation with the other Contracting States.[85] For the sake of 'clarity, speed and efficiency', the Dutch government intends to terminate the intra-EU BITs by concluding one single multilateral treaty.[86] Later, on 15 January 2019, the representatives of 22 Member States signed a declaration, concluding that all arbitration clauses contained in intra-EU BITs are incompatible with the EU law and thus inapplicable.[87] The representatives announced the termination of all intra-EU BITs, either by a multilateral treaty or by means of bilateral treaties. Indeed, on 24 October 2019, the European Commission announced that the EU Member States agreed on a plurilateral treaty for the termination of intra-EU BITs. [88] However, despite political efforts to effectuate the judgment, crucial questions remain unsettled.

Firstly, the extent of incompatibility between intra-EU BITs and the EU law is uncertain. It seems possible that *only* the arbitration clauses of such treaties infringe the EU law.[89] If courts or tribunals in the meaning of Article 267 of the TFEU settle investor claims based on an intra-EU BIT, the primacy of EU law seems far less to be at stake.[90] At the same time, intra-EU BITs regularly grant investors a substantive level of protection that exceeds the standard of protection under EU law.[91] This poses the risk of substantive incompatibility with Article 18 of the TFEU.[92] Unfortunately,

---

[83]See Kaag (2018).

[84]See also Kaag (2018). For a comment on the Dutch announcement, see Davoise and Burgstaller (2018). But despite this announcement, see Lavranos and Singla (2018, p. 350), who observed that 'to the best knowledge of the authors, no intra-EU BIT has been terminated post-*Achmea* so far' although, for instance, the Netherlands-Poland BIT could have been terminated by August 2018.

[85]See Hess (2018, p. 10), who also relied on Art 54 of the VCLT.

[86]See Davoise and Burgstaller (2018).

[87]Declaration of the Representatives of the Governments of the Member States (2019, p. 1). For a discussion of this declaration, see Power (2019).

[88]European Commission (2019). See also the Declaration of the Representatives of the Governments of the Member States (2019, p. 4). According to the latter declaration, the Member States promised to 'make best efforts to deposit their instruments of ratification, approval or acceptance of that plurilateral treaty or of any bilateral treaty terminating bilateral investment treaties between Member States no later than 6 December 2019'.

[89]This was e.g. proposed by Lang (2018, p. 15), with regard to the immediate consequences of the ECJ judgment.

[90]See Glinski (2018, p. 64), who assumed that 'substantive tensions with EU law are far less likely to materialise if the disputes were decided by regular courts'.

[91]Glinski (2018, p. 64) and Wathelet (2017, paras 179 et seq.).

[92]See Glinski (2018, p. 64). To the contrary, see also Stöbener de Mora (2018, p. 366), who assumed that the risk of an infringement appears far-fetched, given that an interpretation in conformity with European law seems feasible.

the ECJ did not address whether arbitration clauses infringe this provision.[93] In absence of any guidance by the ECJ whether or not another provision of the intra-EU BIT infringes Article 18 of the TFEU, one observation appears to be particularly relevant. The majority of the currently existing intra-EU BITs were concluded at a time when only *one* of its parties was a Member State to the EU.[94] The treaties were meant to set incentives for investing in third countries by 'offering reciprocal guarantees against political risks which might negatively affect those investments'.[95] As a consequence, the enlargement of the EU renders it doubtful if such guarantees remain in fact compatible with EU law and particularly with Article 18 of the TFEU.[96]

Secondly, the consequences of terminating intra-EU BITs remain to be ascertained.[97] So-called 'sunset clauses' are meant to protect an investor's legitimate expectation that a BIT would continue to remain in force. For instance, Article 13(3) of the Netherlands-Slovakia BIT reads as follows:

> In respect of investments made before the date of the termination of the present Agreement the foregoing Articles thereof shall continue to be effective for a further period of fifteen years from that date.

Whether Contracting States are able to validly terminate a treaty inclusive of the sunset clause by mutual consent is disputed.[98] In view of this, Member States might still be subject to investor claims even if they terminate intra-EU BITs by consent according to Article 54 of the VCLT.

4.3 *Perspectives for Pending and Future Arbitration Proceedings Under Intra-EU BITs*

Whilst the fate of intra-EU BITs as treaties is one question, the fate of pending and future arbitration proceedings that arose from intra-EU BITs is another.[99] This relates to the question of to what extent arbitral tribunals will follow the *Achmea*

[93] ECJ, *Achmea*, para 61.

[94] European Commission (2015).

[95] European Commission (2015).

[96] However, see also Wathelet (2017, paras 49 et seq.), who suggested that Art 18 of the TFEU is not infringed.

[97] This issue was briefly addressed by Glinski (2018, p. 63).

[98] Regarding this controversy, see Zarowna (2017). Zarowna observed that it 'appears that this issue has not yet been tested by international arbitral practice'. For a less cautious assessment, see Stöbener de Mora (2018, p. 366), who suggested that for the sake of the protection of legitimate expectations, even mutual consent does not render sunset clauses inapplicable. By contrast, the sunset clauses were deemed equally inapplicable and without any effect by the representatives of 22 Member States, see the Declaration of the Representatives of the Governments of the Member States (2019, p. 1).

[99] It was reported, albeit without further reference, that there were 37 pending arbitrations under intra-EU BITs in 2018, cf. De Sadeleer (2018, p. 367).

decision of the ECJ. The view of the European Commission regarding this question is definite. It stated that 'any arbitration tribunal established on the basis of such clauses [from an intra-EU BIT] lacks jurisdiction due to the absence of a valid arbitration agreement'.[100]

It is however questionable if the current *status quo* is that obvious. As shown above, the binding effect of the judgment of the ECJ is limited.[101] Arbitral tribunals thus face a difficult decision: They would have to either terminate the pending proceedings by denying their jurisdiction or affirm their jurisdiction and decide on the merits of the case. If they decide to do the latter, it is advisable for the arbitral tribunals to thoroughly manifest their jurisdiction, as they are responsible for ensuring that arbitral awards are enforceable.[102]

Shortly after the judgment was handed down, Hess suggested that tribunals should refer to Article 30(3) of the VCLT in addressing this question.[103] In simple terms, Article 30(3) of the VCLT governs the relation between two treaties. According to this provision, if the parties to an earlier treaty are also parties to a later treaty, the earlier treaty applies only to the extent that its provisions are compatible with the later treaty. Hess understands the ECJ's decision to the effect that Article 344 of the TFEU constitutes a provision that applies to intra-EU investment arbitration and prevails over dispute resolution clauses in a BIT.[104] It remains to be seen if arbitral tribunals will follow Hess' suggestions in practice and terminate proceedings on this basis. Others suggested that it might be possible for arbitrators to successfully affirm their jurisdiction if the seat and the assets subject to enforcement are located in a non-EU jurisdiction and the domestic courts in the respective jurisdiction are willing to depart from the ECJ's ruling.[105]

So far, the de facto responses of companies and arbitral tribunals are inconclusive. Whilst there are reports about companies withdrawing treaty-based claims against EU Member States,[106] at the same time, there are also arbitral awards affirming an arbitral tribunal's jurisdiction under the ECT.[107]

---

[100] European Commission (2018).

[101] See also Hartkamp (2018, p. 733 et seq.), Lee (2018, p. 147).

[102] For a detailed discussion of the duty of a tribunal to render an enforceable award, see Horvath (2001, p. 135 et seq.).

[103] Hess (2018, p. 13 et seq.).

[104] For a detailed discussion of this approach and a further analysis of Art 59 of the VCLT, see Hess (2018, pp. 12–14).

[105] Dimopoulos (2018).

[106] See e.g. Yong (2018).

[107] See *Vattenfall AB* et al. *v Federal Republic of Germany*, ICSID Case No. ARB/12/12, Decision on the *Achmea* Issue, 31 August 2018, https://www.italaw.com/sites/default/files/case-documents/italaw9916.pdf (hereafter '*Vattenfall AB*'); and *Masdar Solar & Wind Cooperatief U.A. v Kingdom of Spain*, ICSID Case No. ARB/14/1, Award. 16 May 2018, https://www.italaw.com/sites/default/files/case-documents/italaw9710.pdf (hereafter '*Masdar Solar*'). Both cases will be discussed in more detail in the ECT section of this Chapter.

4.4 Enforcement of Intra-EU BIT Arbitral Awards

As demonstrated above, arbitrators will be facing difficult decisions in light of the *Achmea* judgment. Furthermore, the judgment will also affect already concluded arbitration proceedings because the findings of the ECJ have an impact on the enforcement of intra-EU BIT awards. When examining the enforceability of arbitral awards rendered in proceedings under an intra-EU BIT, there are two particularly relevant aspects. Firstly, the country in which a party seeks enforcement is relevant. Secondly, the rules which governed the preceding arbitration are relevant. Particularly if the arbitration was conducted under the Convention on the Settlement of Investment Disputes Between States and Nationals of Other States (ICSID Convention), this facilitates the enforcement.

Regarding the first aspect, it would be appropriate to differentiate between enforcement proceedings inside and outside of the EU. If a party seeks enforcement of an arbitral award outside of the EU, the enforcing court may not consider, not to mention follow, the *Achmea* decision. The New York Convention on the Recognition and Enforcement of Foreign Arbitral Awards (New York Convention), does not allow for refusing enforcement of an award on this basis. Article V(2)(b) of the New York Convention provides for a public policy exemption. However, this exemption is interpreted narrowly.[108] An infringement of EU law does not, in general, violate national public policy of states outside of the EU.[109] For this reason, investors will presumably favour the enforcement of awards based on intra-EU BITs in jurisdictions outside of the EU.[110]

By contrast, if a party seeks enforcement of an arbitral award inside the EU, domestic courts will face a dilemma. Article 267(3) of the TFEU compels the courts of final instance to request further preliminary references if intra-EU BITs other than the Netherlands-Slovakia BIT are in question.[111] In light of the varying particulars of each intra-EU BIT, the *acte claire* doctrine is considered not to apply to the question of compatibility with EU law.[112] At the same time, the New York Convention obliges its Contracting States to recognise and enforce arbitral awards. Yet, in this scenario, Article V(2)(b) of the New York Convention could allow domestic courts of EU Member States to refuse recognition and enforcement of arbitral awards. Whilst the exact definition of the term 'public policy' remains disputed, the principle of autonomy of the EU and its legal order could constitute a matter of public policy.[113]

---

[108] Solomon (2016, p. 143).

[109] De Sadeleer (2018, p. 368). Cf. Lavranos and Singla (2018, p. 354), for tribunals seated outside of the European Union. Cf. Lang (2018, p. 22).

[110] See Lavranos and Singla (2018, p. 354), Lee (2018, p. 149). Finally, see also Stöbener de Mora (2018, p. 366), who suggested that not only enforcement, but generally choosing arbitration in non-Member States might become more appealing.

[111] Cf. Wuschka (2018, p. 40), who assumed that it is 'likely that more references to the CJEU will follow'.

[112] Wuschka (2018, p. 40).

[113] Singla (2018).

In its decision in *Vincenzo Manfredi v Llyod Adriatico Assicurazioni SpA*, the ECJ regarded questions of EU Competition Law as 'a matter of public policy which must be automatically applied by national courts'.[114] This at least indicates that key elements such as the autonomy of the EU and its legal order could also be regarded as a matter of public policy by EU Member States.[115] At the very least, the *Achmea* decision renders enforcement of such arbitral awards in the EU less predictable, if not potentially unattainable.[116]

The above considerations apply to arbitrations conducted under rules other than the ICSID Convention. However, they do not hold true to ICSID proceedings.[117] The ICSID Convention does not provide for review of arbitral awards by domestic courts.[118] Article 53(1) of the ICSID Convention precludes any appeal other than that provided for in the Convention. Article 54(1) of the ICSID Convention obliges the Contracting States to recognise ICSID awards as binding. From the outset, this leaves domestic courts with no choice but to enforce the arbitral award.[119] Yet, tribunals in pending ICSID proceedings are well-advised to address the implications of the *Achmea* decision in future hearings. An insufficient examination of the implications increases the risk that the losing party commences annulment proceedings under Article 52 of the ICSID Convention.[120]

Despite this benefit of ICSID proceedings, 'in reality, the European Commission presents a formidable obstacle even to enforcement of ICSID awards'.[121] Notably, the England and Wales Court of Appeal affirmed a stay of the ICSID enforcement proceedings in *Viorel Micula* et al. *v Romania*.[122] This stay of proceedings was seen as a 'delicate balancing act […] between the UK's obligations under the ICSID Convention and its duties under EU law'.[123] The stay of the enforcement proceedings was

---

[114]ECJ, Judgment of the Court in Joined Cases C-295/04 to C-298/04, 13 July 2006 (ECLI:EU:C:2006:461), para 31.

[115]See Singla (2018), who advocated this conclusion.

[116]See Lavranos and Singla (2018, p. 353), who assumed that tribunals 'proceeding with a finding of jurisdiction under an intra-EU BIT, and possibly under the ECT, would render [the tribunals' awards] potentially unenforceable within the entire EU'.

[117]For authors who assumed that *Achmea* will not have an impact on ICSID awards, see e.g. Bischoff (2018, p. 591), Lee (2018, p. 146). But see also Hess (2018, p. 14), who cautiously stated that the 'situation of ICSID awards which have already been rendered is more complex'.

[118]Reed et al. (2010, p. 180 et seq.). See also Wuschka (2018, p. 40), and finally, Ohler (2018, p. 516), who stressed that the ICSID Convention does not even provide for court review in exceptional circumstances.

[119]This was generally affirmed by De Sadeleer (2018, p. 368), Hess (2018, p. 14) and Wuschka (2018, p. 40). But see Lang (2018, p. 21), for an opposing view. He assumed that EU law, particularly Art 4(3) of the TEU, might oblige Member States to reject enforcement of an ICSID award that infringes EU law.

[120]Cf. Hess (2018, p. 14).

[121]Lavranos and Singla (2018, p. 355).

[122]*Micula* et al. *v Romania*, England and Wales Court of Appeal (Civil Division), [2018] EWCA Civ 1801, 27 July 2018 (hereafter '*Micula*').

[123]Hawes (2018).

affirmed in light of the pending proceedings before the General Court of the EU.[124] The tribunal in *Viorel Micula* et al. *v Romania* awarded the Micula investors damages.[125] The European Commission subsequently declared that enforcement of this award would constitute State aid as per Article 107(1) of the TFEU.[126] The European Commission thus ordered Romania to refrain from paying any damages to the Micual investors and to recover any sum already paid.[127] The Micula investors successfully appealed against this decision before the General Court of the EU.[128] Although the Micula proceedings are not directly related to *Achmea*, these proceedings might allow some projections on enforcement proceedings pursuant to the *Achmea* decision.

Finally, the *Achmea* decision is considered not to have given reasons for annulment of awards that have not been challenged within the statutory time limits. Whilst the *Achmea* decision provides for considerations of fundamental importance, it does not prevent a challenge from being time-barred.[129]

4.5 The Future of BITs Between EU Member States and Third Countries

The *Achmea* judgment concerned an intra-EU BIT. Whilst the number of existing intra-EU BITs is already significant, the number of BITs between EU Member States and third countries (extra-EU BITs) clearly exceeds the former. The Netherlands alone is a party to 78 extra-EU BITs that were in force in 2018,[130] while France is a party to 84 BITs of this kind.[131] Reportedly, the EU Member States altogether concluded approximately 1200 extra-EU BITs.[132] The sheer numbers emphasise the significance of the question as to the impact of the *Achmea* judgment on extra-EU BITs.

To date, the future of extra-EU BITs is uncertain. Generally, extra-EU BITs are meant to remain in force until BITs or Free Trade Agreements concluded by the EU succeed them.[133] The ECJ did not address this issue expressly. Equally, the European

---

[124] *Micula*, para 104.

[125] *Ioan Micula, Viorel Micula* et al. *v. Romania*, ICSID Case No. ARB/05/20, Award, 11 December 2013, https://www.italaw.com/sites/default/files/case-documents/italaw3036.pdf.

[126] European Commission, Decision (EU) 2015/1470, 30 March 2015, https://eur-lex.europa.eu/eli/dec/2015/1470/oj (hereafter 'European Commission, Decision (EU) 2015/1470'), Art 1.

[127] European Commission, Decision (EU) 2015/1470, Art 2(1).

[128] General Court, Judgment of the General Court in Cases T-624/15, T-694/15 and T-704/15, 18 June 2019 (ECLI:EU:T:2019:423).

[129] See Wuschka (2018, p. 38), who noted that anything else would 'violate considerations of legal certainty and good faith'.

[130] See Investment Policy Hub, http://investmentpolicyhub.unctad.org/IIA/CountryBits/148.

[131] See Investment Policy Hub, http://investmentpolicyhub.unctad.org/IIA/CountryBits/72.

[132] For the number, see Lavranos and Singla (2018, p. 351), and Woolcock (2010, p. 53).

[133] See Regulation (EU) No 1219/2012 and further Lavranos and Singla (2018, p. 351).

Commission solely addressed intra-EU BITs and multilateral treaties, particularly the ECT, when expressing its views on the consequences of *Achmea*.[134] Does this silence indicate that extra-EU BITs are not affected by the *Achmea* decision?

In the *Achmea* decision, the ECJ expressly referred to 'international agreement[s] concluded between *Member States*' only.[135] Some scholars noted that this phrasing would consistently mandate that arbitration clauses in extra-EU BITs are compatible with EU law.[136] Pinna further noted that EU law seems to advocate this finding.[137] According to Article 351(1) of the TFEU, the rights and obligations arising from agreements concluded before 1 January 1958 or, for acceding States, before the date of their accession, between one or more Member States on the one hand, and one or more third countries on the other hand, shall not be affected by the provisions of the Treaties of the EU. In view of the time limitation, reliance on Article 351(1) of the TFEU nonetheless only holds true for extra-EU BITs that were concluded prior to the relevant point in time. Nevertheless, another observation advocates the compatibility of arbitration clauses in extra-EU BITs: the opposite could lead to 'a dissymmetric offer to arbitrate'.[138] If an investor from the EU invests in a third country, the offer to arbitrate on behalf of the third country would be valid. Contrary to where an investor from a third country invests in an EU Member State, the offer to arbitrate on behalf of the EU Member State would infringe EU law.[139] Eventually, there is one policy aspect that might deter the European Commission from condemning extra-EU BITs as intensely as it condemns intra-EU BITs. Extra-EU BITs provide investors from the EU with a level of legal protection that often exceeds the legal protection ensured by domestic courts.[140]

However, doubts remain as to the future of extra EU-BITs.[141] It is true that EU law is less relevant in this context. Many extra-EU BITs do not refer to EU law as

---

[134]See European Commission (2018). It should, however, be noted that this communication was limited in its scope. It *a priori* only 'focuses on intra-EU investment and thus does not concern investments made by EU investors in third countries or investments made by third country investors in EU'. It is open to interpretation whether this limited scope indicates the understanding that the *Achmea* decision is equally limited in its effect.

[135]ECJ, *Achmea*, para 31 (emphasis added).

[136]Pinna (2018, p. 92). See also Stöbener de Mora (2018, p. 368), who considered any infringement unlikely since the application of EU law is not an issue in this constellation. Finally, Lang (2018, p. 47), considered such BITs to be unaffected primarily because the principle of mutual trust is inapplicable.

[137]Pinna (2018, p. 93), with reference to Art 351(1) of the TFEU.

[138]Pinna (2018, p. 93).

[139]See Pinna (2018, p. 93). But see also De Sadeleer (2018, p. 367), who observed this 'imbalance' but seemingly reconciled with it. After all, some asymmetries seem inevitable as Lavranos and Singla (2018, p. 351), asserted. The latter scholars noted that regarding claims against EU Member States, non-EU investors receive preferential treatment over EU investors if the extra-EU BITs remain in force.

[140]Cf. Rose-Ackerman and Tobin (2005, p. 6).

[141]See e.g. Ohler (2018, p. 515 et seq.). Ohler assumed that at least if the respondent of an arbitration is a Member State, and the law of the Member State applies to the dispute, extra-EU BITs infringe EU law.

the applicable law.[142] At the same time, it cannot be ruled out that arbitral tribunals under extra EU-BITs may interpret EU law if a question of EU law is relevant to deciding the case.[143] Thus, even if one were to assume that extra-EU BITs and the arbitration clauses therein will generally remain applicable,[144] EU law remains a relevant factor for subsequent arbitration proceedings. Eventually, the ECJ may also rule on the compatibility of extra-EU BITs with EU law. If a non-EU investor seeks recognition and enforcement by a court of an EU Member State of an award rendered under an extra-EU BIT, this court could request a preliminary reference to the ECJ pursuant to Article 267(3) of the TFEU.[145]

4.6 The Future of Investment Treaties Between the EU and Third Countries

Eventually, the impact of the *Achmea* decision on treaties between the EU and third countries is to be discussed. There are two types of such treaties. Firstly, there are bilateral treaties primarily negotiated between the EU and third countries. The most prominent example is probably the already mentioned CETA concluded between the EU and Canada. Secondly, there are other 'mixed agreements'.[146] Mixed agreements are multilateral treaties between the EU, its Member States and third countries. The most prominent example for the latter is the ECT. Both treaties will be analysed in the following.

4.6.1 Bilateral Treaties Between the EU and Third Countries

Firstly, regarding CETA as an one of the most important treaties between the EU and a third country, the ECJ also addressed the question as to its compatibility with EU law. In September 2017, Belgium requested an opinion of the ECJ on the compatibility

[142] Lavranos and Singla (2018, p. 351).

[143] Lavranos and Singla (2018, p. 351).

[144] There are, however, also scholars who assumed that extra-EU BITs equally infringe EU law. See, for example, De Sadeleer (2018, p. 367). De Sadeleer plainly assumed that 'dispute resolution mechanisms provided for under BITs concluded between Member States and third countries will also prove to violate Article 267 and 344 TFEU where the arbitral jurisdiction is liable to concern either the application or the interpretation of EU law'.

[145] Lavranos and Singla (2018, p. 352).

[146] Regarding that term, see e.g. Hess (2018, p. 15).

of CETA's Investment Court System (ICS) with EU law.[147] In its much anticipated *Opinion 1/17*, the ECJ ultimately found the ICS to be compatible with EU law.[148]

As one of its arguments, the ECJ emphasized that the treaty that establishes the ICS is one between the 'Union and a non-Member State'. The principle of mutual trust, which was an important element of the reasoning in the *Achmea* decision, is inapplicable between the EU and a third country. Prior to Opinion 1/17, it was disputed if the *Achmea* decision foreshadowed a conflict between the ICS and the EU law or not.[149] Besides having addressed the issue of international dispute settlement in earlier opinions, the ECJ did so in *Achmea* as well. The ECJ held that an 'international agreement providing for the establishment of a court responsible for the interpretation of its provisions and whose decisions are binding on the institutions, including the Court of Justice, is not in principle incompatible with EU law'.[150] The EU may generally submit to the decisions of such a court.[151] Yet again, the ECJ emphasised the limit of such a conferral of power, namely that the 'autonomy of the EU and its legal order is respected'.[152]

There was a vivid debate in scholarly literature as to whether the ICS under CETA sufficiently respects the autonomy of the EU and its legal order. This debate concerned, most importantly, the relevance of EU law. On the one hand, one could assume that between Canada and the EU, EU law only qualifies as domestic law of the EU.[153] Article 8.31.2. of the CETA establishes that the Tribunal 'may consider, as appropriate, the domestic law of the disputing Party as a matter of fact'. The Tribunal further has to follow the 'prevailing interpretation given to the domestic law by the courts or authorities of that Party'. Finally, 'any meaning given to domestic law by the Tribunal shall not be binding upon courts […] of that Party' according to Article

---

[147] See Department of Foreign Affairs, Foreign Trade and Development Cooperation of the Kingdom of Belgium (2017). Its press release specifies that the request regards the compatibility of the ICS with: (1) the exclusive competence of the ECJ to provide the definitive interpretation of EU law; (2) the general principle of equality and the 'practical effect' requirement of EU law; (3) the right to access to the courts; and (4) the right to an independent and impartial judiciary.

[148] Lavranos and Singla (2018, p. 351). On 29 January 2019, Advocate General Yves Bot rendered his Opinion 1/17 on this matter (Advocate General Bot, Opinion 1/17, 29 January 2019 (ECLI:EU:C:2019:72)). He concluded that the provisions in questions are compatible with TEU, the TFEU and the Charter of Fundamental Rights of the European Union. For short discussions of Opinion 1/17, see Croisant (2019) and Gáspár-Szilágy (2019). Cf. Bodenheimer and Eller (2018, p. 788), who assumed that *Achmea* might constitute a prologue to Opinion 1/17.

[149] Eckes (2018) assumed that the *Achmea* decision foreshadows such a conflict with the EU law. In contrast, see Hindelang (2019, p. 394). He assumed that, albeit it cannot be ruled out that the ECJ will find CETA to infringe the autonomy of EU law, *Achmea* generally 'seems to be only of limited guidance' regarding agreements of the EU with third countries.

[150] ECJ, *Achmea*, para 57.

[151] In this regard, the ECJ expressly distinguished between bilateral agreements between Member States only and agreements concluded by the European Union itself as it emphasised that the Netherlands-Slovakia BIT was 'concluded not by the EU but by Member States', see ECJ, *Achmea*, para 58.

[152] ECJ, *Achmea*, para 57.

[153] See Ohler (2018, p. 516), and Stöbener de Mora (2018, p. 368). Both suggested that this suffices to avoid an infringement of EU law. For a more cautious assessment, see Glinski (2018, p. 66).

8.31.2 of the CETA. On the other hand, notwithstanding this effort to safeguard the primacy of EU law, scholars remained doubtful if it suffices.[154] After all, it is the 'very idea' of an ISDS to grant protection against legislative changes.[155] As this also covers changes in EU law, Article 8.31.2 of the CETA might be insufficient to prevent conflicts with the EU law.[156] Decisions within the ICS are also not subject to any review by courts of the EU.[157] In view of the reasoning of the ECJ regarding Article 267 of the TFEU,[158] it already seemed unlikely that the ECJ regarded the ICS as a court or tribunal of an EU Member State.[159] In addition, there were different opinions regarding the relevance of the principles of mutual trust and sincere cooperation between EU Member States in such a scenario. Whilst some suggested that both principles are less affected in an extra-EU situation,[160] others believed that those principles also oblige EU Member States to individually safeguard the unity of the EU and its objectives with regard to the EU's external relations.[161]

4.6.2 Multilateral Investment Treaties Between the EU, Its Member States and Third Countries

Secondly, the impact on mixed agreements, particularly on the ECT, is also uncertain.[162] Again, the European Commission voiced a clear stance on the question. It assumed the following:

---

[154] See Glinski (2018, p. 66). See also O'Sullivan (2018, p. 15 et seq.), for an earlier assessment of CETA in light of the primacy of the principle of autonomy as established by the ECJ. She noted that '[h]aving compared the concerns of the CJEU in Opinion 2/13 with the solutions proposed in dispute settlement provisions in CETA, the future of the Tribunal appears to rest on a very shaky foundation' (p. 19).

[155] See Glinski (2018, p. 66).

[156] Art 8.9.1. of the CETA equally intends to avoid potential conflicts by affirming the Contracting Parties' 'right to regulate within their territories to achieve legitimate policy objectives'. According to Art 8.9.2. of the CETA, the mere fact that a Party regulates in a manner that negatively affects an investment or the expectations of an investor does not amount to a breach of an obligation under the respective section. But see further Glinski (2018, p. 66), who stated that it remains to be seen whether this sufficiently protects EU law from adverse influences. See also Lavranos and Singla (2018, p. 355), who suggested that the Appellate Tribunal is able to 'interpret and apply EU law as a matter of fact' under Art 8.28 of the CETA.

[157] Instead, Art 8.28 of the CETA establishes an Appellate Tribunal to review awards rendered under the agreement. For a short explanation of the appeal procedures, see Puccio and Harte (2017, paras 3.2.3. et seq.).

[158] ECJ, *Achmea*, paras 43–49.

[159] See Lavranos and Singla (2018, p. 355).

[160] See Glinski (2018, p. 66). Cf. Hindelang (2019, p. 395).

[161] See Eckes (2018).

[162] For a detailed analysis of this question, especially in view of Art 351 of the TFEU, see Lang (2018, p. 22 et seq.) Happold and De Boeck (2019, p. 33), noted that Opinion 1/17 of the ECJ had 'the potential to impact significantly on the extra-EU applicability of the ECT'.

> The *Achmea* judgment is also relevant for the investor-State arbitration mechanism established in Article 26 of the Energy Charter Treaty as regards intra-EU relations. This provision, if interpreted correctly, does not provide for an investor-State arbitration clause applicable between investors from a Member States of the EU and another Member States of the EU. Given the primacy of Union law, that clause, if interpreted as applying intra-EU, is incompatible with EU primary law and thus inapplicable. Indeed, the reasoning of the Court in *Achmea* applies equally to the intra-EU application of such a clause which, just like the clauses of intra-EU BITs, opens the possibility of submitting those disputes to a body which is not part of the judicial system of the EU.[163]

Notably, the representatives of 22 Member States followed the conclusions of the European Commission and considered the arbitration clause in the ECT to be incompatible with the EU law.[164] Indeed, scholars affirmed that 'the basic scenario [...] is largely the same as the one of intra-EU BITs in the *Achmea* case'.[165] To safeguard the primacy of EU law, Article 30(4) lit. (a) of the VCLT could be the crucial provision of international public law.[166] To give Article 344 of the TFEU as *lex posterior* full effect, Article 30(4) lit. (a) of the VCLT could render the dispute resolution clause in Article 26 of the ECT inapplicable.[167]

By contrast, arbitral tribunals take a different view on the ECT.[168] The tribunal in the International Centre for Settlement of Investment Dispute (ICSID) proceeding *Masdar Solar & Wind Cooperatief U.A. v Kingdom of Spain* rendered its award on 16 May 2018.[169] It held that the '*Achmea* Judgment has no bearing upon the present case'.[170] According to the tribunal, the considerations of the ECJ do not apply to multilateral treaties.[171]

On 31 August 2018, the arbitral tribunal in the ICSID proceedings *Vattenfall AB* et al. *v the Federal Republic of Germany* rendered its decision on the *Achmea* issue.[172] In its extensive reasoning, this tribunal affirmed its jurisdiction notwithstanding the ECJ judgment. As one of the several key points, it referred to Article 16 of the ECT

163 European Commission (2018).

164 Declaration of the Representatives of the Governments of the Member States (2019, p. 2).

165 Hess (2018, p. 12). See also Hindelang (2019, p. 394), who suggested that 'intra-EU arbitration based on the ECT should in effect not be treated differently from those addressed in *Achmea*'.

166 As suggested by Hess (2018, p. 12).

167 Hess (2018, p. 13). However, see also Happold and De Boeck (2019, p. 14), who suggested that either the principle of the primacy of EU law, as established by the ECJ, or Art 16 of the ECT could be interpreted as conflict rules that prevail over the general rules of international law. They noted that '[u]nder international law, an expression of the parties' will to provide for a conflict rule, explicit or even implicit, is recognized' and the customary conflict of law rules 'codified fragmentarily in Articles 30 and 59 VCLT' apply only secondarily.

168 Cf. Happold and De Boeck (2019, p. 16).

169 *Masdar Solar*.

170 *Masdar Solar*, para 678.

171 *Masdar Solar*, para 679.

172 *Vattenfall AB*. The tribunal rendered the decision after Germany had invoked a jurisdictional objection.

when examining the relation between the EU law and the ECT.[173] The tribunal read this provision in a way that precludes a contracting party from interpreting the 'EU Treaties so as to derogate from an Investor's right to dispute resolution under Article 26 ECT, to the extent that they are understood to concern the same subject manner'.[174] The tribunal further rejected that as a matter of conflicts of law, EU law prevails over the ECT.[175] In short, the tribunal did not recognise a conflict in the first place. Instead, Article 26 of the ECT and Articles 267 and 344 of the TFEU were deemed to 'operat[e] in their separate spheres without conflict' because the provisions 'do not have the same subject matter or scope'.[176] Nonetheless, even if one were to recognise a conflict, particularly Article 30(4)(a) of the VCLT shall not mandate that Articles 267 and 344 of the TFEU prevail over Article 26 of the ECT. According to the tribunal, Article 30(4)(a) of the VCLT is subsidiary to Article 16 of the ECT.[177] In addition, the tribunal suggested that it is 'by no means clear that the EU Treaties are the "later treaty" under Article 30 VCLT' because the relevant articles are deemed to have 'existed in substantively similar form since a time prior to the conclusion of the ECT'.[178] Finally, one more finding appears to be particularly noteworthy. The tribunal stressed that the EU *itself*, as a contracting party, has 'accepted the possibility of arbitration proceedings under Article 26 [ECT], even against itself, without making a distinction between investors from EU or non-EU Member States'.[179] By contrast, in the eye of the European Commission, this distinction is insignificant. The European Commission's take on it is that 'the participation of the EU in that Treaty has only created rights and obligations between the EU and third countries and has not affected the relations between the EU Member States'.[180]

Happold and De Boeck have pinpointed the underlying problem of this question:

> The analyses used in international law and EU law start from different premises, apply different conflict of laws mechanisms, and consequently lead to different outcomes.[181]

In the end, it might again be up to the ECJ to decide on the compatibility of the ECT with EU law. Spain has requested the Svea Court of Appeal in Sweden to annul the

---

[173] Art 16 of the ECT reads in its relevant parts as follows: „Where two or more Contracting Parties have entered into a prior [...] or enter into a subsequent international agreement, whose terms in either case concern the subject matter of Part III or V of this Treaty, [...] (2) nothing in such terms of the other agreement shall be construed to derogate from any provision of Part III or V of this Treaty or from any right to dispute resolution with respect thereto under this Treaty, where any such provision is more favourable to the Investor [...]".

[174] *Vattenfall AB*, para 195.

[175] *Vattenfall AB*, paras 211 et seq.

[176] *Vattenfall AB*, para 212.

[177] *Vattenfall AB*, para 217.

[178] *Vattenfall AB*, para 218.

[179] *Vattenfall AB*, para 188. See also Stöbener de Mora (2018, p. 367), who suggested that in view of its Contracting States, the ECT is governed by international public law. As a consequence, the principle of *pacta sunt servanda* (Art 26 of the VCLT) was not to allow the EU law to deny tribunals their jurisdiction.

[180] European Commission (2018).

[181] Happold and De Boeck (2019, p. 2).

award in *Novenergia v Spain*. The award had been rendered on 15 February 2015 and was based on the ECT.[182] In the course of the annulment proceedings, Spain asked the Swedish court to seek preliminary reference from the ECJ. The Swedish court granted a stay of enforcement but ultimately rejected Spain's request for preliminary reference to the ECJ.[183] Pending a decision of the ECJ to the contrary, arbitral tribunals are currently encouraged to follow the lead of the *Masdar* and *Vattenfall* tribunals.[184]

4.7 The Impact of the Achmea Decision on Commercial Arbitration

Finally, the impact of the decision on *commercial* arbitration is to be examined. The ECJ itself addressed the realm of commercial arbitration in its decision. In doing so, it affirmed the findings it made in earlier judgments, namely in *Eco Swiss*[185] and *Mostaza Claro*.[186] The ECJ draws a distinct line between commercial arbitration and investment arbitration. Commercial arbitration builds on the express intent of private parties to arbitrate. In contrast to commercial arbitration, investment arbitration is based on treaties, concluded by the EU Member States. The EU Member States thereby remove one type of dispute from the judicial system. However, Article 19(1) of the TEU particularly requires the EU Member States to establish a judicial system that safeguards the uniform application and interpretation of EU law.[187] In view of the autonomy of the EU law, the ECJ does not tolerate the removal of disputes in the realm of investment arbitration. Yet, due to the distinction between investment arbitration and commercial arbitration, the ECJ nonetheless accepts the 'review of arbitral awards by the courts of the Member States being limited in scope, provided that the fundamental provisions of EU law can be examined in the course of that review and, if necessary, be subject of a reference to the Court for a preliminary ruling'.[188] Apparently, this leads to the conclusion that the judgment does not affect disputes in commercial arbitration. This corresponds with the assessment of the

[182] *Novenergia II—Energy & Environment (SCA) (Grand Duchy of Luxembourg), SICAR v. The Kingdom of Spain*, SCC Arbitration (2015/063), Final Arbitral Award, 15 February 2018, https://www.italaw.com/sites/default/files/case-documents/italaw9715.pdf.

[183] Svea Court of Appeal, Decision in Case T 4658-18, 25 April 2019. See also Lavranos and Singla (2018, p. 352), Schwedt and Reichert (2018).

[184] Lavranos and Singla (2018, p. 354).

[185] ECJ, Judgment of the Court in Case C-126/97 (*Eco Swiss*), 1 June 1999 (ECLI:EU:C:1999:269) (hereafter 'ECJ, *Eco Swiss*').

[186] ECJ, Judgment of the Court in Case C-168/05 (*Mostaza Claro*), 26 October 2006 (ECLI:EU:C:2006:675) (hereafter 'ECJ, *Mostaza Claro*').

[187] ECJ, *Achmea*, para 55.

[188] ECJ, *Achmea*, para 54.

ECJ[189] and the existing scholarly literature.[190] Article 19(1) of the TEU does not oblige private parties to safeguard the primacy of the EU law in the way it obliges EU Member States to do so. Private parties should thus have the autonomy to freely choose their forum for dispute settlement.

Nonetheless, it has been noted that the ECJ would have needed to prevent *any* instances outside of the EU legal system to decide on the interpretation of EU law if it were to follow its strict reasoning in *Achmea* consistently.[191] Or, to put it in other words: if the ECJ were to consistently follow its earlier decisions in *Eco Swiss* and *Mostaza Claro*, it would have found that at least non-ICSID investment arbitration is compatible with EU law.[192] Both *Eco Swiss*[193] and *Mostaza Claro*[194] were based on the assumption that the subsequent, limited review by domestic courts (as per Article 267 of the TFEU) suffices in safeguarding the primacy of EU law.[195] The domestic courts scrutinise commercial arbitration either in the course of annulment or enforcement proceedings.[196] In this regard, the New York Convention notably does not differentiate between the review of awards from commercial and non-ICSID investment arbitration.[197] By contrast, the ECJ only regarded the review of awards from investment arbitration as insufficient. After all, in view of the ECJ's distinction between commercial and investment arbitration, the parties in commercial arbitrations have 'nothing to worry about—at least for now'.[198]

5 Conclusion

In the end, the highly anticipated *Achmea* decision probably left more questions unanswered than it had settled. The views on the consequences regarding the various treaties and both the jurisdiction of arbitral tribunals as well as the enforceability of arbitral awards differ significantly. Not only were these differences caused by different legal views, but they also root in divergent objectives. This is especially true to the political agenda of the European Commission on the one hand, and arbitral tribunals on the other hand. In the end, these uncertainties in themselves presumably strengthen the position of respondent States and the European Commission.

---

[189] Cf. ECJ, *Achmea*, paras 54 et seq.

[190] See Hess (2018, p. 6), who noted that '*Achmea* does not change the present situation' regarding commercial arbitration. See further Lavranos and Singla (2018, p. 356), and Ohler (2018, p. 515).

[191] Lavranos and Singla (2018, p. 356).

[192] Cf. Alvarez (2018, p. 153), Bodenheimer and Eller (2018, p. 790).

[193] ECJ, *Eco Swiss*, paras 35, 36, 40.

[194] ECJ, *Mostaza Claro*, paras 34–39.

[195] Sadowski (2018, p. 1055). Cf. Pinna (2018, p. 77 et seq.).

[196] Sadowski (2018, p. 1055).

[197] Alvarez (2018, p. 153).

[198] Lavranos and Singla (2018, p. 356).

When assessing the uncertain legal landscape in the aftermath of *Achmea*, one aspect seems to be particularly difficult. Irrespective of the exact legal consequences, the legal unpredictability encroaches the legal position of investors, causing more difficulties for investors to pursue their rights and protect their investments. This applies all the more as scholars consistently note that the protection of investments under EU law alone is not as effective as the mechanisms of ISDS.[199] There is a stark contrast between the theoretical demands on the protection of investments in the EU and the actual enforceability of these rights. This discrepancy is prominently illustrated by the Article 7 of the TEU procedure against an EU Member State in view of the 'threat of a persistent and systematic breach of the rule of law in Poland'.[200] Yet at the same time, the decision of the ECJ potentially offers the chance to implement effective investment protection amongst the EU Member States, rooted in EU law.[201] This, however, depends on the combined efforts of the EU as a whole—an effort that, at least at the moment, seems hardly achievable.

Acknowledgements The authors would like to thank Raphaelle Teenie Chan for the language revision of this Chapter.

References

Alvarez GM (2018) Note: *Slovak Republic v Achmea*, Judgement of the Court of Justice of the European Union (Grand Chamber) Case No. C-284/16, 6 March 2018. Revista Brasileira de Arbitragem 15:149–155

Bischoff JA (2018) Ein Sturm im Wasserglas? Zur Zukunft der Investitionsschiedsgerichtsbarkeit nach *Achmea v Slovakia*. Praxis des Internationalen Privat- und Verfahrensrechts 38:588–591

Board of ASA (2018) ASA Board Message, The Cost of Achmea. ASA Bull 36:553–557

Bodenheimer RF, Eller KH (2018) Unionsrechtszentrismus und ISDS. Recht der Internationalen Wirtschaft 64:786–792

Croisant G (2019) CJEU Opinion 1/17—AG Bot Concludes that CETA's Investment Court System is Compatible with EU Law. Kluwer Arbitration Blog. http://arbitrationblog.kluwerarbitration.com/2019/01/29/cjeu-opinion-117-ag-bot-concludes-that-cetas-investment-court-system-is-compatible-with-eu-law/

Davoise M, Burgstaller M (2018) Another One BIT the Dust: Is the Netherland's Termination of intra-EU Treaties the Latest Symptom of a Backlash Against Investor-State Arbitration? Kluwer Arbitration Blog. http://arbitrationblog.kluwerarbitration.com/2018/08/11/another-one-bit-dust-netherlands-termination-intra-eu-treaties-latest-symptom-backlash-investor-state-arbitration/

De Sadeleer N (2018) The End of the Game: the Autonomy of the EU Legal Order Opposes Arbitral Tribunals under Bilateral Investment Treaties Concluded between Two Member States. Eur J Risk Regul 9:355–371

---

[199] This disparity was for example noted by the Board of ASA (2018, p. 556), and Sadowski (2018, p. 1040 et seq.) Cf. Hindelang (2019, p. 384).

[200] Sadowski (2018, 1025 et seq.).

[201] Notably, the representatives of 22 Member States announced their commitment to 'intensify discussions without undue delay with the aim of better ensuring complete, strong and effective protection of investments within the European Union', see the Declaration of the Representatives of the Governments of the Member States (2019, p. 3). Cf. Lavranos (2018).

Declaration of the Representatives of the Governments of the Member States (2019) The Legal Consequences of the Judgment of the Court of Justice in *Achmea* and on Investment Protection in the European Union. https://ec.europa.eu/info/sites/info/files/business_economy_euro/banking_and_finance/documents/190117-bilateral-investment-treaties_en.pdf

Department of Foreign Affairs, Foreign Trade and Development Cooperation of the Kingdom of Belgium (2017). CETA: Belgian request for an opinion from the European Court of Justice. https://diplomatie.belgium.be/sites/default/files/downloads/ceta_summary.pdf

Dimopoulos A (2018). *Achmea*: the principle of autonomy and its implications for intra and extra-EU BITs. Blog Eur J Int Law. https://www.ejiltalk.org/achmea-the-principle-of-autonomy-and-its-implications-for-intra-and-extra-eu-bits/

Eckes C (2018) Don't lead with your chin! If Member States continue with the ratification of CETA, they violate European Union law. European Law Blog. https://europeanlawblog.eu/2018/03/13/dont-lead-with-your-chin-if-member-states-continue-with-the-ratification-of-ceta-they-violate-european-union-law/

Editorial Board of the Common Law Market Review (2018) Editorial comments: EU Law between common values and collective feelings. Common Law Market Rev 55:1329–1340

European Commission (2015) Commission asks member States to terminate their intra-EU bilateral investment treaties. European Commission Press Release Database. http://europa.eu/rapid/press-release_IP-15-5198_en.htm

European Commission (2018) Communication from the Commission to the European Parliament and the Council—Protection of intra-EU investment. https://eur-lex.europa.eu/legal-content/EN/TXT/?uri=CELEX:52018DC0547

European Commission (2019) EU Member States agree on a plurilateral treaty to terminate bilateral investment treaties. https://ec.europa.eu/info/publications/191024-bilateral-investment-treaties_en

European Court of Justice (2018) Press release no 26/18: the arbitration clause in the agreement between the Netherlands and Slovakia on the protection of investments is not compatible with EU law. https://curia.europa.eu/jcms/upload/docs/application/pdf/2018-03/cp180026en.pdf

Gáspár-Szilágy S (2019) AG Bot in opinion 1/17. The autonomy of the EU legal order v. the reasons why the CETA ICS might be needed. European Law Blog. http://europeanlawblog.eu/2019/02/06/ag-bot-in-opinion-1-17-the-autonomy-of-the-eu-legal-order-v-the-reasons-why-the-ceta-ics-might-be-needed/

Glinski C (2018) *Achmea* and its Implications for Investor Dispute Settlement. Zeitschrift für Europarechtliche Studien 21:47–68. https://doi.org/10.5771/1435-439X-2018-1-47

Happold M, De Boeck M (2019) The European Union and the Energy Charter Treaty: What Next After Achmea? In: Andenas M, Happold M, Pantaleo L (eds) The European Union as an actor in international economic law. T.M.C. Asser Press, The Hague (forthcoming)

Hartkamp A (2018) Gevolgen van het Achmea arrest voor de praktijk van de investeringsarbitrage binnen de EU. Ars Aequi 7:732–738

Hawes SG (2018) *Micula*: ICSID enforcement before the English Court of Appeal. JDSupra. https://www.jdsupra.com/legalnews/micula-icsid-enforcement-before-the-82280/

Hess B (2018) The Fate of Investment Dispute Resolution after the *Achmea* Decision of the European Court of Justice. Max Planck Institute Luxembourg for Procedural Law Research Paper Series. https://papers.ssrn.com/sol3/papers.cfm?abstract_id=3152972

Hindelang S (2018) The Limited Immediate Effects of CJEU's *Achmea* Judgement. Verfassungsblog on Matters Constitutional. https://verfassungsblog.de/the-limited-immediate-effects-of-cjeus-achmea-judgement/

Hindelang S (2019) Conceptualisation and Application of the Principle of Autonomy of EU Law: The CJEU's Judgment in *Achmea* Put in Perspective. E L Rev 44:383–400

Horvath GJ (2001) The Duty of the Tribunal to Render an Enforceable Award. J Int Arbitr 18:135–158

Kaag S (2018) Kamerbrief over investeringsakkoorden met ander EU-lidstaten: Betreft Investeringsakkoorden met andere EU-lidstaten (Letter to the Second Chamber on investment agreements

with other Member States). https://www.rijksoverheid.nl/documenten/kamerstukken/2018/04/26/kamerbrief-over-investeringsakkoorden-met-andere-eu-lidstaten
Koch C (2009) The Enforcement of Awards Annulled in their Place of Origin. J Int Arbitr 26:267–292
Lang A (2018) Die Autonomie des Unionsrechts und die Zukunft der Investor-Staat-Streitbeilegung in Europa nach Achmea. Beiträge zum Transnationalen Wirtschaftsrecht. http://telc.jura.uni-halle.de/sites/default/files/BeitraegeTWR/Heft%20156.pdf
Lavranos N (2018) After *Achmea*: the Need for an EU Investment Protection Regulation. Kluwer Arbitration Blog. http://arbitrationblog.kluwerarbitration.com/2018/03/17/achmea-need-eu-investment-protection-regulation/
Lavranos N, Singla T (2018) *Achmea*: Groundbreaking or Overrated? German Arbitr J 17:348–357
Lee J (2018) The Empire Strikes Back: Case Note on the CJEU decision in *Slovak Republic v. Achmea BV*, March 6, 2018. Contemporary Asia Arbitr J 11:137–152
O'Sullivan R (2018) Burning Bridges? The Court of Justice and the Autonomy of the EU Legal Order. Hibernian Law J 17:1–24
Ohler C (2018) Anmerkung zu EuGH, Urteil v. 6.3.2018—C-284/16. JuristenZeitung 73:514–517. https://doi.org/10.1628/jz-2018-0075
Pinna A (2018) The Incompatibility of Intra-EU BITs with European Union Law, annotation following ECJ, 6 March 2018, Case 284/16, *Slovak Republic v Achmea B.V.* Paris J Int Arbitr 9:73–95
Power R (2019) The (Final?) Death of Intra-EU Investor-State Arbitration. Kluwer Arbitration Blog. http://arbitrationblog.kluwerarbitration.com/2019/01/28/the-final-death-of-intra-eu-investor-state-arbitration/
Puccio L, Harte R (2017) From arbitration to the investment court system (ICS)—the evolution of CETA rules. Eur Parliamentary Res Serv. https://doi.org/10.2861/856144
Reed L, Paulsson J et al (2010) Recognition, Enforcement and Execution of ICSID Awards. In: Reed L, Paulsson J et al (eds) Guide to ICSID arbitration. Kluwer Law International, Alphen aan den Rijn, pp 179–190
Rose-Ackerman S, Tobin J (2005) Foreign Direct Investment and the Business Environment in Developing Countries: the Impact of Bilateral Investment Treaties. Yale law & economics research paper no. 293. https://ssrn.com/abstract=557121
Sadowski W (2018) Protection of the rule of law in the European Union through Investment Treaty Arbitration: is judicial monopolism the right response to illiberal tendencies in Europe? Common Market Law Rev 55:1025–1060
Schwedt K, Reichert M (2018) The changing landscape of intra-EU investment protection: latest communication by the European Commission and other post-*Achmea* developments. Linklaters Arbitration Links. https://www.arbitrationlinks.com/the-changing-landscape-of-intra-eu-investment-protection-latest-communication-by-the-european-commission-and-other-post-achmea-developments
Singla T (2018) *Achmea*: The fate and future of intra-eu investment treaty awards under the New York convention. Blog Eur Law J Int Law. https://www.ejiltalk.org/achmea-the-fate-and-future-of-intra-eu-investment-treaty-awards-under-the-new-york-convention/
Solomon D (2016) International Commercial Arbitration: The New York Convention. In: Balthasar S (ed) International Commercial Arbitration: A Practitioners' Guide. C.H. Beck–Hart–Nomos, Munich, pp 45–158
Stöbener de Mora PS (2018) Das Achmea-Urteil zum Intra-EU-Investitionsschutz. Europäische Zeitschrift für Wirtschaftsrecht 29:363–370
Thym D (2018) Todesstoß für autonome Investitionsschutzgerichte. Verfassungsblog on Matters Constitutional. https://verfassungsblog.de/todesstoss-fuer-autonome-investitionsschutzgerichte/
Woolcock S (2010) The EU Approach to International Investment Policy After the Lisbon Treaty. http://www.europarl.europa.eu/RegData/etudes/etudes/join/2010/433854/EXPO-INTA_ET(2010)433854_EN.pdf

Wuschka S (2018) Investment protection and the EU after Achmea. Zeitschrift für Europarechtliche Studien 21:25–46. https://doi.org/10.5771/1435-439X-2018-1-25
Yong L (2018) Airbus withdraws treaty claim against Poland. Global Arbitr Rev. https://globalarbitrationreview.com/article/1169853/airbus-withdraws-treaty-claim-against-poland
Zarowna A (2017) Termination of BITs and Sunset Clauses—What Can Investors in Poland Expect? Kluwer Arbitration Blog. http://arbitrationblog.kluwerarbitration.com/2017/02/28/booked-22-february-polish-bits/

André Janssen is a Chair Professor at the Radboud University Nijmegen, The Netherlands. He has previously held positions at the Universities of Bayreuth, Göttingen, Münster, and at the City University of Hong Kong. Furthermore, he was a visiting scholar at the Universities of Nijmegen, Oxford and Turin and member of several international research networks. Janssen taught and presented at international conferences on four continents and published more than 100 books and articles. He is the co-chief-editor of the European Review of Private Law (ERPL), a member of the editorial board of the International Arbitration Law Review (IALR), and the head of the German redaction committee of the Italian law journal Contratto e impresa/Europa.

Christian Johannes Wahnschaffe is a doctoral candidate at the Faculty of Law of the University of Münster, Germany. His current research focuses on the field of arbitration both on the national and on the international level. He is a research assistant to Prof. Dr. James Fowkes, LL.M. (Yale) at the Chair for Foreign and International Law and, in this capacity, the Director of the Karina und Erich Schumann Centre for Advanced International Legal Studies at the University of Münster. Furthermore, he has been a research and student assistant to Prof. Dr. Gerald Mäsch at the Institute of International Business Law. In the latter capacity, he has coached the faculty's team for the Willem C. Vis International Commercial Arbitration Moot for multiple years.

The manufacturer's authorised representative in the EU is Springer Nature Customer Service Centre GmbH, Europaplatz 3, 69115 Heidelberg, Germany. If you have any concerns regarding our products, please contact ProductSafety@springernature.com

Printed and bound by CPI Group (UK) Ltd, Croydon, CR0 4YY
30/09/2026
02225647-0008